The Battle
of Monroe's Crossroads

and the Civil War's Final Campaign

Books by Eric J. Wittenberg

Gettysburg's Forgotten Cavalry Actions (1998)

"We Have It Damn Hard Out Here": The Civil War Letters of
  Sgt. Thomas W. Smith, Sixth Pennsylvania Cavalry (1999)

Under Custer's Command: The Civil War Journal
  of James Henry Avery (2000)

One of Custer's Wolverines: The Civil War Letters of
  Bvt. Brig. Gen. James H. Kidd (2000)

At Custer's Side: The Civil War Writings of James Harvey Kidd (2001)

Glory Enough for All: Sheridan's Second Raid and the
  Battle of Trevilian Station (2001)

Protecting the Flank: The Battles of Brinkerhoff's Ridge and East
  Cavalry Field, Battle of Gettysburg, July 2-3, 1863 (2002)

Little Phil: A Critical Assessment of the Civil War Generalship
  of Philip H.Sheridan (2002)

The Union Cavalry Comes of Age:Hartwood Church to
  Brandy Station (2003)

The Battle
of Monroe's Crossroads

and the Civil War's Final Campaign

Eric J. Wittenberg

SB

Savas Beatie

Cataloging-in-Publication Data is available from the Library of Congress.

ISBN 1-932714-17-0

SB

Published by
Savas Beatie LLC
521 Fifth Avenue, Suite 3400
New York, NY 10175
Phone: 610-853-9131

Editorial Offices:

Savas Beatie LLC
P.O. Box 4527
El Dorado Hills, CA 95762
Phone: 916-941-6896
(E-mail) editorial@savasbeatie.com

Savas Beatie titles are available at special discounts for bulk purchases in the United States by corporations, institutions, and other organizations. For more details, please contact Special Sales, P.O. Box 4527, El Dorado Hills, CA 95762, or you may e-mail us as at sales@savasbeatie.com, or visit our website at www.savasbeatie.com for additional information.

For Susan

Did you ever see a cavalry charge? Imagine a thousand imps of darkness! A thousand fiends incarnate! Drawn up in battle array. In front of them is a line which must be broken. You hear the cannons roar! The bursting of shell! The crashing of the grape and canister! You see the men with saber drawn, with eyes flashing fire; every horse with head erect and champing his bit, as though he, too, were conscious of what was about to take place. They start! The tramping of hoofs resembling the roll of distant thunder; first a trot, then a gallop, then they charge with yells and loud huzzas, and, like maniacs, they rush upon the enemy. See the gaps in the line as the grape and canister crashes through them; you see them close up, boot to boot. There is no halting, but with a determination to do or die they rush their steeds ahead; then you hear the roll of musketry, the rattling fire of pistols, the clank of sabers, the shrieks of the wounded, and the groans of the dying; in a moment the vanquished run madly from the field, pursued by the victors, dealing death to their fleeting adversaries. These are the times that try men's souls, and call for heroic action."

— Confederate cavalryman, November 1898

Contents

Preface and Acknowledgments
xv

Foreword
xxiii

Chapter 1:
Hugh Judson Kilpatrick and his Federal Dragoons
1

Chapter 2:
Wade Hampton and his Confederate Cavaliers
25

Chapter 3:
A Sure Sign of Things to Come
59

Chapter 4:
Groping in the Dark
109

Chapter 5:
"We Fell upon the Camp like a Small Avalanche"
131

Chapter 6:
"One of the Most Terrific Hand-to-Hand
Encounters I Ever Witnessed"
157

Chapter 7:
The Aftermath
187

Contents (continued)

Chapter 8:
A Critical Assessment
213

Epilogue
227

Appendix A: Order of Battle
233

Appendix B: Identified Casualties at Monroe's Crossroads
238

Appendix C: Who was Judson Kilpatrick's
Female Companion in March 1865?
252

Appendix D: What was Joseph Wheeler's
Rank in March 1865?
255

Notes
259

Bibliography
301

Index
323

List of Illustrations

Brig. Gen. Hugh Judson Kilpatrick   3

Troopers of the 5th Ohio Cavalry   9

Maj. Gen. William T. Sherman   10

Maj. Gen. Henry W. Slocum   12

Col. Thomas J. Jordan   16

Brig. Gen. Smith D. Atkins   18

Col. George E. Spencer   19

Lt. Col. William B. Way   21

Capt. Theodore Northrop   22

Maj. Gen. Joseph Wheeler   26

Lt. Gen. Wade Hampton   33

Gen. Joseph E. Johnston   38

Brig. Gen. Thomas Harrison   44

Col. Henry M. Ashby   44

Brig. Gen. William W. Allen   45

Col. James Hagan   47

Brig. Gen. Robert H. Anderson   47

Col. Charles Crews   48

Brig. Gen. George G. Dibrell   49

Col. W. C. P. Breckinridge   50

Col. William S. McLemore   52

Maj. Gen. Matthew C. Butler   53

Brig. Gen. Evander M. Law   55

Col. Gilbert J. Wright   57

Fayetteville Arsenal/Armory   62

Lt. Gen. William J. Hardee   64

Capt. Alexander M. Shannon   87

Shannon's Scouts   88

The Malcolm Blue house   110

Capt. Moses B. Humphrey   116

List of Illustrations (continued)

Brig. Gen. William Y. C. Humes   125

Col. J. Fred Waring   134

Lt. Col. William Stough   151

Maj. Francis L. Cramer   153

Lt. Col. Barrington S. King   166

"Kilpatrick Recaptures His Headquarters"   168

An early 20th Century Union mass grave   179

A modern-day view of a Union mass   180

The Monroe's Crossroads battlefield in 1924   181

U.S. Army monument at Monroe's Crossroads   184

"The Skirmish in Fayetteville"   190

The Market House in the center of Fayetteville   195

List of Maps

Opening moves in the Carolinas, early March 1865   15

Movements up to March 8, 1865   67

Judson Kilpatrick moves out to screen the main Union forces while Wade Hampton's cavalry strike the advance, March 3-4, 1865   69

Captain Northrop's 3rd Division Scouts raid into Wadesboro, March 4, 1865   72

Skirmish at Phillips' Cross Roads, March 4, 1865   75

List of Maps (continued)

Jordan's and Kilpatrick's withdrawal and McBride's
Scout, March 5-6, 1865   77

Tramel raid to Rockingham, March 6-7, 1865   81

Union forces cross the Pee Dee River/Confederates move
toward Fayetteville, March 6-7, 1865   83

Main force movements of Federal and Confederate units throughout South
Carolina and North Carolina, March 6-7, 1865   85

First moves in the area of Monroe's Crossroads, early March 8, 1865   90

Secondary moves, late March 8, 1865   94

Early moves, morning, March 9, 1865   98

Movement of opposing forces, early afternoon, March 9, 1865   100

Movement of opposing forces on the afternoon of March 9, 1865   102

Movement of opposing forces from late afternoon to
early evening, March 9, 1865   106

Movement of opposing forces, late evening, March 9, 1865   108

Movement of opposing forces, night of March 9. and early
hours of March 10, 1865   112

Early moves of Wheeler's cavalry to scout Kilpatrick's camp,
night of March 9 and early hours of March 10, 1865   114

List of Maps (continued)

Wheeler's cavalry closes the net on Kilpatrick's camp,
early morning, March 10, 1865   121

Opening moves of the Confederate cavalry against Kilpatrick   133

The Confederate attack   136

Federal response/ Kilpatrick retakes south end of the camp   156

The Federal repulse of the Confederates   162

The Confederate withdrawal signals the end of the battle   172

The race to Fayetteville after the battle of Monroe's Crossroads   182

Federal attempts to capture Cape Fear River bridges, March 11, 1865   189

Confedertate retreat and the burning of Cape Fear
River bridges, March 11, 1865   197

The Army of Mississippi halts to cross the Cape Fear
River, March 11-15, 1865   202

Federal forces are pushed back and
Confederate forces move forward, March 15, 1865   204

Map Legend

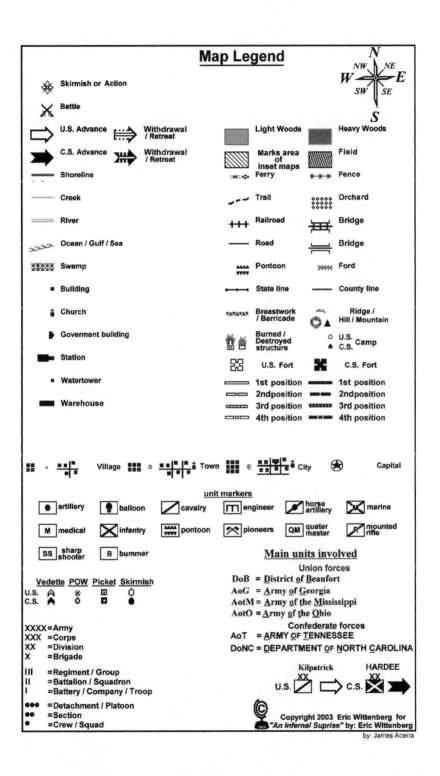

N
NW | NE
W — E
SW | SE
S

✳ Skirmish or Action

✗ Battle

⇨ U.S. Advance   ⇢ Withdrawal / Retreat

➡ C.S. Advance   ⇢ Withdrawal / Retreat

— Shoreline

— Creek

≈ River

〜 Ocean / Gulf / Sea

Swamp

▪ Building

✝ Church

Goverment building

Station

• Watertower

Warehouse

Light Woods   Heavy Woods

Marks area of inset maps   Field

Ferry   ✳✳✳ Fence

Trail   Orchard

+++ Railroad   Bridge

— Road   Bridge

Pontoon   Ford

State line   County line

xxxxxx Breastwork / Barricade   Ridge / Hill / Mountain

Burned / Destroyed structure   △ U.S. ▲ C.S. Camp

U.S. Fort   C.S. Fort

⊏⊐ 1st position   ▬ 1st position
⊏⊐ 2nd position   ▬▬ 2nd position
⊏⊐ 3rd position   ▬▬▬ 3rd position
⊏⊐ 4th position   ▬ ▬ 4th position

Village   Town   City   ★ Capital

unit markers

● artillery	balloon	╱ cavalry	engineer	horse artillery	M marine
M medical	✕ infantry	pontoon	✕ pioneers	QM quater master	R mounted rifle
SS sharp shooter	B bummer

Main units involved

Union forces

DoB = District of Beaufort
AoG = Army of Georgia
AotM = Army of the Mississippi
AotO = Army of the Ohio

Confederate forces

AoT = ARMY OF TENNESSEE
DoNC = DEPARTMENT OF NORTH CAROLINA

	Vedette	POW	Picket	Skirmish
U.S.	⌂	⊗	▫	◌
C.S.	▲	⊗	▪	●

XXXX = Army
XXX = Corps
XX = Division
X = Brigade

III = Regiment / Group
II = Battalion / Squadron
I = Battery / Company / Troop

●●● = Detachment / Platoon
●● = Section
● = Crew / Squad

Kilpatrick   HARDEE
XX   XX
U.S. ⇨   C.S. ➡

Preface

History descended on the two-room wooden home of James and Nancy Bennett near Durham Station, North Carolina, on April 17, 1865. Eight days earlier, Gen. Robert E. Lee had surrendered the tattered remnants of the Army of Northern Virginia at Appomattox Court House. General Joseph E. Johnston, who commanded most of the remaining Confederate forces in North Carolina, realized that once the possibility of a link-up with Lee's army was gone, there was no hope for his vastly outnumbered force. Johnston, however wanted to make peace rather than just surrender his army. Major General William T. Sherman, Johnston's formidable adversary, also wanted to make peace in the hope of avoiding further bloodshed.

Johnston proposed a meeting between the two army commanders, and they selected James Bennett's place, approximately halfway between the positions held by the two foes. Thus, as one of Sherman's staff officers noted, "two great men came together in the heart of North Carolina, intent, with true nobility of soul and in the highest interest of humanity, upon putting a stop to the needless sacrifice of life."[1]

The two generals entered the little Bennett house and began negotiating the terms, not just of the surrender of Johnston's army but of the end of the war and the restoration of the Union. Great things would happen in the small, plain parlor of the Bennett home, events of far-reaching consequence that remain largely unappreciated even today.[2]

Each commander arrived with his staff and a cavalry escort. Lieutenant General Wade Hampton of South Carolina, Johnston's chief of cavalry, and Brevet Major General Judson Kilpatrick, Sherman's cavalry chieftain, accompanied their respective commanders to the meeting at the Bennett house. Hampton and Kilpatrick were both transfers from the Virginia theater of operations, where they tangled a number of times during the first two years of the war. Although it is difficult to imagine more dissimilar personalities than these two men, they were familiar adversaries.

The horse soldiers mingled as they shook hands, shared war stories, and traded souvenirs. Colonel J. Fred Waring, commander of the Jeff Davis Legion Cavalry of Mississippi, engaged Major Llewellyn G. Estes, Kilpatrick's assistant adjutant general, in conversation. To his great surprise, Waring discovered Major Estes was "a pleasant, civil gentleman. I was treated civilly by all the officers I met. We recalled our fights in Virginia." Estes agreed, adding that "it seemed like meeting old friends." Waring found Estes's warmth a bit unsettling. "Queer expression for a man who is ready to cut my throat when we next meet on the field," he observed. "But he is a good fellow, if he is an enemy."[3]

While waiting for Generals Johnston and Sherman to conclude their meeting, Hampton and his son, Lieutenant Wade Hampton, Jr., lounged on a carpenter's bench outside the Bennett house. The elder Hampton wore his best uniform topped by a black felt hat adorned with gold braid and well shined cavalry boots. He left his sword behind that day in favor of a switch—perhaps to send a message that he could still thrash any Yankee who crossed his path. The sight of his men and officers chitchatting with the enemy angered the aloof Hampton, who attitude that day was described as cold and "bold beyond arrogance."[4]

Determined to end the fraternizing, an annoyed Hampton snapped, "Fall in!" When Kilpatrick approached to protest, remembered one witness, "Wade Hampton looked savage enough to eat 'Little Kil,'" which prompted his antagonist to return "his looks most defiantly."[5]

"The war is over," proclaimed Kilpatrick to his old adversary. "Let the men fraternize."[6]

"I do not intend to surrender!" snapped Hampton. He added that he would never fraternize with the Yankees, "but would retaliate with torch and sword" to avenge the style of war the North had waged.[7] With a stern tone, Hampton again snarled to his troopers, "Fall in!"

"General Hampton, you compel me to remind you that you have no authority here," shot back Kilpatrick.

"Permit me, sir, to remind you," answered the South Carolinian, his words dripping with disdain, "that Napoleon said that any general who would permit himself to be surprised is a very poor soldier, and I surprised you [at Monroe's Crossroads]."

"Yes, but what did Napoleon say of one general who after having surprised another, allowed himself to be whipped by his opposite in his shirt and drawers?" Little Kill sneered in return. And so the two old horse soldiers began refighting their campaigns.[8]

Kilpatrick teased his old adversary by referring to an incident in South Carolina a few months earlier. "Well, General, down yonder in Linch's Creek I gave you a splendid entertainment, but you were too strong for me."

"When and where?" demanded Hampton.

"Oh, when I was after your wagon train and fought your cavalry and a regiment of infantry," replied Little Kil.

Hampton laughed. "Beg pardon, General, allow me to introduce you to Col. Gib Wright who was in command that day with one regiment of cavalry and twenty dismounted men."[9] That did it, and the barbs really began to fly.

The longer the discussion lasted the more heated and the louder it became. "I have heard of your promise to pursue me to the death, General Kilpatrick," exclaimed a heated Hampton. "I only wish to say that you will not have to pursue far."

"Well, I'll go where I'm sent," shot back Kilpatrick.

"Oh? You sometimes go where you are not sent?" retorted Hampton, prompting nearby Federals to chuckle in reply.

"You refer to the time you surprised me near Fayetteville?" inquired Little Kil.

"Yes," answered the South Carolinian. "A general surprised is a general disgraced."

"That happened once. It will never happen again," said Kilpatrick.

"This is the second time. Remember Atlee's Station?" taunted Hampton. "General Kilpatrick, when I look at men like you, I feel like Wellington, who said under like circumstances, I thank my God for my belief in a hell." The assembled crowd exploded in laughter, a response that increased Kilpatrick's simmering anger and frustration.[10]

When one of Kilpatrick's taunts finally drew Hampton's ire, the big Confederate rose from the carpenter's bench, loomed over his diminutive adversary, and proclaimed, "Well, you never ran *me* out of Headquarters in my stocking feet!" A Northern horse soldier who overheard the exchange observed that Hampton's retort "was a home thrust and too true to be funny."

Anger clouded Little Kil's ruddy face. The Union commander replied that Hampton had to leave faster than he came, and then "words grew hot" with "both parties expressing a desire that the issue of the war should be left between the cavalry." The row had by this time grown quite loud, and Sherman and Johnston interrupted their conference to separate the two irate cavalrymen.[11]

A few minutes later the respective contingents mounted up and rode off. Another meeting was scheduled for the next day so that Johnston could communicate with Confederate authorities about his negotiations with Sherman. Instead of risking another confrontation with his old adversary, Hampton stayed at headquarters when Johnston rode off to meet with Sherman the second time.[12]

What had happened to cause such a violent reaction between two old foes? The answer is simple. On March 10, 1865, Hampton had launched a surprise dawn attack on Kilpatrick's camp with Maj. Gen. Joseph Wheeler's Cavalry Corps and Maj. Gen. Matthew C. Butler's Division from the Army of Northern Virginia. The dawn assault wreaked havoc and came within a whisker of destroying Kilpatrick's command before being driven off after a hard fight. The fighting had rousted Kilpatrick from his bed and forced him to flee in his nightshirt. He but narrowly escaped the humiliation of capture. To Little Kil's eternal embarrassment, amused Federal infantrymen dubbed the episode "Kilpatrick's Shirt-Tail Skedaddle," something the diminutive Northerner never forgot.

The battle of Monroe's Crossroads was fought near Fayetteville, North Carolina. It is a tale filled with acts of great privation, bravery, bloodshed, sacrifice, and valor. And it is a story that, until now, has never been fully told.

Acknowledgments

I have spent most of my adult life studying Union cavalry actions in the Eastern Theater of the Civil War. In September 2001, just a few days before the terrible terrorist attack that changed our world forever, I went to North Carolina and visited some of the important sites associated with

William T. Sherman's 1865 Carolinas Campaign. As a result, I began studying the Carolinas Campaign in some detail. After reading a number of books on the subject, my interest in the war's final campaign grew. Finally, in May 2002, I had an opportunity to visit the Monroe's Crossroads battlefield, which lies nestled among the artillery ranges on the grounds of Fort Bragg, near Fayetteville. I have visited many Civil War battlefields, but I have never seen one as pristine as Monroe's Crossroads. The United States Army has done an admirable job of maintaining this little battlefield, which it jealously protects.

There have been a number of treatments of the battle over the years, but never a scholarly monograph on this important all-cavalry battle. My friend, Mark L. Bradley, who has done the best studies of the Carolinas Campaign yet written, devoted a chapter to Monroe's Crossroads in his fine work Last Stand in the Carolinas: The Battle of Bentonville. There is a single book, published by the Army for the casual student, and an interesting staff ride manual that does not cover the entire battle. It is more of a battle tour guide and leadership exercise than it is a detailed history of the fight at Monroe's Crossroads. Unable to find the level of detail that I wanted, I ultimately decided to break from my own habit of dealing with the Army of the Potomac's Cavalry Corps, and set out to tackle a scholarly monograph on Monroe's Crossroads of my own.

This battle, which featured nearly 6,000 cavalrymen, involved several of my favorite characters of the Civil War. Union commander Judson Kilpatrick is one of its more notable and memorable personalities, a small man of great appetites and ambitions, failings and flaws. Wade Hampton, the Confederate Cavalry Corps leader, is one of the war's most fascinating figures. At its outset he had no military training or experience, yet the genteel South Carolinian was one of only two Confederate cavalry officers to achieve the rank of lieutenant general. While Monroe's Crossroads was not the first time that these two generals had tangled, it was probably the most memorable. Hampton took advantage of Kilpatrick's shoddy dispositions to launch a surprise dawn charge on Kilpatrick's sleeping camp. That infernal surprise led to a brutal fight that featured mounted charges and dismounted combat as fierce as any infantry battle.

The savageness of this fight left an impression on the participants of both sides for the rest of their lives. "Oh, that I had the power to describe this hand-to-hand fight—the men on both sides were brave and fought with more desperation than I had ever before seen," recalled Ulysses R. Brooks of the 5th South Carolina Cavalry, a man not usually at a loss for words. There were nearly four hundred casualties in a three-hour-long fight. Hampton's thunderbolt meant that the Confederates would win the race for the critical bridges over the Cape Fear River at Fayetteville, briefly saving the strategic town and crucial river crossing for the Confederacy. While the outcome of this battle did not save the Confederacy, Hampton's audacious strike probably prolonged the war in North Carolina by a few weeks.

This book tells the story of the Battle of Monroe's Crossroads in detail. It sets the stage for this battle by showing how the confrontation became inevitable, and shows how Kilpatrick's careless dispositions brought it about. It provides a detailed tactical analysis of the fighting, and also demonstrates how Judson Kilpatrick made a desperate, hair-breadth escape from capture, prompting amused Federal infantrymen to dub this fight "Kilpatrick's Shirt-Tail Skedaddle." It addresses many of the legends that have developed about this battle over the years, and provides a detailed listing of all identified Union casualties in the battle. There are several appendices. One addresses the question of General Joseph Wheeler's rank at the time of the battle, and another discusses the identity of Kilpatrick's female companion on the morning of the battle.

All interpretations set forth herein are solely my own, and as such I take responsibility for them. As with every project of this nature, there are many people to whom I am grateful. First and foremost, I deeply appreciate the guidance, encouragement, and friendship of Mark L. Bradley, whose work inspired me to learn more about the Carolinas Campaign. Mark gave me a guided tour of the battlefield and wrote the foreword to this book. James Acerra's fine map series enhances this book. I thank them both for making this study possible.

Bill Kern, who helped maintain the battlefield for the United States Army, permitted me to visit the small display of battle artifacts recovered from the field, and also arranged for us to have access to the site. Bill's successor, Charles Heath, was also a tremendous help to me, providing me with feedback, access to the battlefield, maps, and photographs, as well as his encyclopedic knowledge of the cultural history of Fort Bragg. I am deeply grateful to Charles. Douglas D. Scott, a talented archaeologist employed by the National Park Service, who performed a detailed study on the site that was very useful in specifically locating specific events on the ground, also reviewed my manuscript.

A number of people also unselfishly helped me to gather information for this book. I could not have done this without the assistance of Tonia J. "Teej" Smith, of Pinehurst, North Carolina, who not only allowed me to use her lovely home as a headquarters for my battlefield visits, but also made numerous trips to various repositories in North Carolina to help me gather primary source material for this book.

I also appreciate the assistance of Bryce A. Suderow, Robert Lee Hodge, and Steve L. Zerbe, all of whom helped me to identify and obtain research materials for use in this project. Maj. Mark A. Smith of the U.S. Army, a fellow student of the Carolinas Campaign, provided me with invaluable material on Capt. Theodore F. Northrop, and also read this work for accuracy for me. My good friends and fellow cavalry historians Jerry F. Meyers, J. David Petruzzi, Chris Hartley, Robert F. O'Neill, Jr., and Horace Mewborn also reviewed my manuscript. So did David Arthur, Gordon C. Rhea, Noah Andre Trudeau, and Edwin C. Bearss, the dean of Civil War historians.

Thomas Elmore, of Columbia, South Carolina, provided me with useful information about Marie Boozer, whom many have speculated to be Kilpatrick's female companion on the morning of March 10, 1865. Kevin D. McLemore, of Fort Campbell, Kentucky, was extremely generous in providing material on his ancestor, Col. William Sugars McLemore of the 4th Tennessee Cavalry, who commanded a Confederate brigade at Monroe's Crossroads. Larry Strayer, of Dayton, Ohio, provided me with the photograph of Kilpatrick's chief scout, Capt. Theodore F. Northrop. Michael Shannon provided me with a photograph of his ancestor, Capt. Alexander M. Shannon, Northrop's Confederate counterpart, as well as evidence that Shannon may have been promoted from captain to colonel in the waning days of the war. David A. Powell provided good primary source material for me, as did Tom Nanzig of Ann Arbor, Michigan, who obtained materials from the Bentley Historical Library and William L. Clements Library at the University of Michigan.

None of my historical work would be possible without the love, support and encouragement of my wife, best friend, and favorite traveling companion, Susan Skilken Wittenberg. Her endless patience with my insatiable need to tell the stories of the horse soldiers of the Civil

War gives me the freedom to do this work, and I am eternally grateful to her for her patience and support. I have lost track of the number of nights that Susan has tolerated my piles of books and file folders while I struggled my way through yet another project. I could not do this work without her. Thank you, Susan.

Foreword

In February 1865, the 60,000-strong Federal grand army commanded by Maj. Gen. William T. Sherman marched north from Savannah, Georgia, en route to Richmond, Virginia, the capital of the Confederacy. One month later Sherman's juggernaut crossed into North Carolina after a devastating and virtually unopposed march through South Carolina. The ineffectual Confederate defense of the Palmetto State was largely the result of Gen. P. G. T. Beauregard's failure to concentrate his forces in sufficient strength to contest Sherman's progress. On February 22, the Confederate army's newly appointed general-in-chief, Robert E. Lee, replaced Beauregard with Gen. Joseph E. Johnston, who had languished in semi-retirement since his removal as the commander of the Army of Tennessee the previous July. Johnston faced the daunting task of stopping Sherman with a scattered command of 25,000 troops consisting of everything from jaded frontline veterans to boys and old men in state reserve units. In the words of Johnston's cavalry commander, Lt. Gen. Wade Hampton, "it would scarcely have been possible to disperse a force more effectually."

While Johnston raced to concentrate his army, he left the thankless task of harassing Sherman's advance to Hampton and his cavalry. Though he did not have a formal military education, Hampton proved his leadership ability during years of hard fighting in Virginia and especially during the 1864 Overland Campaign, after which he was appointed by General Lee to succeed the fallen "Jeb" Stuart as the commander of the Army of Northern Virginia's cavalry. In February 1865, Hampton was transferred at his own request to South Carolina to defend his native soil. He took with him a superb cavalry division commanded by his capable protégé, Maj. Gen. Matthew C. Butler. In addition to Butler's Division, in the Carolinas Hampton also commanded Maj. Gen. Joseph Wheeler's cavalry corps, which had been shadowing and harassing Sherman's army since the March to the Sea. Even as his cavalry fell back before the overwhelming numbers of the Federals, the ever-aggressive Hampton sought opportunities to attack isolated elements of the enemy. By far the best such opportunity presented itself on March 10, 1865, at Monroe's Crossroads in the sparsely settled Sandhills region of North Carolina.

Hampton's Federal counterpart was Bvt. Maj. Gen. Hugh Judson Kilpatrick, a flamboyant and often reckless cavalryman whose men nicknamed him "Kill-Cavalry." While he boasted the West Point pedigree that Hampton lacked, Kilpatrick's botched raid on Richmond in February 1864 led to his transfer to the war's Western Theater—a move generally regarded as a demotion. During the first week of March 1865, Hampton's and Kilpatrick's cavalry skirmished continually in the pine woods of the Tar Heel State. Their running fight culminated in the March 10 Battle of Monroe's Crossroads, the last significant cavalry action of the war. Kilpatrick's recklessness rendered him vulnerable at Monroe's Crossroads, but his undeniable bravery proved to be his salvation. And yet, somehow Kilpatrick failed to glean the most important lesson of the March 10 battle: the Confederates still had plenty of fight left; they would demonstrate as much at Averasboro less than one week later, and again at Bentonville on March 19-21.

Eric Wittenberg has penned the definitive account of this fascinating battle. This which will come as no surprise to the readers of his many excellent books and articles on cavalry operations in the Eastern Theater. Given the inaccessibility of the battlefield to the civilian Civil War buff—Monroe's Crossroads lies smack in the middle of several off-limits drop zones and impact areas on Fort Bragg Military Reservation—*The Battle of Monroe's Crossroads and the Civil War's Final Campaign* is all the more valuable. It is the closest that most students of the war will ever come to walking the ground there.

The Battle of Monroe's Crossroads features a marvelous cast of characters and a riveting story impeccably researched and judiciously interpreted. Wittenberg's study is operational history at its finest.

Mark L. Bradley
Graham, North Carolina

Chapter 1

Hugh Judson Kilpatrick
and his Federal Dragoons

W HEN Maj. Gen. William T. Sherman led his armies into the field in the spring of 1864, he took with him a new set of cavalry commanders. These two senior officers, Maj. Gen. George Stoneman and Brig. Gen. Hugh Judson Kilpatrick, had both served with the Army of the Potomac with mixed results, and had both come west looking for opportunities to distinguish themselves.

Because Stoneman was the ranking general officer in the Federal cavalry in the spring of 1864, he became Sherman's chief of cavalry by default. That summer and with Sherman's blessing to continue Stoneman led a raid toward Macon and on to Andersonville prison, where the cavalryman intended to liberate Union prisoners of war. The raid ended in disaster short of Macon on July 29 when Stoneman and 700 of his troopers were captured and the raid fell apart. Command of Sherman's horsemen fell to Kilpatrick, the next senior general officer. Thanks to Sherman's energetic intercession, Stoneman was exchanged that autumn and given command of the district that included Eastern Tennessee, but he would never again serve in the field with Sherman.[1]

Judson Kilpatrick had come West under uncertain circumstances. He had fought bravely—if not always wisely—in the Eastern Theater and relieved of command as a result. A cloud hung over Kilpatrick's head, one he very much wanted to dissolve.

Hugh Judson Kilpatrick was born in Deckertown, New Jersey, on January 14, 1836, the second son of Simon and Julia Kilpatrick. The elder Kilpatrick was a colonel in the New Jersey state militia who cut an imposing figure in his fine uniform. This image was not lost on little Judson, who at an early age decided he wanted to be a soldier. He spent his childhood attending good schools and reading about military history, eagerly learning all he could about great captains and campaigns.[2]

The boy's most earnest dreams came true in 1856 when he received an appointment to the United States Military Academy at West Point. He graduated from in the Class of 1861, seventeenth in a class of forty-five. "His ambition was simply boundless," recalled a fellow cadet, "and from his intimates he did not disguise his faith that . . . he would become governor of New Jersey, and ultimately president of the United States."[3] A few days after graduating, Judson married his sweetheart Alice Shailer, the niece of a prominent New York politician. He would carry a personal battle flag emblazoned with her name into combat throughout the upcoming war, which would last longer than his marriage to Alice. The young lieutenant and his bride spent only one night together before he rushed off to begin his military career.[4]

A dominant personality trait emerged early in Kilpatrick's career: intense ambition. Recognizing that volunteer service would lead to quicker promotions than the Regular Army, the new graduate asked his mathematics professor from West Point, Gouverneur K. Warren, to recommend him for a captaincy in the newly-formed 5th New York Infantry. On May 9, 1861, Kilpatrick received a commission as captain of Company H, 5th New York. One month later he fought at Big Bethel on June 10 in the Civil War's first full-scale confrontation. The young captain was wounded in the skirmish and earned the distinction of being the first West Pointer on the Union side injured by enemy fire. For someone looking forward to a political career, Kilpatrick was off to a good start.

When he returned to duty he did so as lieutenant colonel of the 2nd New York (Harris) Cavalry. His parting from the 5th New York was not graceful. Kilpatrick had taken sick leave rather than return to duty with his regiment, all the while angling for higher rank in a cavalry regiment while angering Warren in the process. As the second in command of a regiment of horsemen, Kilpatrick served in Maj. Gen. George B. McClellan's Army of the Potomac. He took part in the 1862 Peninsula

Brigadier General Hugh Judson Kilpatrick

Campaign. That summer his regiment left the Virginia Peninsula to serve with Maj. Gen. John Pope's new Army of Virginia. The lieutenant colonel was eagerly searching for opportunities to gain fame and rapid promotion. As it turned out, Kilpatrick almost never got the chance.

In the fall of 1862, Kilpatrick was jailed in Washington D.C.'s Old Capitol Prison, charged with conduct unbecoming an officer. Specifically, he was accused of taking bribes, stealing horses and tobacco and selling them, and impropriety in borrowing money. A less resourceful or ambitious man might have been slowed by these circumstances, but not Kilpatrick. In spite of his incarceration, he managed a promotion to colonel of the 2nd New York Cavalry in December 1862. In January 1863, friends in high places and the exigencies of the war prevailed, and Kilpatrick returned to his regiment untainted by the scandal of a courts-martial.[5] For most young officers such charges would have been career-ending. Kilpatrick had not only survived unscathed, but emerged from prison a full colonel.

By the spring of 1863 the New Jersey native was in command of a brigade. Major General Alfred Pleasonton, the temporary commander of the Army of the Potomac's newly-formed Cavalry Corps, arranged for Kilpatrick's promotion to brigadier general on June 14, 1863. The basis for the recommendation rested upon Kilpatrick's good performance during the May 1863 Stoneman Raid and the Battle of Brandy Station. On June 28, when Maj. Gen. Julius Stahel was relieved of command and his independent cavalry division was merged into the Army of the Potomac's Cavalry Corps, Kilpatrick took charge of the newly-designated Third Cavalry Division. It was in that capacity that he ordered a foolhardy mounted charge across difficult terrain by Brig. Gen. Elon J. Farnsworth's cavalry brigade at the Battle of Gettysburg on the afternoon of July 3, 1863, an attack that accomplished nothing but the pointless death of Farnsworth and many of his brave troopers.[6]

Thanks in large part to the Union victory at Gettysburg, Kilpatrick was not censured for his poor judgment in ordering Farnsworth's charge. When bloody draft riots broke out in New York City a few days later, Kilpatrick was sent to assist Maj. Gen. John E. Wool and assumed command of the Federal cavalry forces gathered to help quell the disturbances.[7] After visiting with his wife and newborn son for two weeks, Kilpatrick returned to duty in Virginia.

The Federal and Confederate armies spent a long and bloody fall jockeying for position. Kilpatrick suffered a crushing defeat at the hands of Maj. Gen. James Ewell Brown (Jeb) Stuart's Confederate cavalry at the Battle of Buckland Mills on October 19, 1863, precipitating a rout known to history as "the Buckland Races."

When the fall campaign season ended with the armies stalemated along the Rappahannock River, Kilpatrick developed a bold scheme to liberate Union prisoners of war from Libby Prison and Belle Isle in Richmond. If he succeeded, great glory awaited him. Colonel Ulric Dahlgren, a flamboyant 22-year-old one-legged cavalry officer commanded one column of the raid, while Kilpatrick commanded the other. Over Alfred Pleasonton's vigorous objections, the raid was approved.[8]

Faced with unexpected Confederate resistance, Kilpatrick was repulsed in front of Richmond and struck hard by Wade Hampton's rebel troopers at Atlee's Station later that night. Dahlgren was thrown back at the southwestern defenses of Richmond and killed in an ambush near Stevensburg in King & Queen County, almost forty miles from the Southern capital. Incriminating documents found on Dahlgren's body suggested that the purpose of the raid was not only the liberation of prisoners of war, but the burning of Richmond and the murder of President Davis and his cabinet. A firestorm of controversy erupted, and Kilpatrick was blamed for the embarrassing debacle. A scathing Detroit newspaper editorial observed that Kilpatrick "cares nothing about the lives of men, sacrificing them with cool indifference, his only object being his own promotion and keeping his name before the public."[9] By this time he had acquired the unflattering nickname of "Kill-Cavalry" because he had repeatedly used up both men and horses in his ongoing pursuit of personal glory. On April 15, 1864, Kilpatrick was removed from command of the Third Cavalry Division.

Meanwhile, General Sherman's western army (he actually led three armies together in one large group on his drive into Georgia) needed a new cavalry commander. The Western Federal cavalry had fared poorly during the first three years of the war, and Sherman had been looking for someone to bring toughness and aggressiveness to his mounted arm. He had several cavalry commanders to choose from, including George Stoneman, Kilpatrick, and Maj. Gen. James H. Wilson, the overall commander of the cavalry assigned to Sherman's theater of operations.

Wilson had succeeded Kilpatrick in command of the Third Division of the Army of the Potomac's Cavalry Corps. Even though Wilson was younger than Kilpatrick, he was a full major general of volunteers while Kilpatrick was only a brevet brigadier general. Not surprisingly, there was no love lost between the two officers. Sherman resolved this potential conflict by placing Kilpatrick directly under his own command, thereby removing him from Wilson's authority.

Not long after joining Sherman, Kilpatrick was badly wounded at Resaca during the opening days of the Atlanta Campaign that May. He did not return to duty until late July 1864. By this time Stoneman was in a Confederate prison, leaving Kilpatrick as the commander of Sherman's cavalry by default—even though Wilson outranked him. Kilpatrick capably led a division of cavalry during Sherman's March to the Sea and in his subsequent advance through South Carolina and into North Carolina during the winter of 1864.[10]

For his part, Wilson remained at cavalry headquarters in Alabama developing a new plan. He put together a 16,000-man mounted army and led it on an extended raid into the heartland of the South, eviscerating what remained of the that portion of the Confederacy. Wilson's army defeated Lt. Gen. Nathan Bedford Forrest's cavalry at Selma, Alabama, on April 2, 1865.

Judson Kilpatrick cut an odd figure. He stood only five feet, three inches tall and weighed about 130 pounds. Despite his diminutive size, he was nevertheless a memorable character in a war filled with unforgettable personalities. "His face was . . . marked . . . showing . . . individuality in every line," remembered cavalryman James H. Kidd. "[He had] a prominent nose, a wide mouth, a firm jaw, thin cheeks set off by side whiskers rather light in color . . . the eyes . . . were cold and lustrous, but searching . . . a countenance that once seen, was never forgotten." He wore a stylish, tight-fitting blue uniform and "a black hat with the brim turned down on one side, up on the other . . . which gave to the style of his own name."[11]

Not everyone sang his praises. Others viewed him less kindly. "He is a very ungraceful rider, looking more like a monkey than a man on horseback," wrote one Federal officer who went on to describe him as "the most vain, conceited, egotistical little popinjay I ever saw."[12] That was not the only negative assessment. "It is hard to look at him without laughing," wrote Lt. Col. Theodore Lyman, a staff officer assigned to the Army of the Potomac's headquarters in the spring of 1864.[13]

Though cheerful and approachable, Kilpatrick also possessed a fiery temper. He was, recalled one man, brave but "flamboyant, reckless, tempestuous, and even licentious."[14] Captain Charles Francis Adams of the 1st Massachusetts Cavalry, the grandson and great-grandson of American presidents and possessed of the notorious Adams's family acid pen, observed, "Kilpatrick is a brave, injudicious boy, much given to blowing, and will surely come to grief."[15] Another Federal officer called Kilpatrick "a frothy braggart without brains."[16]

Henry C. Meyer, who had served with Kilpatrick in the 2nd New York Cavalry and as a member of his staff, had many opportunities to observe "Little Kil" during 1862 and 1863. "He had capacity for rallying soldiers and getting them into a charge," recalled Meyer. "His usual method when meeting the enemy was to order a charge. Sometimes this was successful, and at other times it was not so much so and very costly of men. It was because of this that he secured the nickname of 'Kil-Cavalry.'"[17]

Kilpatrick used language more like a club than a sabre. His profanity was notorious. It was also well known that "a dispatch bearing Kilpatrick's name leads to . . . doubt of its accuracy," one Northern artillerist caustically noted.[18] "His memory and imagination," wrote the ever-tactful Maj. Gen. Oliver O. Howard, "were often in conflict."[19]

The New Jersey general always had an eye for the ladies. Alice Kilpatrick had died unexpectedly on November 22, 1863, and her husband became quite the womanizer after her passing. As the army advanced through South Carolina in 1865, several women joined his retinue. Six weeks after the Battle of Monroe's Crossroads he occupied a wing of a house near Durham with a woman he claimed was Mrs. Kilpatrick, although he had not remarried. Major Lewellyn G. Estes, Kilpatrick's chief of staff, shared a bed with a second woman. "I was at first led to believe that these women were respectable," remembered the owner of the house, "but they soon made their appearance in male attire and the one under General Kilpatrick's charge was known as 'Charley' and the one with [Major] Estes was known as 'Frank' and I soon discovered them to be women of dissolute character." He continued, "They were vulgar, rude, and indecent, but fitting companions for a man of General Kilpatrick's character and they forced themselves upon my family in a low vulgar manner."[20]

"Charley" had black eyes, black hair and a dark complexion. "I have often seen General Kilpatrick in bed with Charley hugged up close," recalled a witness. "I know that Charley was a woman for I have seen her naked and I have seen her making water and she always sat down to do it."[21] Another observer noted, "I . . . often saw General Kilpatrick in bed with Charley . . . General Kilpatrick was very fond of Charley and used to lie pretty close to her in bed."[22] A local black woman also witnessed that another young woman who accompanied Kilpatrick's headquarters named Molly "was in the family way," and that "General Kilpatrick was the father of her child." Molly told the same witness that Little Kil had "done her so [and] now was trying to go back on her but she should stick to him and make him take care of the baby, for it was his."[23]

Captain James H. Miller, who commanded Company L of the 5th Ohio Cavalry, confirmed many of these observations. "It was generally understood in his command that General Kilpatrick had a woman with him all through the campaign dressed in men's half uniform clothes," he later recalled.[24]

Another woman named Alice, who rode in a special carriage as part of the general's headquarters train, also accompanied Kilpatrick. Alice "was rather plain-looking and not over-young," was how one Confederate described her.[25] Kilpatrick introduced Alice as a school teacher from New England who had been stranded in the Deep South with the coming of war. He often said that he was conducting her north to safety. She "had turned to temporarily presiding over Kilpatrick's military establishment," quipped a South Carolinian.[26] Ohio Captain James Miller noted, "It was the general belief of the command that he carried her with him for purposes less honorable than those alleged by him."[27]

Lieutenant Henry Clay Reynolds, a renowned Confederate scout attached to the command of Kilpatrick's West Point friend and classmate Maj. Gen. Joseph Wheeler, had an opportunity to observe Kilpatrick dallying with Alice. Reynolds was captured and forced to follow along on foot, his feet aching as he limped along in another man's shoes. "There was a Yankee school teacher who appealed to Genl Kilpatrick to be carried along with his command till she reached some point on the sea board so she might reach home. He took a carriage and a pair of horses at

USAMHI

Troopers of the 5th Ohio Cavalry

Aiken, S.C. put her in it and had one of his escort drive it." According to Reynolds, "I was immediately in rear of this carriage. Saw Genl K lie with his head in this lady's lap &c."[28] Although nobody has ever positively identified her, one of these three women played a significant role in the Battle of Monroe's Crossroads, to Judson Kilpatrick's eternal embarrassment.

Major General Joseph Wheeler's Confederate cavalry had harried Kilpatrick's advance throughout the Carolinas Campaign, generally making his advance miserable. "The cavalry, protecting the front, flanks, and rear of the advancing army of four great infantry columns through a hostile country, was ever in motion," noted one observer.[29]

As Sherman refitted his army group in Savannah, he began a dialogue with general-in- chief Lt. Gen. Ulysses S. Grant as to his next move. Grant initially considered transferring Sherman's "army group" north to Virginia by sea, where it would then act in concert with Union forces confronting Robert E. Lee's Army of Northern Virginia. "I had no idea originally of having Sherman march from Savannah to Richmond, or even to North Carolina," admitted Grant after the war.[30]

Foremost in Grant's thinking was the weather. The winter of 1864-1865 had been especially bad, with no promise of improvement any time soon. It was one of the rainiest winters anyone could remember, and the roads were heavy quagmires capable of swallowing wagons and horses and pulling and sucking an army to a standstill. Grant knew the torrential rains had rendered most of the roads impassable, and that the terrible weather would adversely affect Sherman's ability to maneuver and fight to advantage.[31]

Sherman was more sanguine. His successful March to the Sea had made clear to him how he expected to conduct operations in the Carolinas. He also appreciated their strategic value and he asked his commander to consider the effect that marching his "army group" through the Carolinas would have on the Confederacy. "Sherman realized that by marching his army through the Carolinas he would

inevitably cut Lee's supply lines to the Deep South and induce hundreds—if not thousands—of Lee's troops from that region to desert," wrote Grant. Sherman's march across Georgia to Savannah demonstrated the

Major General
William T. Sherman

NARA

devastating effect an army could have on an enemy's transportation and supply networks.[32]

If Sherman marched his army through the Carolinas, it would eviscerate what remained of the Confederacy. Grant reconsidered Sherman's proposal and four days before the turn of the new year instructed him to "make your preparations to start on your expedition without delay. . . .break up the railroads in South and North Carolina, and join the armies operating against Richmond as soon as you can."[33]

With the authorization to proceed, Sherman set about making the necessary preparations for his army group's thrust through the Carolinas. In his drive north, he planned to link up with other Union forces advancing inland from the coast of North Carolina. If all went according to plan, they would unite near the railroad junction of Goldsboro. The combined armies would then be linked to the Union-occupied coast by rail, their supplies and communications secure.[34]

Sherman decided to engage in a bit of deception by moving along multiple routes in order to create uncertainty within the Confederate high command (which included his old friends Braxton Bragg and P. G. T. Beauregard) as to his final destination. Once inside the Palmetto State, he intended to feint simultaneously in the direction of Augusta, Georgia, and Charleston, South Carolina. This would force Beauregard to divide his forces to protect both cities, thereby stretching the South's already limited resources to the breaking point. Once Sherman reached the interior of the state, he intended to turn his columns toward the state capitol at Columbia. After capturing Columbia, he would move north into North Carolina. His final campaign objective remained uncertain: either that state's capitol at Raleigh or the important railhead at Weldon. From either destination he would be within one week's march of Grant's armies operating against Petersburg and Richmond.[35]

On February 1, 1865, with the majority of his infantry divisions and Kilpatrick's cavalry across the Savannah River, Sherman ordered his commanders to initiate the campaign on the following day. In spite of all the difficulties posed by weather and logistics, Sherman's "grand army" was on the move. As he had done during the Savannah Campaign, Sherman sent Maj. Gen. Henry W. Slocum and Major General Howard's wings on simultaneous movements that confused the Confederates as to his real objective. The army group's wings moved along a front 40 miles wide.[36]

Major General
Henry W. Slocum

In order to mask the fact that his army's left wing, after crossing the Savannah River at Sisters Ferry and demonstrating toward Augusta, Georgia, was moving east toward Columbia, South Carolina, Sherman ordered Kilpatrick to make a demonstration westward toward Aiken. Joe Wheeler divined Kilpatrick's intentions and concentrated about 4,500 cavalry to oppose the move. As Kilpatrick's unsuspecting column of 3,000 Federal horsemen approached Aiken on February 11, Wheeler deployed his troopers in the side streets and ordered them to remain quiet. Before long the Federals entered the town, with Little Kil riding at the head of his column. Wheeler sprung his trap and charged, surprising and routing one of Kilpatrick's brigades in the first moments of contact. "The next thing in order was for the 92nd Illinois Mounted Infantry to charge into the town; so into the town they went," recalled an Illinois horseman. "Now we felt that we were going into a trap, but Kilpatrick took the lead."[37]

It was a dangerous position for a general commanding a column, and Wheeler's troopers nearly captured Little Kil. "As he came within sight of the line of battle of the Ninth Ohio and Ninth Michigan, the Rebels were actually grabbing for him, as he hugged his horse's neck, and roweled the horse's flanks with his spurs. It was laughable in the extreme," remembered a member of the 92nd Illinois.[38]

"A crush of horses, a flashing of sword blades, five or ten minutes of blind confusion, and then those who have not been knocked from their saddles by their neighbor's horses, and have not cut off their own horses' heads instead of their enemies, 'find themselves, they know not how, either running away or being run away from,'" was how a bluecoat described the melee in the streets.[39] "Every man in the regiment appeared to be conscious that the only way to get out was to assault the rebel line and cut a hole in it," remembered another member of the 92nd Illinois.[40] "So mixed up were the gray and the blue in a confused, helter-skelter, jumbled crowd, pressing on to the brigade, each claiming the other as prisoner, not a shot could be fired by the brigade."[41]

After desperate hand-to-hand fighting in the streets, the press of Wheeler's men began overwhelming the Federals. Kilpatrick's men succeeded in cutting their way free and fled the town. In their wake were 450 killed and wounded troopers. Wheeler only gave up the pursuit when he encountered a pair of Kilpatrick's regiments posted behind breastworks armed with lethal Spencer repeating carbines. Southern losses in the Aiken fighting totaled 251 from all causes.[42]

Not surprisingly, Kilpatrick did not admit defeat at Aiken. "Wheeler has, as usual, reported a victory over my people, whose backs he has not yet seen, and from all that I can learn a portion of our army seems only too willing to believe such reports," he claimed.[43] Not even the news that Lt. Gen. Wade Hampton and a cavalry division from Virginia had reinforced Wheeler's horsemen in February gave Little Kil pause. "I don't fear Wheeler and Hampton combined, even without supports," he boasted in a report to Sherman.[44]

Because of such grandiose proclamations and earlier episodes not unlike Aiken, Sherman retained little faith in Kilpatrick. Sherman's soldiers held a similarly jaundiced opinion of the army's mounted arm. In November 1864, a surprise attack by Wheeler near Waynesboro had nearly devastated Kilpatrick's command, much to the division commander's humiliation. "These cavalrymen are a positive nuisance," commented one of Sherman's staff officers, "they won't fight, and whenever they are around, they are always in the way of those who will fight. . . . Confound the cavalry. They're good for nothing but to run down horses and steal chickens."[45]

Painfully aware of these shortcomings, Sherman had been corresponding with Grant about the problem for some months. As Grant recounted, "The enemy having withdrawn the bulk of his force from the Shenandoah Valley and sent it south, or replaced troops sent from Richmond, and desiring to reinforce Sherman, if practicable, whose cavalry was greatly inferior in numbers to that of the enemy, I determined to make a move from the Shenandoah, which, if successful, would accomplish the first at least, and possibly the latter of these objects."[46]

By February 17, Sherman's army occupied the capitol of South Carolina. Implementing Sherman's policy of destroying anything of value to the Confederate war effort, the blue-backs razed the arsenal and many government warehouses jammed with military supplies. The Federals replenished their supply wagons with captured bags of corn meal and other commissary supplies.[47] As South Carolina's state capital Columbia suffered a fate worse than any other city occupied by Sherman's men, who viewed the city as the birthplace of the hated rebellion. A fire started by the burning of cotton bales spread throughout the city, destroying both public and private property. No one could agree on who was responsible. Sherman blamed Confederate cavalry under Hampton for the conflagration, while Hampton pointed the finger at Sherman's men. Regardless of who caused the fire, the result left many Columbians homeless, hungry, and jobless.

Worried that Sherman might need assistance, on February 20 Grant ordered Maj. Gen. Philip H. Sheridan, who had two large and powerful veteran divisions of cavalry at Winchester, Virginia, to move his command to Lynchburg. "From Lynchburg, if information you might get there would justify it, you could strike south, heading the streams in Virginia to the westward of Danville, and push on and join Sherman."[48]

A few days later, when Sheridan asked where Sherman's army was, Grant repeated his instructions. He added that Sherman had completed the refitting of his army. "I think, however, all danger of the necessity for going to that point has passed. I believe he has passed Charlotte. He may take Fayetteville on his way to Goldsboro," wrote the general-in-chief. "If you reach Lynchburg you will have to be guided in your after movements by the information you obtain. Before you could possibly reach Sherman I think you would find him moving from Goldsboro toward Raleigh, or engaging the enemy strongly posted at one or the other of these places, with railroad communications opened from his army to Wilmington or New Berne."[49]

Sheridan, however, never reported to Sherman and Grant never punished Sheridan for insubordination.[50] Although Sherman wanted Sheridan to take command of the cavalry forces attached to his army, as well as Sheridan's own divisions, Sheridan's refusal to cooperate meant that Sherman would have no choice but to rely on Judson Kilpatrick to carry the burden of his mounted operations for the remainder of the campaign. It also meant Sherman would have to keep his aggressive

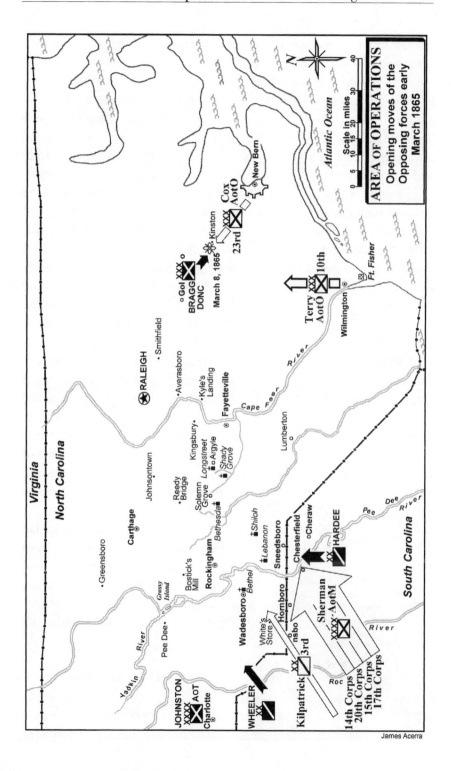

AREA OF OPERATIONS

Opening moves of the
Opposing forces early
March 1865

Scale in miles
0   5   10   15   20   30   40

Atlantic Ocean

New Bern

Cox
AotO

Kinston

23rd

March 8, 1865

Gol
BRAGG
DONC

10th

Ft. Fisher

Terry
AotO

Wilmington

Smithfield

RALEIGH

Averasboro

Kyle's
Landing

Fayetteville

Cape Fear River

Kingsbury

Longstreet

Argyle

Shady
Grove

Johnsontown

*Reedy
Bridge*

Solemn
Grove

Bethesda

Lumberton

Virginia

North Carolina

Greensboro

Carthage

Bostick's
Mill

Rockingham

Grassy
Island

Pee Dee River

Yadkin River

Shiloh

Lebanon

Sneedsboro

Cheraw

Chesterfield

HARDEE

Pee Dee River

South Carolina

Bethel

Wadesboro

Hornboro

White's
Store

nsbo

3rd

Kilpatrick

Sherman
AotM

River

Roc

14th Corps
20th Corps
15th Corps
17th Corps

JOHNSTON
AoT
Charlotte

WHEELER

Kilpatrick

James Acerra

cavalry chief on a short leash because trusting Little Kil to his own discretion had proven disastrous in the past.

With his work in Columbia finished, Sherman began moving toward his next objective, Fayetteville, North Carolina.[51] By March 8 the lead element of Howard's Right Wing had crossed into North Carolina, which "for the first time felt the full weight of Sherman's army." The new and devastating form of total warfare Sherman had inflicted upon Georgia and South Carolina was about to be unleashed on the Old North State.[52]

The two wings of the Federal army advanced to Fayetteville along separate routes. General Howard's Right Wing moved well to the east along two direct roads. Once the Right Wing neared Fayetteville, it was ordered to enter the town from the south. General Henry Slocum's Left Wing moved toward Fayetteville along a single road intending to enter the town from the west. Kilpatrick's cavalry, meanwhile, was to continue operating well to the left rear of Slocum's wing in order to protect the army's trains from Hampton's and Wheeler's marauding cavalrymen.[53]

Although Kilpatrick no longer held Sherman's confidence, there is no evidence that he was aware of it. Under his command was a division of experienced horse soldiers, approximately 4,400 battle-hardened veterans organized into three brigades. He also had an *ad hoc* provisional brigade consisting of the dismounted men of his various regiments, formed into three regiments and armed with infantry weapons. These men had seen plenty of fighting and hard marching during the course of their service with Sherman. Kilpatrick was also blessed with four experienced and competent brigade commanders.

Colonel Thomas Jefferson Jordan commanded the First Brigade. Born in Walnut Hill, Dauphin County, Pennsylvania, on December 2, 1821, Jordan was a graduate of Carlisle, Pennsylvania's venerable Dickinson

Colonel Thomas Jordan

USAMHI

College and had served several terms in the Pennsylvania legislature. His grandfather had been a major and paymaster in the Revolutionary War and his wife was the granddaughter of a Revolutionary War general. Jordan was practicing law in Harrisburg when the Civil War came. Although he had no formal military training, he had served in the local militia for years and was a friend of Pennsylvania Governor Andrew G. Curtin, who appreciated Jordan's intellect and administrative ability.[54]

The day after Fort Sumter fell, Curtin appointed Jordan as an aide to Maj. Gen. William H. Keim, commander of Pennsylvania's military forces. Jordan served Keim well. He carried the first news of the riots in Baltimore to Bvt. Lt. Gen. Winfield Scott, then accompanied Keim and the Pennsylvania forces into Maryland for their 1861 summer campaign against the Virginia forces of Brig. Gen. Joseph E. Johnston. Jordan saw action at Falling Waters and earned invaluable experience.

When that campaign concluded, Jordan was mustered out, received a new commission as a major, and was assigned to assist Col. Edward C. Williams in recruiting the 9th Pennsylvania Cavalry. Jordan was captured in June 1862, and spent five months as a prisoner of war, first at Madison, Georgia, and then in Richmond's notorious Libby Prison. He received a promotion to colonel of the 9th Pennsylvania in early 1863 while still a prisoner of war.[55] Jordan was exchanged in March 1863, and led the regiment through September 1864. He so impressed Maj. Gen. George H. Thomas that Thomas asked President Lincoln to promote Jordan in recognition of his meritorious service at the Battle of Chickamauga in September 1863.[56] By October 1864, Jordan was in command of a brigade of veteran cavalry, which he successfully led on the March to the Sea and then into the Carolinas, defeating Wheeler in combat several times along the way. On February 25, 1865, Jordan received a brevet promotion to brigadier general of volunteers for his meritorious service.[57] The 44-year-old thickly bearded colonel with the receding hairline and sharp countenance was well respected by both his men and his superiors.

Jordan's First Brigade, about 1,500 strong, consisted of a battalion of the 3rd Indiana Cavalry, the 8th Indiana Cavalry, the 2nd Kentucky Cavalry, the 3rd Kentucky Cavalry, and the 9th Pennsylvania Cavalry. These men had fought hard throughout the war, including the 1862 Kentucky Campaign, the 1863 Tullahoma Campaign, Chickamauga, Knoxville, and all of Sherman's campaigns in 1864 and 1865. These veteran horse soldiers knew their business and had proved their mettle on battlefields scattered across many states.

Brigadier General Smith D. Atkins commanded Kilpatrick's Second Brigade. Born on June 9, 1835 in Horseheads, New York, Atkins attended the Rock River Seminary in Mt. Morris, Illinois. Before the war, the young man worked as a newspaper editor and lawyer in Illinois. He was commissioned captain of the 11th Illinois Infantry on April 30, 1861, and promoted to major on March 21, 1862. He spent most of that intervening year serving on the staff of Maj. Gen. Stephen A. Hurlbut. In September of 1862, Atkins was appointed colonel of the 92nd Illinois Infantry. By February of the following year he was in command of a brigade in the Army of Kentucky. Four months later in June he was at the head of a brigade in the Reserve Corps of the Army of the Cumberland.

On July 22 Atkins's regiment was converted to mounted infantry and became part of Col. John T. Wilder's legendary Lightning Brigade, an outfit made up of mounted infantrymen armed with Spencer repeating rifles. Their mobility and firepower made them a prototype for James Wilson's mounted corps. These men performed admirably at the September 1863 Battle of Chickamauga, holding off superior enemy forces with the firepower of their seven-shot Spencer rifles.[58] By the beginning of the 1864 Atlanta Campaign, the Lightning Brigade had been outfitted with traditional cavalry arms and was serving as light cavalry, with Atkins in command of the brigade. He received a brevet to brigadier general of volunteers on January 12, 1865.[59]

Atkins had many friends and admirers throughout the army, but one member of the 92nd Illinois described him as "a peculiar man." Another noted that he was "a talented lawyer by profession and like many men of that profession had used his

Brigadier General
Smith D. Atkins

NARA

talents to save wrong doers from getting justice done them." Although Atkins did not usually imbibe alcohol, his men liked to play tricks on him by spiking his demijohn with whiskey. "He had a slick tongue and was fond of speech making and had a high appreciation of what he said and did," remembered one Union soldier.[60]

Atkins's 1,000-strong Second Brigade consisted of the 92nd Illinois Mounted Infantry, the 9th Michigan Cavalry, the 9th Ohio Cavalry, the 10th Ohio Cavalry, and McLaughlin's Squadron of Ohio Cavalry. Like Jordan's troopers, these men were also veteran units that had seen extensive action in the Western Theater, including the Atlanta Campaign, the March to the Sea, and the early days of the Carolinas Campaign. Several units of Atkins's brigade had served together for some time, but others had joined after the fall of Atlanta.

Colonel George Eliphaz Spencer of the 1st Alabama Cavalry, a loyalist unit from the heart of the Confederacy, led Kilpatrick's Third Brigade. Born in Champion, Jefferson County, New York, on November 1, 1836, Spencer attended college in Montreal, Canada. A lawyer, he later served in the United States Senate. Spencer was commissioned a captain in the U. S. Volunteers on October 24, 1862, serving as an assistant adjutant general and then chief of staff for Brig. Gen. Grenville M. Dodge. In July 1863, Spencer requested a transfer to the 1st Alabama Cavalry, which did not have a permanent commanding officer. That September his request was granted and Spencer was appointed colonel of the Alabama regiment, which was stationed at Corinth, Mississippi.

In early 1864, the 1st Alabama engaged in scouting and skirmishing against Joe Wheeler's cavalry around Rome, Georgia. The Alabamians quickly earned the respect of their veteran comrades (though they would

Colonel
George Eliphaz Spencer

occasionally behave badly around Savannah) and were assigned to Kilpatrick's division that fall, just in time for the March to the Sea. By January 1865, Spencer had assumed command of the Third Brigade. A competent officer, he would receive a brevet to brigadier general of volunteers for his meritorious service during the Carolinas Campaign, primarily for his meritorious service at Monroe's Crossroads.[61]

Spencer's 1,500 men came from three cavalry regiments: the 1st Alabama, the 5th Kentucky, and the 5th Ohio. The latter pair were veterans of many campaigns, including the pursuit of Brig. Gen. John Hunt Morgan's raiders across Indiana and Ohio. They had also served throughout the Atlanta Campaign and the March to the Sea. The 1st Alabama, on the other hand, was a rowdy and undisciplined bunch infamous for their plundering exploits. During the March to the Sea, Maj. Gen. Frank Blair, commander of the 17th Corps, scolded Spencer: "The outrages committed by your command during the march are becoming so common, and are of such an aggravated nature, that they call for some severe and instant mode of correction." The lack of discipline would haunt Kilpatrick in a most unfortunate manner in the coming weeks.[62]

Large mounted forces in the field use and lose many horses, an unfortunate but inevitable consequence of hard campaigning. By March 1865, Kilpatrick's troopers had been campaigning continuously for six weeks, and the attrition on their mounts had been severe. Nearly ten percent of his troopers, or some 400 men, had lost their horses and had been unable to secure replacements. The dismounted men were organized into a provisional brigade consisting of three *ad hoc* regiments. Assignments to the dismounted regiments corresponded to the soldier's regular brigade. For example, if a trooper in Atkins's Second Brigade lost his mount, he was assigned to the 2nd Provisional Regiment. As a general rule, these men continued to carry their cavalry carbines, but to maximize the range of their firepower, some carried Springfield rifled muskets rather than the traditional carbines and sabers carried by horse soldiers.

Lieutenant Colonel William B. Way of the 9th Michigan Cavalry commanded the Provisional Brigade. The 30-year-old native of Rochester, New York, was raised in Pontiac, Michigan. When the war broke out he was mustered in as a first lieutenant in the 1st Michigan Cavalry. By November 1861 he had assumed command of Company C of the 1st Michigan Cavalry. By October 1862 he was a captain, a promotion earned after hard campaigning in the Shenandoah Valley

Lieutenant Colonel
William B. Way

against Thomas "Stonewall" Jackson, and then in Maj. Gen. John Pope's Army of Virginia.. The following month, Way mustered out of service with the 1st Michigan Cavalry. On April 30, 1863, he was commissioned major in the newly-formed 9th Michigan Cavalry. Way distinguished himself during John Morgan's Raid across Indiana and Ohio, when he led a contingent of 200 troopers on a wild chase after the Confederate cavalier and his men, capturing more than 300—including Morgan himself—and killing and wounding many others.[63] On November 30, 1863, Way received a well deserved promotion to lieutenant colonel of the 9th Michigan Cavalry, a role he filled until his appointment to command the Provisional Brigade.[64]

Captain Theodore F. Northrop was the 20-year-old commander of Kilpatrick's 85-man scout detachment. One of eight children, Northrop was born in southeast New York on May 31, 1844, to William and Agnes Northrop. In 1861, when the 2nd New York Cavalry regiment was raised in Essex, New Jersey, the youth enlisted as a private in Company G. A short time later he was promoted to sergeant. By the fall of 1862 Northrop had found a position in Kilpatrick's inner circle as an orderly. When Kilpatrick was imprisoned in November of that year, Northrop submitted an affidavit defending his superior against the charges of dishonesty and theft. Kilpatrick rewarded the young man for his loyalty. "Capt. Northrop was one of the most steadfast of friends," noted a comrade. "Once he formed a friendship it endured through all the storms of life."[65]

The young man was both tough and courageous. During the cavalry fight at Aldie on June 17, 1863, Northrop was severely wounded in the right shoulder. He carried the bullet for more than thirty years before the

Captain
Theodore Northrop

Larry Strayer

troublesome slug was finally cut out. Captured, Northrop was held briefly in Libby Prison before being exchanged to rejoin his command a few days later. As a reward for his valor, Northrop was commissioned second lieutenant with the date of rank made retroactive to June 17, 1863.

On May 2, 1864, Northrop was promoted to first lieutenant and received a second promotion to captain later that fall.[66] He was just twenty when appointed to command Kilpatrick's scout detachment. It was an important role, for the scouts led the way for Kilpatrick's division.[67] "The duty assigned to me was that of procuring information for headquarters in regard to the enemy's movement, locations, conditions of lines of communication and topography," recounted Northrop in 1917. "It was not my duty to engage in an offensive against the enemy."[68] Although quite young, Northrop proved an effective leader in his new role. One of Kil-Cavalry's staff officers praised Northrop's courage, recalling how he "repeatedly carried out successfully missions involving unusual hazards and requiring great daring."[69]

Northrop proudly claimed that his scouts, who were handpicked from each regiment of Kilpatrick's division, were "as brave and as able a body of rough-riders as ever fought on horseback."[70] Much of their time was spent dressed in enemy uniforms and most had mastered a convincing Southern drawl. Their daring allowed them to pass for Confederates and ride into enemy camps. It was a dangerous assignment, because if they were caught they could be executed as spies.[71] Northrop's scouts fanned out across the Southern countryside, stealing and foraging everything that crossed their path. It did not take long before the people of Georgia, South Carolina, and North Carolina came to hate Northrop and his men and dreaded their approach.[72]

Kilpatrick's command also included 94 officers and men of the 10th Battery, Wisconsin Light Artillery, commanded by Capt. Yates V. Beebe, who doubled as Kilpatrick's chief of artillery. Three sections of two guns each of horse artillery accompanied each brigade of cavalry assigned to Kilpatrick's Division, although the dismounted provisional brigade did not originally have guns supporting it. Their two-gun section of 3-inch ordnance rifles had been captured from the Confederates at Lovejoy Station in Georgia in August 1864 and arrived at Monroe's Crossroads at the same time as the brigade.[73] The artillerists were veterans of the Atlanta Campaign and of the March to the Sea and had performed good service during their tenure with Sherman's army.

Although Sherman had little faith in Kilpatrick, the cavalryman's command was composed of reliable veteran troopers who had fought, marched, and ridden their way across much of the South. The men were well-armed, well-equipped, and, with the exception of the Provisional Brigade, fairly well-mounted. By 1865, the Federal government had become proficient in providing remounts to the cavalry, making the existence of the dismounted brigade something of a mystery. Virtually all of Kilpatrick's troopers carried seven-shot Spencer repeating carbines, but there were also single-shot breach-loading weapons such as the Smith, Hall, Starr, Sharps, Joslyn, and Burnside carbines, reliable weapons with an effective range of about 200 yards.[74] Most of the men carried sabers and pistols, typically Colt or Remington .44 caliber revolvers. As noted earlier, the dismounted brigade carried the familiar single-shot muzzle-loading Springfield rifled muskets. They traveled with enough ammunition to keep their cartridge boxes full.[75]

These veteran horse soldiers, confident that was war was winding down, would need all their experience, courage, and weaponry in days ahead.

Chapter 2

Wade Hampton and
his Confederate Cavaliers

Although the attrition of war had worn down the Confederacy and its armies, the cavalry attached to Joe Johnston's army remained a powerful and effective force in early 1865. These combat-tested veterans had seen fighting in scores of battles and skirmishes, as had their commander, 28-year-old Maj. Gen. Joseph Wheeler. Two years ahead of Kilpatrick at West Point, Wheeler had led the cavalry forces attached to the Army of Tennessee for much of the war. Only the late Jeb Stuart had outranked Wheeler in the Southern mounted arm.

The youngest of four children, Joe Wheeler was born on September 10, 1836. He was the son of a prominent Connecticut businessman who had settled on a large plantation near Augusta, Georgia. Wheeler's paternal grandfather had been an American general in the War of 1812, and young Joe inherited his grandfather's appetite for adventure. His diminutive and frail-looking physique earned him the unflattering nickname of "Little Joe." Those who tagged him with the name were in for a surprise because "Little Joe's" size belied his courage: the boy was utterly fearless.

Wheeler's mother died when he was only five and his father suffered a series of financial disasters that left the family bankrupt. A move to Connecticut failed to alleviate the family's plight, and the father returned

Major General Joseph Wheeler

his family to Augusta in an effort to recoup his fortune. When this attempt failed, the 13-year-old Wheeler was sent to Cheshire, Connecticut, to live with two aunts. When he graduated from Cheshire's Episcopal Academy, Wheeler moved to New York City to work as a clerk and live with a sister and her brother-in-law.

In 1854, Wheeler convinced a New York congressman to appoint him to the United States Military Academy at West Point. He proved to be less than a mediocre student, graduating nineteenth of twenty-two in the class of 1859. Ironically, he finished dead last in cavalry tactics. Wheeler was commissioned a brevet second lieutenant and received an assignment to the 1st U. S. Dragoons. In the spring of 1860 he was transferred to the 1st U. S. Mounted Rifles and saw combat against Indians in New Mexico Territory. His aggressiveness earned him the nom-de-guerre "Fighting Joe," a moniker he carried for the rest of his life.[1]

Despite his long ties with the North, when Georgia seceded from the Union in 1861 Wheeler resigned his commission and accepted an appointment as a first lieutenant of artillery in the Confederate army. He was ordered to Pensacola, Florida, where Southern volunteers were trying to reduce Fort Pickens. It was there that Wheeler met Brig. Gen. Braxton Bragg, whose patronage would carry Wheeler to high rank. Within a short time Wheeler was appointed colonel of the 19th Alabama Infantry and received orders to report to Mobile. At the head of his regiment at Shiloh he was struck by a spent ball and had two horses shot from under him.

Late in the summer of 1862, Wheeler assumed command of a brigade of cavalry, screening Bragg's advance into Kentucky. At the Battle of Perryville, Wheeler stared down a Union infantry corps with only five regiments of horse. Impressed with his steely performance and coolness under fire, Bragg appointed the pugnacious little horse soldier to be his chief of cavalry. Wheeler's troopers rode and fought night and day covering Bragg's withdrawal from Kentucky, a strong performance that earned him a wreath around his colonel's stars.

As a brigadier general, Wheeler performed well during the Stones River campaign that winter, waging an effective action that delayed 40,000 Union soldiers for nearly four days. He rode his horsemen around Maj. Gen. William S. Rosecrans and his Army of the Cumberland twice in excursions reminiscent of Jeb Stuart's more famous "Ride Around

McClellan." A week later, Wheeler captured five transports and a gunboat on the Cumberland River, earning a nomination for promotion to major general to date from January 20, 1863.[2] Later that year Wheeler authored a well-regarded cavalry tactics manual for use by Confederate horse soldiers and mounted infantry that was based on the French cavalry system.[3]

Unfortunately, Wheeler's fellow officers regarded him as Bragg's "pet," an association that may well have inhibited his career in the Confederate service. After a clash with Wheeler, Nathan Bedford Forrest refused to serve again under him, and other older officers such as John Hunt Morgan, Earl Van Dorn, and John Wharton also refused to take orders from "that boy."[4] Wheeler's poor performance during the opening phase of the Chickamauga Campaign permitted Rosecrans to steal a march on Bragg and capture Chattanooga without bloodshed, a gross lapse that encouraged many to call for Wheeler's removal as commander of Bragg's cavalry.[5] However, Wheeler survived the cries for his scalp and retained command of the largest force of Confederate cavalry in the Western Theater.

By early 1864, Joe Wheeler was one of the most experienced cavalry leaders in the entire Confederate army. Five horses had been shot from under him and his saddle, equipment, and uniform had frequently been rent by bullets.[6] He had also been wounded three times. Seven of his staff officers had been killed and another three wounded. His participation in numerous engagements and close brushes with death earned the respect of the men under his command, who called him "The War Child."[7] As one of his staff officers recalled, "No officer, since the commencement of the war, has been more exposed to the missiles of death than General Wheeler."[8]

Joe Wheeler stood only five feet, five inches tall and weighed a mere 120 pounds.[9] "His person is small, and in his manner there is nothing manly and commanding," wrote one of his men. Like Braxton Bragg—and possibly a reason for their affinity—Wheeler was of rigid and upright demeanor. "The habits and moral character of Gen. Wheeler are of the most circumspect and high-toned nature," observed a staff officer. "None of the vices of intemperance, or other bad habits common in the country, have been able to allure him from the spotless rectitude which has distinguished him from his earliest childhood."[10]

Although possessed of a "spotless rectitude," the horseman was also a humorless martinet and unpopular with his fellow officers. "As a brigadier he was successful, sober, industrious, and methodical," wrote one critic who objected to Wheeler's promotion to major general. "He succeeded well in organizing, but when the field of his operations was enlarged the draft on his intellect, which is one of mediocrity, became too heavy. He has signally failed to give satisfaction. . . . He evidently handles men awkwardly in battle, for he has but few engaged at a time." After acrimonious debate in the Senate, a direct appeal from Gen. Joseph E. Johnston finally secured Wheeler's confirmation as major general in the spring of 1864.[11]

Wheeler performed competently during the Atlanta Campaign, but the many problems plaguing his command limited its effectiveness. "We have a brave, gallant corps of Cavalry," noted a newspaper correspondent, "but there seems to be something lacking."[12] What was lacking was discipline, and Wheeler's men were quickly gaining a reputation as hooligans. Some Southerners contended that Wheeler's horsemen inflicted as much damage upon the Georgia countryside as did the passage of Sherman's army. Grumbling about Wheeler increased in all quarters.[13] In a letter to the editor of her local newspaper, one woman noted that the people of Georgia were suffering from both the "depredations" of Sherman's army and the "shameful" conduct of Wheeler's horsemen. "While the enemy were burning and destroying property on one side . . . [Wheeler's men] were stealing horses and mules on the other."[14]

A South Carolinian wrote an open letter to James A. Seddon, the Confederate secretary of war, which was published in the *Charleston Mercury* on January 14, 1865. "I cannot forbear appealing to you on behalf of the producing population of the States of Georgia and South Carolina for protection against he destructive lawlessness of members of General Wheeler's command," he began. "From Augusta to Hardeeville the road is now strewn with corn left on the ground unconsumed. Beeves have been shot down in the fields, one quarter taken off and the balance left for buzzards. Horses are stolen out of wagons on the road, and by wholesale out of stables at night." After describing further depredations, the correspondent concluded,

Are General Wheeler and his brigade commanders not responsible to the country for stealing the stock engaged in the production of food for our army, the falling off in the production of corn alone in the States of Georgia and South Carolina may be counted by the hundred thousand bushels. Make the country one immense camp— let everybody be engaged in working for the support of the whole army, but for the sake of our *glorious cause,* given the producer the protection necessary to enable him to make bread for the army and his little family? If General Hampton's cavalry had used Virginia and North Carolina as General Wheeler's men have used Georgia and South Carolina, where would General Lee now be?[15]

"The enemy care nothing for Wheeler and his seven thousand cavalry in the rear," wrote Georgia politician Robert Toombs to Confederate Vice President Alexander Stephens. "They did not obstruct his trains for more than four days, if that; and Wheeler avoided all depots where there were as much as armed sutlers. He has been gone [to Tennessee] for three weeks. I cannot say he has done no good for he has relieved the poor people of this part of the country temporarily from his plundering marauding bands of cowardly robbers . . . I hope to God he will never get back to Georgia." Another citizen complained to President Jefferson Davis that the people of Georgia had ceased caring who won the war since Sherman was not making war any harder on them than Wheeler's "robbers." Major General Daniel H. Hill, commanding at Augusta, wrote in January 1865, that "the whole of Georgia is full of bitter complaints about Wheeler's cavalry."[16]

On February 20, 1865, in the wake of the burning of Columbia, South Carolina State Commissioner W. Leman arrived at the offices of the Graniteville Manufacturing Company to confiscate cloth as payment for state taxes. He found bedlam instead. The company's managers were in the process of handing out the company stores at half price to the employees in order to keep the goods out of Union hands. Above all else, chaos reigned. Into this mess rode some of Joe Wheeler's horse soldiers. Instead of helping restore order, the Rebel troopers precipitated a riot. In conjunction with a mob described as both "White and Black" by a company manager named Gregg, they ransacked the company store, causing damages estimated between $250,000 to $350,000. Only the mustering of the Home Guard and a standoff with Wheeler's men restored order.[17]

Charles M. Calhoun of the 6th South Carolina Cavalry had come from the Army of Northern Virginia to defend his home state. He observed Wheeler's men in the field and came away unimpressed. "While General Wheeler and his command possessed many good fighting qualities, yet neither he nor his men were immune to many bad ones," he recalled. "It is a well-known fact that they as a whole or in part were badly disciplined, and were greatly dreaded even by their friends at times."[18] Calhoun's strong condemnation suggested that something had to be done quickly about Wheeler and his cavalry, especially given the crisis facing the Confederacy.

In the winter of 1864-1865, Col. Alfred Roman, the inspector general of the Military Division of the West, conducted a lengthy inspection of Wheeler's command. He did not like what he saw. Roman determined that Wheeler's Cavalry Corps was poorly organized and poorly armed, with no uniformity in its weaponry. More importantly, Roman noted, "Too much familiarity exists between officers and men. Discipline is thereby impaired. It has become loose, uncertain, wavering. Orders are not promptly obeyed. The military appearance is bad."

Roman continued:

> Much has been said and is still being said of the gross misconduct of Gen. Wheeler's men. Their alleged depredations and straggling propensities and their reported brutal interference with private property have become common by-words in every county where it has been their misfortune to pass. Public opinion condemns them everywhere; and not a few do we find in Georgia as well in South Carolina who look upon them more as a band of highway robbers than as an organized military body.

Colonel Roman saved his strongest criticism for Joseph Wheeler. "No one admires General Wheeler more than I do," he began. "He is a modest, conscientious, industrious officer. He takes a fatherly interest in his command. His activity is proverbial, and is equaled only by his gallantry. But he is wanting in firmness. His mind and his will are not in proper relation to one another. He is too gentle, too lenient, and we know how easily leniency can be made to degenerate into weakness." Roman also observed that "General Wheeler's men like him, but do not appear to be proud of him. They know he will always fight well, but seem to feel he cannot make them fight as well. The proposition that all who are able are not fit to be efficient cavalry commanders," Roman concluded, "is assuming more and more the proportions of a self evident proposition."

Roman ended his eye-popping report with both a stunning and damning condemnation of the Augusta native:

> My honest conviction is that General Wheeler would be a most excellent brigade or division commander, but I do not consider him the proper man to be placed at the head of a large independent cavalry corps. Under him and in spite of his good discipline and soldierly qualities, no true discipline will ever be perfect in his command nor with the whole efficiency of his corps, the entire fighting capabilities of his men, their dash, their intrepidity, be ever fairly and fully developed.
>
> Had I the power to act in the matter, I would relieve General Wheeler from his command, not as a rebuke, not as a punishment, for he surely deserves neither, but on higher grounds, that is, for the good of the cause and for his own reputation. We have no time to lose at this juncture of our affairs. If we intend to resist we must do it gloriously, promptly and fear no personal dissatisfaction in the performance of our duties. We have too much at stake to hesitate a moment.[19]

General Pierre G. T. Beauregard, commander of the Military Division of the West, agreed with Roman's assessment. A few days after receiving the report, Beauregard wrote to Gen. Robert E. Lee, who by this time was the general-in-chief of the Confederate armies. "I earnestly recommend, for the good of the service and cause, that General Hampton be promoted temporarily to command all the cavalry of this department, which cannot be rendered otherwise as effective as present emergencies demand," urged Beauregard. "Major-General Wheeler, who ranks only a few days, is a modest, zealous, gallant, and indefatigable officer, but he cannot properly control and direct successfully so large a corps of cavalry."[20] Lee, who had never overseen any of Wheeler's operations, reluctantly agreed. The general's hesitancy in removing Wheeler was obvious: he loathed even the thought of transferring his superb cavalry commander from the Army of Northern Virginia to fill "Little Joe's" boots.

Forty-six-year-old Wade Hampton was one of the wealthiest men in the South. Tall, handsome, and amiable, he stood about six feet tall and weighed more than 200 pounds. As the war had borne out, the South Carolinian was enormously strong and seemingly tireless. A tale was

USAMHI

Lieutenant General Wade Hampton

repeated often that he had killed a bear with his bare hands. The grandson of a U. S. Army general, Hampton had no formal military training. He graduated from South Carolina College (later the University of South Carolina) and took up the life of a planter and politician.[21] Unlike so many men with wealth and intellect, Hampton was modest and unpretentious, with a subtle self-deprecating sense of humor. He was a refined patrician with manners suited to his high position in society, and was remembered by one who knew him well as a "prince among gentlemen."[22] When the war came Hampton committed himself totally to the cause, personally raising and equipping at great expense the Hampton Legion, an outfit consisting of infantry, artillery, and cavalry units.

On July 21, 1861, Hampton suffered his first of what would be several wounds in the fighting at Manassas. His talents were quickly recognized and he was appointed a brigadier general on May 23, 1862, while commanding an infantry brigade. Eight days later he suffered a second more serious wound at Seven Pines (Fair Oaks). Once he recovered Hampton was confirmed as a brigadier and took command of a brigade of cavalry in Jeb Stuart's cavalry division of the Army of Northern Virginia. The 2nd South Carolina Cavalry regiment, formerly part of Hampton's Legion, served in Hampton's Brigade. The general's younger brother, Lt. Col. Frank Hampton, rode with the 2nd South Carolina. He was mortally wounded in the June 9, 1863, fighting at Brandy Station. The sad event was just one of the many losses Wade Hampton would suffer during the long and costly war. Less than a month later he was leading his troopers at Gettysburg in the fighting on East Cavalry Field on July 3, 1863. In the swirling close-quarter combat Hampton received a near-fatal saber blow to the head and a bullet wound in the side.[23]

The South Carolinian was known for leading charges and personally killed at least thirteen men during the Civil War. "Gen. Hampton always appeared to be unconscious of danger, with the fighting instinct ever uppermost, and to see a body of Yankees was to commence fighting, and if possible to lead the charge," remembered one of his staff officers years later.[24]

Hampton's "lack of . . . military training would prove an impediment at first, until practical experience in the field, developing the natural bent, had supplied its place."[25] One Northern officer suggested that while Hampton was an unschooled soldier who had probably never even read a book on tactics, he "knew how to maneuver the units of his command so as to occupy for offensive or defensive action the strongest points of the battlefield, and that is about all there is in tactics." Hampton, he continued, "appeared possessed of almost an instinctive topographical talent. He could take in the strong strategic points in the field of his operations with an accuracy of judgment that was surprising to his comrades. . . . He would hunt his antagonist as he would hunt big game in the forest. The celerity and audacity of his movements against the front, sometimes on the flank, then again in the rear, kept his enemies in a constant state of uncertainty and anxiety as to where and when they might expect him." The Yankee officer concluded: "With his wonderful powers of physical endurance, his alert vigilant mind, his matchless horsemanship, no obstacles seemed to baffle his audacity or thwart his purpose."[26]

Hampton's skill in leading horse soldiers prompted Lt. Gen. James Longstreet, the ranking corps commander in the Army of Northen Virginia, to declare that the South Carolinian "was the greatest cavalry leader of our or any other age."[27] Others agreed. "He was my ideal of a cavalry officer," declared Col. Thomas T. Munford, who served with Hampton in the Virginia army. "He had all the qualifications, as natural gifts. He was a woodsman and hunter; nature had taught him topography, geography, and astronomy. He saw everything, heard and gave ear to everything, but was cautious about telling his plans. Strategy with him was far superior to cunning. He knew where to fight, where to hit and when to retire." Munford finished his assessment of his superior with glowing words of praise: "He was by all odds the most successful cavalry officer in the Army of Northern Virginia."[28]

After recovering from his Gettysburg wounds, Hampton returned to duty in early November 1863, receiving a promotion to major general and command of a division of cavalry. When Stuart suffered a mortal wound in May 1864 at the Battle of Yellow Tavern, Hampton, as senior division commander, was next in line to assume command of the army's cavalry corps. However, a fierce rivalry developed between Hampton and Maj. Gen. Fitzhugh Lee, the nephew of General Lee. Fitz Lee would likely have been Stuart's choice, but Hampton outranked Lee even though both had been promoted to major general on August 3, 1863. The elder General Lee put off the difficult choice by electing not to appoint a new corps commander. Instead, he maintained his three divisions of cavalry as independent commands, with each division commander reporting directly to army headquarters.[29]

This awkward arrangement not only increased the stress on General Lee but created serious command problems during what is known as Maj. Gen. Philip H. Sheridan's mid-June 1864 Trevilian Raid. In spite of Fitz Lee's conspicuous lack of cooperation, Hampton thrashed the Federal cavalry at the June 11-12 Battle of Trevilian Station. Shortly thereafter Fitz Lee once again failed to coordinate with Hampton, a lapse that permitted the Federal raiders of Brig. Gens. James H. Wilson and August V. Kautz to escape an otherwise well-executed division-sized ambush at Reams Station on June 29, 1864. Several of Hampton's subordinates encouraged him to prefer courts-martial charges against Fitz Lee. The politically astute Hampton chose not to do so, realizing that a courts-martial of the army commander's nephew would likely fail and only serve to divide further an already wounded cavalry arm. General Lee recognized Hampton's abilities and on July 2 asked President Davis for the authority to make Hampton the commander of the Army of Northern Virginia's Cavalry Corps.[30]

Hampton's successes against the Federal cavalry continued through the late summer and early autumn of 1864. From September 11-16, the South Carolinian led a daring thrust deep behind Union lines to steal and safely bring back a large herd of beef cattle to an army desperately in need of the rations. Though Hampton's "Beef Steak Raid" was an unqualified success, other actions that followed extracted a high price. On October 27, General Hampton's son, Lt. William Preston Hampton, was killed in action at Burgess's Mill, where his other son and namesake, Lt. Wade Hampton, Jr., also received a severe wound. Notwithstanding his grief and staggering personal loss, the general somehow remained composed and in the field leading his men.

As a native of South Carolina, Hampton paid special attention to Sherman's presence in Georgia at Savannah. On February 1, 1865, the Union commander left Savannah with some 60,000 men and 2,500 wagons bound for parts unknown. His left wing and Kilpatrick's cavalry crossed the Savannah River at Sister's Ferry and and thrust into Hampton's native South Carolina. "The fact is my darling we are retreating *without* fighting & Sherman is, in fact, now marching through S.C. as easily as he did through Georgia," a frustrated Georgian wrote to his wife.[31]

Sherman's army seemed unstoppable. "Wheeler's cavalry was almost the only obstacle to Sherman's great march to the sea," observed a member of the 8th Texas Cavalry. "They harassed his columns front, flanks, and rear, picking up many prisoners; but three or four thousand cavalry could make little resistance to the onward sweep of 60,000 veterans under one of the greatest captains of modern times." In spite of almost daily combat, Wheeler's dogged band was nearly powerless to stop Sherman's advance.[32] "Was with General Wheeler's army all the way from Atlanta to Savannah and in a continual mix-up with Sherman's cavalry," recalled a member of the 4th Georgia Cavalry.[33]

Frustrated by his inability to protect his home and family, Hampton watched helplessly from Virginia. Unwilling to sit idly by and watch his beloved state be put to the torch, Hampton applied for a transfer to South Carolina. He requested that his able and trusted subordinate, Maj. Gen. Matthew C. Butler, accompany him along with his veteran cavalry division. Nearly half of Butler's command lacked horses and the transfer would enable them to find fresh mounts.[34] "I think Hampton will be of service in mounting his men and arousing the spirit and strength of the State and otherwise do good," General Lee wrote in a letter to President Davis. "I will therefore send him."[35] Hampton later recalled, "I was directed by [Lee] to proceed to South Carolina to assist in mounting and putting Butler's Division in the field 'with permission if a suitable command was given to me to operate it until recalled to Virginia.'"[36] In January 18 letter to his sister, the cavalry commander explained, "I am going to go out to see if I can do anything for my state, as Genl. Lee thinks that I can do good there."[37]

Determined to "fight as long as I can wield my saber," Hampton headed south, though with one major caveat: he refused to serve under Joe Wheeler.[38] That open bit of rebellion threatened to cause a serious command problem because Wheeler outranked Hampton.[39] In late January 1865, Hampton arrived at his home town of Columbia. He received a telegram from President Davis on February 16 informing him that he had been commissioned a lieutenant general, to rank from February 14.[40] Although the promotion was not undeserving, it was politically motivated in its timing. Hampton now outranked Wheeler. "[Lee] had me promoted so as to command him [Wheeler] and all his cavalry," explained Hampton in a postwar letter. "The Genl refused to let me serve under Wheeler."[41]

While he was undoubtedly disappointed, Wheeler took the news well. When Hampton informed him of the change, the diminutive cavalryman responded, "Certainly, general, I will receive your orders with pleasure."[42] Hampton was equally gracious toward his subordinate. "It must be said in acknowledgment of the high-bred courtesy of Hampton that he studiously avoided any show of authority over Wheeler that was avoidable," observed the historian of Wheeler's cavalry corps. "He assumed the duties the government had assigned to him without his consent, but he gave Wheeler free rein. It was only one among other evidences of his greatness."[43]

Although Wheeler took the loss of overall command graciously, his troopers did not. They viewed the move as a slap at their commander.

"His men can but feel that a grave wrong has been done one of the most gallant and meritorious officers in the service," noted one of his horsemen. "They can but feel it was done on incorrect information, or by designing men who had other motives than the good of the service to influence them."[44] Every officer in one of Wheeler's divisions signed a resolution protesting the move. "While we would not underrate the distinguished services rendered or detract from the merited laurels won by General Hampton, we desire to say in most unmistakable terms that we *entertain now,* as we have *always done,* the most *unbounded confidence* in *General Wheeler* as a man and as an *officer,* and where he *leads* we will *cheerfully follow,*" proclaimed the document signed by more than 100 officers of Brig. Gen. William Y. C. Humes's cavalry division.[45] The petition did not change a thing. Hampton, who was now the highest ranking officer in the Confederate cavalry service, assumed command.

Hampton was looking forward to fighting with Joe Johnston again. The South Carolinian had worked closely with Johnston early in the war before both had been severely wounded at Seven Pines on May 31, 1862. The two officers knew, respected, and trusted each other implicitly. According to diarist Mary Chesnut, Hampton told her, "Joe is equal to even Gen. Lee, if not superior."[46] The cavalryman quickly became Joe Johnston's best and most dependable subordinate.

In spite of the best efforts of the Confederates, on February 17 Columbia fell to Sherman's host. Butler's men fought long and hard, but Wheeler's undisciplined command hardly fired a shot, their attention diverted by

General
Joseph E. Johnston

Library of Congress

opportunities for drunken plunder. In the chaos some of the bales of cotton that filled the streets of the city caught fire, and soon about one-third of the town was ablaze. Millwood, Hampton's handsome plantation house, burned to the ground. That same day some of Sherman's men found and burned Hampton's two remaining estates.[47] "I have given far more than all my property to this cause," proclaimed Hampton, "and I am ready to give *all*."[48]

Sherman added insult to injury. "I declare in the presence of my God that Hampton burned Columbia, and that he alone he is responsible for it," proclaimed the Union commander. He later admitted that the charges were false and that he had made them in an attempt to lower the South Carolinian's standing in the eyes of the public. A furious Hampton fired off an angry denial. Sherman had earned the South Carolinian's hatred.[49] Hampton was more determined than ever to resist the advance of Sherman's army—and especially Kilpatrick's hated cavalry—with every ounce of his being.

The South Carolina populace despised Northern foragers, who added insult to injury as they prowled along the fringes of the advancing Union armies. The countryside crawled with "men who made foraging their sole business." Although they operated in organized units under the supervision of their officers, "hundreds were constantly out, independent of all control. Many roamed though the country solely to plunder, and in their nefarious work threw off all restraint—fearing neither God nor man—nor his mythical majesty the Devil."[50] These "bummers," as they were also known, became targets for angry citizens and soldiers. Any Yankee forager caught rummaging through a house or barn faced a certain and unpleasant death. Referring to the Northern foragers, one Georgia officer observed, "None are taken prisoner but all killed."[51]

The issue reached a climax on February 22 when Kilpatrick learned that eighteen of his horse soldiers foraging near Chester, South Carolina, had been captured and killed by Wheeler's men. A few had pieces of paper pinned to their breasts proclaiming "Death to all foragers." Kilpatrick informed Sherman, "Some had their throats cut. I have sent Wheeler word that I intend to hang eighteen of his men."[52] Sherman could not have looked upon this turn of events favorably, but viable alternatives were nonexistent. "It leaves no alternative," he agreed. "You must retaliate."[53]

Wheeler vigorously denied the allegations. "I will have the matter promptly investigated and see that full justice is done," he assured his Union counterpart.[54] Little Kil responded with both restraint and respect. "I feel satisfied that you will . . . investigate the circumstances attending the murder of my men and that the guilty parties will be [caught] and punished . . . I shall take no action at this time."[55] Kilpatrick's charitable reply notwithstanding, the incident only served to deepen the vendetta between Sherman and Hampton.

After capturing Columbia, Sherman's army turned north, heading for North Carolina. Butler's men resisted the Federal advance. Confederate horsemen buzzed along the fringes of Sherman's marching column, and small units operated behind the lines, seeking revenge on Northern "bummers," as they fanned out across the countryside foraging and looting. Again, South Carolinians, furious about the devastation of their state, took out their frustrations on any foragers unfortunate enough to cross their paths. They took "intense pleasure" in "chasing and killing" foragers, "taken often in the act" of committing some offense.[56] All too often, wrote another witness after the war, Northern foragers "fell to the tender mercies of Wheeler's Cavalry, and were never heard of again."[57] The bodies of these unfortunates became a familiar sight along the route of march. On February 23, 1865, Butler's cavalry intercepted a foraging expedition near Lynch's Creek in northeastern South Carolina. Pursuing Union infantry caught up to some of Butler's horse soldiers and claimed that two of their men, who had been captured by Butler, had been "brutally murdered in plain view of our skirmishers."[58]

The barbarous war unfolding in the Carolinas was unlike that being waged almost anywhere else in the country. When Sherman learned of these claims the following day, he sent an angry letter to Hampton under a flag of truce:

> It is officially reported to me that our foraging parties are murdered after capture and labeled 'Death to all foragers.' One instance of a lieutenant and seven men near Chesterville; and another of twenty 'near a ravine eighty rods from the main road' about three miles from Feasterville. I have ordered a similar number of prisoners in our hands to be disposed of in like manner. I hold about 1,000 prisoners captured in various ways, and can stand it as long as you; but I hardly think these murders are committed with your knowledge, and would suggest that you give notice to the people at

large that every life taken by them simply results in the death of one
of your Confederates.

Sherman concluded thusly:

> I have no doubt this is the occasion of much misbehavior on the part
> of our men, but I cannot permit an enemy to judge or punish with
> wholesale murder. Personally I regret the bitter feelings engendered
> by this war, but they were to be expected, and I simply allege that
> those who struck the first blow and made war inevitable ought not,
> in fairness, to reproach us for the natural consequences. I merely
> assert our war right to forage and my resolve to protect my foragers
> to the extent of life for life.[59]

Hampton, already furious about the devastation of Columbia and his
family homes, responded sharply to Sherman's message:

> In it you state that it has been officially reported that your foraging
> parties are 'murdered' after capture. You go on to say that you have
> 'ordered a similar number of prisoners in our hands to be disposed
> of in like manner'; that is to say, you have ordered a number of
> Confederate soldiers to be 'murdered.' You characterize your order
> in proper terms, for the public voice, even in your own country,
> where it seldom dares to express itself in vindication of truth, honor,
> or justice, will surely agree with you in pronouncing you guilty of
> murder if your order is carried out. Before dismissing this portion of
> your letter, I beg to assure you that for every soldier of mine
> 'murdered' by you, I shall have executed at once two of yours,
> giving in all cases preference to any officers who may be in my
> hands

Hampton denied having any knowledge of the alleged murder of Union
prisoners, but decried the practice of burning homes and foraging:

> It is a part of the system of the thieves whom you designate as your
> foragers to fire the dwellings of those citizens whom they have
> robbed. To check this inhuman system, which is justly execrated by
> every civilized nation, I have directed my men to shoot down all of
> your men who are caught burning houses. This order shall remain in
> force so long as you disgrace the profession of arms by allowing
> your men to destroy private dwellings.

Hampton went on to argue that his men had every right to defend themselves and their homes. "In conclusion, I have only to request that whenever you have any of my men 'murdered' or 'disposed of,' for the terms appear to be synonymous with you, you will let me hear of it, that I may know what action to take in the matter. In the meantime I shall hold fifty-six of your men as hostages for those whom you have ordered to be executed."[60]

The vitriolic exchange set the tone for the rest of the campaign. There were no further executions, but Hampton had made it clear that neither he nor his command were to be dictated to, and that they brooked no threats. Hampton, meanwhile, searched long and hard for an opportunity to avenge the many losses he had suffered at the hands of the advancing Federals. His opportunity to strike a blow was fast approaching.

*   *   *

The veteran cavalry command wielded by Hampton consisted of four divisions numbering more than 4,000 sabers. Three divisions came from Wheeler's Corps, and the other division, Butler's, had ridden south with Hampton from the Army of Northern Virginia. Hampton made a point of riding with Wheeler's horse soldiers in an effort to instill discipline and efficiency into their ranks. He did so even though Wheeler's people resented his presence. Hampton demonstrated the true measure of his military greatness during his time in the Carolinas. Although the power of Johnston's army was being bled away each day, Hampton's cavalry remained Johnston's largest and most effective arm.

Brigadier General William Young Conn Humes commanded one of Wheeler's three divisions. Although he is known for his cavalry career, Humes spent the first half of the war as an artillerist. Born in Abingdon, Virginia, on May 1, 1830, he graduated second in the Virginia Military Institute's class of 1851. After a year in Knoxville, Tennessee, he moved to the western end of the state and settled in Memphis, where he studied law, was admitted to the bar, and opened a law office. In 1861, Humes received a commission as a lieutenant of artillery in the Confederate service. He was quickly promoted to captain and captured when Island No. 10 fell on April 8, 1862. A short prison stint on Johnson's Island in Sandusky Bay on Lake Erie followed before he was exchanged on September 20.

For a time Humes commanded what was known as a "consolidated battalion" of exchanged prisoners slated to join Maj. Gen. Sterling Price's Army of the West. Little is known of his outfit, but it probably served as infantry. The early weeks of 1863 found Humes in Mobile overseeing artillery and earthworks until Joe Wheeler asked in March of that year that he serve as his chief of artillery. Humes was wounded in a fight at Farmington on October 7, 1863, during Wheeler's Middle Tennessee Raid. His actions won the plaudits of his superior, who praised Humes for his "great gallantry." Humes received a promotion to brigadier general to date from November 16 and was given command of a brigade of Tennessee cavalry in Wheeler's corps. Difficult service followed under James Longstreet in East Tennessee. By the spring of 1864, Humes was back with the Army of Tennessee in North Georgia. His duties were significantly enlarged when he was given a division of cavalry a short time before the Atlanta Campaign erupted.

Humes participated in nearly every engagement of the Atlanta Campaign. "Throughout the whole campaign from Dalton to Atlanta the cavalry were kept busy, sometimes guarding the flank of the army, at times making raids to the rear of the enemy, and at other times meeting Federal raiders and defeating them," noted a biographer. Humes's command accompanied Wheeler on his disastrous raid into North Georgia, Tennessee, and northern Alabama in the late summer of 1864. His troopers harassed Sherman's men on the March to the Sea, earning the division commander a recommendation for promotion to major general. According to one writer, like many citizen-soldiers, Humes "learned to look upon danger and death as matters that could not be helped. Just as men strive to win their way in business by diligent application to duty, so men strove to win their way to promotion by proving themselves efficient and bold in battle."[61]

Humes's Division consisted of three brigades. Brigadier General Thomas Harrison's was comprised of Texans and Arkansans. Its commander was born in Jefferson County, Alabama, on May 1, 1823, but was raised in Monroe County, Mississippi. He moved to Texas in 1843, where he studied law before returning to Mississippi to serve in Jefferson Davis's 1st Mississippi Rifles during the Mexican War. At the end of that war Harrison returned to Texas, settling first in Houston and later in Waco, where he practiced law and took up politics. Because he had been the captain of a volunteer militia company, he was quickly commissioned

Brigadier General
Thomas Harrison

Confederate Military History

a captain in the 8th Texas Cavalry—the renowned Terry's Texas Rangers. By April 1862, Harrison was a major and assumed command of his regiment during the second day at Shiloh when the colonel was wounded. Harrison was appointed colonel just before the Battle of Stones River in December 1862. By July 1863 he was in charge of a cavalry brigade, which he capably led under Wheeler at Chickamauga and during the campaigns in Georgia and the Carolinas. "On January 14, 1865, he was commissioned brigadier-general," records one history of his service, "an honor that he had long merited, having been in command of a brigade for more than a year."[62] Harrison's hard-fighting brigade, which Wheeler's men called the "charging Brigade," consisted of the 8th Texas, 11th Texas, 3rd Arkansas, and the consolidated 4th/8th Tennessee.[63]

Colonel Henry M. Ashby commanded Humes's Tennessee

Colonel
Henry M. Ashby

Confederate Veteran

Brigade. Only 24 years old, Ashby hailed from Knox County, Tennessee. In the spring of 1861 he raised a company of cavalry in Knox County and was given a captain's commission or his efforts. This company became part of the 3rd Battalion Tennessee Cavalry, later consolidated into the 2nd Tennessee Cavalry Regiment. Ashby was appointed colonel of the 2nd Tennessee in May 1862. Serving in Wheeler's command, Ashby led his regiment in East Tennessee and Kentucky and in the Battles of Stones River and Chickamauga. While participating in a raid deep into Kentucky, the bone of Ashby's right heel was shot off, a painful wound that crippled him for life.

When Wheeler reorganized his corps in the spring of 1864, Ashby assumed command of a brigade in Humes's Division that May. "With this brigade Col. Ashby rendered conspicuous service under Gen. Wheeler, hovering on Sherman's flanks and rear down through Georgia and up through the Carolinas." Ashby earned the respect of all who served under him. "From the first to the last of his service Col. Ashby was on the front, always in the face of the enemy; and his ability, vigilance, and efficiency are attested by the fact that at no time during the four years of service was any body of troops, large or small, under his command surprised by the enemy," remembered one of Ashby's staff officers. "Personally he was one of the most genial of gentlemen, and no officer of any rank was more devotedly loved or implicitly trusted by his troops. Few officers were better known in the Army of Tennessee, and his superb horsemanship . . . was the admiration of all who knew him. Whether in camp, on the march, or in combat, Henry M. Ashby was a born soldier."[64] In the

Brigadier General
William Wirt Allen

Confederate Military History

Carolinas, Ashby led the consolidated 1st/6th Tennessee, the 2nd Tennessee, and the 5th Tennessee regiments.

Brigadier General William Wirt Allen commanded Wheeler's second division. On September 11, 1835, Allen was born in New York City into a family that was among the earliest settlers of Montgomery, Alabama. He graduated from Princeton in 1854 and read law after leaving college, although he chose not to practice. Instead, Allen took up planting and was engaged in this pursuit when war found him in 1861. He entered the Confederate service as a lieutenant in the Montgomery Mounted Rifles in April 1861, reporting to Bragg in Pensacola, Florida. Allen remained with Bragg until the next fall, when he was elected major of the 1st Alabama Cavalry. He had a horse shot from under him at the Battle of Shiloh in April 1862, and was wounded slightly at Perryville six months later on October 8. When he returned to duty, Allen took command of the mounted forces attached to the left wing of Bragg's army. Allen was badly wounded on the first day at Stones River. "As a soldier he was cool and fearless in danger and tireless in the performance of duty. As a citizen he was cordial in manner and of ardent public spirit," noted a biographer.[65]

On February 26, 1864, Allen received an appointment as brigadier general and led a brigade during the Atlanta Campaign. Later that summer he assumed command of a division and led it throughout the March to the Sea and into the Carolinas. On March 4, 1865, Allen was appointed major general with temporary rank, but the appointment was not confirmed by the Confederate Senate. "I would add that I was in active service and on duty in the field from the beginning to the close of the war, except when disabled by wounds received in action," wrote an aged Allen in 1894. "I was shot three times and had horses shot [from] under me ten times."[66]

Colonel James Hagan commanded one of Allen's brigades. Born in Ireland in 1821, Hagan and his parents immigrated to the United States when the boy was an infant. The family settled in Pennsylvania, where his father took up farming. Upon reaching adulthood, James joined his uncle's business in New Orleans and eventually settled in Mobile, Alabama. After gallant service in the Mexican War, Hagan took up planting and in 1854 married the beautiful and socially prominent daughter of the attorney general of Alabama. With the outbreak of war Hagan enlisted as a captain of a cavalry company raised in Mobile

Colonel
James Hagan

More Generals in Gray

County, Alabama, and was later elected major when the 1st Alabama Cavalry was formed under William Wirt Allen's command.

Not long after the Battle of Shiloh in early 1862, Hagan was appointed colonel of a new regiment, the 3rd Alabama Cavalry. From that point forward he served with Wheeler's cavalry in all its campaigns, taking charge of a brigade of Alabama horse soldiers in 1863. Hagan was wounded in battle twice in Tennessee (and would be a third time at Monroe's Crossroads). "Being a man of generous nature and manly impulses, he was greatly admired and loved by his soldiers," remembered Joe Wheeler long after the war. "He knew how to obey as well as command, and set before his men an example of the implicit obedience due by a subordinate to a superior officer."[67]

Hagan's veteran brigade consisted of the 1st, 3rd, 9th, 12th, 51st, and 53rd Alabama Cavalry regiments, and Alabama and Georgia companies from the

Brigadier General
Robert H. Anderson

Confederate Military History

Colonel
Charles Crews

USAMHI

10th Confederate Cavalry Regiment.

Brigadier General Robert H. Anderson commanded a brigade of Georgia horsemen in Allen's Division. He was born in Savannah on October 1, 1835. After attending local schools Anderson received an appointment to the United States Military Academy. He graduated in 1857 and spent his Regular Army career in the infantry in the Pacific Northwest before resigning his commission in 1861 to enlist in the new Confederacy. He was appointed a lieutenant of artillery, but soon thereafter received a promotion to major in September 1861. Anderson served as Maj. Gen. W. H. T. "Shot Pouch" Walker's adjutant, and was then transferred to a line regiment, the 5th Georgia Cavalry, in January 1863. The 5th Georgia joined Wheeler's corps and became part of Allen's Brigade. When Allen assumed division command, Anderson succeeded him in command of the brigade. On July 26, 1864, he was promoted to brigadier general and served well throughout the Atlanta Campaign and the March to the Sea. Anderson was a competent officer with a solid command consisting of the 3rd, 5th, and 6th Georgia Cavalry and the Alabama and Mississippi companies of the 8th Confederate Cavalry.[68]

Allen's third brigade was entirely composed of Georgians and led by Col. Charles C. Crews. Thirty-five year old Crews was born in Harris County, Georgia, and raised in Ellerslie, where he studied law and medicine. He graduated in 1853 from Carleton Medical College and set up a practice in Cuthbert, Georgia. In January 1861 he was elected ensign in a cavalry militia company before being commissioned a captain in the 2nd Georgia Cavalry in March 1862. He was captured during a raid into

Kentucky that fall. After being exchanged in November, Crews was promoted to colonel of the regiment only to be severely wounded in the hip on January 3, 1863. After a painful convalescence he returned to assume command of a brigade consisting of the 1st, 2nd, 4th, and 12th Georgia cavalry regiments in 1864. Crews led a brigade for an extended period of time and received several citations for gallantry from Wheeler. Crews had a habit of attracting enemy metal and was wounded yet again, this time in South Carolina in 1865. Late war records are woefully incomplete, but it appears that Crews was not with his brigade when it entered North Carolina. His command was known to be an especially unruly unit, perhaps the worst offender of all of Wheeler's undisciplined corps. The record is so muddy that it is unclear whether this brigade was even with Wheeler's Corps in March 1865, and there is no evidence that it was engaged in combat at Monroe's Crossroads.[69]

Brigadier General George G. Dibrell also commanded a division of Wheeler's troopers. Born in Sparta, Tennessee, on April 12, 1822, Dibrell overcame a minimal education to become a successful merchant and farmer. In 1861 he was elected to the Tennessee State Convention as a Union delegate. When the convention voted in favor of secession, Dibrell enlisted in the Confederate army as a private. Not exactly suited to such a lowly rank, the Tennessean recruited and raised the 8th Tennessee Cavalry in early 1862 and accepted an appointment as its colonel. The 8th Tennessee served with Nathan Bedford Forrest. On March 25 near Florence,

Brigadier General
George G. Dibrell

Alabama Department of
Archives and History

Colonel William Campbell
Preston Breckinridge

Filson Club

Dibrell defeated two Union
gunboats and a body of raiders,
earning high praise from the
demanding Forrest. In 1863,
Dibrell assumed command of
one of Forrest's brigades, with
which he continued, in the words
of a Tennessee historian, "to
sustain his high reputation in the
campaigns of Forrest and
afterward of Wheeler."

In the autumn of 1863,
Dibrell's cavalrymen joined
Gen. Joseph E. Johnston's command at Dalton, Georgia, where they were
assigned to Wheeler's Cavalry Corps. The Tennessean fought across
much of Georgia and then all the way to the outskirts of Savannah in the
campaign that followed. Colonel Roman, the Western Theater's
inspector general, described Dibrell as "perhaps the hardest fighter" in
Wheeler's entire command. On January 28, 1865, Dibrell received a
well-deserved (and long in coming) commission to brigadier general, to
date from July 26, 1864.[70]

Dibrell's cavalry division consisted of two brigades, one of
Kentucky troopers and the other of Tennessee men. Colonel William
Campbell Preston Breckinridge headed up the brigade of Kentucky horse
soldiers. A man of boasting a prominent pedigree, Breckinridge was a
first cousin of Confederate Secretary of War John C. Breckinridge and
part of a powerful and influential Border State family. His father, Rev.
Robert J. Breckinridge, "was one of the most eloquent and influential
Presbyterian preachers of his day, and his grandfather, John
Breckinridge, was one of Kentucky's most distinguished Senators,
Attorney-General under Jefferson, and one of his chief advisors in the

acquisition of Louisiana," proclaimed an article in *Confederate Veteran*. Breckinridge was also related to Patrick Henry on his mother's side as well as influential South Carolina Senator William Campbell Preston.[71] Born in Baltimore, Maryland, on August 28, 1837, Breckinridge's mother died when he was but seven years old. The tragedy left a grieving father to raise the boy.[72]

Breckinridge attended schools in Chambersburg, Pennsylvania, and Woodford County, Kentucky, before graduating from Centre College in Danville in 1855. He planned to become a doctor but changed his mind after just one year of study.[73] "[W]hen a mere lad at college, [William] won a reputation as one of the most eloquent of the young men Kentucky had ever known," and later earned the title of the "Silver-Tongued Orator of Kentucky," wrote a historian of the famous family. Breckinridge graduated from law school at the University of Louisville in 1857 and ran a successful practice in Louisville until the beginning of the Civil War. On March 17, 1859, Willie (as he was known) married Lucretia Clay, the granddaughter of the late Sen. Henry Clay. Sadly, Lucretia died in childbirth one year later. He wed again two years afterward.[74]

Like so many Kentucky families, the Breckinridges were deeply divided by war. William's brother Joseph Cabell Breckinridge served in the Union cavalry, while William and his other brother Robert Jefferson Breckinridge Jr., served the Confederacy.[75] In July 1861, to the great disappointment of his staunchly Unionist father, William recruited a company that became part of the 9th Kentucky Cavalry (Confederate). During Bragg's September-October 1862 invasion into Kentucky, Breckinridge recruited a battalion that was consolidated with a second battalion to form the 9th Kentucky Cavalry. The new organization was assigned to Brig. Gen. John Hunt Morgan's command.[76] "The regiment was composed of young men recruited in the Blue Grass region of Kentucky, the sons of farmers, mechanics, and professional men, and many young men who quit college to enter the service," recalled a member of the 9th Kentucky. "From its organization until the close of the war this regiment was engaged in active and arduous service. No other cavalry regiment in the Confederate army did more hard fighting and important service, and none was more distinguished for gallantry and endurance."[77]

By December 1862 Colonel Breckinridge was leading a brigade in Morgan's command and participated in the Kentucky "Christmas Raid"

Colonel
William L. S. McLemore

Kevin McLemore

of 1862-1863. His regiment joined Wheeler's Cavalry Corps in 1863, participating in Wheeler's many campaigns, including Chickamauga, Chattanooga, the Atlanta Campaign, and the March to the Sea. When Brig. Gen. John S. "Cerro Gordo" Williams was relieved of command of Wheeler's Kentucky brigade for disobedience to orders, Breckinridge took charge of the brigade, which he led for the rest of the Civil War.[78] Breckinridge's brigade included the 1st, 2nd, and 9th Kentucky Cavalry regiments, and the 4th, 5th, 6th, and 9th Kentucky Mounted Infantry Regiments.[79]

The commander of Dibrell's former brigade was Col. William L. S. McLemore. The thirty-three-year-old McLemore was tall, fair-skinned, dark haired, and had flashing blue eyes. He was a successful attorney from Williamson County, Tennessee. At seventeen, he enrolled at Transylvania University in Lexington, Kentucky, followed by the Cumberland Law School in Lebanon, Tennessee, in 1849. After completing his legal education in 1851, McLemore opened a practice in Franklin, Tennessee. Three years later he made an unsuccessful run for attorney general for a three-county district. In 1856 he was elected county court clerk, a position he held until 1860, when he declined re-election and resumed practicing law. The following year McLemore became editor of a local newspaper and was also sworn in as an assistant attorney general for the Confederate States of America.[80]

In 1861, McLemore enlisted in Company F, 4th Tennessee Cavalry, and served under both Forrest and Wheeler. His unit was one of two designated as the 4th Tennessee Cavalry, and was known as a "crack regiment." To distinguish the units, they were usually referred to by the names of their respective commanders. Thus, McLemore's command was known as the "Starnes-McLemore Regiment." In 1862, he received a promotion to captain and assumed command of Company F, although he also led the regiment when the regimental commander was wounded. While serving under Forrest, McLemore's 4th Tennessee helped capture Col. Abel D. Streight's mounted command. When Col. J. W. Starnes was killed in action on June 30, 1863, during the Tullahoma Campaign, McLemore was eventually promoted to colonel on February 25, 1864, upon the written recommendation of Nathan Bedford Forrest. "He has proved himself in every respect worthy and capable to fill the position," wrote Forrest.[81] McLemore assumed command of Dibrell's Brigade after Dibrell's promotion to division commander. McLemore had three horses shot from under him in battle but was never wounded.[82] McLemore's

Library of Congress

Major General Matthew Calbraith Butler

Brigade of Tennessee horse soldiers included Allison's Squadron (Hamilton's Battalion and Shaw's Battalion), the 4th Tennessee Cavalry, and the 13th Tennessee Cavalry.[83]

Major General Matthew Calbraith Butler commanded the cavalry division from the Army of Northern Virginia. Butler was a 28-year-old lawyer from Greenville, South Carolina. Like his mentor Wade Hampton, Butler attended South Carolina College and had no military training prior to the war. However, he could boast a fine military pedigree as the nephew of War of 1812 naval hero Commodore Oliver Hazard Perry (and his father was a naval surgeon). Butler married the daughter of South Carolina governor Francis W. Pickens, ensuring him a bright future in state politics.

Butler was appointed a captain in the Hampton Legion in 1861 and quickly received a promotion to major. When the cavalry contingent of the Hampton Legion was split off and redesignated the 2nd South Carolina Cavalry, Butler became its colonel. He was severely wounded at the Battle of Brandy Station in June of 1863 when a round shot carried away his right foot. "It used to be said his skin glanced bullets," explained one of his troopers, "and that it required a twelve-pounder to carry away [the foot lost at Brandy Station]."[84] The crippled Southern officer returned to service in September 1863, received a promotion to brigadier general, and assumed command of a brigade of South Carolina cavalry.

Butler's Brigade performed extraordinary service in Virginia in 1864, bearing the brunt of the brutal two-day fight at Trevilian Station on June 11-12, 1864. "Butler's defense at Trevilian was never surpassed," proclaimed Hampton.[85] Following Hampton's promotion to corps commander, Butler received a promotion to major general on September 19 and took command of Hampton's old division. In January 1865, Butler rode his command to South Carolina, where he assumed command of the cavalry division assigned to the Department of South Carolina, Georgia, and Florida. When Hampton assumed overall command of the Confederate cavalry, Butler's slender division of but 1,200 men joined Wheeler's cavalry.[86] Although illness took him away from his division a few days after Monroe's Crossroads, "from the fall of Columbia to the surrender of Johnston at Durham, Butler was ever at the front, harassing and impeding Sherman's advance," wrote one of his staff officers.[87]

Butler, recalled one eyewitness, "showed no emotion as he scanned the field of battle" armed with only a silver riding crop, calmly taking in the situation and carefully planning his response.[88] One observer noted of Butler, "so fine was his courage, so unshaken his nerve, that, if he realized the danger, he scorned it and his chiseled face never so handsome as when cold-set for battle, never showed if or not his soul was in tumult." Butler was the sort of leader who sat his horse quietly while shot and shell stormed around him and other men ran for shelter.[89] His men loved him for his common touch. "Often did I see him after the fatiguing events of the day lying upon the ground with no shelter but the vaulted sky above, sharing the hardships with his men, ever hopeful, ever ready to lead his sadly diminished ranks where an effective blow might be struck," wrote one of his soldiers three decades after the war. By 1865, Butler was known as "Hampton's Right Bower."[90]

Brigadier General Evander M. Law commanded one of Butler's two brigades. Born in Darlington, South Carolina, on August 7, 1836, Law graduated from The Citadel in 1856, where had served as an instructor of belles lettres during his senior year. After spending several years teaching and helping to found a military high school in Tuskegee, Alabama, Law recruited a company of state troops in 1861 and led them to join Braxton Bragg's force at Pensacola. Law was elected lieutenant colonel of the 4th Alabama Infantry and received a severe wound at First Manassas on July 21, 1861. Promoted to colonel of the regiment in November of that year, he led his Alabamans in nearly all of the Army of Northern

Brigadier General
Evander M. Law

USAMHI

Virginia's battles of 1862. On October 2 Law was commissioned a brigadier general in command of a brigade in Maj. Gen. John B. Hood's Division. When Hood was severely wounded at Gettysburg, Law took command of the division, explains one source, "in the famous assault on the Federal position on Little Round Top, a movement which he protested against before it was ordered, but carried out with a skillful handling of his valiant men, who lost 2,000 of their number. On the third day his prompt dispositions defeated the flank attack of Federal cavalry."

Law led the division capably until Hood returned to duty later that summer. When Hood was badly wounded a second time at Chickamauga Law once more assumed command of the division. He fought gallantly as a brigade commander throughout the Overland Campaign of 1864, during which he received a second wound. After his recovery Law asked to be relieved of command in order to join Joe Johnston's army in defense of his home state. As Sherman's army approach he was assigned to command at Columbia, and in February assumed the reins of command of Butler's cavalry brigade."[91] According to a complimentary article in *Confederate Veteran*, Law was "one of the handsomest of men, as straight as an arrow, with jet black beard, and dashing appearance. The grace of his manner was flawless."[92] Law's Brigade consisted of the 1st, 4th, 5th, and 6th South Carolina cavalry regiments and the 19th South Carolina Cavalry Battalion—rugged veterans all.

Colonel Gilbert J. Wright led Butler's second brigade. Wright was born in Lawrenceville, Georgia, on February 18, 1825. When the Mexican War broke out in 1846, he enlisted in Company A, 1st Georgia Infantry. He fought in several battles and received a severe neck wound. Although he returned to duty with his regiment after a period of recuperation, he suffered from a painful stiff neck for the rest of his life. When the war ended Wright returned to Georgia, read law, and joined the bar in 1848. A walking paradox, he served as judge and mayor of Albany, Georgia, but also killed a close friend in a drunken brawl.

Wright helped to organize a company of the Cobb Legion Cavalry in 1861 and was appointed a lieutenant. He served in all of the campaigns of the Army of Northern Virginia until 1865. Wright received a promotion to captain in 1862 and to major in 1863. He was wounded in battle several times, earning the respect of his brigade commander Wade Hampton. On October 9, 1863, Wright was promoted to colonel of the Cobb Legion and assumed command of his brigade when Brig. Gen. Pierce M. B.

Colonel
Gilbert J. Wright

Georgia Historical Society

Young was transferred to command the North Carolina cavalry brigade. Wright was badly wounded yet again on May 30, 1864. "Gib" Wright led the brigade at intervals throughout the rest of 1864. In January 1865, when the brigade was transferred to South Carolina, he assumed permanent command. According to one of his troopers, Wright's "unique personality . . . vigorous intellect and . . . untiring energy made a remarkable impression upon all with whom he came into contact." Though not a professional soldier, Wright possessed a "bulldog courage" and "stentorian voice" that were conspicuous in battle. A South Carolina horse soldier described him as a "stern old soldier."[93] Wright was apparently promoted to brigadier general during the war's final months, but he never received the commission.[94] His a sturdy and reliable brigade consisted of the Cobb Legion, Phillips Legion, Jeff Davis Legion, and the 20th Georgia Cavalry Battalion.

The grayclad horse soldiers riding under Wheeler and Hampton carried a hodgepodge of weapons. Roman's inspection report of January 1865 indicates that Wheeler's troopers carried "arms of eight or nine different calibers, but mostly of calibers .57 and .54," including a large number of captured Federal weapons. Most of these arms were Enfield, Springfield, and Austrian rifle-muskets rather than cavalry carbines. In January the corps numbered 6,607 weapons in serviceable condition, including 3,896 rifles, 500 carbines, and 1,978 pistols. "When the war closed in 1865," recalled one of Wheeler's Alabamans, "more than fifty per cent of the arms, accoutrements and equipment generally of the Confederate cavalry, bore the imprint of the United States."[95] According to this accounting there was a deficiency of about 1,447 rifles/carbines and 3,747 pistols, meaning that most of Wheeler's command did not have a full complement of weapons at that late stage of the war. In addition, only fifty or sixty members of Anderson's Brigade carried sabers. Any fighting by Wheeler's men would have to be done with firearms.[96] Law's Brigade of Butler's Division carried two-band Enfield rifles and no sabers.[97] Only Wright's Brigade carried the full array of traditional cavalry weapons: sabers, pistols, and carbines.

The Southern horsemen were also short on ammunition. They carried an average of 35-40 rounds per man, but Wheeler's reserve train hauled only about 40 rounds per man. This meant that extensive resupply during or after a severe firefight would have been a difficult proposition.[98] Because the Confederate government dictated that cavalrymen were responsible for supplying their own mounts, replacing killed, wounded, or crippled horses was a daunting task—especially in 1865. "When a soldier owns the horse he rides, when experience teaches him that though bound to pay for its loss in action, the Government is never ready to do so, that soldier will invariably take so much care of his horse so as to feel at least disinclined to risk him in a battle," Colonel Roman astutely observed. "That soldier therefore cannot do as good service as if he knew that as many horses might be shot under him just as many more would the Government give him."[99] Men who had lost their mounts had two choices: struggle along with their command as a dismounted trooper or obtain leave to try to find a replacement. Either way, the goverment remount policy hampered the effectiveness of Confederate cavalry.

Hampered though it was, the Southern cavalry was ready to vigorously engage its Union counterpart. Most of these commands had fought many times across several states in a wide variety of battles. They knew each other well. And they would meet one another again, one more time, in one of the largest (and last) cavalry battles of the war.

Chapter 3

A Sure Sign of Things to Come

On February 23, 1865, Gen. Joseph E. Johnston stepped off the train in Charlotte, North Carolina. At the request of newly-appointed General-in-Chief Robert E. Lee and with the approval of Secretary of War John C. Breckinridge, two days later "Old Joe" officially assumed command of the Department of Georgia, South Carolina, and Florida as well as the Department of Tennessee and Georgia. Several Confederate Congressmen had interceded with President Davis in an effort to oppose Johnston's appointment. With his high command's strong endorsement of Johnston, Davis reluctantly agreed to his appointment, "with the understanding that General Lee would supervise and control the operations."[1] By that point in the war Davis had few other viable alternatives.

Opinion as to Johnston's ability in the field varied widely. Lieutenant General James Longstreet described him as "the ablest and most accomplished man the Confederate armies produced."[2] Stephen R. Mallory, the Confederate Secretary of the Navy, held Johnston in similar esteem. "Of medium height, about five feet eight, and weighing about 150 pounds, he had a well-formed and developed figure; a clean, elastic step; an erect, manly, graceful carriage; and an impressive air of com mand," recalled Mallory. Johnston, he continued, was

> bronzed by the sun and hardened by exposure, he seemed in the best
> condition to meet any possible demand upon his physique; while his

grave, handsome face and bright eye, telling of intellectual power and cultivation, were frequently lighted up by a flashing, sunny smile, which betrayed, in spite of an habitual expression of firmness and austerity, a genial nature, and a ready appreciation of humor."[3]

A week after his appointment became official, Johnston took charge of the forces of the Department of North Carolina. He enjoyed the support of the Tar Heel State, which rallied to his banner. "The advance of this great general to the command of the Southern Department, has given an impulse to the popular confidence, not even anticipated by his most sanguine friends," crowed a Raleigh newspaper editor. "All men, however their predilections, whether for or against him, will rally to his support; and bear him on the discharge of his high trust in the arms of a universal confidence."[4]

Popular support notwithstanding, Johnston's task was a daunting one: stop Maj. Gen. William T. Sherman's army group from overrunning the Carolinas. With a much larger army under his control, Johnston had failed to stop Sherman in Georgia. After capturing Atlanta, the Union commander had rampaged across the state on his March to the Sea before burning and pillaging his way through South Carolina. Sherman's men viewed South Carolina as the birthplace of the rebellion, and they had exacted their revenge. "South Carolina, or some parts of it, has paid well for the active part taken by her chivalry in bringing about the Rebellion," noted an officer of the 9th Michigan Cavalry. "I hardly think the people of that state will care to have 'Sherman's company' march through there again."[5]

Residents of North Carolina feared they would face the same ugly fate. "We hope for the best, but we confess that Sherman will not be routed, or even checked . . . Goldsborough, Fayetteville, and even Raleigh are in danger," observed the editor of the *North Carolina Standard*. "We fear that what has been will be; in other words, that the enemy will overrun this country."[6]

Johnston had a no illusions about his return to command. "This was done with a full consciousness on my part, however, that we could have no other object, in continuing the war, than to obtain fair terms of peace; for the Southern cause must have appeared hopeless then, to all intelligent and dispassionate Southern men," Johnston recalled in his memoirs. "I therefore resumed the duties of my military grade with no hope beyond that of contributing to obtain peace on such conditions as, under the circumstances, ought to satisfy the Southern people and their government."[7]

With only a scattered force of perhaps 25,000 of all arms, Johnston faced Sherman's army of more than 60,000. The Confederates had contested Sherman's march through South Carolina as strongly as possible. In an effort to boost sagging civilian morale, one newspaper editor wrote, "Sherman . . . has found a lion in his path, in the person of a gallant Confederate General supported by thousands of men."[8] In his struggle Johnston relied heavily on Wade Hampton and his veteran cavaliers, who dogged the Federal advance every step of the way. Sherman realized that even though he outnumbered his opponent more than two to one, he would still have his hands full in making his way through North Carolina en route to linking up with Grant's army in Virginia. "I knew full well at the time that . . . if handled with skill and energy, [Johnston's army] would constitute a formidable force," Sherman recalled years later, "and might make the passage of such rivers as the Santee and Cape Fear a difficult undertaking."[9]

Sherman decided it was prudent to stay near the Atlantic coast and his lines of resupply from the north. He therefore turned east and headed toward Fayetteville. From there, Sherman planned to threaten both Goldsboro and the state capital at Raleigh. There was a substantial arsenal-armory in Fayetteville that made the town an important military target. Sherman wanted to destroy the arsenal to prevent it from playing any further role in arming the rebellion.[10] The Cape Fear River, which emptied into the Atlantic just south of Wilmington, was navigable as far north as Fayetteville and provided a good channel of supply and communication with the vast Federal depot that had been established since the capture of Wilmington on February 22.[11]

After reaching Fayetteville, Sherman planned to feint toward Raleigh but march northeast to Goldsboro which, as he later explained, was "a point of great convenience for ulterior operations, by reason of the two railroads which were there, coming from the sea-coast at Wilmington by way of New Bern."[12] In capturing the junction of the Wilmington & Weldon and the Atlantic & North Carolina Railroads, Sherman would deprive the Confederacy of two major railroads in North Carolina while simultaneously acquiring railroads for his own benefit.[13]

If his feint succeeded, Sherman would reach Fayetteville before Johnston. Union troops would seize the bridges over the Cape Fear River

The remains of the Fayetteville Arsenal/Armory.

and pin the Confederates on the western side of the river. Meanwhile, Federal troops under Maj. Gen. John M. Schofield would advance from Wilmington and New Bern. It was at that point in the campaign that Sherman intended to concentrate all of his forces and move his mammoth command into Virginia, link up with the Federal armies operating against Lee, and deliver the coup de grace to the Confederacy.

Sherman's army advanced in two wings. The left wing was comprised of the Army of Georgia and consisted of the 14th and 20th Corps. The right wing, the Army of the Tennessee, consisted of the 15th and 17th Corps. The plan was to demonstrate toward Charlotte after leaving Columbia while Schofield's force advanced simultaneously on Goldsboro from the coast. Kilpatrick's cavalry division would ride far in advance of Sherman's main columns, screening them from the probing Confederates and creating the illusion that Sherman was marching on Charlotte. After crossing the Catawba on a broad front, Sherman intended to make a sharp turn toward the northeast and head straight for Fayetteville, where he planned to resupply his army from steamboats ascending the Cape Fear River from Wilmington. Sherman's hope was that the movement would confuse his already outnumbered enemy and further divide their limited resources.[14]

Johnston, however, was not easily fooled. "The route by Charlotte, Greensborough, and Danville is very difficult now," he wrote to General Lee on March 1. "It would also leave your army exactly between those of General Grant and General Sherman. It seems to me, therefore, that he, General Sherman, ought not to take it." As Johnston astutely reasoned, "His [Sherman's] junction with Schofield is also an object important enough, I should think, to induce him to keep more to the east. Such a course would also render his junction with General Grant easier."[15]

Local newspapers were not fooled either. "It is useless to disguise the belief that Fayetteville is seriously threatened," noted a Fayetteville editor on March 1, "for if the report be true that the advance of Schofield on Goldsboro is checked, and he does not move into South Carolina to the relief of Sherman, it is evident, we think, that he will move, by the left flank, on Fayetteville." Another correspondent noted that Sherman "will use his utmost efforts to deceive our commanders; and it is therefore impossible to determine his point of destination. Vigilant eyes are watching his movements, and he will find a brave and determined army hanging on his flanks, and rear, wherever he may go." The editor remained confident in Johnston's ability to protect the town from Sherman's depredations. "We feel assured that no hostile army will ever occupy Fayetteville, but this is only an individual opinion, and it is well to make 'assurances doubly sure.' We shall make no preparations going on for our defense, but we feel it our duty to warn people that they must be active and energetic."[16]

Although he had divined Sherman's general intentions, Johnston still had to devise a feasible defensive strategy. Lieutenant General William J. Hardee's 6,000-man corps, which had evacuated Charleston on the night of February 17-18 only hours after Sherman's soldiers had entered Columbia, was assigned to shadow Sherman's advance. Hampton placed Butler's cavalry division on the right flank of Sherman's army. "The service of this cavalry was, to retard the enemy's progress, and as much as possible to protect the people of the country from exactions of Federal foraging-parties, and robbery by stragglers," explained Johnston.[17] The Confederate horse soldiers were to resist Sherman's advance with all their remaining strength, hovering around the edges of the Federal column like a swarm of angry hornets ready to exact a heavy toll whenever an opportunity presented itself.[18] Specifically, the cavalry's task "was to confine to the smallest possible limits the area of his

Lieutenant General William J. Hardee

devastation," noted one of Butler's troopers. "To hover by turns around his front, his flanks and his rear; to pounce upon his foraging parties, who were burning and harrying; to dash between his marching columns and cut off marauders; to save the lives and property, as far as practicable, of women and children."[19]

Hardee's Corps traveled by rail and reached Cheraw, South Carolina, on March 1. The infantry was just ten miles south of the North Carolina line and barely ahead of Sherman's marching vanguard. That same day Hampton instructed Wheeler to operate on the left flank of Sherman's advance. Wheeler was instructed to "leave a party to follow the rear of the enemy on the Wadesboro road to pick up stragglers and worry the enemy." Hampton intended to join Wheeler's Corps, uniting the entire Confederate cavalry command for the first time.[20]

On March 2, the head of Sherman's 20th Corps slogged its way into Chesterfield, South Carolina, its advance contested by Butler's dogged horsemen. "The Yankees are unable to move on account of the mud," noted one of Butler's regimental commanders, "it having rained more or less for 6 days & is still drizzling, dark clouds hanging low with prospects of more rain. The roads are cut up deep with mire." The officer concluded, "No one seems to know where Sherman will move whether to Wilmington or Lynchburg or Charleston. He is making a demonstration against this place now at Monroe Union Co. [North Carolina]."[21] The confused state of affairs in the Carolinas was evident in the Southern officer's assessment of the situation, for Union forces had been occupying Charleston since the night of February 17-18. Despite Johnston's general appreciation of his enemy's plan, Sherman's feints seemed to working. The larger question was whether Sherman would be able to take advantage of his opponent's lack of accurate field intelligence.

The swollen Great Pee Dee River caused Hampton and Wheeler to diverge "far to the left of [Sherman's] direct route, to the fords near and above the grassy islands," meaning that the two wings of the Southern cavalry would not reunite until March 8.[22] Sherman, meanwhile, ordered Kilpatrick and his cavalry division to keep well to the left of the 14th Corps. Sherman also gave Little Kil permission to ride to Fayetteville via New Gilead, and then to Solemn Grove, instructing his cavalry commander to conserve his horses for the difficult campaigning that lay ahead.[23] The notion that they were conserving strength, however, was unnoticed by the men. "The general direction was northeasterly, although the route traveled was a continual zigzag, through water and mud that seemed to have no bottom," recalled the historian of

McLaughlin's Squadron of Ohio Cavalry, which served with the 9th Michigan Cavalry. "The roads were simply infamous."[24]

Hardee withdrew on March 3, leaving Butler's dismounted cavalry to try to delay Sherman's march. That same day elements of Sherman's infantry advanced on the town of Cheraw, where they encountered Butler's cavalry entrenched on a hill about five miles from the town. The determined Federals drove off Butler's skirmishers and entered the town. The retreating Confederates took up a position on high ground along the east bank of the Great Pee Dee River and set the covered bridge across the stream ablaze. Unable to pursue, Sherman's infantry watched as the Confederates withdrew, contented with holding the town and foraging for whatever they could find in the way of supplies and plunder.[25]

While the uneven fight for Cheraw was underway, portions of Kilpatrick's division entered North Carolina, camping four miles above the state line on the road leading to Hornsboro, South Carolina. "I want you to interpose between Charlotte and Cheraw until we are across," Sherman instructed Kilpatrick that morning.[26] Cornelius Baker, a trooper with the 9th Pennsylvania, noted that his regiment had left "at 5 o'clock on an expedition for horses. We went near Wadesboro and captured a lot of horses and mules." The brigade then rode to Chesterfield, where it crossed the state line and camped for the night.[27]

Spencer's brigade also had a hard time of it. "We resumed our line of march on the left through a clay country with horrible roads and traveled a distance of ten miles," reported Colonel Spencer. Hampton's cavalry had been dogging the fringes of the Federal advance and no sooner had Spencer deployed his pickets than the Confederates attacked. "The command was quickly thrown into position and we awaited an attack," reported Spencer. "A small force of the enemy attempted to charge the extreme right of our line, when a few shells from Lieutenant [Ebenezer] Stetson's section quickly scattered them." Spencer's weary horsemen spent the night in line of battle, waiting for a resumption of the attack that never came.[28]

Kilpatrick evidently did not realize the magnitude of the danger facing his command, for he did not picket the approaches to his camp. "My command is all in camp, and I believe my position a good one; covering, however, as I do so many roads, I shall have comparatively but a small force to resist any determined attack upon either one," he wrote Sherman.[29]

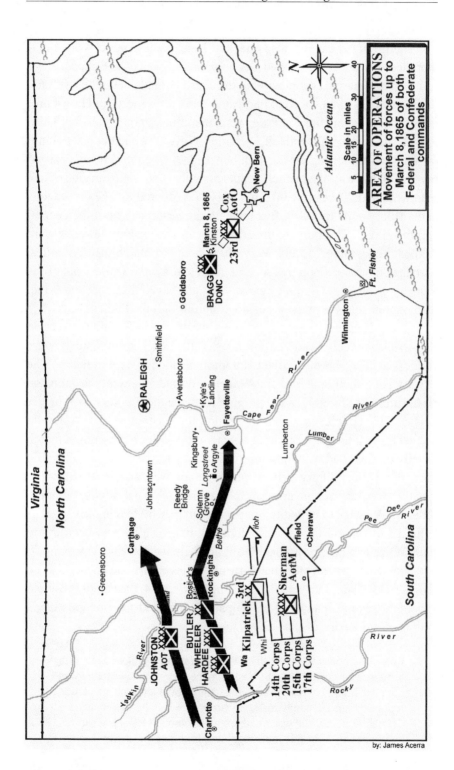

by: James Acerra

The grayclad cavalry also attacked Lieutenant Colonel Way's dismounted brigade, which had accompanied Spencer's brigade. "We resumed our march, accompanying the Third Brigade upon the left flank until March 3, when we went into camp three miles north of Hornsboro, taking position on the road we were marching upon, with the Third Brigade upon our right and left," reported Way. "We had but just got into position, with a strong picket, well barricaded, when the enemy charged my picket, but was handsomely repulsed, with a loss upon our side of one man wounded." About 11:00 p.m., Way was ordered to take the wagons and artillery and "move on five miles to the headquarters of the general commanding." The rain continued falling in sheets and the roads were "almost impassable." It took Way seven hours to march just five miles, with the command stopping "several times to draw the artillery out of the mud by hand."[30] Miserable, exhausted, and soaked to the bone, the dismounted soldiers pressed on, slogging through the thick mud.

Wade Hampton spotted an opportunity to inflict damage upon Kilpatrick's widely scattered brigades. Little Kil's arrangements were careless at best, and the vigilant Hampton decided to exploit them. "The cavalry is on the Landsford and Wadesboro road," he wrote to Johnston on the night of March 3, "and I propose to attack them as soon as Wheeler gets up." He concluded with a suggestion for his commander: "Can you not get the troops from Charlotte over to join Hardee? They might march rapidly on this road, which will be covered by the cavalry, and then join him. If all the infantry can be put together we can punish Sherman greatly, for his troops are much scattered."[31] That night Hampton directed Wheeler to expedite his pace of march by leaving his wagons behind and closing up on the Federal column. If all went according to plan, Wheeler would be prepared to attack Kilpatrick the next morning.[32]

Kilpatrick, on the other hand, firmly believed that the enemy was no longer in his front. Early on the morning of March 4, the day of President Lincoln's second inauguration, Kilpatrick reported the previous day's actions to Sherman:

> I have the honor to report that General Hampton attacked me with his entire command at 4 P.M. yesterday near my headquarters. I was not in position, but was just leaving camp; however, such attack was repulsed, until I could mass my troops, when he again made a deliberate attack, and was finally repulsed about 7 P.M. last evening. I expected to fight this morning, but I find that the enemy has left

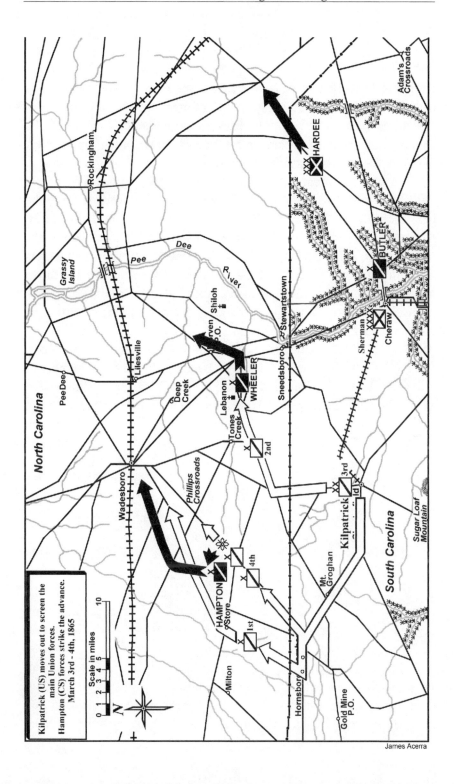

Kilpatrick (US) moves out to screen the
main Union forces.
Hampton (CS) forces strike the advance.
March 3rd - 4th, 1865

James Acerra

my front, and I believe him to be moving for Wall's Ferry, via Wadesboro.

Kilpatrick's claim that he was attacked by Hampton on March 3 is curious because the Southern leader never mentioned having done so in any correspondence or report. Perhaps it was another case of Little Kil's memory and imagination being in conflict. About Hampton having "left" his front, Kilpatrick was simply wrong.[33]

The men of Jordan's First Brigade spent the night of March 3 at Phillips's Cross Roads on the Wadesboro Road. They awoke early the next morning to the rattle of gunfire. Lieutenant Colonel David H. Kimmel and his 9th Pennsylvania Cavalry were camped well behind the rest of the brigade, leaving a gap in the Federal line that the Southerners had found and attacked. About 200 Confederates spread out and drove into the gap, firing as they advanced. Attacked from behind, Kimmel's pickets fell back toward the bulk of the regiment, their defense stiffening until the initial Southern attack was repulsed. While the Southerners were deploying a line of skirmishers and probing the Pennsylvania front, Kimmel sent his adjutant, Lt. Isaac D. Landis, with an equal number of troopers to try and outflank and capture the enemy pickets. Landis moved as ordered, but quickly realized that his small force had advanced behind Col. William McLemore's entire Tennessee brigade. Outnumbered and in danger of being cut off, Landis wisely withdrew.[34] Kimmel, meanwhile, prepared his regiment to receive an attack but the enemy failed to launch a second effort. "Our company went on picket and the rebels charged them," recounted trooper Cornelius Baker, "We lay in the barricades all nite."[35] The grayclad troopers contented themselves with exchanging heavy picket fire with Kimmel's men.[36]

The beginning of Abraham Lincoln's second term and the inexorable advance of Sherman's army caused consternation among the Confederate soldiers. Most of them were realists and understood that the outcome of the war had already been decided. "This is indeed a gloomy beginning to Mr. Lincoln's 2nd turn," noted one of Wheeler's Georgians. "Does it portend evil to his or our country?"[37]

Kilpatrick certainly hoped so. Early that morning he ordered Maj. James G. McBride of the 9th Michigan Cavalry to take a 100-man scouting party on a nine-mile ride to Wadesboro. McBride's written instructions were simple: "clean out the town." To stay in touch with the rest of the command, the Wolverines carried skyrockets they could use at night as signals.[38] McBride and his little force rode without incident to Wadesboro, where they destroyed a grist mill, a sawmill, a tannery, several large government stables, and all the other public property in the town. "The heart sickens to look upon and contemplate the ruin they have left behind," noted the local newspaper. "The houses they visited, of the rich and poor alike, were pillaged of whatever provisions were about them, smoke houses were broken open and despoiled of their contents, corn cribs emptied, or where the corn was not removed, the buildings were fired and their contents destroyed; fodder, mills, gin-houses and cotton screws, with large amounts of cotton, were burned—in fact the section of the country we have designated was left a complete wreck."[39]

What Kilpatrick did not know was that while McBride was burning sawmills, Confederate cavalry was working its way into position to decisively attack him. When he learned that Wheeler had attacked Jordan's camps, Kilpatrick smartly decided to consolidate his command and find a better defensive position. Jordan's brigade pulled back and linked up with Brig. Gen. Smith D. Atkins and his Second Brigade. While Wheeler's men pressed Atkins, Jordan assumed a new position two miles behind him, leaving Atkins to disengage and follow. Atkins's leapfrogged his command rearward behind Jordan, leaving that officer to face the approaching enemy. Kilpatrick brought up the rest of his division and prepared for a general engagement. Wheeler's men bore down and lightly attacked Jordan's new line several times, but was repulsed on each occasion.[40] "Pickets had a lively time for a while," noted the adjutant of the 8th Indiana Cavalry in his diary.[41] At 2:25 p.m. Wheeler scribbled a quick report to Hampton: "The enemy have left their lines of works. All heard of as yet were 100 men at the first works."[42]

A squadron of Federals, Companies E and H of the 9th Michigan Cavalry of Atkins's brigade, had a tough time of it that afternoon. The two company commanders, Capts. John J. Hinchey and Howard M. Rice, were not informed of the leapfrog move to the rear and so had remained in position, fighting vigorously against Wheeler's cavalry. The withdrawal of the rest of the command exposed their rear and an overwhelming attack crashed into them from behind. Seeing no alternative but to slash their way to safety, Hinchey and Rice ordered their men to draw sabers. The bugles sounded the charge, and off went the intrepid Michigan men. "In the charge Captain Rice lost 2 men killed

note of interest:
Due to the death of Lieutenant Griffin, Union forces made a sweep of the town, looting provisions and personal items. One townsman was shot for his property.

**Captain Nothrop's (US)
3rd Division Scouts raid
into Wadesboro, N.C.
Mar. 4th, 1865**

Copyright 2003 by James Acerra for *"An Infernal Surprise"* by: Eric J. Wittenburg

—Northrop's Scouts dash into Wadesboro, where they meet local Home Guardsmen. A melee breaks out in the streets. Lt. Amos Griffin, a Confederate deserter serving as one of the Scouts, is killed. Griffin was the sole Union casualty in the skirmish at Wadesboro;

—Northrop rounds up prisoners, including the man who shot Griffin, and takes them away. The Scouts threatened to execute the man as soon as they return to their command. Other members of the Home Guard are also taken captive as the Scouts depart;

—Angered by the loss of Griffin, the Scouts loot Wadesboro (including the sacristy of the Episcopal Bishop of North Carolina). A civilian is killed when he refuses to give up his watch and money. The Scouts commandeer a carriage to haul off their loot.

—The engagement at Wadesboro is brief but deadly.

and 11 from the command missing," explained the official report. "Captain Hinchey had his horse shot and quite a number of his men also lost their horses." The survivors—and the rest of the regiment—rode ten miles to Bethel Church, fighting a running rearguard action with Wheeler's men the entire way.[43]

Just five minutes later Wheeler scribbled a note to Hampton requesting reinforcements. "We find artillery here, and have but two small regiments," he wrote. "Can you not send more forces up? The enemy have retired from four lines of works. Each line of works was for about 100 men."[44] Wheeler had surrounded most of Kilpatrick's division and was in position to move in for the kill—if only he had sufficient forces to do so.[45]

Colonel Way reacted to Wheeler's growing threat by bringing up his dismounted brigade. His men lined up alongside the first brigade, and the combined force threw together a strong rail barricade around the Federal position.[46] "We had hardly completed our barricade before our pickets were attacked and driven in," recounted Way. "The enemy formed all along our front and seemed to be preparing for an attack, when the artillery of the First Brigade opened, which with a brisk fire from the line caused him to withdraw his main force, though he kept a skirmish line in our front."[47]

Lieutenant Charles Blanford commanded Jordan's horse artillery, which consisted of a section of howitzers. He and his gunners had passed a quiet morning, enjoying a respite from the toils of the march. About two that afternoon, with "heavy skirmishing around the lines . . . I broke camp and marched two miles and a half at a trot, where I took up position for the night behind rail barricades, supported by the Eighth Indiana Cavalry," reported Blanford. "About dark the enemy came charging upon our front, mounted, when I was ordered by Colonel Jordan to open fire on them; after firing a few rounds the enemy drew off, and did not molest us again during the night."[48]

Unable to receive sufficient reinforcements to press his advantage, and with only two regiments at his disposal, Wheeler gave up an hour later. "Having run against some artillery, and not having sufficient force to drive the enemy from his position, I have taken up a position and will await your orders," he reported to Hampton. "The enemy were driven from four lines of works by flanking him, but when we came upon artillery he showed himself rather bold. He advanced upon us, but only a short distance."[49]

Wheeler maintained a desultory fire until about 9:00 p.m., when he broke off the engagement and withdrew to bivouac in a nearby field.[50] Given the overall state of affairs the morale of some in his command was higher than he had a right to expect. "I am in good spirits," noted one of his officers in his diary that night. "The cloud that is hovering around us is dark, but I have no doubt concerning our future."[51]

Fully expecting Wheeler to resume his attack the next morning, Jordan and Way remained in line of battle all night. "Wheeler and Hampton had a very much larger force than Kilpatrick," recalled a member of the 92nd Illinois, "and with our pickets driven in before dark, and the enemy encircling our barricaded position, it looked like a battle at daylight, or before, and the men lay behind the barricade resting on their arms." The Federals were able to relax sooner than they thought. "We heard their bugles sounding and soon all was quiet," recalled a thankful member of the 8th Indiana Cavalry in his diary.[52]

To intimidate the Confederates, Kilpatrick ordered his command to send up different color rockets, which were answered by the contingent of the 9th Michigan Cavalry that had ridden off on the mission to Wadesboro. The sky lit up in a brilliant display of color. "Rockets in front of them, and rockets behind them—it might mean a trap for [the enemy]. In a little while we could distinctly hear them withdrawing their troops who encircled our position."[53]

Jordan's alerted pickets killed a wayward Confederate soldier and captured several others. "All ready for an attack since 4 A.M.," noted a Hoosier horseman.[54] Jordan sent his wagons to the rear "and prepared for the struggle, but daylight revealed . . . that the enemy had decamped during the night."[55] Although Kilpatrick probably did not realize it, he had but narrowly avoided a much more serious setback. If Wheeler and Hampton had joined forces, and the entire column of Southern cavalry had been available, Kilpatrick's sloppy dispositions might well have exposed him to disaster. And the horse soldiers had only just entered the Old North State.

Returning from their expedition to Wadesboro, McBride's Michiganders did not encounter any Confederates until they neared the morning's picket lines. Instead of finding friendly pickets, however, they found Wheeler's troopers. "Deeming it impossible, [McBride] rode up

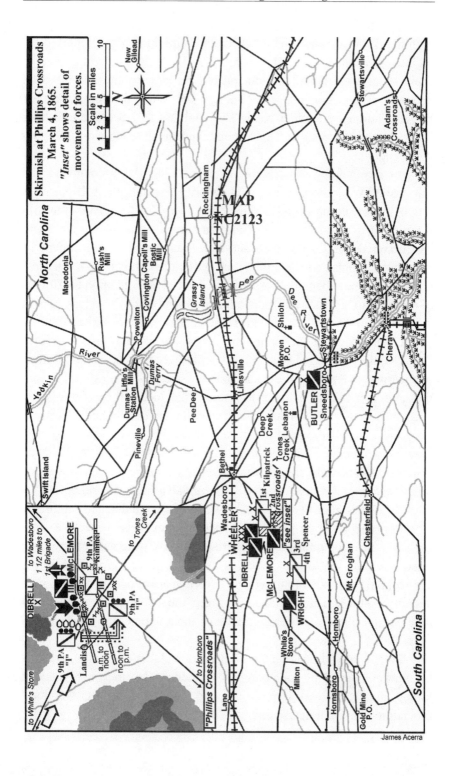

James Acerra

with the advance, when the rebels opened fire upon him," reported his regimental commander, Col. George S. Acker. "By a gallant charge he drove them back, but seeing our pickets no longer there and the dead bodies of two of our men, he withdrew and joined the command near Bethel Church by another road. The coolness and courage of Major McBride and the men under his command on this occasion is highly commendable."[56]

The day before, another contingent of Kilpatrick's command had also visited Wadesboro. Captain Theodore F. Northrop led Kilpatrick's scouts, an elite group of eighty selected troopers.[57] A lieutenant of the 5th Kentucky Cavalry from North Carolina named Amos M. Griffin, who had deserted the Confederate service, commanded a detachment of Northrop's scouts and was killed during a brief skirmish. "We learned," noted a local newspaper editor, "[that Kilpatrick looked upon Griffin] as of more use to him than any man in his command, and whose loss, he was understood to remark, crippled him more than if he had lost a brigade."[58]

As the scouts made their way across the pine forests of North Carolina, they fanned out like a horde of hungry locusts. Some of them, on their way to Fayetteville, dashed into the streets of Wadesboro. Seeing the approach of the Yankee horsemen, the local Home Guardsmen scrambled to meet the threat. "There were not ten of us who had arms in our hands," recalled one of them, "and when the enemy were first seen they could not have been more than a hundred yards from us. A stampede instantly took place by the crowd, and we found ourselves standing alone in the middle of the street, bullets whizzing all around us, and before we could bring our guns to our shoulder we were surrounded and captured." Northrop and his men swiftly rounded up their prisoners. "We were carried to near the public well, where the enemy were assembling their prisoners, and we found ourselves among a mixed crowd of Home Guards, old men, boys fourteen and fifteen years of age, and negro men and boys—these latter brought in from the country with them and mounted on mules and horses, many of them apparently just from the plow."[59]

A member of the Home Guard heard the clatter of hooves, grabbed his musket, opened his door, and shot Lieutenant Griffin from his saddle, killing him. "He was a renegade and deserter from our service," proclaimed the local newspaper. "So perish all such."[60]

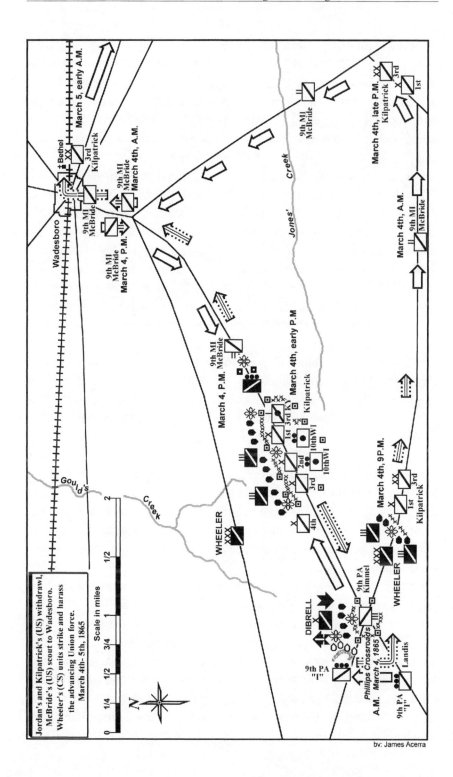

bv: James Acerra

Predictably, an Ohio newspaper offered an entirely different perspective. "The loss of Lieutenant Griffin was most serious and was deeply felt by the entire command," reported a correspondent traveling with Kilpatrick's headquarters.[61] "It was a gallant little fight," noted one of the scouts, "but our Lieutenant was killed—the only man hurt in the engagement, on our side. We captured a great many prisoners, horses, and negroes, which we carried back to the camp."[62]

Infuriated by the death of Griffin, Northrop and his scouts looted Wadesboro. Thomas Atkinson, the Episcopal bishop of North Carolina, had his house and possessions pillaged by Northrop's men, who took the bishop's watch, clothes, jewelry, and horse. They cleaned out every home in the town that seemed worth robbing, and even a few that did not. The scouts broke into storerooms and took whatever they wanted. "A Mr. James C. Bennett, one of the oldest and wealthiest men in Anson County, was shot at the door of his own house because he did not give up his watch and money, which had been previously taken from him by another party," recounted Bishop Atkinson[63] Another man of the cloth, Reverend S. C. Bland, the rector of Wadesboro's Calvary Episcopal Church, recorded, "This day a portion of General Kilpatrick's command was sent to sack our village, which they did and robbed the church of the few dollars on hand. General Kilpatrick was an officer of Sherman's Army, and was acting under orders of his commander-in-chief. This is one of many churches robbed."[64]

Northrop's men commandeered a carriage from a civilian and used it to carry off Griffin's body.[65] His killer was quickly located and arrested, and the Yankees made dire threats against him and the townspeople. The Federals told the man's family that he would be executed as soon as they got back to their command, and dragged the unfortunate Home Guardsman man away with them. Both he and the other town soldiers swept up in Northrop's initial dash into the town dejectedly joined the large contingent of prisoners marching with Way's dismounted Union brigade.

Wheeler's command arrived in Wadesboro that night. "The people gave us a heartfelt welcome," commented one Georgia horseman, "they having had a taste of Yankee kindness that day."[66] The next day some of Capt. Alexander M. Shannon's Scouts passed through the town while tracking the enemy. The wife and two daughters of the Home Guardsman who had killed Griffin "stood on the street corner and, in tears, [and] told us of their fear that the threat [to hang him] would be carried out." A number of the Shannon's Scouts vowed to rescue the man if they could.[67]

Wheeler's attack on Kilpatrick's camps near the state line was ample warning that the feisty Confederate cavalry remained a force to be reckoned with. The Union horseman should have realized that Hampton and Wheeler were seeking opportunities to attack him, and he should have been more careful in his dispositions. Considering his experience and the situation facing him in North Carolina, there would be no excuse for him to be surprised.

Kilpatrick's division moved out at 6:00 a.m. on March 5, riding eight miles to Morven's Post Office. The column camped there, awaiting the construction of a pontoon bridge across the swollen river. The crossing was delayed because there was not enough bridging to span the Great Pee Dee.[68] As they waited to cross, Kilpatrick's men lay uncomfortably on the soggy ground, clutching their reins, because they were not permitted to go into camp or even to establish a bivouac for fear that the Confederate cavalry might fall upon them unexpectedly.[69]

While Kilpatrick waited, Hampton remained active. Just after midnight he had instructed Wheeler to "close up everything on this road and camp wherever you can find forage." After telling Wheeler where he could find a supply of corn, Hampton instructed his lieutenant "to be ready to move in at daylight in the morning" and to push into Wadesboro, all the while sending out scouts to locate the enemy column. That afternoon, Wheeler reported that "the only place we can ford the river is at Grassy Island," eleven miles from Wadesboro. Since Grassy Island was closest to his position, Wheeler would head there and attempt to cross the Great Pee Dee.[70] The Federal 14th Corps was less than two days' march behind him.

A virgin pine forest filled the area between the Great Pee Dee and Cape Fear rivers. "Here are extensive forests of trees from twenty inches to three feet in diameter and at least seventy feet without a limb, but spreading at the top with a dense mass of interlocking limbs, clothed in evergreen leaves so dense as to exclude the sun," remarked Col. William D. Hamilton of the 9th Ohio Cavalry. "The ground is covered from 4 to 6 inches deep with 'pine needles' rotting at the bottom but soft and clean on the surface." The pitch and resin from these pine trees was collected for naval stores. The highly flammable material also made these pine forests a tempting target for the Federals, who remained determined to punish the citizens of the Confederacy. There were also many turpentine factories along the numerous streams crisscrossing the area. These facilities tended to attract Yankee torches. As the men fired the buildings and the woods, the thick canopy created by the mature trees trapped the smoke from the fires, creating "a feeling of awe as though one were within the precincts of a grand old cathedral," Colonel Hamilton recalled.[71]

General Butler's Southern cavalry division rode to the railroad town of Rockingham, North Carolina, on March 5. "Our cavalry column was hailed with joy by the women and children particularly, for we saw very few men," recalled a member of the 6th South Carolina. "They were quite liberal in supplying us with hot biscuits just from the oven. It was almost impossible to keep the men in line, with the plates of hot rolls, and biscuits being brought out to them as we passed through."[72]

"We marched to Rockingham upon the advance of the enemy upon our pickets," Col. J. Fred Waring of the Jeff Davis Legion wrote in his diary. "We shall suffer soon unless we get a supply of horse shoes." Waring also noted that Butler's favorite courier had been shot through the throat by a Federal picket the night before.[73]

While his men were enjoying local hospitality, Butler was reporting that Hardee's column had cleared Rockingham before noon. Butler remained in Rockingham overnight with a brigade of cavalry to protect Hardee's rear. "The enemy crossed at Cheraw yesterday morning and drove in my pickets at daylight, two miles from the river, on the road to Fayetteville," reported Butler. "From the columns of smoke seen below, they appear to be marching toward Fayetteville." Noting the dispositions of Sherman's infantry corps, Butler concluded, "Sherman, I have no doubt, is making for Fayetteville."[74]

Wheeler's corps came up to support Butler's horsemen. "Poor country and the ugliest women I ever saw," complained one of Wheeler's officers. "Today is Sunday. If I could see Ma and loved ones far away I would be happy." The Southern horsemen remained in Rockingham all the next day, resting their mounts and preparing for their next move.[75]

There no longer seemed any doubt that Sherman's destination was Fayetteville. It was now a race to see who would reach the critical bridges across the Cape Fear first. The Cape Fear was fast and deep at Fayetteville, and without the bridges Sherman would have to bring up bridging materials to get across. General Beauregard, Johnston's

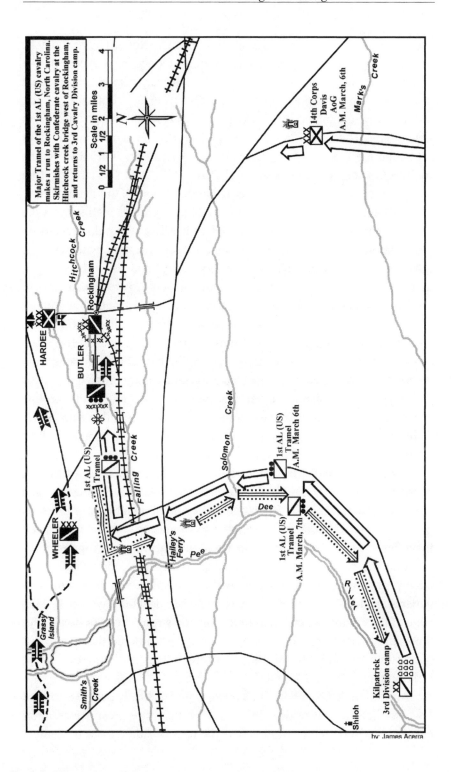

Major Tramel of the 1st AL (US) cavalry makes a run to Rockingham, North Carolina. Skirmishes with Confederate cavalry at the Hitchcock creek bridge west of Rockingham, and returns to 3rd Cavalry Division camp.

Scale in miles

0   1/2   1   1/2   2   3   4

N

Hitchcock Creek

Rockingham

HARDEE

BUTLER

14th Corps
Davis
AoG
A.M. March, 6th

Marks Creek

Falling Creek

Solomon Creek

1st AL (US)
Tramel

WHEELER

1st AL (US)
Tramel
A.M. March 6th

Dee

Halley's Ferry

Pee

1st AL (US)
Tramel
A.M. March, 7th

River

Grassy Island

Smith's Creek

Kilpatrick
3rd Division camp

Shiloh

by James Acerra

second-in-command, was with the garrison at Charlotte. The next day he sent Hardee concise instructions. "March at once on Fayetteville, if possible; if not, then on to Raleigh."[76] Hardee responded the next morning. "Agreeably to instructions from General Johnston, I am moving my command, via Monroe's Bridge and New Gilead, to Fayetteville," he wrote. "I hope to reach Fayetteville in three or four days (not counting today). Major-General Butler's cavalry will move on the road to Graham's Bridge and parallel roads."[77] And so Hardee's foot soldiers moved out, hoping to beat Kilpatrick troopers to Fayetteville.

On the morning of March 6, the Federal engineers realized that the level of the broad and high-running Great Pee Dee was unlikely to drop any time soon. If it did not, it was an open question whether their pontoons would work. "The river is about four hundred yards wide and quite swift," noted a Hoosier. "It is quite difficult to get the anchors to hold their places and not allow the bridge to break loose and swing round, or break into sections."[78] Since there were not enough pontoons, the resourceful Federal engineers covered the bottom and sides of forty-two army wagons with cotton cloth, linked them to the pontoons, and completed the bridge.[79] The blueclad horsemen finally crossed the Great Pee Dee near Sneedsboro, about one mile south of the North Carolina state line. After crossing they continued about six miles into North Carolina before halting for the night six miles from Morven's Post Office.[80]

That same night, Maj. Sanford Tramel, the commander of the 1st Alabama Cavalry (U.S.), received orders from Colonel Spencer to take fifty men and advance on Rockingham, a ride of about twelve miles. If possible, ordered Spencer, Tramel was to capture the town. "I advanced to within three miles of the place without meeting any opposition," reported the major. "I there found the road strongly picketed by the enemy, and immediately ordered my men to charge, which they did in a gallant manner, driving the enemy from post to post until we reached the edge of the village, where we found a line too strong for us to break with the small force at my command; consequently I ordered the men to fall back slowly, which they did in good order. I then returned to camp, arriving there at 4 A.M. on the 7th."[81]

And so the Yankee horsemen made slow but steady progress toward Fayetteville and the critical bridges over the Cape Fear River, their passage cutting a wide swath across the countryside. "Corn is plenty,"

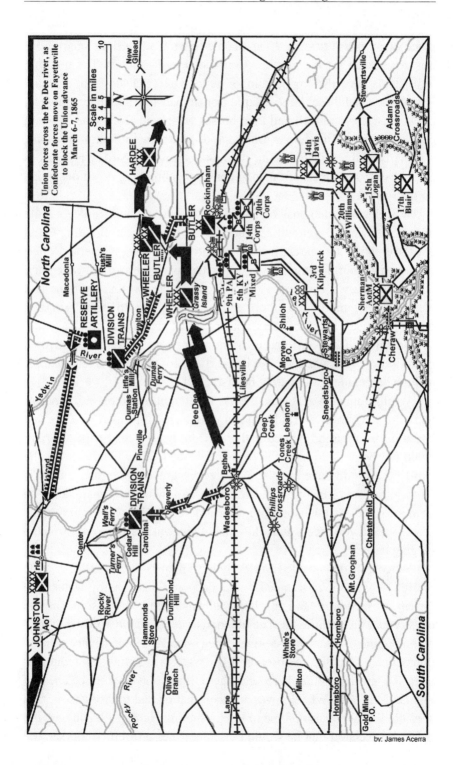

Union forces cross the Pee Dee river, as Confederate forces move on Fayetteville to block the Union advance
March 6-7, 1865

by: James Acerra

noted one Federal trooper. "The people 'have made a right smart crop' this last season for the glorious Confederacy. *We* take it. The obliging individuals have also 'made' a lot of pork. We let that alone, of course!" Kilpatrick's saddle soldiers suffered from exhaustion and other ailments, but at least they ate well and their horses were well fed.[82] One of them, caught while stealing horses from one of Sherman's infantry divisions, was marched through the infantry camps wearing a placard on his back as punishment. The stress of the long march was breaking down discipline on both sides.[83]

Wheeler was also busy on March 6. Anxious to find Hardee's route of march toward Fayetteville, Wheeler had to cross the flooding Great Pee Dee River to search for the infantry. Brigadier General Robert Anderson's Georgia brigade was the first to reach the swollen waterway. "One evening we came to a deep, broad river, swollen by rains and melting snow, impossible to ford and very dangerous to swim," recalled one of Anderson's staff officers. Anderson had his brigade bivouac while he and some of his staff and couriers rode along the river to judge its condition. "There was a freshet in the river, covering the river swamps, and the other side could barely be discerned."

While Anderson evaluated the risk of attempting a crossing, Wheeler and a dozen couriers and aides rode up. Anderson informed Wheeler that based on information he had gathered from nearby residents, the river could not be crossed until the freshet subsided. They Confederates, he explained, would have to wait. Wheeler disagreed. "Sherman's army is on the other side," he retorted, "and I must know what they are doing so as to inform Gen. Johnston." Wheeler ordered Anderson to return to his brigade and await orders and told some of his couriers to try and cross the surging river.[84]

Wheeler had persuaded an elderly local man to act as a guide, but the old fellow was soon swamped by the deep and fast-flowing water. The torrent washed him and his horse downstream, where some of the cavalrymen pulled him out. The old man understandably refused to try a second time. "The oldest river men declared the river entirely impracticable," noted an observer. "The water was raging, extending far over the swamp, with here and there little outstanding patches of highland visible." Wheeler was adamant that he had to cross as soon as possible for there was no time to lose in finding Hardee. Fed up with the delay, he declared that he would cross the water himself. With that, the

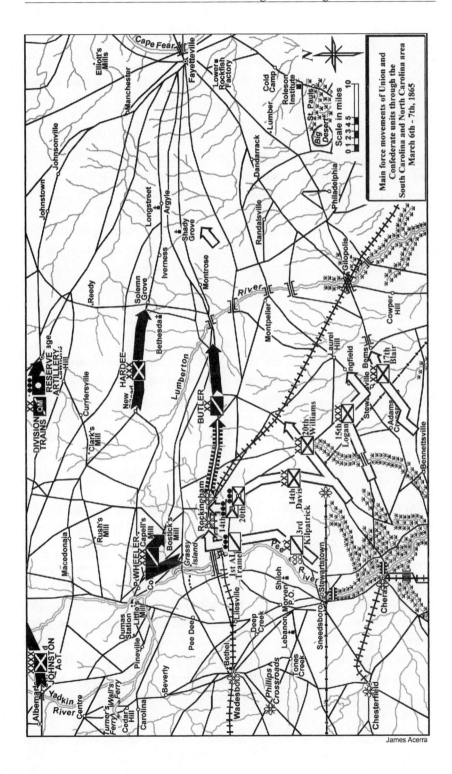

Main force movements of Union and Confederate units through the South Carolina and North Carolina area March 6th - 7th, 1865

James Acerra

Southern general spurred his horse into the swollen river. Edward H. McKnight, Company K, 8th Texas Cavalry, had wandered down to the riverbank to water his horse. Acting impulsively, he turned to his comrade, James B. Nance of the 4th Tennessee and said, "Let's go with him."[85]

Seeing the two men plunge into the rampaging river, Wheeler called out, "Boys, hold your horses' heads upstream and let them float across!" From past experience, the three men knew how to guide their horses across a river so that the swift running current would not trip or overturn the animals, thereby drowning both horse and rider.[86] The diminutive Wheeler could barely be seen in the raging torrent. "Nothing was visible above the water except the heads of the riders and the noses and tips of the ears of the horses," recalled one impressed observer. "The first landing was on an island, midway. Wringing the water from clothing and emptying boots occupied a few minutes while the horses rested."[87]

After their brief respite the trio mounted up and plunged once more into the frigid torrent. A few more minutes of swimming and they found themselves on the river's far bank. Wheeler and his two companions stopped at a nearby farm house and had a pleasant dinner, tricking their host into thinking they were Yankees. The owner complained about Wheeler's command, little realizing who shared the table with him. Wheeler's men were "worse than Yankees, stealing all a man had," proclaimed the farmer. An amused Wheeler smiled and agreed, saying that yes, Wheeler's men were bad indeed. With that, the tired little general retired for the night.[88]

Wheeler's troopers were not about to abandon their commander. Now that everyone knew the river could be crossed, the remainder of the corps began making its way across the swollen Great Pee Dee. The next morning, March 7, Wheeler and his horse soldiers resumed their pursuit of Kilpatrick's column while searching for Hardee's infantry. Wheeler established his headquarters at the nearby home of Alfred Dockery, a prominent prewar member of Congress and gentleman planter who generously offered his residence as a base of operations.[89] "Stayed with Mr. Dockery, who, with his family, we found most hospitable and kind," recalled a grateful Georgian.[90] Wheeler found a few minutes to send a report to Hampton. "I think it will be advisable at least to keep these roads picketed until the whole command is across the river."[91]

Wheeler's dogged pursuit impressed the people of North Carolina. Although his men had earned a terrible reputation for their depredations in Georgia and South Carolina, a local newspaperman came to Wheeler's defense. "We are disposed to think that 'Wheeler's Cavalry' have been, to a great extent, unjustly censured," wrote the editor of the *Western Democrat,* a Charlotte newspaper. "All thieving that is done, or depredations of any sort that have been committed, is charged upon Wheeler's cavalry, although in some instances, it is known that they were far away. We learn that Wheeler's men have been close on the flanks of the enemy ever since they left Columbia and we know (from official reports) that they have fought the enemy wherever opportunity offered. We suspect that the sins of others are often laid on Wheeler's men," he concluded.[92]

Captain Alexander Shannon led Wheeler's scout detachment. The 25-year-old Shannon was born in Arkansas on May 7, 1839, but moved to Texas at the age of fourteen. He settled in southwest Texas, where he acquired a fine ranch on the banks of the San Antonio River. Shannon was a Mason and a Democrat who had originally opposed secession. After Texas seceded, however, he raised a company for Brig. Gen. Henry Sibley's command and soon transferred to Terry's Texas Rangers, participating as a first lieutenant in all of the storied regiment's engagements.[93] Shannon received a promotion to captain in 1863.[94]

"Shannon's Scouts was one of the most colorful and effective organizations performing both reconnaissance and commando service in the Confederate Army," writes a modern historian.[95] Formed in August 1864 by Gen. John Bell Hood, Shannon's initial force of thirty

Captain
Alexander Shannon

Michael Shannon

USAMHI

Five of "Shannon's Scouts."

men was drawn from a company of the 8th Texas Cavalry, but other horse soldiers of Harrison's Brigade reinforced the Texans. Shannon's Scouts dogged Sherman's foraging parties and routinely attacked units four times their size, killing, wounding, and capturing nearly 150 Federals in the process. "Shannon's selection of the men he had with him soon won for him and his scouts a reputation with our army, and especially with the enemy, second to no scout ever sent out by any army," declared H. W. Graber, a proud member of Shannon's Scouts.[96]

A passage from a letter written by Enoch John, one of Shannon's Scouts, on December 18, 1864, reveals the hard nature of the war waged by these men. "I have enjoyed myself for this trip but think, sometimes, I am getting hard-hearted," he wrote. "But I notice the tears of a lady always bring tears to my eyes and the smoke and flames of a dwelling prevents the prayers of the Yankees for their lives, even when on their knees, being heard, and steadies my nerves to kill them all . . . I have a brace of pistols that never snap." This was the hard hand of war. In some quarters the black flag had been raised, and Shannon's men acted accordingly.[97]

Taking a page from other successful Confederate partisans like Col. John S. Mosby, Shannon's Scouts often employed hit-and-run tactics. "Witnesses stated that Shannon's rule was immediately to attack any enemy force encountered and if it proved too strong to withdraw," wrote one historian of the unit. If endangered, the Scouts remained concealed, waiting for a chance to pounce on stragglers. Shannon often divided his command into squads that operated independently, and by the time the armies had entered North Carolina, Shannon regularly made a point of retaining elements of his command in camp to meet emergencies.[98]

Shannon proved to be such a thorn in Kilpatrick's side that Little Kil offered a $5,000 reward for his capture. Months later, under a flag of truce, Shannon responded. "I want to thank you for the signal honor," he told Kilpatrick, "but I'm going to go you one better: I'm going to get you for nothing."[99] Shannon was never able to fulfill his promise, but he remained an irritant to Kilpatrick and his horsemen. Shannon's Scouts had crossed the swollen Great Pee Dee River on flatboats the day before and were waiting for Wheeler to join them. It came as a surprise, then, when they learned their commander had already crossed the waterway and had spent the night at Dockery's nearby home.

The Scouts successfully located Wheeler, remembered one Southern trooper, "but they hardly had time to feed their horses before the picket reported Yankees just down the road robbing a house."[100] Wheeler cautioned the Scouts, "Don't call me General; I'm Private Johnson with you boys today," before leading twenty of Shannon's men in a small ambush against some of Kilpatrick's troopers pillaging a residence near Rockingham. The Confederates routed the stunned Yankees and killed or captured thirty-five in a spirited skirmish. Two troopers from the 9th Pennsylvania Cavalry were killed, as were two of the 8th Indiana Cavalry. Mathew S. Ross of Company G surrendered, but one of Shannon's men shot him in the back of the head nonetheless, the ball lodging between his skull and the skin of his forehead. "He lived until after dark that night when he died. His death has cast a gloom over his comrades and is a severe blow to his own dear brother George of the same company," lamented Williamson D. Ward of the 8th Indiana. "We know that the news of his death will be sad indeed to his parents and friends at home."[101]

Shannon's favorite stallion "Mohawk" took a round in the neck during the melee, but Shannon picked himself up, changed horses, and continued the fight.[102] "The chase was kept up until the advancing Federal forces were seen across the open road forming a line of battle for

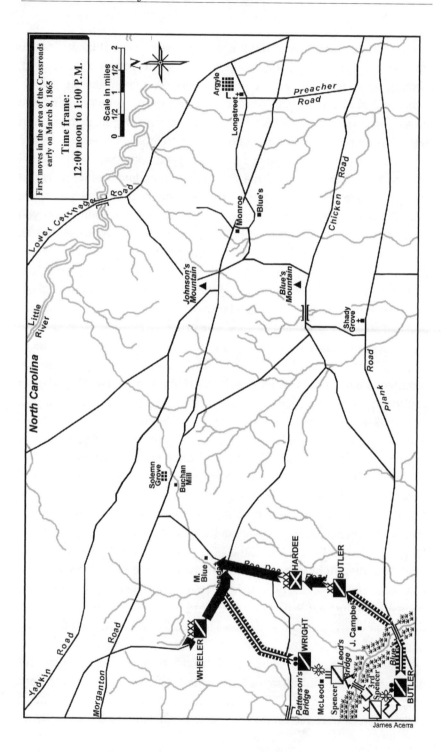

James Acerra

their reception," recalled one of Wheeler's men, so the [Scouts] hastily retired."[103]

That morning Little Kil and his staff were riding with Colonel Jordan and his brigade. About 10:00 a.m. Jordan's lead regiment, the 9th Pennsylvania Cavalry, along with a detachment of the 3rd Kentucky and a few "bummers" from some of Sherman's infantry regiments collided with Butler's cavalry division occupying Rockingham. "The rebels showed their teeth," noted an Ohio trooper and member of Kilpatrick's escort company.[104] The Federals drove Butler's veterans from the town and captured it without much difficulty.[105] "We retired without fighting," recounted one of Gib Wright's officers.[106] "A large cotton factory, which had been running day and night, making cloth for the Confederate army, was burned," noted the Ohio trooper.[107]

Ulysses R. Brooks of the 6th South Carolina Cavalry described the Rockingham affair as "a pretty hot skirmish." Unable to control his horse, Brooks ended up leading a charge against some Yankee horsemen who had just opened a captured barrel of wine. "Fortunately, our men coming behind me with a rebel yell created a panic among the Yankees and they stampeded, thereby saving me from death or capture," the South Carolinian recalled with gratitude.[108]

The Confederate cavalry maintained an aggressive posture, and the fact that it was contesting every step of the march frustrated Kilpatrick. He still had to cover the advance of the infantry, however, so he paused to assess the situation and cover Slocum's advance. "Here the cavalry amused Hampton and Hardee until Major-General Slocum had crossed Lynch River," recalled the surgeon of the 9th Pennsylvania Cavalry.[109]

Kilpatrick reported on his whereabouts and activities that morning and Sherman responded later that day. "I am well pleased to learn that Hardee is making well north. Though willing to fight Joe Johnston who commands in chief, I would prefer to work over to the new base to clear our columns of the impedimenta and make junction with Schofield, who is doubtless working up toward Goldsborough," explained Sherman. "If I can get that point secure . . . you will perceive what a base I will have. Raleigh will be easy of conquest and we can drive all Carolina north of Roanoke, where the concentrated armies of the Confederacy will have contracted foraging ground." Sherman also informed his cavalry chief that he was heading for Fayetteville. He instructed Kilpatrick to keep up the appearance of pursuing Hardee, to go easy on the citizens of North

Carolina, and to avoid unnecessary destruction of private property. "There is a body of infantry and cavalry left down in the pocket about Florence that might be caught, but it won't pay to chase them—horse flesh is too precious," Sherman concluded. "Keep your horses in the best order for the day when we must have a big fight—not, however, on this turn."[110]

After hacking its way through the thick North Carolina pine forests, the Union infantry expected to reach Fayetteville by March 10. "Our progress was necessarily slow on account of a large force of cavalry in our front," recalled a member of the 52nd Ohio Volunteer Infantry of the 14th Corps, "stubbornly resisting our advance, in order to let Johnston concentrate on the east side of the Cape Fear River."[111] The Ohioan had nailed the question exactly: could Hampton and Wheeler hold back the advance of Sherman's army long enough to permit Joe Johnston to concentrate his forces and offer a credible battle?

On the other side of the Great Pee Dee, Hampton hovered on the fringes of Kilpatrick's advance. He now had Wheeler's Corps and 500 horsemen of Butler's division on the east bank. Probably because of his lack of service with Wheeler, Hampton felt that unless he could get all of Butler's command, which had accompanied Hardee and the infantry, he would have a difficult time harassing the advance of the Federals. That afternoon, Hampton fired off a note to Hardee seeking the return of Butler and his horse soldiers. "I have succeeded with great difficulty in getting most of my command across the river to-day,"wrote Hampton, "and I hope the whole of it will be over to-night." He then joined Butler's division, to the delight of the men in the ranks.[112]

Hampton reminded Hardee that "The Fourteenth Corps [crossed] at Wall's Ferry last evening, that corps being on the left. Kilpatrick is now at Rockingham. General Wheeler killed ten of his men a few hours ago, and drove the rest close up to the town. I shall get everything together near here to-night, and then be ready to move as circumstances require. I wish to have Butler with me, so as to operate to more advantage. Can you not let me have a small battery till mine comes up?" Hampton told Hardee precisely where his command lay. "I am now near Bethel Church, on the road to Rockingham, and three miles below Grassy Island Ford. As soon as my command can be concentrated I shall move round the left flank of the enemy to his front."[113] If Hampton could get in front of Sherman's infantry he could slow its advance, which was exactly what Johnston wanted him to do.

Hardee responded favorably, telling Hampton that he was presently twenty-eight miles from Fayetteville and that his command would arrive there on March 9. "I am glad you are across the river," said Hardee. "General Johnston wishes you to get in front of the enemy and to move in front of him if he should advance on Fayetteville; if on Wilmington, to 'dog his rear a few marches.'" The infantry general concluded by telling Hampton, "Let me know what can be done to aid you."[114]

By the next morning, March 8, all of Sherman's "army group" had entered North Carolina and was moving northeast, closing on Fayetteville. That same day, Maj. Gen. Jacob D. Cox's Federal 23th Corps collided with Braxton Bragg's troops at Wyse's Fork, a crossroads near Kinston. Bragg's men routed part of Cox's command, capturing a cannon and 800 prisoners. Cox's troops dug in and resumed skirmishing the next day. On March 10, while the opposing cavalry forces clashed at Monroe's Crossroads, Bragg launched an attack that was repulsed. When Bragg learned that Cox had received reinforcements, he broke off the battle and withdrew. Although Bragg lost the fight at Wyse's Fork, he had delayed the Federals for the better part of three days. Bragg retreated toward Goldsboro, and Johnston began concentrating his scattered forces in an effort to stop Sherman's seemingly inexorable advance.[115]

The important race for the Cape Fear bridges, however, had already been decided and Hardee was the winner. His troops entered Fayetteville that morning. It was a good day for the Confederate horse, too, as the Great Pee Dee River had finally subsided enough to permit Hampton and Wheeler to unite their commands for the first time. Johnston told Hampton that it was more important to menace the enemy's right flank than his left in order to prevent his communicating with the coast, and he wanted Hampton to concentrate his cavalry as soon as possible in the enemy's immediate front. Johnston also noted that Union cavalry appeared at 11:00 a.m. on the March 8 at McEachin's and other bridges over Lumber River, and that they drove back a detachment of the 5th Tennessee Cavalry to Antioch Church. "This detachment is now the only force known to us between this place and the enemy," Johnston wrote.[116]

Wheeler informed Hampton that he believed the enemy was headed for Fayetteville via the road from Rockingham, and that there was little forage available along that route. He also told him that he would cover his

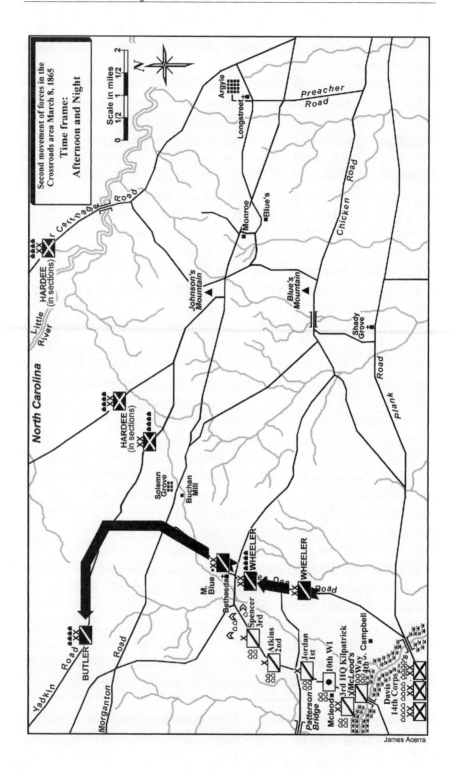

James Acerra

line of march with elements of his command, with an eye toward controlling the various river crossings that Kilpatrick would need in order to continue his advance. "I think we should take possession of these bridges immediately, before the enemy can take possession of, or citizens destroy, them," suggested Wheeler.[117] In the meantime, Butler's Division would link up with Wheeler's Corps. The junction was an important one, for it would allow the entire Confederate cavalry force to operate as a unified command for the first time. By this time both Hampton and Wheeler had determined that Kilpatrick's command was pinched between Hampton's cavalry and Hardee's infantry. "Immediate action to place the whole cavalry between Kilpatrick and Hardee was plainly imperative," remarked one observer.[118]

The grayclad horsemen set off toward Fayetteville on the Plank Road.[119] "Met the enemy at 12 o'clock. Charged and drove them for 2 miles," one of Wheeler's officers recorded in his diary. "Captured 14 prisoners. Our loss, one good soldier." The Southerners broke off the engagement and retired six miles before setting up camp. "Gen. Hampton up all night," noted the same officer.[120] "We had been in our saddles for twenty-four or thirty-six hours, with but little rest, dogging [the enemy's] footsteps," recalled a member of the 6th South Carolina Cavalry. "Seeing a light in front, a charge was made, but no enemy was found, but instead we found many nice eatables, canned goods, etc." The famished Confederates took a moment to enjoy their bounty before moving out once again.[121]

As the Confederate cavalry rode to interdict Kilpatrick the unsuspecting Federals pressed on, Spencer's Third Brigade leading the advance.[122] Spencer's men forced their way across the swollen Drowning Creek, which was really more of a swamp than a definable waterway and nearly half a mile wide. Contingents of Hampton's cavalry, meanwhile, buzzed angrily along the edges of Spencer's column, harassing the Federals every step of the way. "I believe it is about the worst road we have ever found," commented a Federal horseman on both the muddy terrain and the threatening enemy.[123]

Hoping to stop and rest for a while, Spencer searched for a good position on high ground. He spied a ridge and headed for it. As his men climbed the rising terrain the colonel spotted a farmhouse surrounded by people—though civilian or military he could not discern. Spencer ordered his men to advance at the gallop, and they dashed off toward the farmhouse, which was owned by a family named McLeod.

"About noon of the 8th of March a . . . squadron of Wade Hampton's men galloped into the yard and mother and my sister Flora here got them up a good supper," recalled Evander McLeod, son of the farm's owner, who had just returned home after being paroled at Fort Fisher. The Southern troopers were Gib Wright's men, probably of the Jeff Davis Legion. "They were splendid dashing young fellows, from Mississippi, who said our patrols were in touch with Yankee cavalry all through Pee Dee country, and that they would be along directly," recalled McLeod. They said to mother, 'Stand up to them, old lady. They will try to scare you, but they won't kill you.'"[124]

And then Spencer's men paid the family a visit. Wright's men had already left. Evander picks up the story at that point:

> Along after noon we began to hear the sound of shooting in the distance. I broke and ran just as hard as I could pelt for the horses, which my brother and another fellow were guarding down the creek. The Yankees rode into the yard, ran pelter into the house, drew their shining swords and demanded of mother 'her gold, her sons, and her horses.' Mother stood up to them all right, and told them to wipe their feet before they came into the parlor.[125]

While Spencer's brigade enjoyed the bounty of the McLeod farm, the rest of Kilpatrick's division struggled along in an effort to catch up. They had to contend with a flooded Deep Creek and Devil's Gut, two more formidable impediments. "We rode hard all day through the rain and met with very poor success," noted Pvt. James S. Thompson of the 8th Indiana Cavalry.[126] Wednesday, March 8 was "one of almost inconceivable hardship," grumbled the historian of McLaughlin's Squadron of Atkins's Second Brigade.[127]

Much to their chagrin, the Northern horsemen had to contend with the deepest, muddiest, and worst swamp of the campaign. "This has been decisively the worst day we have had since we left Marietta," noted a member of the 10th Ohio Cavalry of Atkins's brigade. "Well we got safely across the swamp but we had still another swamp to cross through mud and rain till when we got to where we intended to stop. We found the Johnnies in full possession and we fired a few rounds and was glad to leave them, they followed a short distance and left us to pursue our way and lonely and dreary it was."[128] Lieutenant Colonel Robert H. King of the 3rd Kentucky Cavalry echoed the Ohioan's sentiments. "During this time our march was over the worst roads it has ever been my fortune to travel," complained King. "For two nights the men were dismounted in mud and water, drawing our artillery and wagons through swamps."[129]

About 8:00 that evening Kilpatrick and his staff arrived at the McLeod house. "A little after dark a body of officers covered with mud and wet to the skin, dashed up to the house, and without ceremony took possession," recalled Evander McLeod. "There were about twelve of them, led by a stocky bald headed man of medium height, who took instant charge of everything. He ordered dinner, but the girls wouldn't cook it. A soldier came in with a bushel of sweet potatoes, which he said were to be prepared for the General and his Staff. But the girls threw them in a pot and all got together with their mother in the east room," continued the paroled former Confederate soldier. "It was Judson Kilpatrick, in command of all of Sherman's cavalry. He was really very decent to the women. He left them unmolested in their room."[130] Evander's sister Flora, who was about sixteen years old, remembered that Kilpatrick had the family "move out of half the house to give up that half to him and his staff for sleeping, but . . . none of the family was touched or harmed in any way."[131]

While Little Kil was eating his boiled sweet potatoes, his men were slogging through thick mud and inky darkness. They had a difficult time of it. Colonel Jordan reported, "I had to dismount my command to draw the artillery and wagons through the swamp, more than half a mile wide; the men were many times in mud and water up to their armpits."[132] Complained one of Jordan's Hoosiers, "We had to drag our artillery across by hand. The horses would just swamp down and could not draw the load. The men were dismounted in the mud and water up to their waists pulling away at the wagons and cannons." Of his plight as a soldier he concluded, "The people at home quietly sleeping in their downy beds little realize what the soldiers were doing for them to save our country."[133]

"The wagons and artillery could only be dragged along by the men laying hold of ropes, which were run out ahead of the teams, while others laid their hands to the wheels," recalled one miserable Ohioan. "Often the vehicles stuck immovably and had to be pried out with levers and spikes. Such a wild scene of splashing and yelling and swearing and braying has

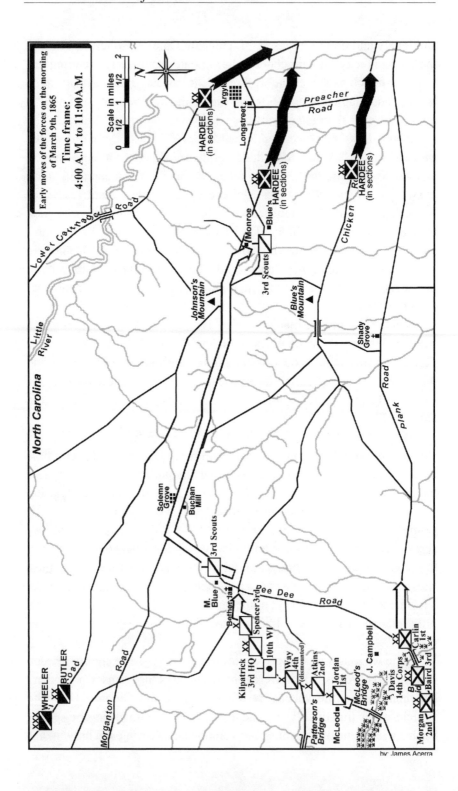

by: James Acerra

rarely greeted mortal eyes and ears."[134] Trooper Warren McCain of the 3rd Indiana Cavalry contracted a serious illness as a result of overexposure to the freezing waters and chilly evening air. "Those night marches in such miserable swamps were enough to kill man and beast," he remembered with a shudder.[135]

Lieutenant Colonel Way and his dismounted brigade probably had the worst time of all. At least the mounted troopers had their horses to raise them above some of the frigid mud and water. Way's men had no such luxury. "[We] continued our march in a severe rain-storm," reported Way. "The roads were very bad and the swamps had become almost impassable from the rains that had fallen." His exhausted men finally camped near the headwaters of the Lumber River at 11 p.m.[136] Jordan's brigade held the rear of Kilpatrick's column that day and did not reach its camp site on the opposite side of Drowning Creek until 4:00 a.m. on March 9.[137] "Had a hard time in crossing swamps," noted one of Jordan's Hoosiers, "and while doing so massed the troops on one of [Revolutionary War] Genl [Francis] Marion's camp grounds it is said."[138]

Colonel Jordan and his weary troopers got less than a four-hour respite before reveille was sounded. By 8:00 a.m. they were back in the saddle heading east as the rest of the division fell in behind them. "In the morning the men arose, stiffened, cold and hungry," wrote the historian of McLaughlin's Squadron. "Without breakfast they saddled, mounted, and again plunged into the mire, slowly and painfully urging their toilsome way."[139] Rain-swollen creeks and waterways continued to hinder their progress, prompting Kilpatrick to call them "the most horrible roads, swamps and swollen streams."[140] Looking to pick up the pace of march, Little Kil sent scouting parties to look for parallel routes to avoid overtaxing the roads. The farther his men spread out, however, the more the Federals risked attack by marauding Confederate cavalrymen hovering just beyond the fringes of Kilpatrick's column.[141]

While his men suffered, Kilpatrick enjoyed a pleasant day riding in a horse-drawn carriage in the company of a woman named Alice. Lieutenant Henry Clay Reynolds, one of Shannon's Scouts, had been captured the night before. Although Reynolds was the first of Shannon's men captured, Kilpatrick did not realize what a prize he had in his custody. "Reynolds was an experienced and successful cavalry officer who had often bettered the Yankees in battle and had led many successful

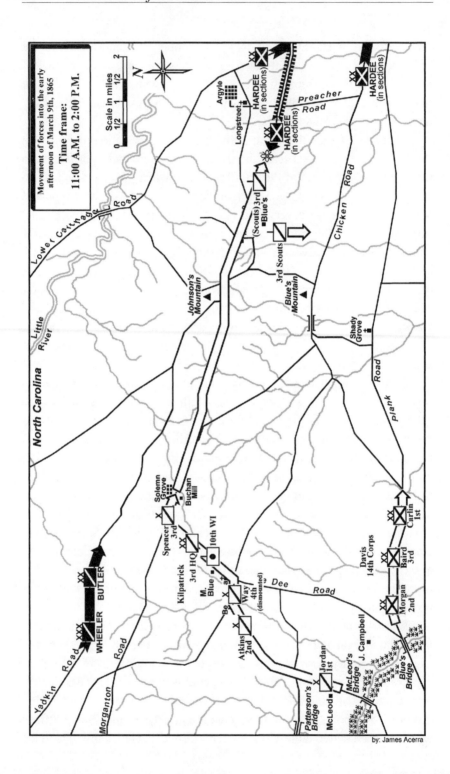

by: James Acerra

scouts," noted an historian of Shannon's command.[142] Reynolds was wearing a handsome pair of high-topped cavalry boots when he was captured, "the like of which it would not be easy to find in any shoe store in the Confederacy." One of his captors promptly relieved him of his prized boots, leaving the Scout to march along on foot behind Kilpatrick's carriage in an ill-fitting pair of brogans that blistered his soles and wore off the nails of his big toes. From his vantage point Reynolds could clearly see Kilpatrick lying with his head in Alice's lap and his feet hanging out the window of the carriage, oblivious to either his men's hardship or to the dangers presented by lurking Confederate cavalry. This sort of inattention was nothing new to Little Kil's command, and would permit a tired and footsore Reynolds to escape later that night, determined to avenge the loss of those prized boots.[143]

With Butler's Southern division of horsemen once again combined with Wheeler's corps, Hampton and Wheeler could begin searching for an opportunity to punish Kilpatrick. The Federal horsemen were far in advance of the rest of Sherman's army, alone and exposed, caught in the no-man's land between Hardee's 6,000 infantry at Fayetteville and Sherman's blueclad host. Kilpatrick's column was strung out across the countryside and, though doing what it could to protect its flanks, offered an inviting target. The fact that the Federals were in unfamiliar territory, contending with nearly impassable roads and terrible weather, only worsened their plight.

* * *

Monroe's Crossroads is on the Morganton Road about fourteen miles west of Fayetteville. In 1865 it was the site of Charles Monroe's 500-acre farmstead, one of the many modest farms in the Sandhills region of the Atlantic Coastal Plain. Poor farmers of Scottish descent made up the largest portion of the local population. The terrain features gently rolling hills consisting of sandy loam deposits that support little other than dense pine forests and wiry grasses. While none of the elevations in the area are dramatic (typical differences in elevation are less then 100 feet), the rolling hills are continuous and only from the crest of an especially high ridge can one see for any significant distance. Shallow but deeply entrenched creeks carve the countryside. Johnson's Mountain, which dominates the area, stands about six miles west of Longstreet Church on

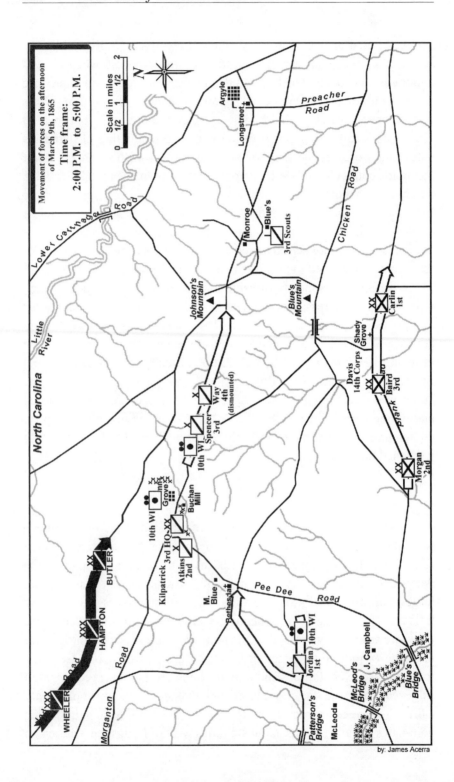

Movement of forces on the afternoon of March 9th, 1865

Time frame:

2:00 P.M. to 5:00 P.M.

by: James Acerra

the Morganton Road. Nicholson Creek runs north to south near the site of the two-story wood framed Monroe farm house and outbuildings.

The Monroe home (which no longer stands) was just south of the intersection of the Morganton and Blue's Rosin roads a few hundred yards west of the intersection of the Morganton and Yadkin roads.[144] Approximately one-half mile to the west of Monroe's Crossroads, the Yadkin Road splits off again, heading in a northwesterly direction. A single resident, Neill Monroe, occupied the main house. A resourceful old slave named Hannah lived in a log cabin behind the main house, which stood atop a low ridge; it was a wise place to build, for it was the driest ground in the area. An impenetrable swamp fed by Nicholson Creek was just a few hundred yards southwest of the Monroe home.[145]

Riding far in advance of the main body of Kilpatrick's division, Captain Northrop and his scouts arrived at Monroe's Crossroads about 11:00 on the morning of March 9. They remained there until dark, "hourly expecting the arrival of the command." Concerned about the overdue division, Northrop sent two of his men to seek out the column; he heard nothing further from them. Since they were nearly ten miles ahead of the main column, Northrop had his men dismount and rest themselves and their horses. Even though the Monroe house looked comfortable, Northrop disliked the position. "I considered it too much exposed, and crossed the swamp to a quiet place."[146] About half a mile away Northrop found a combination mill-dam and bridge. "I passed over this with the scouts and prisoners, of whom I had collected about thirty that day," he recalled. Northrop followed a plantation road to a small house, where he found accommodations for his little contingent.[147]

Because Colonel Jordan's First Brigade had been in the lead the day before, Spencer's Third Brigade took the lead on March 9. About 2:00 p.m. Spencer's column reached Solemn Grove, also known as Solomon's Grove, a hamlet consisting of a store, a post office, several homes, and a mill. Spencer's brigade was several hours in advance of the rest of the division. Lieutenant Colonel Way and his dismounted men brought up its rear and did not arrive at Solemn Grove until about five that afternoon. The heavy rains continued, making sure the roads remained a miserable quagmire. Spencer realized that it would take time for the rest of the division to catch up, so he sent out scouts and told his men to dismount and rest themselves and their horses. He established his headquarters on a hill south of the road, overlooking a stream that provided a good water source for his tired mounts.

Spencer's scouts caught up to Hardee's rear guard and, after a small skirmish, captured a few prisoners. The captives reported that most of Hardee's infantry had passed through the area the day before, making their way toward Fayetteville, and that Confederate cavalry was operating several miles from his left flank. According to the captives, the Southern horsemen were heading toward Fayetteville to link up with Hardee's foot soldiers. Alarmed at his isolation, Spencer began establishing a defensive position, deploying a section of guns on a nearby hill and orienting his regiments on the stream crossing to cover the eastern approaches.[148]

As he was finishing these dispositions Kilpatrick and his staff and escort rode up. Spencer quickly briefed the division commander, whose choices were at best unpleasant. He could press on and risk having his column cut to pieces by three divisions of aggressive Confederate cavalry operating in his rear, or he could stop and try to intercept the Southern horsemen.[149] Either choice meant a fight on uncertain terms. The road network complicated matters for Kilpatrick. Three major roads criss-crossed the area, which meant that he would have to cover each with one of his brigades, further scattering his force. The aggressive Kilpatrick decided an attempt to intercept the Confederate cavalry was worth the gamble. It was a risky proposition and violated one of the primary tenets of contemporary military thought. Since Napoleon's day, military colleges had taught their students not to divide their forces in the face of an enemy of equal or superior strength.[150] General Robert E. Lee had done so successfully on several occasions including Chancellorsville in May 1863, but Judson Kilpatrick was no General Lee.

If he were to have any hope of intercepting Hampton, Kilpatrick would have to block three separate routes: the Morganton Road, upon which Spencer had traveled that day; the Chicken Road, to the south; and the Yadkin Road, leading away to the north. Kilpatrick assigned Spencer to march along the Morganton Road beyond its intersection with the Yadkin Road and camp near the Charles Monroe Farm, blocking the Yadkin route. Atkins and the Second Brigade would follow, blocking the Morganton Road, and Jordan's First Brigade would divert to the Chicken Road which, although Kilpatrick did not know it, was the route most of Hardee's infantry was using. Each brigade would take a two-gun section of artillery to bolster its firepower. Lieutenant Colonel Way's dismounted brigade, which was escorting 150 Confederate prisoners, would join Spencer's horsemen on the Yadkin Road.[151]

By late afternoon on March 9 the Northern cavalry column had moved out, its elements heading for their assigned destinations.[152] Hampton's troopers dogged the Federals, moving on parallel roads and carefully watching their progress. "We could occasionally see their column in the distance," recalled a member of the 10th Ohio Cavalry. "It was simply a race between the two commands which should strike the old State road." Kilpatrick tore himself away from Alice and rode with Spencer's Third Brigade, which had the lead. Atkins's Second Brigade followed close behind. Jordan's First Brigade acted as the division's rear-guard. "Several times during the day our foragers ran against those of the enemy, and several prisoners were taken on both sides," remembered one Union horseman[153] Nervous about the prospect of another clash with his old adversary Hampton, Little Kil spent the afternoon dashing back and forth between his scattered brigades, checking on his dispositions and preparing to give battle if necessary. "The roads were in an almost impassable condition," recalled one of Atkins's men.[154] It rained hard that afternoon, adding to the misery of the Northern horse soldiers who managed only about ten miles through the thick muck.[155]

Wade Hampton was also worried. His scouts had determined that Kilpatrick had gotten between the Confederate cavalry and Hardee's infantry, leaving the rear of Hardee's column exposed and vulnerable. Furthermore, he had promised Johnston that he would engage and punish any isolated detachments of Sherman's army he encountered. In order to protect Hardee and fulfill his promise to Johnston, Hampton had to move quickly. As trooper Z. T. DeLoach of the 5th Georgia Cavalry put it, "Wade Hampton, the Senior Cavalry General, bunched up what cavalry he could and cut out to surprise the Yankees while they were in camp."[156] Hampton knew it would be difficult. March 1865 had thus far been an abnormally rainy month, and the elements made rapid movement all but impossible.[157] Still, Hampton made remarkably good time on that long and wet March day. "General Hampton rode ahead of the command all day by himself," recalled one of Butler's troopers, "and the men would look at each other and say: 'Look out, boys, old Wade is fixing a trap for them; we will be into it tonight,' while others would say: 'We will give it to them tomorrow.'"[158]

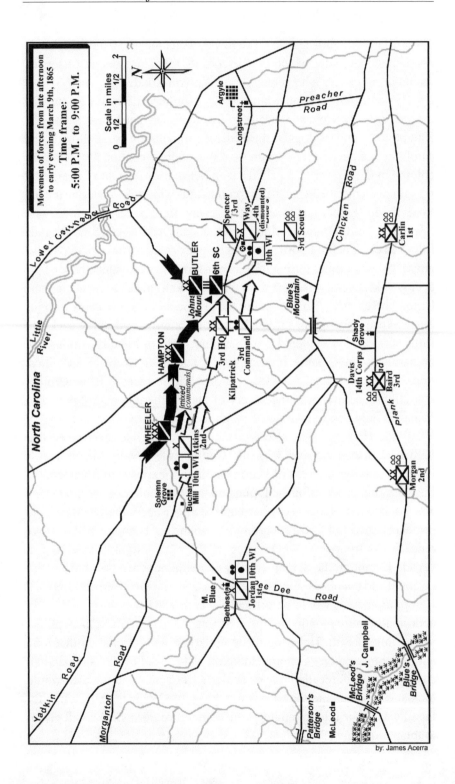

by: James Acerra

The big South Carolinian pressed his command toward Kilpatrick's division and Fayetteville. Butler's Division led the way, marching in column of fours.[159] Wheeler's Corps followed at a distance, marching slowly through the rain all day. It headed directly toward Fayetteville, "resting occasionally, as though there was no occasion to hurry."[160] The horsemen were passing through a very poor country where there was little hope of finding provisions for the men or fodder for the horses.[161]

The people of Fayetteville remained uncertain about their fate. Although the townspeople had been speculating for more than a week that Fayetteville was Sherman's destination, there was enough doubt to underscore that Sherman's deception had confused the public. On March 9, the editor of a Fayetteville newspaper, who was either fooled or simply deluding himself, wrote, "We do not think that Sherman will march on Fayetteville immediately, if at all. He will either form a junction with Schofield and march Northward by the coast route, or he will pause where he now is and recruit the failing strength of his army." The editor concluded, "As almost everyone is expressing an opinion as to the point where the next great battle will be fought, we state, as our opinion, that it will be at or near Fayetteville, or Goldsboro—more probably the latter."[162]

Meanwhile, Wade Hampton and Judson Kilpatrick reached for each other in the rain and gathering darkness.

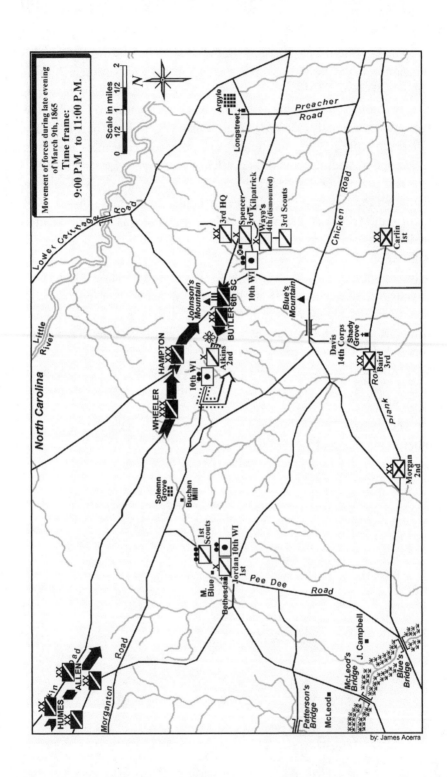

Movement of forces during late evening
of March 9th, 1865
Time frame:
9:00 P.M. to 11:00 P.M.

Scale in miles

North Carolina

Lower Cattawa *Road*

Little River

Johnson's Mountain

WHEELER

HAMPTON

10th WI

Atkins 2nd

BUTLER 6th SC

10th WI

3rd HQ

Spencer 3rd Kilpatrick

Waye's 14th (dismounted)

3rd Scouts

Argyle

Longstreet

Preacher Road

Blue's Mountain

Davis 14th Corps

Carlin 1st

Baird 3rd

Shady Grove

Chicken Road

Solemn Grove

Buchan Mill

1st Scouts

M. Blue

Jordan 10th WI 1st

Bethesda

Pee Dee Road

Morgan 2nd

plank

Patterson's Bridge

McLeod

McLeod's Bridge

J. Campbell

Blue's Bridge

Morganton Road

Morganton Road

Franklin

ALLEN

HUMES

by: James Acerra

Chapter 4

Groping in the Dark

A bout 5:00 p.m. on March 9, 1865, Lieutenant Colonel Way's dismounted troops, together with their bedraggled contingent of 150 prisoners of war, slogged through a cold driving rain into Solemn Grove. While the exhausted soldiers enjoyed a short but much-needed rest, Kilpatrick briefed Way on the state of affairs confronting the cavalry. Spencer's Third Brigade had been preparing to ride out of Solemn Grove, but now that Way had arrived it was determined that his dismounted troopers would lead the way; Spencer's men, with a section of horse artillery, would follow them. The dismounted men would not get much of a break from their labors.[1]

The Federals used Malcolm Blue's sturdy farm house at Solemn Grove as their headquarters. Belle Blue, age ten, watched the Federals fan out across the family farmstead like locusts. "The soldiers took charge of everything in sight," recalled Belle. "They allowed the family half of the house and took over the rest of the building. The Yankees began coming at about nine A.M. and kept arriving all day. All the food and provisions were taken over and the negroes were kept busy all day cooking for the army. The soldiers dug up lard and provisions that had been buried, then ransacked buildings, tore up Bibles and wreaked havoc just for devilment." Belle had an older brother in the Confederate service, and she was worried the Yankees horse soldiers would destroy the family farm if they found out.[2]

The Malcolm Blue house

As they had done all across the Carolinas, Kilpatrick's men foraged the nearby countryside, taking whatever they wanted. Although they spared most of the farm buildings, the Federals helped themselves to whatever items of personal property struck their fancy. They killed every hog, cow, and chicken in Malcolm Blue's pens. One of Blue's neighbors, John M. Ray, surrendered at gunpoint a handsome coat of otter fur to a Northern officer because it "pleased the eye" of the Northerner. Another neighbor, Archibald Buchan, was left destitute by the foragers. Once they left he was reduced to picking up kernels of corn scattered by the horses of Kilpatrick's command and grinding them to make a few handfuls of meal. Some area residents successfully hid their livestock and property in the woods with the help of loyal slaves.[3]

Kilpatrick instructed Colonel Spencer and his staff to bivouac at Green Springs, a popular camp site on the Morganton Road just south of Charles Monroe's house about twelve miles distant.[4] While Spencer's brigade moved out Kilpatrick lingered, waiting for Atkins's brigade to arrive. Soon afterward a group of scouts rode up and alerted Kilpatrick that Atkins was not far behind. Kilpatrick rode out to meet and instruct him to move out as soon as his regiments had closed up enough for effective communication. Atkins indicated that he understood his orders and about 7:00 p.m. set out to obey them, heading east on the Morganton

Road toward Monroe's Crossroads.[5] Kilpatrick wheeled his mount and spurred off toward the same crossroads accompanied by his headquarters escort, a company of the 5th Kentucky Cavalry.

Although he did not know it, Kilpatrick had the Confederate cavalry sandwiched between his First and Third Brigades on the one side, and the Second Brigade on the other. Had he known this, he might have exploited the situation. However, because he had failed to throw out a rear guard or take other steps to protect his rear, he did not realize the trap he had inadvertently set for the Southern horsemen. This lack of diligence would cost his command dearly.[6]

While Spencer and Atkins rode away from Solemn Grove, Colonel Jordan marched for the Chicken Road. Jordan's men faced a significant obstacle in the Devil's Gut, a steep-banked stream a few miles southwest of Solemn Grove. The First Brigade had to contend with its slippery banks and flooded water, and Jordan's men had a difficult time crossing. Jordan dismounted his troopers and had them cross on foot, the men pulling their wagons and a section of artillery across and up the slippery banks. It took them two hours to cross Devil's Gut. "We have crossed two of those sluggish streams with their swampy margins," noted a Hoosier in his diary. "We only marched about ten miles."[7] Once across they remounted and headed for Bethesda Church. After advancing two more miles Jordan and his exhausted command threw in the towel and set up a cold, miserable, and soggy bivouac at Rockfish Church.[8] "Rained all day and we are in a poor country without any feed for our horses tonight," complained Williamson Ward of the 8th Indiana Cavalry.[9]

By 9:00 p.m. that night Colonel Way and his dismounted men had reached Monroe's Crossroads. "The night was dark and the rain fell in torrents, making it impossible to form a correct idea of the country," he reported. Way's men were walking with difficulty through the inky darkness when they spotted shadowy figures in the distance. Unsure of whether they were friend or foe, Way warily awaited their approach. To his relief the small group of men proved to be a scouting party sent to lead the way to the intersection of Blue's Rosin Road and the Morganton Road. Way gratefully followed them to the Charles Monroe farm house. When he reached the place Way directed his men to the right of the road and ordered them to fall out. His command established its camp in line of battle parallel with the Morganton Road and in front of the Monroe

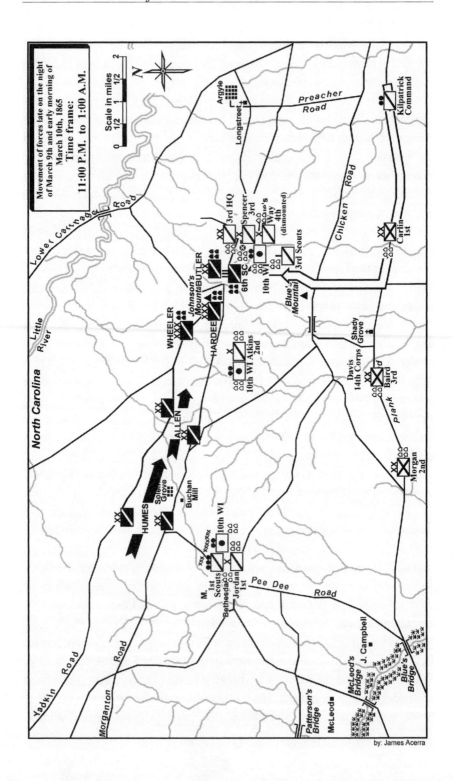

by: James Acerra

house. The wagons and 150 Confederate prisoners accompanying his column fell out around the house.[10]

Spencer's mounted horsemen followed, arriving a few minutes after the dismounted contingent. They marched past Way's camp and turned into a stand of open first-growth long needle pine trees just extensive enough to hold the three regiments of Spencer's brigade and their horses. They established their camp on a plateau south of the Monroe home, on ground that gently sloped to the west and toward an impenetrable swamp to the southwest. "No signs of the enemy were visible at the time we encamped," noted Maj. George H. Rader, commander of the 5th Ohio Cavalry.[11] The 1st Alabama (US) headed down the slope to the west before dismounting while the 5th Kentucky rode south and the 5th Ohio filled in behind the other two regiments. Lieutenant Ebenezer Stetson's two guns of the 10th Wisconsin Battery unlimbered in the road near the Monroe house, their tubes facing north. The horses were unhitched.[12] Colonels Spencer and Way and their staffs established their headquarters in the farm house. The soggy Yankee horse soldiers hunkered down to yet another cold miserable night. They pitched what tents they had and then did what they could to shelter themselves from the torrential rain, hanging their rubber ponchos on anything they could find.

And then Spencer made a critical error: he failed to post vedettes north of his camp. One of the oldest precepts of warfare is to be ready at all times. "It is but a doctrine of war not to assume the enemy will not come, but rather to rely on one's readiness to meet him," wrote Sun Tzu in 500 B. C., "not to presume that he will not attack, but rather to make oneself invincible."[13] Spencer may never have read Sun Tzu, but the governing army regulations specified that he should send out vedettes well to the front of his camp in order to detect the advance of the enemy, should they be operating in the area. "To keep an enemy in ignorance of the state of our forces and the character of our position is one of the most indispensable duties in war," wrote Dennis Hart Mahan, a professor of military tactics at West Point. "It is in this way that we oblige him to take every possible precaution in advancing; forcing him to feel his way, step by step, and to avoid risking his own safety in hazarding those bold and rapid movements which, when made against a feeble, or an unprepared enemy, lead to the most brilliant results."[14]

The doctrine of the day called for vedettes to be placed at those points where they could see the farthest ahead, taking care to maintain contact

Early moves of Wheeler's (CS) forces to scout Kilpatrick's (US) camp on the night and early morning of March 9th and 10th, 1865. Time frame: 10:00 P.M. to 12:00 A.M.

by: James Acerra

with the next vedette post in line. Their positions were such so that the men could spot the approach of the enemy without being seen themselves. "They are concealed from the enemy as much as possible by walls, or trees, or elevated ground," wrote Mahan. "It is generally even of more advantage, not to be seen than to see far. They should not be placed near cover, where the enemy may capture them."[15] Vedette posts usually consisted of two privates and a corporal or sergeant, with a grand guard just behind the lines that periodically relieved the vedettes at the front, and which also provided reinforcements for the vedette posts when needed. Typically, vedette posts were placed about thirty yards apart.

Vedettes had to be prepared to open fire at any moment and challenge anyone approaching their positions. At night, half the vedettes were on the vedette lines while the rest rested with their weapons within easy reach. Their mounts were kept bridled at all times, but could be turned out to eat. Those on the vedette line had to remain awake and vigilant. Some remained mounted all night. An hour before daylight, every vedette was to be mounted and prepared to face an enemy attack. If attacked, they usually were ordered to fall back fighting, thus buying time for the main body to receive the attack.[16]

Had Spencer made his dispositions according to the manual, he would have been prepared to meet any threat posed by the Confederates. For reasons that remain unclear, however, Spencer placed his pickets half a mile south, leaving the Morganton Road—the main artery—unguarded and open to the enemy.[17] Spencer's camp was ripe to be overrun, and was only partially protected by the dense swamp. Clearly the Federal horsemen had failed to learn a lesson from Wheeler's assault on their camps on March 4, when the brigades of Kilpatrick's division had been widely scattered and had not adequately prepared for an attack. It was a recipe for disaster—that is, if Wade Hampton could exploit the situation.

*   *   *

Captain Shannon and Hugh H. Scott led Hampton's headquarters' scouts in front of the advancing column of Southern cavalry. Butler's Division, with Law's Brigade in front, held the vanguard of the main Confederate column. Captain Moses B. Humphreys, who commanded the 6th South Carolina's Cadet Company from The Citadel, had the point company. Wheeler's Corps brought up the end of the column. Butler's

The Citadel

Captain Moses B. Humphreys

men heard occasional firing in their rear, but the column was too attenuated for them to know what was going on behind them. The Confederate horsemen marched in column of fours, meaning there was a substantial distance between the head of the column and the rear.

Between sunset and dark, Captain Humphreys halted at a road intersection and called for Butler to come up to see the glittering target that lay just ahead. When he reached the intersection Butler spotted signs that a large mounted force had recently passed through the area. In the distance the one-footed veteran general could see enemy camp fires flickering dimly in the cold rain.[18]

Most of Wheeler's cavalry was marching southeast along the Yadkin Road, paralleling Atkins's Union movements on the Morganton Road. In places the two roads were less than one mile apart. In the darkness and rain, however, neither Atkins's Yankees nor Wheeler's Rebels realized their adversaries were so close. They were so close that "during the march after nightfall, while riding leisurely along, I discovered a Yankee riding in our columns by my side, which I reported to our commander at the head of our column," wrote a shocked trooper of the 6th Georgia Cavalry of Anderson's Brigade. "A halt was made and a detail of picked men given me with orders to go back after our rear guard, which we supposed had a number of prisoners. On going back no guard was found, but in lieu of that a column of Yankees who had captured our guard and prisoners. Returning and reporting this, we were halted. The Yankees were marching on a parallel road and soon mixed up with us."[19]

At some point during the advance Lt. Henry C. Reynolds of Shannon's Scouts, who had escaped from Kilpatrick's camp the night before, found Wheeler's column. Reynolds reported directly to Wheeler, telling him of his adventures since his capture. Wheeler "was greatly amused at all Genl Kilpatrick had to say about him." Kilpatrick had said that he and Wheeler had been classmates at West Point, and had boasted "how many times he had beaten him &c. &c. I knew just the contrary, but couldn't say so just then," recounted Reynolds.[20] The amused Wheeler vowed to defeat his old friend in battle once more, as he had done on other battlefields in Georgia and South Carolina.

Wheeler still did not know what Hampton's plans were or where the South Carolinian wanted him to place his command. At 7:00 p.m. Wheeler scribbled a note to Maj. Henry B. McClellan, Hampton's adjutant. "General Dibrell has not yet arrived at this point," wrote Wheeler. "He has been delayed by some wagons of General Butler's command in his front. If possible will you please direct me where I can encamp my command? I will direct General Dibrell to stop at Blue's."[21]

Seeing the enemy campfires flickering in front of him, Butler ordered his men to halt, "word being sent down the line in whispers that no man was to talk or strike a match. Everything seemed still as a graveyard," recalled a trooper of the 6th South Carolina Cavalry.[22] While he conferred quietly with Humphreys at the intersection, Butler heard the unmistakable sound of cavalrymen approaching from his right. "As the horses' feet went slushing through the mire, the sound of other hoofs, muffled by mud, coming from the opposite direction was heard, and silently the command was halted by whispers passed back down the line," recalled a member of the 4th South Carolina Cavalry.[23] "It was too near dark to see more than a moving detachment of horsemen, and I inquired of Humphreys if he had anybody on that road," recalled Butler. Humphreys indicated that he did not. Butler rode out alone to the fork of the road toward the advancing Federal detachment. When the horse soldiers were within hailing distance, he called out, "Who goes there?"

When the approaching troopers responded, "Fifth Kentucky," Butler realized that they were Kilpatrick's horsemen. He directed the man at the head of the column to advance so he could speak with him. A lieutenant and his orderly rode up, right into the midst of Humphreys's waiting men, who quickly disarmed the unfortunate Federals and captured them. "I thereupon, in an undertone, directed Humphreys to send out, surround the squad of the 5th Kentucky, which proved to have twenty-eight men, and make them prisoners." As Butler recalled, "This he did without firing a shot, and they were brought in with their flag."[24] It was "the coolest thing I ever witnessed," recalled a South Carolina veteran.[25]

Although Butler had no way of knowing it, the squad of Kentucky horsemen was Kilpatrick's headquarters escort company, meaning that Butler had narrowly missed capturing the Federal cavalry chief himself.[26] Butler quickly rode off to find Hampton to report what had happened and to point out the opportunity for a surprise attack that had presented itself.

Once he heard Butler's report, Hampton decided to attack the unsuspecting Federal camp at daylight the next morning. The two South Carolinians were conferring when Wheeler and his chief scout, Captain Shannon, joined them. Wheeler had come to report his own contact with Kilpatrick's troopers riding on a parallel road. As the trio of generals discussed their options, some of Butler's scouts spurred up and breathlessly reported that they had followed the tracks of Kilpatrick's cavalry for several miles, and they led to a large camp south of the Morganton Road. The scouts also told the generals they had approached the camp without being seen or heard, and that some of their number had stayed behind to watch the Federals for signs of activity.

The news was almost too much to hope for: Kilpatrick's camp was virtually unguarded. Hampton, Wheeler, and Butler set about developing their dawn assault. "Speed is the essence of war," wrote Sun Tzu. "Take advantage of the enemy's unpreparedness; travel by unexpected routes and strike him where he has taken no precautions."[27] The Confederate plan followed these ancient tenets of war to the letter. The plan Hampton settled upon and executed "was a masterpiece," recalled the historian of the South Carolina cavalry brigade.[28]

The Confederates, explained Hampton, would deploy in an L-shaped position, a classic formation for launching an ambush. Butler would bivouac his men (without lighting fires) within striking distance of Kilpatrick's camp, north of the Morganton Road about a quarter-mile west of Monroe's Crossroads. Before daylight he would close up his division in column of regiments in the dense pine woods on the left side of a secondary road that ran parallel to the Morganton Road and north of a house there. His men formed the short shank of an inverted "L," with the short side on the north and the long side on the west. Meanwhile, Wheeler's men—the long shank of the upside down "L"— would move into position below the Morganton Road to attack Kilpatrick's camp from the west across the upper reaches of swampy Nicholson Creek. Butler's division was not advance until the head of Wheeler's column came up.[29] Hampton and Wheeler, along with Captain Shannon and Hugh H. Scott, reconnoitered Kilpatrick's camp by riding within sight of the enemy's camp fires. It was a daring plan, and one that promised success if executed promptly and with vigor.[30]

Butler's men eased forward about a quarter of a mile, with a line of dismounted skirmishers leading the way on both sides of the road. At their assigned destination the Confederate horsemen dismounted and made a soggy bivouac in the cold rain, trying to sleep as best they could without fires to warm them. About ten that night one of Kilpatrick's lieutenants stumbled into the advance guard of Confederate skirmishers and was captured. "He was brought to my Head Quarters where I had a pine root for a pillow on the road side," recalled Butler. The South Carolinian interrogated the prisoner and learned that he was Kilpatrick's acting quartermaster, who had been sent back to search for a broken-down wagon. The prisoner informed Butler that Kilpatrick had established his headquarters in the Monroe house, on the far side of the swamp.

With this important information in hand, Butler ordered a reconnaissance about midnight. Much to his pleasant surprise, the scouts determined that Kilpatrick had failed to picket his front. Butler sent a few dismounted men ahead to make certain any Federal trooper seeking to visit the pickets posted to the south was quickly snatched to prevent the alarm from being raised.[31] A plausible scheme was taking shape in Butler's mind. Without wasting time he next sent for Col. Gilbert J. Wright and directed him to send one of his most dependable squadron commanders to Butler for orders. Wright dispatched Capt. Samuel D. Bostick,commander of Company D, of Wright's own Cobb's Legion Cavalry. Butler informed Bostick of the Rebel plans and told him that at daylight he was to lead his squadron into Kilpatrick's camp, surround Kilpatrick's headquarters, and hold the position until the rest of the command came up. Butler envisioned nothing short of Kilpatrick's capture. Butler instructed Wright to follow closely behind Bostick and send one regiment at a time into the sleeping Union camp. Butler, meanwhile, would follow with Law's Brigade. His dispositions set, Butler returned to his tree root pillow.[32]

Butler's men moved into a position perpendicular to the swamp, where they spent an unpleasant night.[33] "In some woods on each side of the road the division bivouacked, horses remaining saddled, men awake to keep them quiet, or dozing, sitting on the ground with bridle-rein in hand, or under leg, ready to mount at a second's notice," recalled Edward L. Wells of the 4th South Carolina Cavalry. "No fire must be lit for warmth or cooking and no match struck for a pipe; so ran the orders, for this is to be a surprise-party pure and simple."[34]

Wells's men established a miserable bivouac at the intersection of the Rosin Road and the unnamed secondary road that ran parallel to the Morganton Road, a short distance north of the sleeping Federals. "We could see the enemy's camp fires, possibly a mile off," recalled Charles M. Calhoun of the 6th South Carolina Cavalry. "Feeling fatigued and sleepy, I sat on the ground, resting my head against my horse's front legs, sleeping soundly."[35]

Because of the atrocious road conditions and the darkness of the night, Wheeler's column was strung out across the countryside for miles. It would take hours for his rear elements to reach Monroe's Crossroads. "The fearfully bad roads and heavy rains . . . delayed us," recalled one of Wheeler's horse soldiers.[36] Wheeler sent a courier to Col. George W. McKenzie, commander of the 5th Tennessee Cavalry, with orders for the colonel to report to Wheeler's headquarters. McKenzie instructed his adjutant, W. G. Allen, to ride with him. The two officers rode to Wheeler's headquarters, where the general laid out Hampton's plan of

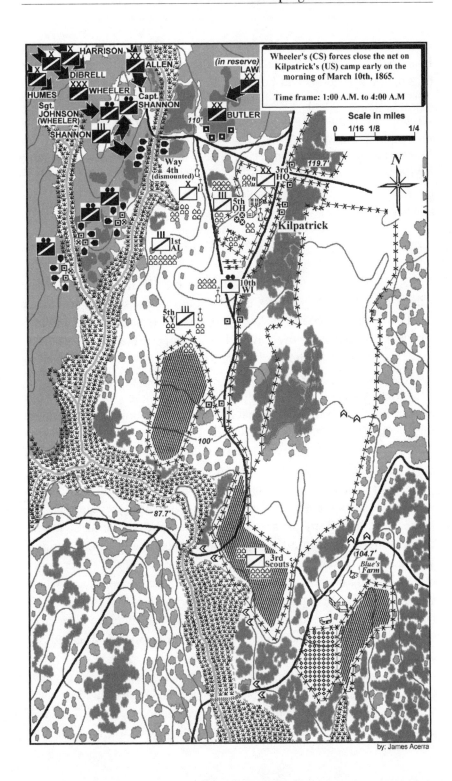

Wheeler's (CS) forces close the net on Kilpatrick's (US) camp early on the morning of March 10th, 1865.

Time frame: 1:00 A.M. to 4:00 A.M

by: James Acerra

attack. "Showing Colonel McKenzie as well as he could the location of Kilpatrick's camps," Allen recalled, "he gave him orders to go to the rear of Kilpatrick's camps and be in position by daylight." McKenzie told Allen to ride to each of his company commanders with orders to saddle up and fall in quietly and the regiment moved out as soon as it was mounted. A guide directed them toward the intersection of the Morganton and Rosin Roads. "When near the point we were to occupy, we bogged, so that but few of the men got through."[37] Because the dense swamp proved to be a formidable obstacle, the attack would have to be delayed.

*   *   *

The Confederate forces were moving quietly into position when Kilpatrick finally arrived at Charles Monroe's house after making a detour through the woods. He knew his headquarters escort was missing, which suggested an enemy force was operating in the area. Yet "[o]ur brave commander, 'Little Kil,' seemed to get an idea that there were no rebels around," recalled a member of the 1st Alabama Cavalry.[38] Kilpatrick went to see Spencer "and asked him some questions concerning the enemy, stating that he thought his camp too far from the First Brigade," wrote another trooper. "The Colonel assured him he would be able to cope with any force that could be brought upon him and [be] reinforced by the balance of the division."[39]

Kilpatrick accepted Spencer's assessment at face value and took no steps to tighten security for his camp or to make certain that the approaches had been properly and fully picketed. Perhaps it was overconfidence on Little Kil's part, or perhaps it was simply fatigue. Whatever the reason, he did not realize the implications of the presence of a large body of enemy troops. "By one of those circumstances which speak more for Kilpatrick's courage and energy than for his caution, he had pushed a brigade of his command across an ugly swamp to an intersecting cross-road, and a highly important position," observed one of Sherman's staff officers.[40]

Unaware of the danger that lay before him, the light-hearted division commander played a tune on the banisters of the house with his saber.[41] With that, he and Alice went to bed. They occupied the second story of the house while his chief of staff, Major Estes, took the first floor. The latter was joined by Colonels Spencer and Way, the division medical officer, Dr. Clinton Helm, and several members of Kilpatrick's staff. None of them had even an inkling that Hampton and his cavalry were but a short distance away plotting their destruction.

* * *

Wheeler, meanwhile, was briefing Captain Shannon on the plan for the dawn attack. He instructed his lead scout to conduct a thorough reconnaissance of the ground west of the swamp and learn as much about the Federal camp as he could. Like Butler, Wheeler wanted to capture Kilpatrick, so he told Shannon to try and bag the Federal pickets without firing a shot to increase to odds of locating Kilpatrick's quarters.[42]

Shannon gathered his Scouts and briefed them on their mission. Once filled in on the plan, Scouts R. A. Jarmon, Lou Compton, Emmitt Lynch, John Hagerty, Joe Rogers, and B. Peebles headed into the woods following a ridge running along the west side of the swamp. They rode the length of the enemy camp, guided by the dim flickering campfires of Kilpatrick's soldiers. Some even walked boldly into the camp as if they belonged there.[43] About 500 yards into their ride the Confederates spotted a group of men in the thick woods ahead. Shannon's troopers rushed forward and surrounded the group, quietly taking the Federals prisoner before they could send up the alarm. The quick action left the west side of Kilpatrick's camp completely exposed. More of Shannon's Scouts came up to join them and they continued to round up Federals. An officer of the 8th Confederate Cavalry estimated that Shannon's Scouts captured seventy-five pickets in their stealthy reconnaissance of the Federal vedette line.[44] The lack of pickets on the north front of the camp and the capture of the pickets on the west side meant that the Southern horsemen would be able to ride up to Kilpatrick's tents with nothing but the swamp to slow them down.[45]

On his ride back north Shannon stopped opposite the Monroe house. He peered into the darkness, hoping to see whether Kilpatrick or the Confederate prisoners of war were near the structure. Shannon asked for volunteers to approach from the swamp and, if possible, enter the camp. Several scouts volunteered for the mission. They dismounted, split into small groups, and plunged into the thick swamp. Shannon found some high ground and sat down to watch and wait.

Unable to curb his excitement in the rear, Wheeler rode up looking for his chief scout. "At this time, as on other occasions, General Wheeler was known by his scouts, at his request, as 'Sergeant Johnson,'" one of the Scouts recalled years later.[46] One of them, A. F. Hardie, sat on his horse about 100 yards from the sleeping Union camp intently watching for any movement. "We heard someone coming from the direction of our command on horseback," Hardie recalled. "We sat alert, with pistols cocked, waiting for him to ride up, as we were too close to the enemy to challenge him." The Scouts recognized Wheeler, who knew most of Shannon's men by name.

"This is Hardie, General."

"Where are the enemy?" inquired Wheeler.

Pointing to Kilpatrick's camp, Hardie replied, "There they are, General."

An incredulous Wheeler said, "What, that near and all asleep? Won't we have a picnic at daylight!"

"What brigade is in [our] front, General?" asked Hardie.

"The Alabama Brigade."

"I wish it were the Texas Brigade, because they are armed with six-shooters," Hardie replied.

"The Texas Brigade is just behind the Alabama and will charge on the right," responded Wheeler, who spurred off to find Shannon.[47]

When Wheeler approached, Shannon rose in his stirrups and quietly informed him that several men were approaching from the direction of the swamp. Two of the Scouts, Joe Rogers and B. Peebles, were on their way back from their excursion. Both men were leading several captured horses, which they proudly showed off to Wheeler. Stunned by the fact that the two Scouts could simply walk into the Federal camp and walk back out with a number of horses, Wheeler asked the two whether they knew the location of Kilpatrick's headquarters and the Confederate prisoners. To the general's delight, the pair reported that Kilpatrick occupied the house and the prisoners were just behind it. Wheeler complimented the men on their haul of horses and, in an inspired moment, instructed Shannon to "place his scouts in close as if they were pickets."[48]

With that, Wheeler turned and headed back up the Morganton Road to see how much of his division had come up. He knew that without any Union pickets to detect his movements on the west side of the swamp, he could begin moving his horse soldiers into position without being seen. Harrison's Texas Brigade led the way. Wheeler instructed Harrison to remain on the ridge opposite Kilpatrick's camp, which lay no more than 400 yards distant. "General Wheeler called for four men from my regiment to go on foot, as horseback was considered too risky, to spy out the situation of the enemy, telling the volunteers to meet at a designated place," recalled Natt Holman of the 8th Texas Cavalry. "The command was then ordered to close in quietly on Kilpatrick's camp and wait the return of the scouts that had been sent forward. After several hours, the men returned, riding bareback, and each led a horse that he confiscated for his trouble. The Terry Texas boys had much aversion to walking. They reported the condition to their commander as they viewed the darkness. Everything was put in order for the charge to be made at daylight."[49]

Wheeler intended to attack the camp with five separate columns. According to his plan, General Humes's Division would deploy his two brigades (Ashby and Harrison) on the extreme right of Wheeler's position, along the southern end of a north-south ridge facing east toward the swamp in their immediate front. They would have to cross the marshy terrain that fed Nicholson Creek in order to make the attack. Neither Wheeler nor Humes realized that the recent heavy rains had flooded the low ground, which on the night of March 9 was full of deep frigid water running with a strong southward-flowing current. Nor did they realize that the drop-off from the ridge to the swamp was abrupt and steep. Although everyone had been dealing with deep and very

Brig. Gen.
William Y. C. Humes

Confederate Military History

treacherous waters throughout the Carolinas Campaign, both Wheeler and Humes expected the swamp to pose only a minor impediment to their attack. Their incorrect assumption and failure to properly scout the ground represented a mistake almost as egregious as Kilpatrick's failure to adequately picket his front.

Humes's brigades silently filed toward their assigned jump-off positions along the ridge, the noise of squeaking leather and the snorts of the Southern horses drowned out by the incessant rain. Harrison's Texans led the way, with Ashby's Tennesseans bringing up the rear. Unfortunately for Humes, the regiment leading Harrison's column strayed into a second swampy area formed by a tributary feeding directly into Nicholson Creek. When the Confederate horsemen realized their mistake they guided their mounts back to solid ground. Moving farther south was simply not feasible. Terrain dictated the location of the right flank of Wheeler's offensive. In the darkness, however, no one realized an additional 200 yards of swamp separated them from Kilpatrick's sleeping camp. Ashby's Tennessee Brigade occupied the ground north of the Texans. Allen's Division of two brigades (Anderson and Hagen) rode through much of the night to arrive at its jump-off point. Before dawn the rain finally stopped and a dense fog settled over the swamp. Including both Butler and Wheeler, nearly 4,000 Confederates had converged around the bog.

Other than the fact that an unsuspecting Federal camp awaited them across the swamp, the men of Wheeler's command had no idea what lay in front of them. "Just as night approached, the column was halted, men ordered to dismount and remain in column, holding their horses," recalled one of Wheeler's staff officers. "When it was black night and there were no signs of moving, some of the troopers slipped from the road into the pine woods, found fragments of lightwood, brought them to the road and started fires." The idea spread quickly, and soon, little campfires started sparking. "Before the troopers had time to warm themselves, or dry their clothes, an order was passed from the rear of the column to 'put out the fires.' The flames were extinguished but the men, holding the reins of their horses, cowered over the smoking brands so long as any heat rose from them. Thus passed the cold, damp night."[50]

The usual rumors and speculation circulated among the rank and file. "At 3 A.M. March 10, we halted, [were] ordered to dismount, and [to] be as quiet as possible," recalled Pvt. Joseph A. Jones of Co. K, 51st

Alabama Partisan Rangers. "In this position we remained until the appearance of day, when we mounted and as quietly as possible we moved to the top of a hill in front of us. Upon reaching the top we beheld the sleeping camp of . . . Kilpatrick's Cavalry, all well armed and mounted. I saw but one Federal soldier stirring. It was a complete surprise."[51]

Brigadier General William W. Allen's Division deployed on the left of Humes's Division fronting the swamp. Arriving during the early morning hours, Allen could see the sleeping camp in front of him. Stunned by the absence of Federal pickets, Allen also began devising a plan to capture Kilpatrick. "Just before day we were halted, and in a few minutes we were moved out of the road into a thick, scrubby growth of timber with orders not to speak above a whisper," recalled Posey Hamilton of Hagan's Brigade. "In a few minutes we came into an open place where the small growth had been cut out, nothing left but large pine timber, where we halted for a short time, and a detail of twenty picked men reported to Lieutenant Tom Stewart." Hamilton and Ed Knight were the only members of their company sent to report to Stewart. "The objective was to ride up quietly to Kilpatrick's tent and capture the General and others with him," Hamilton recalled. "What we took for Kilpatrick's tent was on a round knob in the pine timber about three hundred yards from where we waited to make the advance guard."[52] Evidently no one had told them Kilpatrick was sleeping in the house.

Although dawn—and the time of attack—had almost arrived, some of Wheeler's command had not yet reached the vicinity of Monroe's Crossroads. With fifteen miles to cover through thick fog and inky darkness, it was impossible for Brigadier General George Dibrell's Division to arrive in time to join in the attack. "About 2 in the morning was aroused by report of enemy approaching and in a short time heard firing which forced us out," recorded a Georgia horse soldier in his diary.[53] Dibrell's inability to reach the field meant Wheeler would have to go into battle with only two of his three divisions and a deep swamp on his front. All the cavalry leader could hope for was that Dibrell's troopers would arrive in time to strengthen his intended sledgehammer blow at some point during the battle.

*   *   *

While Wheeler and Butler labored to get their men into position, the Union brigades of Atkins and Spencer were doing their best to shadow and interfere with General Hardee's column of march. The horsemen were heading northeast on two separate but parallel roads between one and two miles from the tramping enemy infantry.[54] "We could occasionally see their column in the distance," recalled a trooper of the 10th Ohio Cavalry. "It was simply a race between the two commands which should first strike the old State road . . . Several times during the day our foragers ran against those of the enemy, and several prisoners were taken on both sides." As darkness fell on March 9, Spencer's Federals established camp but Atkins and his brigade continued advancing slowly toward Monroe's Crossroads. The swampy ground and deeply cut creek bank delayed Atkins's progress and isolated him from Spencer's encamped brigade.[55]

A concerned Atkins sent his adjutant ahead to investigate a house along the route of march. The residents informed the adjutant that "a body of cavalry had passed a short time before, taking the left-hand road; that three miles out he would find a large plantation with an abundance of forage."[56] This was welcome news to Atkins's weary horsemen, who were eager to bed down for the night. However, "before the head of Atkins's brigade reached the designated camping ground, long lines of fires were observed in the woods."[57]

About 11:00 p.m., one of Atkins's scouts rode up with disturbing news: a large enemy camp lay just ahead. Atkins rode out with the scout to see for himself. The two soldiers trotted past the skirmish line and stopped at the bottom of the next ridge, slowly and quietly walking their horses to the top. Before them lay the rear of what was undoubtedly Hardee's Confederate camp. Astoundingly, the Southern officers had not taken any precautions to cover the rear of their encampment. The Rebels were exposed to attack had Atkins been inclined to launch one. He could see the grayclad soldiers trying to sleep and he saw others crossing the Morganton Road, which suggested there was another camp on the far side.

Atkins rode back to his brigade to report that a large enemy force blocked the road in front of them. He sent his transportation and ambulances to the rear and deployed the 10th Ohio Cavalry into a line of battle. He also sent a courier to warn Jordan of the danger in his front.[58]

Before too many minutes passed scattered picket fire rang out in the darkness. "For a full half hour both sides kept up a random fire, when we were ordered to withdraw to the crossroad," recalled a Buckeye.[59] The brigade would have to countermarch and try to find a way to outflank the enemy. Atkins had his brigade in motion quickly, riding down a poor and seldom-used trail heading into a dark and dense pine forest. "We countermarched back to the forks and attempted to move out on the right hand road, and actually did march several miles with the woods on our left full of Johnnies cooking their suppers and getting ready for bed," recalled another Ohioan. "Some were so close that we could distinguish their faces in the firelight and make out what they were saying." The blueclad troopers had to hold on to their accouterments to keep them from clanking.[60] "Passed close by four times our number of Johnnys under General Hardee," noted a member of the 10th Ohio Cavalry in his diary that night.[61]

The road ended a few hundred yards into the woods, forcing Atkins and his horsemen to ride cross-country through thick vegetation. His command quickly bogged down in swampy terrain, his wagons and artillery mired up to their axles in Carolina mud. "After marching about three miles we turned to our left, striking a swamp which, on account of the recent heavy rains we found almost impassable for a man on horseback," reported Col. William D. Hamilton, commander of the 9th Ohio Cavalry. "Our artillery stuck, the horses floundering in the mud and water until it was with great difficulty they could be saved from drowning."[62] Atkins had few viable options. He couldn't stop where he was and he couldn't go back, so he was compelled to march on with the hope of reaching solid ground. "The brigade came up and dismounted, supposing the Third Brigade was before us, and as it was past midnight, some of the rear regiments began to prepare for camp," recalled an Ohio trooper. "Atkins, not intending to be surprised the second time, had made careful observation, and while doing so had captured a courier with a message from Hampton to Hardee."[63]

Without realizing it, Atkins had caught up to the rear of Hampton's long cavalry column as it moved toward Monroe's Crossroads and had somehow gotten into the midst of the Confederates. "We had filled the gap in the Rebel column," recalled a member of the 92nd Illinois. One of Wheeler's staff officers mistook Atkins's brigade for Rebels. Hoping to hurry the Southern column along he moved in while cursing the laggard cavalry to pick up the pace. The aggravated Federals promptly captured him. Fearful that their cover had been blown, Atkins dismounted his men, deployed a section of artillery, and waited for an attack that never materialized. His deployment in the darkness prevented him from pushing on until morning.[64]

Jordan's brigade also had had a trying day. "Rained hard & had much trouble in crossing swamps," recounted Adjutant Chapin of the 8th Indiana Cavalry. Jordan had learned that a large force of the enemy was nearby. "Hardee is reported to be 15 miles from us on the left, marching on Fayetteville," noted Chapin in his diary.[65] Unable to make adequate progress, the Pennsylvanian established his camp near Bethesda Church, about five miles southwest of Solemn Grove and thirty-three miles from Fayetteville. All night long reports filtered in of enemy activity to the north, and the cautious Jordan ordered hasty breastworks built just in case the enemy decided to attack them. "About 1 A.M. I discovered that the enemy had passed on the Morganton road, about two miles and a half in my front, with infantry and cavalry, cutting off my communications with the Second and Third Brigades," Jordan later reported. It looked as though he was indeed about to face an enemy attack, and he prepared accordingly. His men spent a restless night behind logs, sticks, and banks of mud. Although no attack came, reports of a large enemy force in the vicinity froze Jordan's brigade in place and prevented it from joining Kilpatrick at Monroe's Crossroads.[66]

Atkins and Jordan tried to warn Kilpatrick of the danger he faced, but they failed. "General Atkins and Colonel Jordan discovered about 9 o'clock that while the enemy was amusing them in front he was passing with his main force on a road to his right," noted Kilpatrick in his after-action report. "These officers at once pulled out and made every effort to join me before daylight but failed to do so, owing to the bad roads and almost incessant skirmishing with the enemy, who was marching parallel to him, and at some points not a mile distant."[67]

With Atkins and Jordan stopped in the road, Hampton isolated Kilpatrick and his two small brigades. The pieces for a potential Federal disaster had fallen into place. While the unsuspecting Kilpatrick cavorted with Alice on the second floor of the farmhouse, the Confederates closed in on his camp, awaiting only the dawn.

Chapter 5

"We Fell upon the Camp
like a Small Avalanche"

The first traces of dawn colored the eastern sky at 5:20a.m. on Friday, March 10, 1865. Hampton and his Southern horse soldiers stood poised for the attack.[1] The rain had stopped, but the cold thick fog that concealed them from any stirring Federals also made things difficult for the Confederates.[2] "After some minutes a portion of the division which was to lead in the attack moved down the road on a slow walk in the direction of the Federal camp and halted just outside it," recalled Edward L. Wells, 4th South Carolina Cavalry, Law's Brigade. "Here a few words were addressed to the men by [Hampton] in his quiet, clear, incisive voice, he looking, every inch of him, the beau idea of cavalier."[3]

While Wheeler's men were forming for the assault the general dashed off to find Hampton. When he found the South Carolinian chatting with Butler along the Morganton Road, Wheeler reined in and saluted. "With your permission I will dismount my men, making the capture of the entire camp sure," Wheeler proclaimed.

Hampton responded quietly. "General Wheeler, as a cavalryman I prefer making this capture mounted."

The diminutive Georgian saluted again and replied, "General Hampton, all is ready for action; have your headquarters bugler blow the charge."[4] Wheeler wheeled his horse and dashed off to rejoin his command, which was anxiously awaiting his orders to attack.

Hampton decided to ride into the action at the head of Gib Wright's Brigade, while Law's South Carolina brigade remained north of the Morganton Road waiting to reinforce Wright's attack and provide a gathering place for any prisoners of war taken in the charge. Hampton's chief scout, Hugh H. Scott, joined Butler. "Scott, you have been trying for some time to get stripes on your collar," said the general. "Now if you will bring Kilpatrick out and deliver him to me, I will promote you on the battlefield." Fired by the promise of immediate promotion, Scott dashed to his position with Captain Bostick's squadron at the head of Wright's Brigade, where he focused his attention on the fog-shrouded Monroe house.[5] The Yankees in the house, reported a Confederate long after the war, "were buried in the profound slumber of supposed security."[6]

After leaving Hampton and Butler, Wheeler galloped back to his command waiting on the reverse side of the ridge along Nicholson Creek. Humes's Division was formed in line of battle on the far right, with Harrison's Texas Brigade in front holding the extreme right. Wheeler, along with his headquarters escort and Shannon's Scouts, would lead Allen's Division in the center. Dibrell's Division, which was just arriving on the field, would remain in reserve to reinforce the initial attacks if necessary. It had been an exceedingly long night, but everything was finally ready. Silence fell over the two contingents of Confederate horsemen as they anxiously awaited the order to charge.

Hampton fell in at the head of Butler's command. "Follow me, men," cried Hampton, his voice ringing out clearly for all to hear. "Charge!" Butler dashed to the head of his waiting horsemen. "Troops from Virginia! Follow me! Forward, march!" he cried, followed almost immediately by a single word: "Charge!"

"At daylight, we were ordered to mount and march," recalled a member of the Cobb Legion Cavalry of Wright's brigade. "We were marching by fours (the writer was in the first fours). We galloped by Kilpatrick's reserve pickets without the firing of a gun and charged right into their camps just as they were on the eve of rising."[7]

Butler's horsemen eagerly put spurs to their mounts and surged forward. "In a moment the cavalrymen were dashing with a magnificent Confederate yell through Kilpatrick's camp." Hampton was the first to enter Kilpatrick's camp, fighting "as though a private."[8] One of the legion's officers recalled that "we fell upon the camp like a small avalanche."[9] The surprise was overwhelmingly successful. "Our brigade

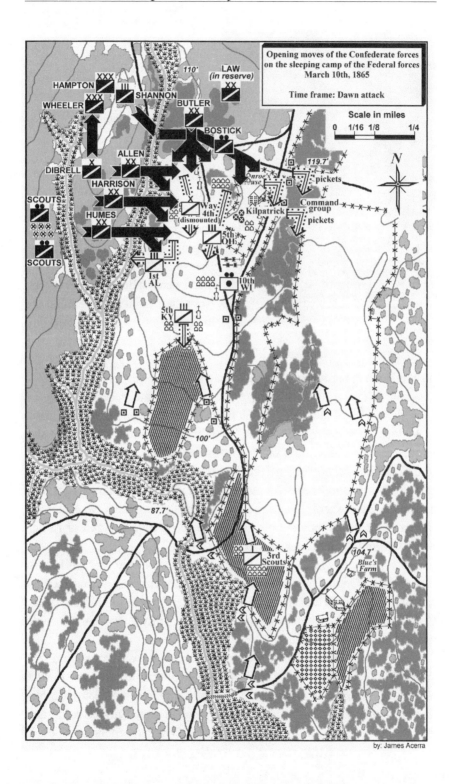

by: James Acerra

Colonel
J. Fred Waring,

Georgia Historical Society

swept out everything clean,"
recalled Col. J. Fred Waring, the
commander of the Jeff Davis
Legion Cavalry of Wright's
Brigade.[10] "Great numbers of the
men were sabered while rising
from their blankets," recalled the
historian of the 5th Ohio
Cavalry.[11]

Only a few guards and cooks
were milling about when the Confederates struck. Everyone else was still
sleeping or resting in their tents. "The troopers, thus rudely awakened,
rubbed their eyes and peered out from under the canvas flies in droll
bewilderment at the row,"[12] a member of the 4th South Carolina Cavalry
later wrote. "If all the foul fiends from the nether world had accompanied
[the Confederate horsemen] the Federals could not have been more
surprised or demoralized. The camp-guards, if there were any awake, had
no time to give warning, and the men under the tent-flies were literally
ridden over; or, as they sprang out half-asleep, were sabered or ridden
down before they knew what was doing."[13]

Unfortunately for the Confederates, Butler's charge rapidly lost
momentum. "On our right we failed to rout the enemy entirely on account
of a ravine where Wheeler's men were to enter," noted a Georgian of the
Cobb Legion. "Their horses would mire, hence only a few of them could
enter and they were killed."[14]

South and west of Butler's command along the eastern edge of the
swamp, Wheeler ordered his two divisions to attack simultaneously with
Hampton's assault. Starting at a walk, then increasing to a trot, and
finally breaking into a gallop, the gray cavalry crested the ridge and
descended upon the sleeping Yankee camp. "We had orders not to enter

the camp until ordered to do so," recalled Sgt. Nathaniel A. Hood of the 51st Alabama. "We passed along the edge of the camp for some two hundred yards, coming to a road leading up to the cabin, some two hundred yards to the right."[15] Colonel James Hagan's Alabamans led the way. "All was still," recalled a Georgian of Anderson's Brigade. "Our advance guard is in their camp, yet no one stirs!"[16] "When we charged in among them, we concluded that we had the entire thing in our hands," wrote George Guild, one of Wheeler's Tennesseans.[17] "No stir at least was made until after we delivered our first volley," recalled W. H. Davis, another Tennessean, "when their Spencer carbines commenced a lively rattle."[18]

Although the totality of the surprise stunned even the Confederates, not every Southerner had an easy time of it. Wheeler's horse was the first to hit the bog, but the little cavalryman put spurs to the animal and surged forward through the thick muck.[19] "Arriving at the marsh only a few of us could founder through," recalled Capt. Wilbur F. Mims of Company H, 3rd Alabama Cavalry. "Vainly did our gallant colonel call for his men to charge. There was not more than half a dozen, the others were in the marsh." Hagan and Maj. John D. Farish, commander of the 3rd Alabama, were soon wounded in the fitful chaos brought about by the marshy terrain. "The hindrance to a successful charge caused great confusion," observed Mims.[20]

Trooper Posey Hamilton of Hagan's Alabama Brigade thought he knew which tent Kilpatrick was in, so and he and his friends determined to nab the unsuspecting Federal commander in his bed. Like so many Confederates that morning, Hamilton and his companions had not been told Kilpatrick was inside the Monroe House. "Our advance was following Lieutenant Stewart in silence and going directly toward General Kilpatrick's headquarters, using a dim road or path," recalled Hamilton. "We soon came up to where the Yankees were lying under good blankets fast asleep, and while we were passing by we said nothing and did not intend to molest them. Our objective point was the big tent, and thus far we were moving in fine order and thinking we were going to make a good haul. We knew we were being led by a cool, brave officer, and that we could depend upon him. Lieutenant Stewart knew that he had twenty men following him that he could depend upon to stand by him in a desperate undertaking."[21]

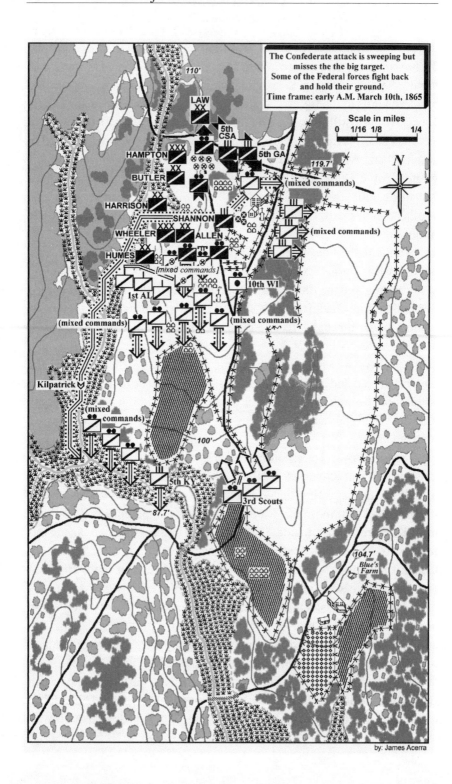

by: James Acerra

When Wheeler's bugler, a man named Pelote, sounded the charge above a chorus of Rebel yells, Allen's Division surged forward out of the fog. "Today I feel the blood tingle in my finger tips as that bugle call returns to me," recalled Edward Kennedy of Shannon's Scouts.[22] Allen's men also bogged down in the swamp west of the Federal camp. "The marsh was very difficult to cross," recalled an Alabama Confederate. "A large part of Allen's Division succeeded in crossing, but many of the poorer or weaker horses failed to cross, because of the condition of the ground."[23]

General Anderson's troopers managed to find a narrow trail through the swamp, but they had to squeeze together to make it across.[24] The horsemen from his 5th Georgia Cavalry approached so stealthily that none of the sleeping Federals stirred until "one of our couriers (following the General) put the point of his saber through the blanket of one of the sleeping guards, who started up, and, by his outcry, woke the sleepers." Anderson headed toward the Monroe house, where a determined little band of Yankees opened fire on him. His response was to order the Georgians to charge. "The regiment came up in column of fours at a gallop," recalled one of Anderson's staff officers. "As they approached us another party of Federals from another hill to our right began a brisk fire from their repeating carbines, and, in spite of all that I could say to the Captain of the leading troop of the Regiment as I rode beside him, he made his troop deflect from the house and turn towards the fire coming from the second hill." With the staff officer's curses echoing in their ears, the entire 5th Georgia followed, plunging into swampy ground, "which checked their charge, threw them into confusion and they were repulsed."

As the Georgians fell back Anderson ordered another of his regiments, the 5th Confederate Cavalry, to assault the enemy in their front. Accompanied by General Allen, Lt. Col. John S. Prather and the 5th Confederate troopers clattered up in column of fours, deployed into line, drew sabers, and surged forward. "As they charged I saw a large man, bareheaded and without a coat, on a large dapple gray horse, without a saddle or bridle, urging the Federals to stand firm. In spite of the Federals fighting on foot with repeating carbines, the 5th Confederate, mounted and using pistols only, broke them and after a brief scrimmage they fled." With the way now clear, Allen headed for the Monroe house. As he approached the structure, his horse was shot from under him. Allen survived the fall unscathed and had his orderly remove the saddle and bridle and put it on a horse taken from Kilpatrick's headquarters.[25] Amazingly, few Federals were yet aware they were under attack—despite several minutes of firing. Perhaps the hills, mist, and wet terrain absorbed the discharges of pistol and carbine and thus deadened their blasts. Kilpatrick's bugler was seized just as he was bringing his horn to his lips. He never got the chance to warn the rest of the camp.[26]

One Yankee drew a bead on an officer of the 6th South Carolina Cavalry sitting his horse, watching his men dash through the Federal camp. Glenn E. Davis, a private of Humphrey's Cadet Company, sprang from his horse onto "the Yankee's head, both coming to the ground and the rifle exploding in the air," remembered one witness. "On the ground they had a regular old time muster-ground fight, the determined Confederate had one of his fingers bitten off by the Yankee," before young Joel T. Salley ran up and dispatched the Northerner.[27]

Private Isaac H. Moses, also of the Cadet Company, was known as "Lord Shaftsbury" because of his scholarly writing style. During the struggle for possession of Kilpatrick's camp Moses had his horse shot from under him. As he pulled himself out from under the poor screaming beast, a large Yankee armed with a saber confronted him. Moses lowered his head and threw himself at the Northerner, grabbing him around the waist and knocking him to the ground. The more powerful Yankee soon pinned Moses to the ground, but Cpl. Bill Martin, another Cadet Ranger, saw Moses's predicament and "lifted the Yank off 'Shaftsbury' with his revolver."[28]

Sergeant Gabriel M. Hodges of the Cadet Company lost his horse in the fighting for Kilpatrick's camp and was shot in the side. The wounded sergeant kept his feet and his wits and captured another horse. Mounted a second time, he continued fighting until a bullet smashed into his shoulder, disabling him. Remarkably, the second bullet entered his uniform coat through a hole cut by a bullet that had hit him at Trevilian Station the previous June.[29]

Still convinced the large tent on the high ground was Kilpatrick's headquarters, Lieutenant Stewart and his Alabamans headed straight for it. By this time every Federal in the area knew they were under attack. "The Yankee camp looked like a cyclone had struck it all at once," recalled trooper Posey Hamilton. "Their blankets were flying in the air, and the men were running about in every direction . . . while the men from the big tent were legging and heeling it down the hill to beat the band. If this was not a stampede on foot, then I never saw one. Our advance guard had to get out of the way of bullets fired by our own men, as we were directly between them and the big tent. Right here the duty of our guard ended. We could do no more, and we had to look out for ourselves."[30]

Humes's surprise attack slammed into the 1st Alabama (U. S.) Cavalry's camp. Captain John Latta, commander of Company C, 1st Alabama, heard the first shots ring out and jumped out of his tent crying, "Fall in! Fall in!" Latta's company was joined by Companies D and I, which joined them on the firing line. Latta marched his little force a short distance to the right, looked back, and spotted Wade Hampton's headquarters flag riding into his rear and a horde of grayclad troopers following close behind. With enemy approaching on at least two fronts, Latta decided Hampton posed the most serious threat and ordered his people to face about and commence firing. The Rebels "killed five men on the ground where my company had slept. This was the first shot they had received, and they got it while calling on us to surrender; but we hadn't any notion of complying," recalled Latta, who mounted his horse in the thick of the fighting before taking a shot in the arm. Latta's orderly was killed at his side. Though the small Alabama force had blunted part of the Southern charge, plenty of hard work remained, for most of Spencer's brigade was still fleeing in the face of Hampton's seemingly irresistible charge. "My opinion is that the whole brigade would have been captured if I had not been so prompt in getting those three companies into shape," Latta later boasted. "There were not enough unwounded commissioned officers left to command the companies after the battle."[31]

Old Hannah, Charles Monroe's aged black cook, was outfitted in a white turban and apron making bread and brewing coffee in the yard outside the house when the bulk of the Confederate tidal wave swept through Kilpatrick's camp. The sight of the onrushing horsemen was like a shot of adrenalin through the old woman's frame. Forgetting her advanced age, Hannah lifted her skirt and ran for the field behind the backyard fence. The lady of the house, Neill Monroe, also beat a hasty retreat, choosing the safety of a neighbor's home rather than an open-air sanctuary.[32]

Spencer's brigade indeed had a hard time that morning. Major George H. Rader, the commander of the 5th Ohio Cavalry, remembered the sudden Confederate onslaught that crashed into his camp before the sun was even peeking over the trees. "My command was taken completely by surprise," he admitted, "the enemy being in force in every part of my camp. The officers and men were completely bewildered for a short time."[33] Another major, Christopher Cheek of the 5th Kentucky, also of Spencer's command, sounded a similar note. "At early dawn, on the morning of the 10th instant, we were awakened from our slumbers by the deadly missiles and fiendish shouts of the rebel cavalry charging into our camp in three different places, rear and both flanks." Cheek recalled that many of his men scattered "almost in a state of nudity, not having had time to dress themselves before the rebels were upon them."[34] One of Cheek's men described the determined Southern charge as "perfectly irresistible."[35] And for a short time that was exactly what it was. Colonel Spencer's camp was chaos as the Confederates dashed through, shooting and sabering right and left. "In the cavalry camp the firing became very severe, and for a time the enemy gained and held nearly two-thirds of their camp," reported Spencer.[36]

The Southern onslaught was so sudden that many Yankees were shot or sabered where they slept, and so never had a chance to escape. Others, "being surprised, hustled out from under their little tents, some with pants on, others with only their night clothing, carrying their guns, and ran across the ridge," recalled E. W. Watkins of the 6th Georgia Cavalry. "No firing was done as we went in on them. They ran out, leaving all horses and equipage."[37]

One drowsy fellow blinked the sleep from his eyes as he struggled to understand what had disturbed his slumber. The Federal mistook Butler's charging troopers for the Sheridan's cavalry, which he and his comrades expected would soon reinforce them from the Army of the Potomac. "Hello, boys, you've come, have you?" he inquired. When he realized they were not Sheridan's men but the enemy, he yelled, "I'll be damned! They are Johnnie Rebs!" A moment later he was a prisoner of war.[38]

The driver of one of Kilpatrick's headquarters wagons was sleeping soundly under the white canvas top, snugly curled up in a pile of soft straw. "He must have been very much fatigued, from doing nothing, or perhaps had taken an overheavy nightcap to guard against the dampness," recalled a smug South Carolinian. "At length, becoming aroused by all the din around him, he pushed aside the curtains and looked sleepily out, blear eyed and frowsy from his morning nap, at a loss to make out the meaning of such a hurly burly, and with no idea of hurting any one." Unfortunately, the attacking Rebels did not realize that this poor teamster had innocent intentions. "One of our men happened to be riding by so near that the fellow almost touched him with his sleepy head as he popped it out between the curtains, and, startled by it into instinctive self defense, promptly put an end to him, so that the poor wretch never really got really well awake at all." With tongue planted firmly in cheek, the South Carolinian concluded, "It was much to be regretted, but the moral is, it is a bad thing to sleep too late in the mornings."[39]

Kilpatrick's headquarters guard, O. P. Ball and Lafayette Caldwell, Company M, 9th Pennsylvania Cavalry, had just been relieved from guard duty when Hampton's cavalry rode into the Federal camp. The Pennsylvanians walked to where they had left their saddles, put their arms down, and set out in search of breakfast. When they spotted approaching men clad in blue overcoats, they mistook them for Northrop's returning scouts and paid them no attention "until they came right up, and pointing revolvers in their faces demanded their surrender," explained George Ward Nichols, one of Sherman's staff officers. "There was no firing up to that time. It was not clear daylight." The two men had no choice but to surrender and were marched off as prisoners of war before they could call out the alarm.[40]

Hearing unusual noises and the pounding of hooves in his camp, Judson Kilpatrick left Alice and the warmth of his bed to find out what was going on. Barefooted and clad only in his nightshirt, Kilpatrick made his way downstairs and stepped outside on the Monroe's front porch. What he saw stunned him: enemy cavalry was mingled with his troopers, swords slashing and pistols drawn. "Here is four years' hard fighting for a major general's commission gone up with an infernal surprise," was the first thought that went through Little Kil's mind as he watched helplessly from the porch.[41] The next day, while writing his report of the battle, Kilpatrick had a rare moment of candor. "Just before daylight the enemy charged my position with three divisions of cavalry, Humes's, Allen's, and Butler's," he wrote. "Hampton led the center division (Butler's) and in less than a minute had driven back my people, and taken possession of my headquarters, captured the artillery, and the whole command was flying before the most formidable cavalry charge I ever have witnessed."[42]

As Kilpatrick stood and gaped at the swirling combat, Captain Bostick and his squad of Georgians dashed up. "Where is General Kilpatrick?" inquired the captain.

Thinking quickly, Kilpatrick responded, "There he goes on that black horse," pointing to a man riding off toward the swamp. Bostick wheeled and dashed off in pursuit, leaving the Federal commander behind. Abandoning Alice to her fate, Little Kil jumped astride the nearest horse and dashed off toward the safety of the swamp, still clad in only his nightshirt. "Kilpatrick himself barely escaped capture," noted one of his men. "Though minus coat and hat—he had not yet completed his toilet—he took leg bail, and made a bee line for the timber, through which his troops were scattered."[43] A Confederate spotted the fleeing officer and chased after him, firing his revolver and crying, "Go it, Yank; you do run like hell!"[44] "Thus by a ruse," recalled Matthew C. Butler, "[Kilpatrick] saved his bacon."[45]

Kilpatrick may have "saved his bacon," but his escape was anything but easy or guaranteed. His horse quickly bogged down in the thick mud, sinking to its knees. Fearing capture, the general leaped from the animal's back and skedaddled deeper into the swamp on foot, with the curses of the Southerners echoing behind him.[46] "On foot I succeeded in gaining the cavalry camp a few hundred yards in the rear," recounted Kilpatrick, "and found the men fighting with the rebels for their camp and animals and we were finally forced back some 500 yards farther to a swamp impassable to friend or foe."[47] Kilpatrick collected himself and began rallying his troops for a counterattack.

Edward L. Wells of the 4th South Carolina Cavalry had also witnessed Kilpatrick's dash for safety. As Wells later wrote, he watched "a sorry looking figure in his shirt and drawers" run from the front porch of the house and, springing astride a horse, "tarried not on the order of his going" as he sped for safety through the fog and gun smoke. "No one stopped him, thinking it not worth while in presence of such abundance of better seeming game," recalled Wells. "Only one man recognized in the humble runaway the quondam bumptious Major General and future politician, and he gave chase. His pistol being empty he meant to ride him down, and would have done so, but unhappily his horse fell on the wet, slippery ground, and he had the mortification of seeing General Kilpatrick disappear."[48]

Kilpatrick had fled the scene with only the shirt on his back. All his horses and personal effects fell into the hands of the swarming Confederates who quickly claimed them as prizes. "The General left his sword, uniform, boots, also a woman, presumably his wife," recalled one of Wheeler's horsemen.[49] Private W. S. Redderick, Company D, 5th Tennessee Cavalry, was one of the first Southerners to reach the Monroe house. Two 51st Alabama Cavalry troopers, Lt. S. D. Bethune and Sgt. Nathaniel A. Hood, were also quick to dash up to Kilpatrick's headquarters and there discovered Little Kil's saddle, holsters, and pistols lying on the ground. Hood cut the holsters from the saddle and placed them on his own. "I wish to say that I am sure that I was among the first 'Rebs' to reach Kilpatrick's headquarters," Hood proudly claimed in an article published many years after the war.[50] The general's saber ended up in the hands of a South Carolina infantry captain who kept it until 1911.[51]

Someone cut loose Little Kil's prized horses and the frightened animals ran free. Sim Lambrecht, Company D, 3rd Alabama Cavalry, captured the general's handsome bay stallion, while Aleck McArthur of the same company caught Kilpatrick's beloved Arabian stallion "Spot," one of Little Kil's most prized possessions.[52]

W. G. Caruthers, Company D, 2nd Georgia Cavalry, was riding with Wheeler and Maj. Gen. William W. Allen when the first shots sounded that morning. Caruthers recalled that Allen crossed the swamp south of the Morganton Road with Hagan's Alabama Brigade, which held the left flank of Wheeler's line, riding close behind him. As they passed the Monroe house Allen announced to anyone close enough to hear him that his horse had been shot. What he apparently did not explain was that he had also taken a ball in the hand. Seeking another mount for the general, Caruthers saw Kilpatrick's large black horse tied close to the house. Caruthers was making for the handsome stallion when he spotted a Confederate trooper leading the animal away. When Caruthers told the man that Allen had lost his horse and needed another mount, the trooper reluctantly gave up his prize. The horseless general removed the bridle from his disabled mount while Caruthers unbuckled the saddle. Together, they placed the accouterments on the black horse. "I assisted Gen. Allen to mount," recalled Caruthers, "as he had been badly shot in the hand. I then mounted my own horse, and seeing another gray horse standing near with saddle and halter on, took charge of him and directly turned him over to one of our boys whose horse had been killed, with the request that if we got out safely he [would] let me have the horse."[53]

The Monroe house and its surrounding grounds acted a like a magnet for Southern horsemen. One of Hampton's staff officers joined the dash for the structure. "Though bullets were flying thick and fast all around us, I noticed a bullet headed negro cooking breakfast and rode up to the fire to see if I could transfer anything to my haversack for my breakfast later, and I was astounded by the absolute indifference of the cook to the danger around him, when he easily could have found safety behind the brick chimney of the house a few feet away." The officer continued, explaining that "he went on cooking just as quietly and coolly as if not under fire." The staff officer grabbed some food before wheeling his mount to look for more opportunities to plunder.[54]

The ecstatic Confederate prisoners who had recently fallen into Union hands realized that their day of liberation had arrived. "As soon as our men who were prisoners heard the shots they told the guards: 'That is Wheeler charging; you had better save yourselves,'" recalled one of Shannon's Scouts. "The guard dashed away and the prisoners began to help themselves to arms, horses, and whatever they wanted."[55]

The former prisoners were in sorry shape. Most were barefooted and bareheaded, hungry, and their clothing was in tatters.[56] Cheering, the freed prisoners ran toward their liberators. The escapees included Flynn Davis, a brother of Col. Zimmerman Davis, the commander of the 5th South Carolina Cavalry, and two brothers, Frank and Reuben Niernsee.[57] The Wadesboro man who had shot Lieutenant Griffin was also among those freed; the Confederate had fulfilled the promise they had made to his wife.[58] In the dim early morning light, however, the Southern horsemen did not realize that the men bearing down on them were friends. The prisoners bolted at the first sound of the Rebel yell. "This somewhat disconcerted some of our men at first," remembered on Southerner.[59]

The prisoners, "frantic with joy, rushed forth to meet their deliverers," recalled a South Carolinian. "One poor fellow, the foremost of them all, ragged, half starved, and lately wretched but now nearly crazed with delight, attempted to embrace a horse's neck, but mistaken in the obscurity for an assailant, met his death at the rider's hand. Perceiving too late his error, the slayer sprang to the ground and bent remorsefully over the corpse, only to recognize in the ghastly features of the dead a near neighbor and lifelong friend."[60]

The Confederate regiments bringing up the rear of the attack thought the freed Southern prisoners were comrades falling back after a repulse. "I had not advanced far into the camp when I was astonished to meet a hundred and thirty or forty Confederates rushing wildly toward us," recalled Butler. "At first I thought [Col. Gib] Wright had been repulsed, but it turned out they were prisoners whom Kilpatrick had taken, and whom Wright's vigorous and unexpected onslaught had released from their guards, and they were making good their escape." Butler ordered these men to the rear and continued on, determined to capture the Federal artillery. He halted Law's Brigade at the entrance to the camp to round up the freed prisoners and herd the Federals swept up in the overwhelming Southern charge.[61] By so doing, however, Butler kept about one-half of his troopers out of the fight, which quickly sapped the strength of his surprise attack.

One former prisoner named Flynn Davis was famished. Other than an occasional nibble at an ear of corn snatched along the road, he had not eaten anything in three days. "The first thing he did when the fighting commenced in the camp was to seize a camp kettle that some of the Yankees had on a fire, and sitting on the ground with the kettle was eating its contents ravenously when a bullet went through it," recalled Davis's friend Ulysses R. Brooks. A moment later General Butler rode upon the scene. When he spotted Davis he asked, "Well, Davis, what are you doing?"

"I am getting a little bit, General," replied Davis, "the first in three days; will be with the boys in a minute."

Butler chuckled and rode off. True to his word, Davis put down the kettle a few moments later, found a carbine and a horse, and went off to exact revenge on the Federals for the ill treatment he had endured as a prisoner. He asked one of the recently freed prisoners if he had seen an especially cruel Federal guard, and the man pointed out the Northerner's location behind a nearby tree. To his disappointment, Davis discovered that the man was already dead. "The released prisoners paid him special attention as soon as the Rebel yell of Butler's men was heard in the camp," Davis recalled.[62]

The scene in Kilpatrick's camp was extreme confusion and tactical anarchy. "The rush of columns to the breach, officers cheering the men on; pauses, breaks, wild and angry threats, upbraiding calls, fresh rush on rush, now here, now there; fierce shouts above, below, behind; shrieks of agony, choked groans and gasps of dying men and horses hurled down with rattling missiles of death," recalled Ulysses R. Brooks of the 5th South Carolina Cavalry.[63]

The terrain played a major role in how the action unfolded. Between Charles Monroe's house and the Union artillery atop the knoll a few hundred feet to the south was a deep ravine running westward toward the swamp. The natural slope of the ravine funneled Butler's southbound troopers into Wheeler's eastbound attackers as they emerged from the swamp. The mingling of the two Confederate forces threw the horsemen into a state of mass confusion. The Southern command and control, already weakened by the swampy terrain and limited visibility, broke down completely.

By this time most of the Union horsemen had scattered and fled for the safety of the swamp, with screaming Southerners hot in pursuit. Those that stood their ground engaged the mounted Confederates as best they could. Impromptu duels and hand-to-hand combat raged about the Union camp. An unarmed General Butler watched as a mounted Federal charged toward him. An unknown Confederate advanced to meet the attacker and Butler said to himself, "They are about matched; I will see it out without interfering."

The two men rode within ten feet of each other, pistols drawn. The blueclad soldier fired first, followed instantly by a shot from the Southerner. "The Federal fired a second time and the Confederate fired almost simultaneously," Butler recalled, "and, I discovered, hit his antagonist, but the Federal managed to fire a third shot and with the report of the Confederate's third fire the Federal tumbled from his horse, mortally wounded. I dismissed the matter from my mind, and was surprised afterward to learn the Confederate was my brother, Capt. James Butler. It was the gamest fight I ever saw, and there I was, a silent spectator, without suspecting that my own brother was one of the parties to a duel a l'outrance."[64]

General Butler's aide-de-camp was his youngest brother, Capt. Nat Butler. Handsome, gallant, fair-haired, and blue-eyed, the staffer was but 19 years old in March 1865. Nat began serving as his aide once Butler returned to the army after recuperating from his crippling foot wound suffered at Brandy Station.[65] When Nat returned after carrying a message for the general, he held up his right arm and announced, "I am wounded." The amount of blood seeping down his brother's coat sleeve indicated the injury was a serious one.

"Why have you not gone to the rear for treatment?" asked the general.

Nat replied, "I cannot go to the rear without your permission."

Butler immediately ordered the youth to the rear beyond range of the enemy's rifles to seek out medical assistance. Fifteen days later Nat's arm was amputated. The effects of the wound and subsequent amputation lingered with Nat the rest of his days.[66]

One South Carolina horseman watched General Butler with admiration during the fast-moving combat. "During all the hurly-burly of the fight Butler was calmly directing the operations of his command," he wrote. "Butler during this campaign was always to be seen among the bullets, with merely a lady's silver-mounted riding-whip, with which he would point out from time to time to those around him what was to be done." Much of the time Butler spent seated calmly on his horse while bullets buzzed around his head like angry hornets.[67]

Fog and acrid black powder smoke hung low over Kilpatrick's camp, trapped by the canopy of tall pine trees towering overhead. Before long it was almost impossible to see more than a few feet in any direction. As one trooper remarked, "If you missed your aim your bullet was liable to kill friend or foe."[68]

A lone Federal major groped his way on horseback through the thick smoke. When he realized he was approaching Confederates, the officer wheeled his horse around and fled. Armed with a saber and a pistol, Pvt. Abe Broadwater of the 6th South Carolina Cavalry put spurs to horse and set out after the Yankee. When Broadwater caught up with the major he demanded his surrender. The officer complied. Even though Broadwater did not demand it, the major turned over his wallet, which contained $135.00, as well as a fine silver pocket watch. "You might as well have it, for when I am sent to prison I know I will lose it," explained the dejected major. "All the favor I ask of you is to be a kind master to my horse, to which I am greatly attached."[69]

George Shuman, another Federal major, watched as officers and men were shot down all around him. "Several men were killed along side of me," he wrote, "but God in his mercy spared my life, although I was sitting still on my horse not over 15 yards from the rebel lines. I was so close that the balls passed all over my head." As the fortunate major later observed, the wounded were all behind him, which meant the Southerners had aimed too high or too wide to hit him.[70]

At first the Southerners overwhelmed the terrified and disoriented Yankees, but "[p]resently they began to rally in knots, and then the hand to hand skirmishing became pretty brisk, as compliments were being exchanged at close quarters," recalled one of Law's South Carolinians. "It was especially lively near a little house which loomed up through the mist and around which were tied many horses." The South Carolinian saw a brawny Federal leap astride a barebacked horse, draw his revolver, and pitch in. "He and one of our men 'tackled,' and by common consent were left to fight it out alone for what seemed minutes, but which were doubtless only seconds. At length he [the Federal] fell under his horse's feet, having died pluckily, as a true soldier should, to save his chief."[71] One of Wheeler's Alabamans recalled that the area around the big tent they had erroneously believed was Kilpatrick's headquarters was the subject of "fighting like the mischief."[72]

Lieutenant Henry C. Reynolds of Shannon's Scouts watched the maelstrom of violence swirling before him. Wheeler recognized Reynolds and rode up to him. "Come with me," ordered the general. "I have neither staff nor escort."

"General, we are between our lines and the enemy's," responded Reynolds, "and both are shooting this way."

"Never mind that; we must keep our men advancing," answered Wheeler.

The two rode on, cheering the Confederate horse soldiers the entire way.[73] With the intrepid Reynolds at his side, Wheeler personally pitched into the melee and "engaged in some dozen encounters, killing two and capturing a number with his own hand," recalled the historian of Wheeler's Corps.[74]

While countless other personal battles lost to history raged, the Confederates surrounded the Monroe house. Although Little Kil had already ridden to relative safety, Colonel Spencer and Lieutenant Colonel Way, Dr. Helm, and their staff officers were still trapped inside the house, as was poor Alice. "The camp of the dismounted men was instantly captured; also the headquarters of the division and brigade, and with the wagons and artillery," reported Colonel Spencer.[75] Spencer, Way, Helm, and their staffs barricaded themselves inside the second floor of the house. As it stood, matters seemed hopeless. According to an Illinois official account, "They were about to descend and surrender, when they heard a Rebel soldier, who had been stationed as a guard at the house, order another Rebel soldier, who came into the house, and wanted to go upstairs, to get out of the house, the guard saying that General Hampton had taken that house as his head-quarters, and had ordered that nothing in it be disturbed."[76]

The Federals remained undiscovered and undisturbed upstairs while the Confederates controlled the downstairs and surrounding grounds. Even though the Rebels did not enter the house and capture these officers, the Federals were virtual prisoners, leaving their brigades without commanders at a critical moment.

Although her beau had abandoned her to the tender mercies of the Confederates, Alice remained cool-headed. She walked outside just as Wade Hampton reined in. Hampton took her for the lady of the house and, ever polite, inquired whether there were any Yankees in her house.

"There are two wounded Yankees in my room," replied the plucky and resourceful Alice.

"Very well, madam," responded Hampton. "I will station a guard at your door, with orders to protect you and your house from my men." The general called for guards, instructed them as to his wishes, and rode off. Alice's quick thinking had saved the two brigade commanders from capture.[77]

"I suppose I was so confidently expecting Wheeler's Division and so intent in securing everything outside it did not occur to me to have the house examined," recounted Butler.[78] One of Sherman's staff officers had a slightly different perspective on things. "It is sufficient evidence of the desperate defense of our soldiers, that the Rebels had no time to enter the house, so that the officers there were not captured."[79] In all likelihood, it was probably a combination of both negligence and discharging carbines that kept the top floor free of inquiring Rebels.

Spencer, Way, and their staffs remained trapped on the upper floor of the house until after the battle ended. The victorious Confederates firmly held the Federal camp and the section of horse artillery assigned to Spencer's brigade.[80] Hampton's men captured the cannons before the gunners could fire a single round.[81] "At one time we had the enemy's artillery and wagons in our possession," declared Wheeler, "the wagons were cut down and the mules driven off."[82]

With bullets hissing all around her, Alice remained on the front porch desperately searching for her carriage. A chivalrous Southern officer spotted her and, fearing for her safety, galloped to the porch and dismounted. He escorted her through a shower of flying splinters ripped free by the bullets thudding into the walls of the house, and led her to a drainage ditch running along the Rosin Road. From that spot Alice watched the rest of the battle unfold in comparative safety. "It was noticed, however," recalled one of Butler's men, "that in spite of the risk thus incurred, she persisted in lifting her head from time to time and peered above the ditch to see what was going on, thus showing, as some said, that female curiosity is even stronger even than love of life."[83]

Although Alice's quick thinking and subsequent flight from the house had saved Colonel Spencer and the others from capture, they were prisoners nonetheless. Left to their own devices, Spencer's leaderless men took cover behind trees and stumps while waves of Confederate cavalry charged them, slashing and hacking with their sabers. The dazed Federals were in a life-and-death struggle, a desperate effort to fend off the onrushing enemy.

According to Colonel Way, Butler's initial charge struck without any warning whatsoever. "So sudden and unexpected was the charge that for a time all was confusion," reported Way. "The officers did all it was possible to do under the circumstances, calling upon the men to secure their arms and fall in, but being in an open field it was impossible to form, and we were obliged to fall back to some woods about 500 yards distant." The gray wave swept up Maj. Charles A. Appel of the 9th Pennsylvania Cavalry, who commanded the second regiment of the dismounted brigade, as well as Dr. C. C. Lathrop, the brigade surgeon.[84]

Major Christopher Cheek, commander of the 5th Kentucky Cavalry, watched the dismounted men scatter like chaff before the Confederate whirlwind. "To the right of our camp we could see the dismounted brigade, commanded by Lieutenant-Colonel Way, Ninth Michigan Cavalry, who had encamped in our rear, flying in every direction, the rebel cavalry in hot pursuit," Cheek later wrote.[85] Way's terrified soldiers high-tailed it in a southeasterly direction, dashing pell mell through the 5th Ohio Cavalry's camp site in a frantic attempt to find safety in the swamp.

Silas Bullock was the victim of unfortunate timing. The 22-year-old quartermaster sergeant of Company C, 9th Michigan Cavalry, had survived a lengthy stint as a prisoner of war and had only recently been formally exchanged. He returned to duty with Way's dismounted brigade just days before the Rebel cavalry struck at Monroe's Crossroads. The Confederate attackers swept him up and quickly returned him to captivity. Although Bullock escaped after only two days and made his way back to his regiment, he had lost nearly all of his personal effects. To his good fortune, Bullock's second stint as a prisoner was much shorter than his first.[86]

With Colonel Way trapped inside the Monroe house, command of his dismounted brigade devolved to the brigade's second-ranking officer, Lt. Col. William Stough of the 9th Ohio Cavalry. Born in Cumberland County, Pennsylvania, the 44-year-old Stough had relocated to Williams County in northwest Ohio as a child. He grew up to be a successful merchant, cabinet maker, and farmer. With the coming of war Stough received a commission as a captain in the 38th Ohio Infantry and, when the 9th Ohio Cavalry was formed in the summer of 1862, transferred to the new regiment. Stough proved himself a brave and competent officer in a number of fights and was promoted to major in September 1864. Less than one month later he received a second promotion to lieutenant colonel. Monroe's Crossroads would be his finest hour.[87]

When the Ohioan heard the fighting echoing in the camp, he halted his fleeing men, rallied them, and ordered the dismounted troopers to form for battle. If only they would stand and

Lieutenant Colonel
William Stough

NARA

fight, thought Stough, they might yet save the guns and even retake Little Kil's camp.

*   *   *

The attack launched on the far right flank of Joe Wheeler's line was not going as well as Butler's assault from the north. While Stough's Federals rallied, the Confederates of Humes's Division, with Harrison's Texas Brigade in front, spurred their horses blindly forward. The riders promptly crashed into a thicket, the heavy pine branches unhorsing and injuring several men. Unwilling to struggle through the thick fog and dense forest, some of Humes's people fell back, leaving the remnants to press forward.

After braving the thicket, Harrison's Texans entered the swampy barricade separating them from Kilpatrick's camp. Some of them spurred their horses forward while others dismounted in an effort to lead their animals into the cold waters. Those who were thrown from their mounts emerged shivering, casting about for their horses which may or may not have reached the other side. "We saw horses all covered in mud except their heads and necks, and their riders trying to save themselves by clinging to tufts," recalled horse soldier Posey Hamilton. "In fact, it is said that skeletons of a horse and rider were found in that awful mire five years later."

Once clear of the sucking waters of the swamp, Harrison's Texans struck the camp of the 1st Alabama Cavalry. The sudden appearance of the Rebel cavalry panicked the sleepy Alabamans who, far removed from the vicinity of the Monroe house, did not yet know they were under attack. Quickly gathering their wits, the Federals grabbed their weapons and took up positions behind trees, stumps, and even in depressions in the ground, firing their carbines and pistols into the screaming saber-waving demons that seemed to have sprung up from the grounds around them. "As the battleground was in the pine woods and very open, our boys fought Indian fashion," recalled a member of the 1st Alabama, "getting behind trees and other objects, without order of battle, at first, so complete was the surprise."[88]

"While gallantly cheering his men Maj. Francis L. Cramer was wounded and taken prisoner," noted Maj. Sanford Tramel, who briefly succeeded Cramer as commander of the 1st Alabama Cavalry. Cramer

Major
Francis L. Cramer

USAMHI

himself recalled the event. "During the fight I was captured by the enemy and held as prisoner until [March 14th], when I succeeded in making my escape, and after three days lying in the swamps and traveling nights, I succeeded in rejoining my command," he wrote. "After my capture Capt. J. J. Hinds took command of the regiment and retained it until my return, and I am indebted to him for the gallant manner in which he handled the command during the remainder of that severe and terrible fight."[89]

Surprised by the stout resistance of the Alabama Yankees, the Texans began withdrawing toward the safety of the swamp they had just worked so hard to pass through. Instead of letting his men become pinned down in the quagmire, however, Humes ordered them to pull back and regroup. As the Southerners reformed Humes and his brigade commanders rode north in an effort to locate a better—and drier—place to cross the swamp. The withdrawal of Humes's Division freed the Federal 1st Alabama and elements of the 5th Kentucky to turn around and help repulse Butler's men, who still had the better of the fighting for the main camp.[90]

As Humes was withdrawing across the swamp, most of Spencer's brigade was scrambling down the back side of the ridge in an effort to join Lieutenant Colonel Stough and the dismounted men rallying in the swamp. Other Federals formed small pockets of resistance. Major Rader's Buckeyes had been camped along the ridge about 150 yards south of the Monroe house. They took advantage of the nearby farm buildings, hiding in the barn and other structures, while others used fence posts, tent poles, and parts of downed tents as crude shelters.[91] The rest of

Spencer's men either stood their ground and fought or headed for the safety of the ravine.

While the Federals retreated and reformed in the ravine south of the house, the victorious—and hungry—Confederates began plundering the Yankee camp. "Our boys for a time had things their own way," noted the the 6th South Carolina Cavalry's Charles M. Calhoun. "Finally there were few of the enemy to be found. It surely was a grand achievement, and would have had no dark side had our troops then been called off, for up to this time our loss was quite small indeed. It must be remembered that our men were starved out," continued the private. "There was nothing in the commissary and less in our stomachs, for virtually we were then living on air and but little water, not being allowed at times to quench the thirst of man or horse when crossing a stream." When the famished Southerners took possession of a camp rich in everything to satisfy a hungry man, they greedily partook of their new-found bounty.[92]

Stopping to loot an overrun enemy camp was a phenomena officers had been wrestling with since antiquity. The Civil War had witnessed its share of similar occurrences, with perhaps the most striking example being the first morning at Shiloh on April 6, 1862, when victorious Confederates abandoned their successful dawn attack to plunder enemy tents and campgrounds. The same thing, though on a much smaller scale, took place on March 10, 1865, at Monroe's Crossroads. The result was also the same: discipline and tactics quickly broke down in the face of scarce food and riches.[93]

Trooper E. W. Watkins, one of Wheeler's men, was one of those who stopped to enjoy the fruits of Little Kil's camp. "I dismounted, picked out the best horse I could find, saddled him with the best saddle, picked out good equipage, saddlebags, blankets, etc., and mounted," he recalled. "Having a led horse now, I was not in much fix for fighting, and too many others were like me in equipping themselves instead of fighting." Watkins rationalized his conduct by claiming that he had lost two good horses over the course of the war, and that he was just making good his loss.[94] "The enemy, eager for plunder, failed to promptly follow us up," Kilpatrick accurately reported.[95] With so much Federal bounty beckoning them, many of Butler's and Wheeler's troopers simply abandoned the attack. The brilliant surprise attack, so carefully planned and executed, had run out of steam.

An alarmed Matthew Butler, who had fought on numerous fields in several states, quickly realized what was happening. After "Wright had rushed through like a whirlwind," the attack bogged down.[96] Hampton had held Law's brigade in reserve to guard prisoners, leaving Butler with only Wright's Brigade as the tip of his offensive southbound spear. "There I was with no power to reap the fruits of Wright's brilliant dash," lamented Butler.[97] Unless Wheeler's men came to Butler's aid, his juggernaut would lose its momentum. Butler quickly instructed his orderly, Ulysses R. Brooks, to find Wheeler and ask him to hurry to Butler's support. Brooks dashed off in search of the general. "I did not deliver the message," recalled the orderly, "because I met General Wheeler and his staff, followed by General Dibrell, at the head of his brave men." As Brooks witnessed, Wheeler was already urging his troopers to reinforce Wright as quicky as possible. Wheeler had also directed Dibrell's Division to come forward and join in the fighting. Wheeler hoped that if he committed his reserve at this crucial point, the renewed impetus would carry his men to victory.[98]

After dispatching Brooks to find Wheeler, Butler grew more frustrated as he watched a golden opportunity slip through his fingers. "I then hoped for the arrival of Wheeler's command from the other side," recalled Butler. Wheeler soon rode up with a few of his staff and escort and asked Butler about the status of his division.

"Scattered like the devil," replied Butler. "Where is yours?"

Wheeler told Butler that he had encountered a bog through which his division could not pass, and that he had ordered his people to make a circuit to the left and come around on Butler's flank. Butler realized it would take precious time for Wheeler's troops to make the flanking movement, and that the Confederate attack might well fail as a consequence. The fruits of the surprise attack on Kilpatrick's slumbering camp were quickly slipping away, and there was nothing that the frustrated Butler could do about it.[99]

The impenetrable swamp, the loss of command and control, and the breakdown in discipline had robbed the Confederate charge of its momentum and threatened to spoil Hampton's plan. The battle had reached its climax.

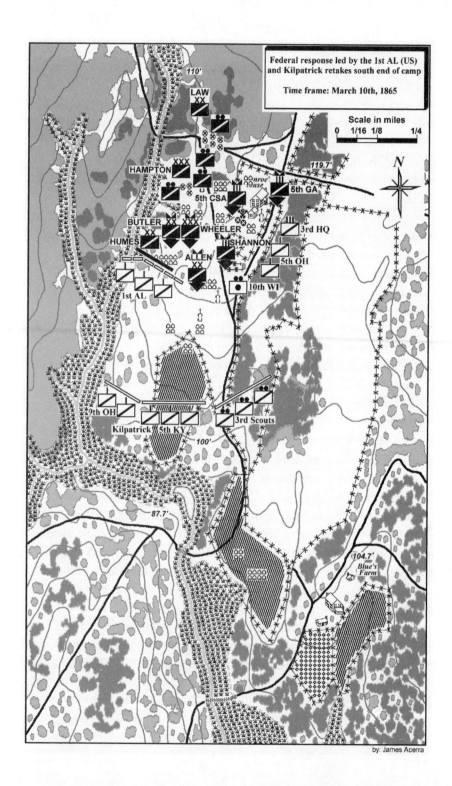

Federal response led by the 1st AL (US)
and Kilpatrick retakes south end of camp

Time frame: March 10th, 1865

Scale in miles

0   1/16 1/8   1/4

N

110'

LAW
XX

119.7'

HAMPTON
XXX

Monroe'
House

5th GA
III

5th CSA

3rd HQ
III

BUTLER
XX   XXX

WHEELER
XX

HUMES
III

SHANNON
III

ALLEN
XX

5th OH
III

1st AL

10th WI

9th OH

3rd Scouts

Kilpatrick 5th KY

100'

87.7'

104.7'
Blue's
Farm

by: James Acerra

Chapter 6

"One of the Most Terrific Hand-to-Hand Encounters I Ever Witnessed"

C old and barefooted, Judson Kilpatrick found himself on the edge of the swamp, spattered with mud and clad in nothing but his nightshirt. "Kil got his mad up," noted an Ohio horse soldier.[1]

After the shock of the whirlwind Confederate attack had worn off, Kilpatrick realized that unless he did something to rally his men and turn the tide, this embarrassing surprise would end in a devastating personal defeat. Finding a group of about twenty-five armed men huddled at the edge of the marshy ground, Little Kil determined to organize them for a counterattack. He faced a daunting task. Around him was a motley array of terrified fugitives, some clad only in their drawers, and others only half-dressed, some mounted, others sharing horses, still others on foot. Aided by Colonel Stough and Lt. Louis Geague, of Company E, 9th Ohio Cavalry, Kilpatrick rallied and reformed them.

According to one of his horse soldiers, Kilpatrick "also secured a horse, a very tame and dilapidated one, I must confess, and truth requires that it should also be owned that he had to ride him bare-back. His appearance on this occasion was in striking contrast with that usually presented by him. Nevertheless, the boys rallied around Kilpatrick, and, commanding them to follow him and charge, they rushed boldly, impetuously forward."[2]

Once gathered and rallied, the men opened on the Confederates milling about the Union tents at the top of the ridge. The fire drove Wheeler's and Butler's men from the southern end of the camp. The firing slowly grew in intensity as more men rallied and joined the line. A respectable line of battle soon began to form, giving heart to Kilpatrick, who continued to rally fugitives. Before long he cobbled together enough men to order an advance. When the order was given the Federals slowly moved up the ridge, firing as they moved. "Little Kilpatrick's brave cavalrymen rallied under the leadership of their tried commander, retook the hills upon the left, and then, with one wild shout, swept down upon the rebels, who were swarming about the captured artillery and Kilpatrick's former headquarters," recalled an Ohio horse soldier.[3]

Some of the Federal fugitives had earlier crossed Nicholson Creek in an effort to reach Captain Northrop's scouts. Roused from his slumber by the sounds of heavy gunfire and the shouts of the fleeing men, Northrop blinked the sleep from his eyes and tried to figure out what was going on. Breathless fugitives inquired, "Where is the infantry?" They "told us General Kilpatrick and the 3d Brigade had been all but captured, and they seemed to think they alone had escaped," recalled Northrop. He realized that if he waited for the infantry to come to the rescue it would be too late, so he decided to do what he could to assist Kilpatrick and his embattled command.[4] "We mounted and started for the camp, hoping that we might recapture some of the prisoners," Northrop later wrote, "but we soon heard the fighting and knew by that that all had not been captured."[5]

Northrop and his scouts made their way through scores of fugitives as they galloped toward the sound of the firing. Some joined them but most kept running for the rear. Northrop splashed across Nicholson Creek near Blue's Rosin Road and dashed up the ridge with his scouts, where they met unsuspecting Confederates. "I decided I would not stop until I had reached the house on the battlefield where I knew headquarters would be," Northrop recalled, but at the top of the ridge and seeing Confederates throughout the camp, Northrop and his men prudently decided to halt their advance.[6]

The arrival of the scouts heartened the troopers comprising Kilpatrick's ragtag battle line, which sent up a cheer when the handful of reinforcements were spotted. "We were followed by from one hundred fifty to two hundred mounted men who had escaped from this captured camp," recalled Northrop. "We had to pass through the men who had been driven from the camp to the swamp, where they had made a stand and at this time were fighting on the defensive. We dashed through them. They thought it was the arrival of the 1st Brigade, and they sang out, 'Here comes the 1st Brigade!' and, led by General Kilpatrick, they followed us in a charge."[7] For his role in rescuing Kilpatrick's command Northrop received a brevet to major.[8]

Posey Hamilton and Ed Knight, the Confederates who had been so determined to reach the big tent they had mistakenly taken for Kilpatrick's headquarters, were now trying to make their way back across the chaotic camp to rejoin their Alabama regiment. Without warning they found themselves facing Northrop and his men. "A Yankee company had moved in and formed in line, all mounted on good horses, well dressed and armed with pistols, between us and the big tent," recalled Hamilton. "We were coming back toward them for two hundred yards, and they were firing at us with pistols at a rapid rate. A few more [comrades] were following us, and some of them were wounded and dropped out."

Hamilton and Knight continued pressing forward to within sixty yards of the enemy before turning east and riding within forty yards of Northrop's command. "They had almost ceased firing at us at that time," Hamilton recalled. "Neither of us or our horses was hit." Somehow the Alabamans had escaped Northrop and his men. "While we were maneuvering in front of that Yankee cavalry company," Hamilton continued, "General Wheeler's men were over the hill west of the big tent fighting like the mischief." After Hamilton and Knight evaded Northrop's pursuit and reached the top of the hill, they met their division commander, General Allen, who was riding Kilpatrick's prized black horse. The two men realized that, for the moment at least, they were safe.[9]

Lieutenant Ebenezer Stetson commanded the two-gun section of artillery attached to Spencer's brigade. When the gray wave crashed into the sleeping camp at dawn, Stetson and his artillerists scrambled for shelter under the Monroe house. After the horrified Stetson watched the Confederates capture his guns early in the fighting, he looked for an opportunity to retake them. There was no greater disgrace for an artillerist than to lose his cannon, and Stetson was bound and determined to have them back.[10]

As Northrop and his scouts engaged the Confederates, Stetson saw his opportunity. With bullets whizzing through the air Stetson and a few men of the 5th Kentucky Cavalry reached one of his guns, unlimbered it, and loaded it with canister.[11] After inserting a friction primer into the vent, the intrepid lieutenant aimed the piece in the general direction of the enemy and pulled the lanyard. The gun belched flame and hot metal, wreaking terrible havoc on the Confederates massed in his front. "Lt. Stetson . . . never fires but what he makes an impression upon the enemy," remembered a Northern cavalryman.[12] The blast of canister was a sound thus far alien to the combat swirling at Monroe's Crossroads, and the deep throated voice of the artillery piece caused soldiers on both sides to pause and look for the source of the discharge. "This was a rallying signal for the entire command," noted Colonel Spencer, "and immediately a sufficient force was placed in support of the battery and a withering fire of grape and canister was opened upon the enemy."[13]

When other Federals saw Stetson beside his gun, lanyard in hand, they cheered and surged forward to support him. "Lt. Stetson quickly fired a round of grape and canister into the rebel ranks," noted the 5th Kentucky Cavalry's Maj. Christopher Cheek, "which greatly encouraged my men, and demoralized and discouraged the rebels to an equal extent."[14]

Undaunted and miraculously untouched by the bullets whizzing around him, Stetson began reloading his rifled cannon. Sergeant John W. Swartz, the chief of the section, recognized the sound of his own guns and reacted by dashing toward Stetson. Several of his artillerists followed in his wake. As Stetson worked on one piece, Swartz and his men unlimbered the second gun and trained it on the Confederates milling about the camp. Because the terrain funneled toward the swamp, the butternut horsemen presented an easy target for the deadly blasts of Stetson's guns. "Lieutenant Stetson kept up such a savage discharge of shell and grape that it made it more than unhealthy for the rebels to remain," recounted a newspaper correspondent.[15] Trapped in a crossfire between the Federal artillery and the small arms of Kilpatrick's troopers, the Rebels suffered horribly. The recapture and firing of the artillery threatened to galvanize Union opposition. The Confederates would have to silence the Federal guns—and quickly—before the tide turned against them.

A number of the Rebels took cover behind one of the Monroe outbuildings, where they fired on Stetson and his men. The well aimed shots picked off some of the artillerists. Several Southern officers, meanwhile, prepared to charge the guns in an effort to capture them at the point of the sword, if necessary. One of the officers was Lt. John P. DeVeaux, "on all occasions one of the bravest men I have ever known," recalled the historian of the South Carolina brigade. DeVeaux, he continued, "never hesitat[ed] an instant to risk his life for a friend." The boast was not idly made, for Butler regularly selected DeVeaux for the most dangerous missions.[16]

Determined to take the section by storm, DeVeaux called upon his comrades to join him in the effort. In the noise and confusion, however, only Capt. Moses B. Humphrey of the 6th South Carolina Cavalry and Glenn Davis, who served in Humphrey's company, could make out what DeVeaux was trying to communicate. Armed only with pistols, the trio spurred their horses and galloped toward the rifled guns. "The Yankee lieutenant serving the gun pulled the lanyard and discharged the load of shrapnel when they were a short distance from the muzzle of the cannon," wrote the historian of Butler's command. The blast killed DeVeaux's horse and struck the lieutenant in five places. Miraculously, no bones were shattered and no vital organs were hit. "When we saw DeVeaux and Humphrey shot down, some of our men charged up to this battery, served so gallantly by this brave and cool Yankee, and while he was in the act of reloading, killed him with a pistol shot." Butler personally witnessed the incident and later said that it was a shame to have to kill such a brave fellow.[17]

Captain Humphrey was in his penultimate year at The Citadel when war came in 1861. He led the Cadet Company of the 6th South Carolina Company and was badly wounded at Trevilian Station on June 11, 1864, but returned to duty later that fall. Butler, who was not the most effusive of men with praise, said of the young captain, "I have never seen a man of more fortitude than Capt. Humphrey." With DeVeaux down, Humphrey continuing galloping bravely for Stetson's guns. A piece of metal, whether from canister or small arms is unknown, shattered his arm. When he was told after the battle that it would have to be amputated Humphreys steadfastly refused, saying that he preferred death to the loss of a limb. Unfortunately, a serious infection set in and he died a few days later, "because he feared not death, but shrank from dismemberment."[18] Humphrey's beloved horse Yago was also mortally wounded in the hell-for-leather charge at the guns. Both were buried in the same grave.[19]

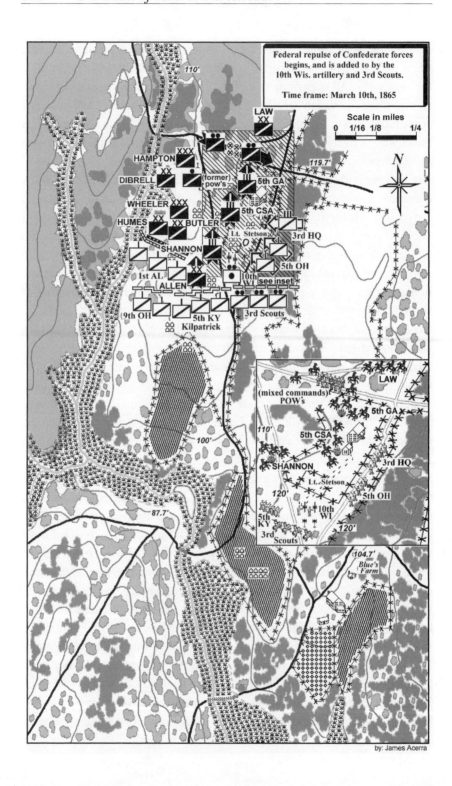

by: James Acerra

Some of Wheeler's men also tried to silence Stetson's guns. "Orders came to cut down the artillery," recalled Sgt. Nathaniel A. Hood, a member of the 51st Alabama. "I held the horse for my Lieutenant while he aided in cutting it down, which was under heavy fire." McLemore's 4th Tennessee had formed mounted near the edge of the woods and near the camp. "I think the 4th did the most gallant fighting that I ever saw men do standing in line on horses," Hood remembered. The heavy fire of the Tennesseans cut down all but one of Stetson's gunners and disabled one of his pieces. Several butternut horse soldiers charged while the lone artillerist "was attempting to reload [and] was killed by a pistol shot."[20]

A critical moment in the fighting had arrived. Wheeler realized that if he could hold these guns and outflank the Federal left, Kilpatrick would have to abandon his camp. Determined to break or drive back the makeshift Union battle line, Wheeler gathered up scattered elements of Allen's Division and began forming them for the attack. Wheeler's bugler sounded the charge a second time and the grayclad horsemen galloped forward, with Wheeler personally leading them. "No officer was more conspicuous on the field than General Wheeler," recalled a Georgia horseman. "He charged into the camp with the first squadron, and killed several Yankees in close encounter, and was at one time entirely surrounded by the enemy, but escaped unscathed."[21]

This time, however, the Federals were ready. As the Confederates rode toward them Kilpatrick's troopers blazed away with their Spencer carbines and Springfield rifle-muskets. Although the determined Confederates forced Colonel Stough's dismounted men to seek cover among the thick pines, the Federals rallied and laid down a severe fire. The firing was so heavy and well delivered that the Southerners were convinced they were facing infantry instead of dismounted cavalry.[22]

Stough's men fired a volley, followed it with a bayonet charge, and drove the Confederates from the guns.[23] Three decades later in the *National Tribune*, Federal trooper J. H. Gardner of the 1st Alabama Cavalry explained that the Rebels believed the reinforcements were from Sherman's army. "When the dismounted cavalry came out of the swamp they thought it was the Fourteenth Corps, as it was next to the cavalry's right at that time."[24] Another veteran writing after turn of the century had nothing but praise for the officer who led the dismounted cavalry. "It was fortunate that Col. Stough with his dismounted cavalrymen armed with Springfield rifles was so close at hand, and under command of so cool and brave an officer as Col. Stough," wrote Smith D. Atkins. "His appearance with his rifles with fixed bayonets and at right shoulder shift so disconcerted the overwhelming force of Confederate cavalry that it hastily retreated."[25] In addition to Stough's men, Stetson's guns had also helped to turn the tide. As a Hoosier horsemen with a good view of the battlefield noted in his diary, "After they were fired on by our artillery, they presented the aspect of a mass of disorderly fugitives."[26]

Despite the sudden shift in momentum, the Confederates continued attacking, though with less ardor and fewer men. Trooper Z. T. DeLoach of the 5th Georgia Cavalry, Anderson's Brigade, charged with his comrades. "In that fight they shot my mule down and I ran to get one of the Yankees' horses, but before I could unhitch it they shot [it too]," he recalled. "I heeled it from there to the branch, but I could not get a ride and I had to get to one side and let all pass, the Yankees too." DeLoach escaped in the confusion, making it to safety on foot.[27]

Wheeler and his men approached the blue line with sabers drawn, hacking away at the dismounted Yankees. This time they stood to their task and inflicted casualties at short range against their mounted opponents. Wheeler's attack quickly ran out of steam. With his losses mounting, he prudently broke off the offensive and ordered his men to withdraw. Those who had lost their mounts were forced to retreat on foot or receive rides from their comrades.

Fighting Joe was not finished, however. Badly in need of reinforcements, he dispatched courier after courier to find Dibrell and guide him to the field. Timely arrival of reinforcements might yet tip the balance in the Confederates's favor.[28] Once back out of range Wheeler rallied his troopers yet again, pulling them together for another charge against the reinforced Yankee line. The butternut horsemen coalesced around Wheeler, forming a line of battle and readying themselves for yet another mounted assault. When Pelote's bugle sounded a third time the Rebel horses surged forward anew. Wheeler and his screaming men dashed at Stough's line, their sabers glinting in the early morning light.

The intrepid Colonel Stough and his dismounted troopers were ready and waiting to meet them. Volley after volley rang out, emptying saddles and shattering the momentum of the charge. Dead and wounded Confederate riders and horses littered the ground. "We soon found ourselves being driven back by the dismounted men that we had not counted on, not knowing they were in such force," recalled Lt. Henry C. Reynolds, who was at Wheeler's side during the attacks against Stough.[29]

As the powder smoke dissipated, the cost of the third charge became evident. Colonel James Hagan, one of Allen's brigadiers, was on the wet ground with a serious wound. Around him lay many of his officers and men. General Humes, who had impetuously joined the charge, was shot through the leg. Slumped over the neck of his horse and weak from the loss of blood, Humes directed his troopers to withdraw from the shadows of the enemy line.

General Butler, meanwhile, watched helplessly as the Federals repulsed Wheeler's second charge. Determined to do what he could to support Wheeler, he gathered as large a detachment as possible from Gib Wright's Brigade and organized them to attack. When the South Carolinian gave the order to charge his men swept forward in good order. Wheeler spotted Butler's attack and rode forward to cheer the men on, his "hat raised as they charged by," recorded a South Carolinian. With Butler leading the way, Wright's troopers rushed Stetson's guns. "Most of our men were dismounted and thrown forward as infantry to hold the ground until the captured horses, artillery, and wagons could be removed or destroyed," recalled Edward L. Wells of the 4th South Carolina Cavalry.[30]

During the charge, Capt. M. C. Dixon of the 4th South Carolina Cavalry, "a brave and gallant officer," was wounded in the hip and arm. He lingered for a few days before dying of his wounds. "His was an enviable career," wrote Charles M. Calhoun of the 6th South Carolina Cavalry. "He did his duty faithfully." Major Thomas Ferguson, the commander of the 6th South Carolina, also went down with a serious wound.[31]

Thirty-two-year-old Lt. Col. Barrington S. King commanded Cobb's Legion of Wright's Brigade. His parents were from Connecticut but had moved south to Georgia many years before the war, where they operated successful textile mills and founded the town of Roswell. King trained as a physician and was practicing medicine in Columbia, South Carolina, when the war broke out. He enlisted as a private in Company C of Cobb's Legion on August 1, 1861, served as the battalion's acting surgeon until March 1862, and was promoted to captain. On October 9, 1863, King was promoted to lieutenant colonel and served capably throughout the brutal Virginia campaigns of 1864. When Wright took command of the brigade

Lieutenant Colonel
Barrington S. King

Georgia Historical Society

King succeeded him as commander of the Cobb Legion.[32] King had had some health problems that winter, and after a stint in the hospital had only rejoined his regiment on the previous day.[33]

With Wade Hampton urging him on, King led his Georgians headed straight for a horseless line of Yankees supported by Stetson's guns. "The Cobb Legion gallantly charged upon that splendidly equipped battle line of dismounted Westerners," recalled an eyewitness, "steadily advancing while their artillery, which we ought to have looked after better at the start, was playing upon our support murderously."[34]

S. W. Bailey, a member of Cobb's Legion, was in the charge that morning and remembered it for the rest of his life. "And right here was my closest call in the war," he recalled years later. "I had crossed over the ravine on a bridge, when we recrossed our men had gone. I had then to go back alone as fast as my horse would carry me in a line parallel with and near the enemy's camp. Zip, zip went many a bullet close to my ears." Bailey saw King forming his horse soldiers for the charge and fell in with them, the men yelling as they dashed for the guns.[35]

During the brief interlude following the previous Confederate charge, the intrepid Stetson had re-manned and reloaded his field pieces. As King and his men thundered toward them, Stetson unleashed another blast of canister. One of the lead balls found its mark and knocked King from his saddle. The missile had severed his femoral artery. As a physician, King would have quickly guessed that the wound was mortal, and he would have been right. The doctor-turned-soldier bled to death within a few minutes. "Say to my wife. I die willingly defending my country," he is said to have uttered as his life spilled out into the muddy Carolina soil. Bailey saw Lt. Wiley Chandler Howard grab the mortally wounded colonel's horse and lead it to safety a short distance away, "to the very spot where we buried him."[36]

King's loss was deeply felt within the brigade. Colonel Wright lamented King as "a tried and true friend" and a "staunch and noble patriot. I would that the blow would have fallen on one whose services to their country were less valuable, but such is the fate of war, her victims are the noblest spirits."[37] King's death and the steady enemy fire took the steam out of Butler's charge, which broke apart before reaching the Federal line. The combination of rifle-musket, carbine, and artillery fire was simply too much for the Southern horsemen to overcome.[38]

Private Bailey of Cobb's Legion was wounded in the arm during the brief attack. "Being in front I was last to retreat and in turning around right at Kilpatrick's headquarters, a ball went through my horse's nostrils; another entered his jaw bone as I turned another ball pierced my saddle wallets," he recalled. "I rode a short distance, dismounted, and turned my wounded horse loose." All the while enemy bullets continued whistling past Bailey, who spied a gray horse running unmounted. Grabbing the horse's reins, Bailey jumped on his back and made it safely back to his regiment. He would ride that horse until the end of the war.[39]

From Butler's perspective, the quick and bloody repulse demonstrated that the Federal defenders now outnumbered the attackers. "Kilpatrick's 1,500 dismounted men had recovered from the shock of our first attack and gathered themselves behind pine trees, and with their rapid-firing Spencer carbines attacked us savagely and drove us out," Butler believed. "They had got to their artillery and, with their carbines, made it so hot for the handful of us we had to retire. In fact, I lost sixty-two men there in about five minutes' time."[40]

Still clad only in his nightshirt, Judson Kilpatrick placed himself at the head of his men. Inspired by the sight of their mud-spattered general, however inappropriately dressed, "the men were now perfectly wild with excitement," observed an Ohio horse soldier. "[W]hen their commander rode along the line and shouted to them that the day was theirs, they could not be restrained, but dashed forward, [and] drove the enemy from every quarter."[41] Although the Buckeye witness exaggerated the ease with which the Federals recovered the field, he captured perfectly the

Harper's Weekly

Kilpatrick recaptures his headquarters.

enthusiasm the men experienced with Kilpatrick back leading them. Although his careless dispositions had placed his command at hazard at the outset, Little Kil was equal to the task of recovering his camp. "We retook the artillery, turned it upon the enemy about our headquarters, not twenty steps distant, and finally forced him out of the camp with great slaughter," he later reported.[42]

"With Kilpatrick in the lead we charged, dismounted as we were, retook our headquarters, and although repeatedly charged by Butler and Hampton, we repulsed every charge," related Pvt. George C. Jenkins, Company M, 1st Alabama Cavalry. The Alabama Yankees laid down such a severe fire that they forced Harrison's and Ashby's troopers, many of whom were still mired in the swamp to the west, to dismount and seek shelter. The Alabama fusillade helped save Kilpatrick's command by preventing Wheeler from receiving badly needed reinforcements at the critical moment of the fight.

Before the Confederate attacked ended, however, Private Jenkins found himself in a duel with a "fine looking rebel officer." The tall Southerner (whom Jenkins recalled as having a clean-shaven upper lip and long chin whiskers) shot Jenkins in the left arm during their exchange. "I would like to know if either of my shots struck him," Jenkins noted, "for when I fired the third shot he fell on his horse's neck, either from the shot or to avoid another." Jenkins never learned his adversary's identity or fate.[43]

The stand of the 1st Alabama impressed Judson Kilpatrick. "Genl Kilpatrick was with our regiment & has since said he never thought or expected a cavalry regiment to stand under the circumstances," proclaimed one of the Alabamans a few days after the battle. "The regt. that was ahead of us broke & ran right through our ranks. We remained front & repulsed the rebs."[44]

"My officers and men were completely bewildered for a short time," admitted Maj. George H. Rader of the 5th Ohio Cavalry, "the enemy being in force in every part of my camp . . . but through the almost superhuman efforts of some of the officers, the men soon rallied and contested the ground inch by inch with the enemy, and finally assisted by the men and officers of the First Alabama and Fifth Kentucky Cavalry, the enemy was forced to retire after one of the most terrific hand-to-hand encounters I ever witnessed, leaving his dead and wounded on the field."

The fighting was indeed conducted at very close quarters. Corporal M. Hayes of the 5th Ohio Cavalry was close enough to shoot a rebel color bearer, tear the colors from the standard, and dash back to his command without suffering a scratch. Hayes presented his trophy to Major Rader, who later commended the corporal in his battle report. Rader also praised Capt. Joseph E. Overturf who, along with Capt. Jerome J. Hinds of the 1st Alabama Cavalry and Capt. John A. P. Glore of the 5th Kentucky Cavalry, had rallied the command and saved it "from total annihilation." The Buckeyes paid a heavy price that morning, suffering four killed, eleven wounded, and eighty-one missing. They also lost sixty-eight horses.[45]

Captain Robert Miller commanded Company L, 5th Ohio Cavalry, an outfit that had not been routed by the initial Confederate surprise attack. Miller's company held its position in line and was "the only command not wholly stampeded and part of my company took the rear on the first assault." Miller's horse was shot out from under him in the melee. As his men drove back the Confederates, Miller, he later wrote, "was the first man at [our] Head Quarters building in its recovery by charge of my troops except one or two men disabled by wounds who were left there. I rode up to the House, and told a wounded soldier to hand me [Kilpatrick's headquarters] Flag. He did so, while the contest was still unabated—and I took and held the flag for two hours until the battle was over, when I returned it to one of the Staff Officers or the color bearer—I do not remember which."[46]

For about ninety minutes the Federals punished the men of Wheeler's command trapped in the swamp fed by Nicholson Creek.[47]

"Quite a battle took place, lasting for an hour or more, till, with . . . assistance from their infantry, they were able to drive us out of their encampment," remembered George B. Guild of the consolidated 4th and 8th Tennessee, Harrison's Brigade. Like many Southern soldiers that day, Guild incorrectly identified Way's dismounted troopers as Federal infantry.[48] Most of James Hagan's 3rd Alabama had failed to make their way across the bog. The few who managed it found the enemy aroused and bravely resisting the Confederate attack. "Assuming a position in a pine forest, they poured a hot fire into our little squad," recalled a veteran of the 3rd Alabama. "Vainly did our gallant colonel call for his men to charge. There was not half a dozen, the others were in the marsh. The situation was extremely critical." Both Hagan (as earlier noted) and Maj. John D. Farish, the commander of the 3rd Alabama, were wounded in this action. Farish's severe thigh wound eventually cost him his leg.[49]

In spite of the stinging repulses and challenges of terrain, Wheeler rallied his men again and prepared to make yet another charge. Wheeler and Lieutenant Reynolds rode in front of the butternut cavalrymen to inspire them as Federal bullets hissed all around. Worried for the general's safety, Reynolds turned to Wheeler and said, "We had better ride in rear of our line." Wheeler, however, would have none of it. "No, Reynolds, we can't hold them in any other way," he responded, meaning unless they led from the front, the Southern horsemen would not vigorously assault the enemy line. Reynolds had no choice but to share in the general's danger.[50]

Inspired by the courage of their little commander, the Confederates steadied themselves and a severe firefight at some distance resumed. Because neither side was willing to give ground, casualties on both sides continued to mount.

Since the first surprise attack early that morning, the Confederate high command had been unable to craft a new plan to defeat Kilpatrick's re-energized cavalry. Heavy losses in officers and horses, coupled with difficult terrain, limited Southern tactical options. "Brigadier Generals Humes and Harrison, Colonels Hagan and Roberts and Major Farish had been badly wounded," recounted Wheeler. "The Alabama Brigade had lost its commander and every field grade officer. Brigadier General Allen's and Colonel Ashby's horses had been shot."[51] After such heavy losses in his officer corps, Wheeler realized it would be difficult to maintain command cohesion.[52] Hampton, Butler, and Wheeler knew that

Yankee infantry was moving on nearby roads, and were convinced that Stough's men—their bayonets gleaming in the pale morning sunlight—were infantry from the Fourteenth Corps who had reinforced Kilpatrick's horse soldiers.[53]

While Wheeler worked to reorganize his scattered command and oversee the removal of some of his wounded from the battlefield, Wade Hampton rode up at the head of Dibrell's Division. Dibrell's Tennessee and Kentucky brigades (led by Cols. William S. McLemore and William Campbell Preston Breckinridge, respectively), had been held in reserve since its arrival on the field earlier that morning. Now Dibrell was available for action and sorely needed. Should his troopers be inserted into the battle? Hampton and Wheeler discussed their options and came to the conclusion that nothing more could be gained by continuing the fight. The element of surprise was gone, the Federals were well-armed veteran troops, and infantry had apparently reinforced Kilpatrick or soon would be. Reluctantly, Hampton decided "that in view of the probability that Federal infantry would soon be on the scene," he had to break off the engagement and withdraw.[54]

"Hampton naturally withdrew when he concluded he had effected all that was practicable," declared Edward L. Wells of the 4th South Carolina Cavalry, "not intending to engage in a battle with all the infantry as well as cavalry of Sherman's army."[55] The fire laid down by the dismounted men of Stough's tiny brigade had been so severe that the Confederates were convinced they were infantry reinforcements.

Hampton and his commanders had good reason for concern. The South Carolinian knew from scouting reports that a large force of enemy foot soldiers was nearby. Brigadier General James D. "Old Jimmy" Morgan's division, part of Maj. Gen. Jefferson C. Davis's Fourteenth Corps, was marching on the Plank Road. Although they had not yet reached the field, Morgan's men were so close they could hear the sounds of the battle raging about five miles to the north as they stepped through the mud, most of their thoughts known only to themselves. "Heavy firing was heard on our left," reported Maj. Aaron B. Robinson, commander of the 121st Ohio Infantry. A courier from Kilpatrick dashed up looking for General Morgan. After Morgan heard the report he halted his division and informed his second brigade commander, Brig. Gen. John Mitchell, that Kilpatrick had been attacked and needed the infantry's help.[56] Mitchell later reported that the "brigade was ordered in haste to go to the

The Confederate withdrawal signals the end of the battle of Monroe's Crossroads.

Time frame: March 10th, 1865

Scale in miles
0   1/16 1/8   1/4

by: James Acerra

relief of . . . General Kilpatrick's cavalry force, which was moving on the left flank of the army."[57] The Union infantry struck out at the double-quick. "We made a forced march of six miles to help him out," recalled one of Mitchell's Ohioans.[58] Wade Hampton did not know the specifics of any this on March 10, but he correctly assumed that reinforcements had to be heading to Kilpatrick's support.

With his decision made, Hampton sent a courier to Butler and with instructions to break off the combat and withdraw from the field. Wheeler directed Dibrell to cover the Confederate cavalry as it pulled back. Colonel McLemore's small Tennessee Brigade deployed in line of battle while Bugler Pelote sounded the recall and the Confederate cavalry began retiring toward the road north of the Monroe house. "We carried away many hundred prisoners (nearly as many as the entire attacking force), and numbers of horses, among them three of Kilpatrick's private mounts, the gallant black already alluded to, a piebald, and a bay," enthused one South Carolinian.[59]

According to one historian, Dibrell's troopers "for an hour and ten minutes made one of the best horseback fights made during the war" while covering the retreat of the Confederate cavalry.[60] Although Dibrell was ready and willing to intercept any pursuit offered by Kilpatrick, there was little in the way of fighting. Little Kil was content to let the grayclad horsemen leave the field unchallenged. The Federals were exhausted, short on ammunition, and satisfied with reclaiming their camp.

Once his men were formed, Hampton ordered the troopers to head straight east for Fayetteville. "We then retired at our leisure," recalled one of Wheeler's men.[61] With Wheeler personally supervising them, Dibrell's rear guard remained at the ready until the main body had moved beyond any immediate danger.[62] After a few token parting shots, Dibrell's Tennesseans and Kentuckians wheeled and rode off after the main column. The Federals made only a half-hearted show of pursuit before returning to camp. McLemore's Brigade "held back a whole division of Yankee infantry for upwards of an hour," a Tennessee horse soldier later boasted with considerable exaggeration.[63]

After the Confederates withdrew, the Federals who had survived the morning attacks breathed a collective sigh of relief. The Battle of Monroe's Crossroads, the Eastern Theater's last large-scale cavalry battle, was over.

* * *

The withdrawing Confederates did what they could to impede the advance of Sherman's infantry. Hampton's horsemen fired a large turpentine factory to prevent it from falling into Union hands and with the hope that the flames would deter the Federals from pursuing. "It was a terrible conflagration," remembered one of Mitchell's Buckeye foot soldiers. "The blaze rose four miles toward heaven, leaping and roaring like a bursting volcano. So great was the heat from the burning casks and tar pits, that we were compelled to turn to the right eight miles down Fallis Creek, crossing at a ford, the water being so hot from the heated air of the mighty burning cauldron, that it took the hair off the horse's legs as they forded it."[64]

Freed from their clapboard prison, Colonels Spencer and Way cautiously emerged from the Monroe house. The devastation wrought by the battle shocked both officers: dead and wounded men and horses littered the ground and equipment and weapons were scattered in every direction. Dazed Federal troopers searched for their comrades and belongings among the corpses and debris. Judson Kilpatrick joined the two officers shortly after they emerged from the Monroe house, and the three men made arrangements for the care of the wounded. Little Kil's red battle flag was once again fluttering above the campground.[65] Kilpatrick wanted to tend to his wounded and bury the dead as quickly as possible so he could move out and reunite with the scattered units of his command. After being ambushed and coming within a whisker of defeat, the last thing Kilpatrick wanted was for Hampton to regroup and strike him again while the Union forces were still disorganized.

More than 320 dead horses were scattered about the battlefield. Desperate for shelter, men of both sides had used dead horses as crude breastworks during the fight. The Yankee horsemen were angry and frustrated at having been surprised and were determined to vent their frustration. One of Neill Blue's daughters recalled that at the end of the battle, the Yankees returned to her father's house, "hatless, coatless, and in a perfect rage; cursing their ill luck and everything in sight, including those of their comrades who at the sound of the guns instead of going to fight had gone in the other direction."[66]

Although some of the Yankees were indeed embarrassed by the surprise and thus "in a perfect rage," the Federals held the battlefield at the end of the engagement and could thus claim victory. After that fact sunk in a certain pride swept through the ranks. "Fought 3 hours whipt the rebels drove them out of our camp," declared Sgt. Josiah D. Wilson of the Federal 1st Alabama Cavalry.[67] "I remember that we had them whipped and the field all to ourselves by 11 o'clock without help," proclaimed Sgt. W. C. Leonard of the 9th Ohio Cavalry, a member of Way's dismounted brigade. "I think the First Brigade and the dismounted men, with the battery, did the job."[68] Even the Confederates were impressed with the Federals' tenacity. Shortly after the battle, Col. J. Fred Waring of the Jeff Davis Legion scribbled into his diary, "The enemy to their credit [rallied] promptly after the first surprise."[69]

Way's dismounted brigade had performed admirably throughout the fight, much to the credit of Colonels Way and Stough. "Colonel Stough deserves great praise for his coolness and good sense, in deploying his little command so opportunely," declared a member of the 92nd Illinois Mounted Infantry.[70] Stough received a brevet to brigadier general of volunteers as a reward for his gallant and meritorious performance in the battle.[71]

Lieutenant Stetson was also one of readily identifiable heroes of the fight. "I cannot let the gallant conduct of Lieutenant Stetson go without mention, who, unaided and alone, crept through the ranks of the enemy and unlimbered and fired one of his guns," proclaimed Colonel Spencer. "To this fact, more than to any other, I ascribe a terrible disaster turned into a brilliant victory."[72] Stetson's artillery command lost ten men captured and thirty horses killed and captured, and one of his guns was left disabled.[73]

Kilpatrick was justifiably proud of his horse soldiers. "This battle speaks for itself and needs no comment from me," he wrote before going on to comment at some length. "I will simply add that less than one-third of my entire command was unexpectedly attacked before daylight by the entire rebel cavalry force led by Hampton in person, the pet and pride of the Southern chivalry, and no matter what the facts may be regarding the conduct of my people under the first terrible onset of the foe, they can proudly boast that without assistance they regained their camp, animals, artillery, and transportation, and drove the enemy in confusion from the ground he had taken by surprise and force of numbers alone."[74]

The Northern media lauded the troopers for a job well done. "The whole affair was indeed most brilliant," one Cincinnati newspaper correspondent declared, "and reflects great credit upon the cavalry, and adds yet another laurel to many won by them since leaving the hills of Georgia."[75] Another Ohio newspaperman echoed the refrain. "The fight and successful stand made by Kilpatrick after he had been surprised are regarded as among the most gallant deeds of the campaign."[76] Little or nothing was mentioned about Kilpatrick's failure to properly picket his lines, or that the surprise and subsequent near-defeat could easily have been prevented.

The Confederates fully realized that a great opportunity had slipped through their fingers. "We never felt satisfied over having failed to capture General Kilpatrick and all the occupants of the big tent," recalled Alabama trooper Posey Hamilton, who was still laboring under his misconception that Little Kil had slept under canvas rather than in a warm bed in the arms of a woman. "There were a great many lost on both sides, and we never thought the capture of four hundred men compensated us for the loss sustained." Hamilton blamed the outcome of the battle on Wheeler's failure to get his entire command into the fight, as did a lieutenant of the 6th South Carolina Cavalry.[77] "The cause of our being so badly used up—it was agreed that Genl. Wheeler should attack the camp on one side and General Butler on the other, so Butler's brigade was held with the expectation of help from General Wheeler," the lieutenant asserted, implying that had Dibrell's Division—which had been detached for provost duty—pitched into the fray, it might have tipped the balance of the fighting.[78] "It made us sore that, with such an advantage, we had not accomplished more than the release of our [captured comrades], and the bringing off of a lot of Federals none of whom were high enough in rank to be of any value to us," grumbled a Georgia staff officer.[79]

Figuring out precise numbers and losses for Monroe's Crossroads is difficult, especially since few reports were filed for the late-war action—especially for the Confederate side. Losses on both sides seem to have been under reported. Kilpatrick officially listed nineteen killed (including four officers), sixty-eight wounded, and 103 missing, for a total of 190 from all causes. No report for Colonel Way's dismounted brigade has been located. Colonel George Eliphaz Spencer, leading Kilpatrick's Third Brigade, however, reported eighteen killed, seventy wounded, and 105 missing. When these are added to Kilpatrick's losses, Union casualties look like this: thirty-seven killed, 138 wounded, and

208 missing/captured. No official report for Stetson's 10th Wisconsin Battery has to date surfaced.[80]

Confederate losses are even more problematic. According to the historian of Wheeler's Corps, "1,189 men of Wheeler's command (not including Butler's troops) went into the action, their loss being 12 men killed, 60 wounded and 10 missing; 59 horses killed and 52 wounded." No casualty reports for Butler's Division have been located.[81]

The Federals left several accounts relating to the enemy dead and wounded—occasionally with precise numbers relating to dead Rebels left on the field. According to one Federal, "Their wounded must have been very great. They carried their wounded off the field as they retreated." Major Christopher Cheek, commander of the 5th Kentucky Cavalry, reported that "Thirty-three dead rebels were counted within the limits of my camp after the fight was over, including many officers."[82]

Some Confederates believed their losses could have been much smaller. "It is sad on reflection to know that had we received the proper support, which was so near and yet so far, or if we had not been allowed to remain on the ground so long, our losses would have been scarcely anything," complained one of Butler's South Carolinians.[83] "I have always believed if Wheeler could have crossed the bog," contended Butler, "we could have bagged Kilpatrick's entire command with his Artillery and transportation."[84] Given the surprise involved, it is difficult to disagree with Butler's assessment.

*   *   *

While the Confederates were plundering Kilpatrick's camp during the fighting, General Atkins's Second Brigade broke its miserable bivouac along Chicken Road and headed out to support Colonels Spencer and Way. Colonel William D. Hamilton of the 9th Ohio Cavalry was eating a breakfast of fresh honey and corn when Kilpatrick's adjutant, Maj. Llewellyn G. Estes, dashed up on foot in his shirt sleeves and out of breath to announce that Spencer's brigade "had been attacked before daylight and their headquarters, with their horses and equipment had been captured; that the general and most of the staff had broken for the brush, half dressed, and he had run back to hurry us up." After so many days of hard marching, Atkins recalled that his brigade was "not in very good condition to hurry."[85]

Hearing heavy firing to the north, Atkins and his men rode as quickly as they could. Before long they encountered terrified refugees from Kilpatrick's camp, who reported that "General Kilpatrick with their brigade had been attacked early in the morning, 'routed and badly used up.'"[86] Atkins hastened his brigade toward the sound of the guns. "We were in hopes of a good night's rest but alas we are just ordered to saddle up and we expect the Johnnys upon us every moment," groused a member of the 10th Ohio Cavalry, "so we will get no sleep again tonight unless it be our Long Sleep." Atkins and his men had to struggle across five difficult swamps before reaching Monroe's Crossroads.[87] When they arrived they learned that the fight had ended and that the Rebels had been repulsed. Happy to avoid any chance of suffering the "long sleep," Atkins's men dismounted and fed their horses.[88]

Colonel Jordan and the First Brigade also got an early start that morning. Mounting up at 6 a.m., Jordan and his men took the Plank Road toward Sandy Grove Church. Three hours later Jordan reached Chicken Road, two miles from (and running parallel to) the Plank Road. "During the march I had heard heavy firing," Colonel Jordan reported, "which proved to be an attack by the combined forces of Wheeler and Hampton on the Third Brigade and dismounted men, but before I could join them the action was over and the enemy driven off." Rumors and speculation about Kilpatrick's plight flew up and down the length of Jordan's column.[89]

Understandably, Jordan's men felt a keen sense of urgency. "I heard heavy cannonading about three miles on my left," recalled one of Jordan's Hoosiers, who became separated from the column and so headed toward the sound of the firing. "I halted and listened attentively for a minute," he continued. "The bugle sounded 'charge.' I could hear the clattering noise of small arms and the men yelling as is common in a charge. I knew it was Kilpatrick and Wade Hampton, for they were in close proximity. I put spurs to my horse and arrived just as Kilpatrick recaptured his artillery and opened fire on them."[90] The main body of Jordan's brigade did not arrive at Monroe's Crossroads until nearly 2:00 p.m.[91]

Having marched cross-country, Mitchell's infantry brigade had the shortest distance to travel and reached Kilpatrick about 10:00 a.m., before either Jordan or Atkins arrived. "We marched briskly and in little over an hour reached the scene of the action, but found the enemy had been repulsed with severe loss, and our cavalry in quiet possession of the field," reported Major Robinson of the 121st Ohio Infantry.[92] The amused infantrymen could not help but noticing that Little Kil "looked a little worse for wear, as we saw him without hat, coat, or shoes."[93]

A worried Kilpatrick asked Mitchell to stay until the cavalryman was confident that the situation was under control. Mitchell deployed a skirmish line around the camp, establishing a protective cordon that had been missing the night before.[94] Kilpatrick stood on the porch of the Monroe house "and detailed in his own peculiar style the particulars of being run into the swamps and rallying his men," recalled a soldier of the 98th Ohio Infantry. "We got up the joke that we had come to help Kilpatrick let the rebels go, and it was substantially true, for he was in their rear, and they only wanted him out of their way." The foot soldiers voted to protect Alice in appreciation of her pluck that morning.[95] Mitchell put his men to work burying the dead in shallow mass graves near the Monroe house. Men and horses were often buried together, their

An early 20th century view of one of the several Union mass graves on the Monroe's Crossroads battlefield.

bodies covered with sandy soil. Kilpatrick's surgeons, meanwhile, tended to the wounded.

The arrival of Jordan and Atkins reunited the cavalry division. Kilpatrick ordered the two brigade commanders to deploy in a defensive position while Spencer and Way broke camp and prepared to march. "Lay in camp until 11 AM buried our dead," recorded a Federal Alabaman.[96] The two mounted brigades relieved Mitchell's infantry, which marched to rejoined Morgan's division "on the Fayetteville plank road at the Fourteen-Mile Post," reported Mitchell.[97]

Soon after the battle, 15-year-old Neill S. Blue emerged from the swamp where he had hidden to watch the fighting. The youth explored the battlefield and saw the location of the unmarked Union graves. Young Blue counted nearly forty fresh mounds scattered around Charles Monroe's property. He marked the grave sites for posterity, assuming that relatives might one day want to retrieve the bodies of their loved ones. Most of the Confederate dead were later disinterred and either moved to cemeteries near their homes or to the graveyard at nearby Long Street Presbyterian Church.[98]

A modern photograph of the largest Union mass grave on the battlefield.

Fort Bragg

The Monroe's Crossroads battlefield as it looked in 1924.

After the surgeons had treated the wounded, those unable to ride on horseback were loaded into ambulances. Spencer informed Kilpatrick that his brigade was ready to march. Little Kil mounted a borrowed horse and rode to the head of the division, shouting orders as he went. And so the Federals departed, leaving Charles Monroe's farmstead in shambles.

With the division strung out along the road the Federals headed south. Kilpatrick marched five miles south to Chicken Road and then turned east, where the head of his column caught up to Major General Davis's Fourteenth Army Corps. Word of Kilpatrick's debacle spread quickly through Sherman's army. "Little Kil was caught napping that time, and the boys think it is a good joke," observed an amused foot soldier in the Fifteenth Corps.[99] After hearing what happened that morning to the cavalry, the infantrymen quickly dubbed the battle "Kilpatrick's Shirt-tail Skedaddle," something that infuriated the cavalry commander, who already felt humiliated enough after his near-disaster.

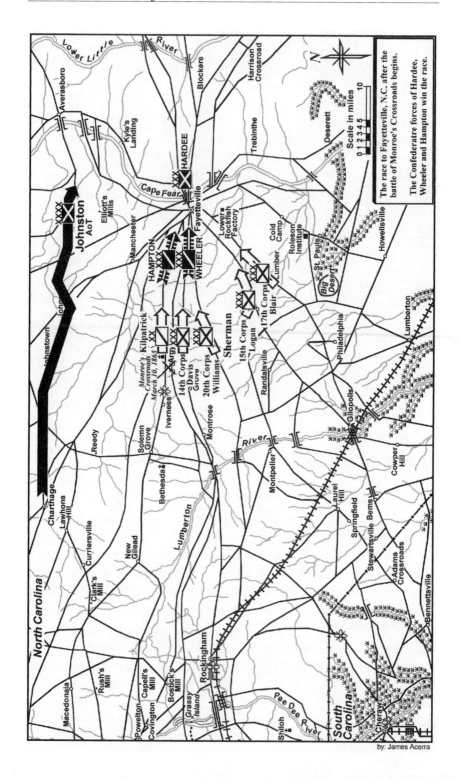

by: James Acerra

"The report is Kilpatrick was surprised before breakfast," chortled an Ohio infantryman.[100] For his part, Kilpatrick vowed revenge on Wade Hampton and his Confederates.

After an eight-mile ride, Kilpatrick ordered his division to cross Little Rockfish Creek and make camp. Small bands of Confederates occasionally dashed up on the column and fired into it, withdrawing before the Federals could respond. The Southerners wounded a few Yankees, including a sergeant in the 8th Indiana Cavalry, who was shot in the leg.[101] Exercising extreme caution, Kilpatrick's troopers threw up hasty wooden breastworks and hunkered down for the night. Little Kil had now united his command and carefully selected a good defensive position that also covered the infantry's route of march. The morning's rude surprise had taught him a bitter lesson. Meanwhile, badly wounded men such as Sgt. John W. Swartz, the heroic artillerist who had helped repulse Butler's attack on the Federal camp, were taken to the nearby home of William Shaw. Swartz and two others died that night and were buried in the yard.

When Hampton and his cavalry rode directly to Fayetteville. "After riding hard all day reached Fayetteville," an exhausted Georgian noted in his diary that night.[102] The weary Southerners presented a sorry sight. "After the excitement was all over we were much amused to discover that, having cowered over the lightwood brands during the night, our faces were blackened with smoke and soot, which the rain had partly smeared and partly streaked, so that we looked like Indians in their war paint," recalled a Georgia staff officer.[103]

Because of the heavy casualties suffered at Monroe's Crossroads, Hampton's column had to move slowly to accommodate the wounded. Many of the more severely wounded were left in houses along the route of march.[104] The sun was setting on March 10 when the Southern horsemen passed through Lt. Gen. William J. Hardee's picket line west of Fayetteville. "Passed through Fayetteville; quite a patriotic town," remarked one of Wheeler's weary horse soldiers. The troopers established their camps and fell to the ground in exhaustion.[105]

Having reached Fayetteville before the Federals, the Confederate cavalry was safe for the moment. "General Hampton in town, enemy reported with whole force within 5 miles of place, which was not fortified & nothing but a rickety bridge over which to cross to the other side," observed an anxious Maj. Gen. Lafayette McLaws, commander of one of

A U.S. Army monument to the horse soldiers who
fought at Monroe's Crossroads.

Hardee's divisions. "Ordered to retire that night, arty and wagons to
move at once, my command to bring up rear of infantry. Hampton's
cavalry the rear of everything else."[106]

The cavalry's lengthy wagon train of wounded rumbled into town.
"It was on this day that a skirmish was fought at Longstreet, twelve miles
from Fayetteville," recalled Fayetteville resident Josephine Bryan
Worth, referring to the fight at Monroe's Crossroads. "Toward the close
of the day the melancholy line of ambulances came in bearing the
wounded, and, to me the still more melancholy file of [Federal] prisoners.
I would have liberated them all if I could. I had not made the acquaintance
of Mr. Sherman's bummers then."[107]

The train of ambulances presented a terrible sight to the women of
Fayetteville, who were unaccustomed to seeing mangled men suffering
from severe battle wounds. "About 9 o'clock they sent for me to come to
the hospital," recalled hospital matron Mrs. James Kyle, "and the
horrible scene I witnessed there I shall never forget. . . . I stayed with [the
wounded] until just before daylight and did all I could to relieve their

wants. Even then I did not hear a single murmur. Such fortitude has no parallel in history."[108]

Once settled in at Fayetteville, Wade Hampton penned an account of the day's actions, which Confederate general-in-chief Robert E. Lee read several days later. "General Hampton attacked General Kilpatrick at daylight this morning and drove him from his camp," Lee reported to Secretary of War John C. Breckinridge, "taking his guns, wagons, many horses, several hundred prisoners, and releasing a great number of our own men who had been captured. The guns and wagons could not be brought off for want of horses."[109]

March 10, 1865 had been a brutal day for Union and Confederate horse soldiers alike. Though none of them could have known it, they waged what proved to be the last large-scale cavalry engagement in the Eastern Theater. While the outcome of the war was not altered by the fight around Charles Monroe's house, the lives of Wade Hampton and Judson Kilpatrick had become forever intertwined because of it.

But it is not the end of their story. More remains to be told of events before their encounter at the Bennett Place just six weeks later.

Chapter 7

The Aftermath

Although he left the Monroe's Crossroads battlefield to Judson Kilpatrick, Wade Hampton achieved his strategic goal. His dawn attack had stopped Kilpatrick and his horse soldiers for an entire day, and Little Kil's command was no longer interposed between Hardee and Hampton. For that day, at least, Fayetteville had been saved for the Confederates. By halting the Federal horsemen Hampton had cleared the all-important road to Fayetteville for the passage of the Confederates, buying sufficient time for Hardee's troops to cross the Cape Fear River in safety.

General Joe Johnston had ordered Hardee to withdraw up the Raleigh Plank Road along the east bank of the Cape Fear, and to remain between Sherman and Goldsboro or Raleigh, depending on where the Federal host was moving. Johnston had also instructed Hardee to burn the bridge across the Cape Fear and to delay the enemy's advance as much as possible without endangering his own command. On the early morning of March 10, while the fighting still raged at Monroe's Crossroads, Hardee deployed his two understrength divisions to defend Fayetteville, but by dawn on March 11 all but his cavalry rearguard had safely pulled out. Because Hampton had cleared the road for him, Hardee was able to withdraw his command, unmolested by Sherman's advance.[1] However, Hardee had to abandon large stocks of military supplies as well as most of the manufacturing equipment and machine tools from the arsenal-armory, although these were probably doomed in any event.[2]

As for Kilpatrick, it was probably a good thing that he had stopped to lick his wounds instead of pressing on toward Fayetteville. Had he challenged Hardee's evacuation of the city he would have found himself caught between two superior enemy forces (Hardee in his front and Hampton in his rear) and well beyond any Federal infantry support.

*   *   *

Wade Hampton slept in a Fayetteville hotel that night and rose early on March 11. His exhausted staff and his Iron Scouts spent the night in a nearby home, leaving Hampton to dine alone with trusted scout Hugh H. Scott. The two men enjoyed a leisurely breakfast at their hotel. Although Hardee's Corps had already crossed the river, the rear guard—consisting of Butler's Division and Wheeler's Corps—had not yet done so. "It was of vital importance that the bridge should be held, until the cavalry could cross," Hampton recalled years later.[3]

Sherman had ordered his left wing commander, Maj. Gen. Henry W. Slocum, "to do all that is possible to secure the [Clarendon] bridge across the Cape Fear River."[4] Accordingly, on the night of March 10 Capt. William H. Duncan, the Army of the Tennessee's chief of scouts, received orders to report to army headquarters with all available mounted men. Duncan led "an organization of great celebrity in the West, made up of the best men of Western regiments," recalled an Ohio officer. "These daring fellows," he continued . . .

> are known as the scouts of the Army of the Tennessee. The organization to which these dauntless heroes belong is uniformed in Confederate clothing, and the men adopt the dialect of the poor people of the South. Being accepted by the inhabitants as straggling rebels, they are entrusted, without question, with the entire stock of information of military movements which they possess. Many of the scouts have even had the audacity to visit the headquarters of the rebel Generals, and in one instance, we remember one of them carried off the officer's monthly return of the strength and equipment of his command.[5]

By all accounts, these daring fellows were the right men to dash into the town and hold it until Sherman's army came up to occupy it in force.

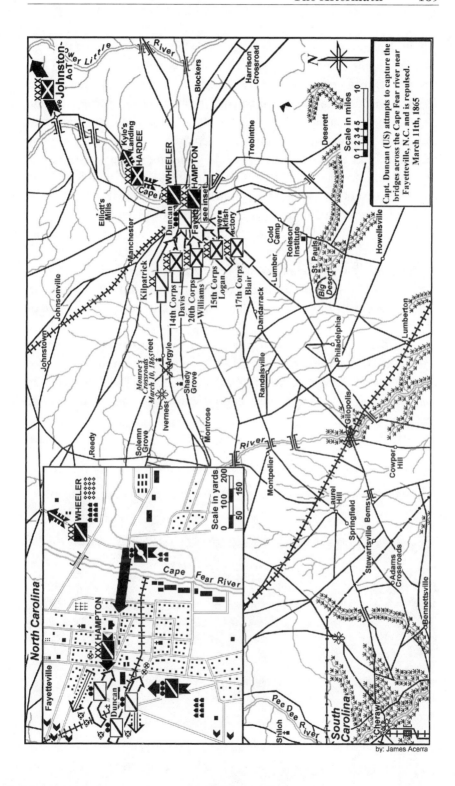

by: James Acerra

With about one hundred men, including his own company of the 10th Illinois Cavalry, and Capt. John L. King's company of the 4th Ohio Cavalry, Duncan prepared to ride.[6] The next morning, Maj. Gen. Oliver O. Howard, commander of Sherman's right wing, instructed Captain Duncan to scout in the direction of Fayetteville. The day was bright and clear, and Duncan and his command departed early. King's company took one road toward the town, while Duncan's troop took another. Duncan and his men passed through a thin picket line unmolested and "did not stop until we were on the main street in Fayetteville, leading to a fine bridge crossing the Cape Fear River at the lowest end of the street."[7] The entrance of Federals into Fayetteville shocked the Confederate defenders, who were unprepared for their sudden appearance.[8] "We charged into town and captured it," recalled one of Duncan's men.[9]

Their meal finished, Scott and Hampton emerged from the hotel in time to hear shots ring out inside the town. Turning toward the sound of the gunfire, they saw some of Wheeler's horsemen retreating toward them, with enemy cavalry hot on their heels. The burly lieutenant general borrowed a horse from a courier. "My saber was in my ambulance as I did not expect to have any use for it that morning," he recalled.[10] Armed only with his pistol, Hampton unsuccessfully tried to rally some of the panicked butternuts.

"General, there are not over ten or fifteen Yankees here," advised Scott. "Give me four or five men and I will whip them right out of town."

Skirmish in Fayetteville, North Carolina.

"You scouts follow me, and I will lead this charge," replied Hampton, whose blood was up as it always was when combat was in the offing.

"We have often read of a warrior's eyes figuratively flashing fire, but it is literally true that on this occasion his eyes emitted sparks of light and his grand personnel claimed the devotion instinctively rendered to the born leader of men," recalled one of Butler's South Carolinians in a poetic flight. "No wonder that, from Manassas to Appomattox, he possessed the faculty of infusing into his followers the inspiration of the God of Battles."[11]

Edward L. Wells, W. H. Bellinger, and William H. Fishburne, three members of Hampton's headquarters escort (the Charleston Light Dragoons, Company K, 4th South Carolina Cavalry) were more than willing to help their general throw the enemy out of Fayetteville. A few of Wheeler's troopers also offered to pitch in.[12] "Charge them!" cried Hampton, and the little band of cavalrymen dashed at the pursuing Yankees with their pistols drawn. "The eight Confederates flung themselves upon the foe, playing a lively instrumental accompaniment with their pistols to the vocal music of a splendid battle-yell," Wells recalled.[13]

The Confederates charged and "had a hand-to-hand fight" with the Yankees, recalled a Federal named Collins.[14] Scott and the dragoons fired their pistols into the faces of their foes, knocking several from their saddles. Hampton himself dropped two enemy troopers and cut down another pair with a saber he had picked up along the way.[15] The brawny South Carolinian had now killed more than a dozen Yankees in personal combat during the war. The rattled Federals withdrew toward the bridge over the Cape Fear and spread out in a thin line of battle, waiting for Hampton to charge them again.

"General, here they are behind us," declared Scott, wheeling about. Duncan had evidently divided his command before attacking and Federals were now approaching from the other end of the street.

"Men, sit still and pick them off one by one as they come down," ordered Hampton.

The Confederate horsemen pulled up and blasted away at the Federals with their pistols, emptying their weapons and several more saddles. "I saw one Yankee jump off his horse and run into a back yard and put his horse in a stable," recalled Scott. "After the fight was over, I went back to this yard and found the fellow in a kitchen behind a safe and I brought him out."[16]

By this time more Confederates had ridden to the sound of the guns. Realizing that discretion was the better part of valor, the Federals broke off the skirmish and withdrew. "They drove us back to the outskirts of the town, and we held it until our infantry came up five hours later," wrote one of Duncan's men.[17] Hampton and his little band rounded up a dozen prisoners, including Captain Duncan, the commander of the expedition. The Federal captain had turned in his saddle and was watching some of Hardee's infantrymen depart "when five of their cavalry dashed up in my front, ordering me to surrender, in language more forcible than moral. They did not give me time to change my mind, so I put the spur to my horse and started after my men." The captain tried to make his way to safety, emptying his revolver in the excitement. He had another, but never got a chance to draw the weapon. An unidentified member of Wheeler's command captured Duncan before he could pull the pistol from its holster. "He had followed me out quite a distance," recalled Duncan. "The road was turnpiked, with board fences on both sides, he threw his horse across the road, had his saber drawn, and called out to me to halt." Duncan's horse was so winded it could not dash away. Left with no alternative, Duncan surrendered.[18] The Confederate trooper took Duncan to Hampton, and "he gave me the sword belt & pistol sheath of the captain, which I still have," recounted Hampton in 1892.[19]

Hampton asked the captain his name and Duncan answered him.

"You belong to General Howard's headquarters?" inquired the South Carolinian.

"Yes, sir."

Hampton and one of his staff officers led Duncan back to Hampton's headquarters at the hotel, where Duncan witnessed Hampton and Hardee engaged in a loud and animated discussion. "I was called up before them and asked if I found any picket on the road over which we came into town," recalled the captain. According to Duncan's account, he told the two generals that there was an infantry picket, but that it did not offer resistance. "If the infantry picket line had rallied and followed us into Fayetteville, they might have prevented us from getting out; but they went to the right, and crossed the Cape Fear River south of town, and joined General Hardee's camp, which was across the river, and not far from the bridge that I had sent Captain King to hold or destroy."[20]

Duncan spent the night at Hampton's headquarters. The next morning, an officer conducted him to where the command's horses were kept. Pointing to one, the officer asked Duncan whether he had ever seen that horse before. "I told him that I thought it was General Kilpatrick's horse (a strawberry roan)." The officer informed Duncan about the infernal surprise that had been sprung on Kilpatrick's camp, and how they had captured almost everything. "It was a nice story for their side," sniffed a suspecting Duncan, "but I was a great admirer of General Kilpatrick, and I thought he might, in telling the story, make it appear better for his side."[21]

The Confederates had also captured noted Union spy David F. Day, the chief scout of the Seventeenth Corps who was caught wearing a Confederate uniform. Day's story is an interesting one. He was only eighteen years old in 1865, and later claimed to be second-in-command of the Fayetteville expedition, during which he had received a saber cut to his foot and had his head grazed by a bullet.[22] Day had enlisted in the 57th Ohio Volunteer Infantry at the tender age of sixteen. A former commander remembered him as "an exceedingly active, courageous, and efficient soldier."[23] In nearly three years of service he had never missed a battle "except the time he was a POW at Andersonville."[24] Day claimed that he was one of the first to escape from the hellish Georgia stockade. He had been wounded in combat four times and taken prisoner three times. At Vicksburg, Day was the first in his unit to volunteer for the "Forlorn Hope" tapped to lead the infamous May 22 assault against the Stockade Redan. Day was wounded severely in the wrist when the rifle-musket he was holding was hit by a round. The teenager used his bayonet to dig into the Confederate works to protect himself from Confederate fire. Once darkness fell, Day safely made his way back to the Union lines. His valor in the Vicksburg Campaign eventually earned him the Medal of Honor. The young man went on to become one of the best known and most successful scouts in Sherman's army.[25]

Day had been captured while wearing a Confederate uniform, and pursuant to the laws of war he could have been summarily hanged without a trial as a spy. However, Day and Duncan escaped that evening while in the hands of reserve troops before Hampton could string up the former soldier. The two scouts eventually made their way back to Sherman's army.[26]

Duncan's task force suffered heavily in the Fayetteville fracas. "Being about 65 strong we yielded up 42 lives and every round of ammunition, the opposing and successful force being Gen. Wade Hampton's command," recounted Day in a post-war application for the Medal of Honor.[27] Hampton's only loss was a faithful steed mortally wounded in the clash.

"A close shave to get out of town," noted Maj. Gen. Lafayette McLaws in his order book. "Hampton had difficulty in crossing his cavalry, had to charge the enemy to effect it."[28] But for Hugh Scott's vigilance Hampton might have been captured. The daring of Duncan's little band impressed Hampton, who later recalled it as "one of the most dashing daring deeds he witnessed during the war."[29]

Young Josephine Bryan Worth enjoyed a birds-eye view of the passage of the Confederate horsemen. "Hampton's cavalry were camped west of the town and had not yet passed through, so close were the contending armies together. After this, for an hour or more we saw no more Yankees and the Confederate cavalry passed by, the horses in ranks and every man with his sabre held up over his shoulder, the noise of their harness and accouterments making a sort of rushing sound almost as soon as they came in sight," she recalled. "After these well-ordered ranks came a more disorderly body of cavalry—Wheeler's I presume—many of them ragged, some of them hatless, and most of them with two or more horses."

Even in the face of impending crisis, Wheeler's men could not pass up the opportunity to do a bit of foraging. According to a local woman, "One of them stopped at our gate and asked for a hat, and about fifty, more or less, stopped to see what kind of hat he would receive. Now, the only masculine headgear about the house was a wheat-straw hat, whole but rather the worse for the wettings it had received. I ran and got that; it was received with shouts of 'New spring hat from Nassau,' 'Ain't it pretty, now,' 'Give it to me,' &c. As the soldier received it he waved it around with three cheers, in which he was joined by all the rest. It is needless to say that I retired in confusion," she concluded demurely.[30]

As the horsemen deployed to cover the river crossing, Wheeler unlimbered some of his horse artillery. "Captain," Hampton instructed the commander of one of the horse batteries, "bring up a section of your battery and give them a few shots." The general was not far from the river on the south side of the Market House located on the town square in the

The Market House in Fayetteville, North Carolina.

center of Fayetteville when a Northern soldier came around the corner and spotted him. The Federal squeezed off a shot that narrowly missed Hampton and lodged in a wooden pillar in front of the Market House. Hampton calmly leveled his pistol at his antagonist and dispatched the man with a single shot. After that bit of cool marksmanship the general spurred his horse and dashed across the bridge to safety.[31]

That afternoon, Federal infantry approached and opened fire on the few Confederates still protecting the span. Wheeler waited until the column had deployed into a line on a front several hundred yards wide, "making a mass of blue which filled the streets from side to side," recalled one of Wheeler's staff officers. "Then he gave the order to fire. I don't know if the missile was a shell or a solid shot . . . It struck the Federal column, ricocheted, and struck again and again. We saw at least three gaps in the blue column where it struck. The column dissolved—all dodging into the houses or side streets for shelter, except those struck by the cannon ball." The amused Confederates chortled at the sight of the scrambling Yankees. "It was too serious a matter to laugh at," recalled George Guild of the consolidated 4th and 8th Tennessee, "but it really was amusing."[32] The gunners limbered up and dashed across the bridge, with Wheeler and his staff following closely in their wake.[33]

As the last of the Confederates forces defending Fayetteville crossed the river, the rearguard torched the bridge. "The Bridge burned beautifully," proclaimed Col. J. Fred Waring, commander of the Jeff Davis Legion. "Mr. Sherman will find use for his pontoons."[34] Once again Kilpatrick had failed Sherman, permitting the Confederates to escape unmolested and burn the bridge behind them. "Perhaps he remembered too well that dark cloudy morning, when, awakened by the reveille of clattering hooves, he sprang on a bare-back horse in shirt and drawers (quite undress parade)," observed Wells.[35]

The Federal cavalry had not marched until nine o'clock that morning. "Getting a late start and giving us plenty of time for breakfast," quipped a member of the 10th Ohio Cavalry. The Yankees rode about eight miles and camped three miles west of Fayetteville.[36] Later that day, the vanguard of Sherman's army group entered the town, followed by Little Kil's division later that afternoon. "We expected to have right smart of a fight at [Fayetteville] but they offered no resistance," recounted an infantryman with the 94th Ohio regiment. "We marched into the town without any trouble."[37]

After the last of the Confederate cavalry had evacuated the town and the Federal infantry had arrived, the mayor of Fayetteville surrendered the place to Col. William E. Strong, a member of Howard's staff. When Maj. Gen. Henry W. Slocum arrived a bit later, the mayor surrendered the town a second time. The United States flag was raised over the Market House, the recent scene of the street fighting. Slocum quickly imposed martial law and the 4,000 residents came under Union control.[38]

"On the 11th of March, after some lively skirmishes, we entered Fayetteville, a river town of much note; here we were delayed sufficient time to have a rest of ten hours, whilst the pontooneers were busily engaged in laying pontoons across Cape Fear River (the bridge being burnt by the retreating army)," recounted a member of the 77th New York State Volunteers. "About sunset, the pontoon-bridge was laid, and crossed by the First Brigade, Second Division, Fourteenth Army Corps," he continued. "Crossing in such haste was not expected by the enemy, for we came across the enemy's pickets about three miles from the bridge. Re-enforcements were continually increasing the force ahead of us, so that they became very stubborn and tried to check our advance; although

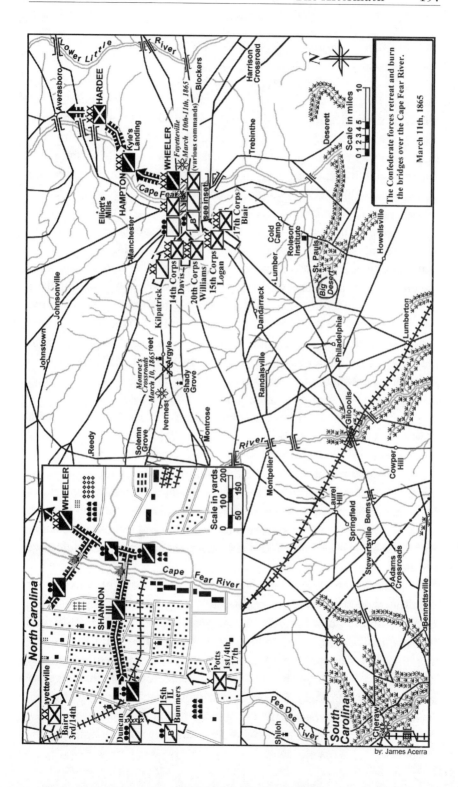

The Confederate forces retreat and burn the bridges over the Cape Fear River.

March 11th, 1865

by: James Acerra

the roads were in a miserable condition (through rain), we moved ahead with but slight trouble from the enemy."[39]

A few hours after Sherman secured the town, the Federal tug *Davidson* reached Fayetteville after steaming upriver from Wilmington. Sherman's line of communications was now secure.[40] "Some say that we are going to stop here," commented trooper W. W. Pritchard. "I think not. I have an idea that we will leave the rebels go now and go to Wilmington to recuperate."[41] Pritchard was engaging in some wishful thinking. The ragged and exhausted horses and men needed rest, even if it meant allowing the Confederates to escape once more.

Although Kilpatrick did not know it, Federal scouts nearly avenged his "shirt-tail skedaddle." When Duncan's men charged into Fayetteville that morning, General Matthew Butler and Lt. E. Thornton Tayloe were asleep. The two men were naked, with a laundress outside scrubbing their uniforms and undergarments. A courier burst into their room shouting, "The Yankees! The Yankees!" The two men grabbed their only available clothing—boots, overcoats, and hats—and dashed outside, mounted their horses, and galloped off.[42] In these closing days of the war, Butler was having his share of close shaves. The day after this narrow escape, his horse was shot out from under him.[43]

Major General Slocum, the commander of Sherman's Left Wing (Army of Georgia), occupied the town and the Federals did not clear Fayetteville until March 15.[44] "We have had a hard time for the last six weeks," noted a member of the 92nd Illinois Mounted Infantry, "and now we will have 2 or 3 days to rest then forward again."[45] While Kilpatrick's horsemen appreciated the opportunity to rest and refit after their travails, that pause also meant that Hardee's foot soldiers and Hampton's cavalry would have an opportunity to rest and select and prepare strong defensive positions.

"Think we will leave tomorrow, we think now of making for Goldsboro on the Neuse River, but it is all guess-work," predicted a Buckeye on the 14th of March.[46] Another speculated the Federals would "move on toward Goldsboro where it is understood we will end this long and tiresome campaign."[47] Although they looked forward to finally reaching Goldsboro, the horsemen knew what sort of a challenge lay ahead of them. "From here I think we will go to Goldsborough at which place it is said the Rebs will make a stand, but as at least places have been mentioned already where we would be stopped without fail and the enemy usually left just before we got there," recalled one Yankee. "I begin to doubt whether they will attempt to oppose Sherman's march."[48]

Local citizens told the Federal cavalry that Hampton had stripped his Monroe's Crossroads prisoners of nearly all of their clothing before parading them through the town naked, subjecting them to the catcalls and jeers of the local populace. This infuriated Kilpatrick, who retaliated in kind two days later by showing off some of his prisoners in like fashion.[49]

Using the respite to pen a report of the fighting at Monroe's Crossroads, Kilpatrick claimed an outright victory. "I am now within two miles of the road mentioned," he wrote, "and as soon as my command has fed will move to intercept that portion which has not yet passed. I have written you in detail, that you may fully know all that has taken place. . . . We have marched over the worst roads I ever saw, and have had scarcely forage for the past two days, Hardee having taken nearly everything in the country. My command very much needs rest."[50]

As for Alice, she took her leave of Little Kil and headed for Northern parts unknown once the Union cavalry reached Fayetteville. Kilpatrick would have to find someone else to share his bed for the rest of the campaign.[51]

Although he was less than pleased with Kilpatrick's performance, and particularly with his lack of vigilance, Sherman nevertheless responded favorably to his account of the March 10 fight. "I have just received your report and read it with great satisfaction. I feared it was worse, as the enemy claims from 200 to 400 prisoners, which were conducted through Fayetteville. You may rest a couple of days, and then be ready to cross the river." Sherman gave his cavalry chieftain further instructions. "The enemy have sent a good deal of ordnance up toward the coal mines on the railroad. I would like to have it and the cars and locomotives destroyed, but can hardly spare time. We will lay the pontoons tomorrow and cross Monday."[52]

*　*　*

Joe Johnston realized his plight in North Carolina was a desperate one. By March 11 he had established his headquarters at Raleigh. In a lengthy letter to Robert E. Lee, Johnston outlined the disposition of his scattered forces and indicated his course of action. He estimated

Sherman's army at 45,000 strong (it was closer to 60,000). "Under such circumstances I will not give battle to Sherman's united army unless your situation may require such a course; but will if I can find it divided. Of this please advise me. I need not say that your opinions will have a control equal to that of your official authority."

Johnston was keenly aware that if Sherman and Schofield (who was moving in from the coast) merged their armies, Johnston would be unable to prevent them from marching into Virginia. "In that event . . . you will meet us at the southern edge of Virginia to give battle. Would it be practicable, instead, to hold one of the inner lines of Richmond with one part of your army, and meet Sherman with the other, returning to Richmond after fighting?" asked Johnston of Lee. The chances of linking up with Lee's army were slim and Johnston knew it, but he was determined to hang on as long as this slender hope remained.[53]

At Fayetteville, meanwhile, Sherman waited for supplies to come up the Cape Fear from Wilmington. He spent much of March 12 writing letters. "We reached this place yesterday at noon," Sherman informed Grant. "Hardee as usual retreating across the Cape Fear burning his Bridge, but our pontoons will be up today and with as little delay as possible I will be after him towards Goldsboro. Joe Johnston may try to interpose between me here and Schofield about Newbern," he concluded, "but I think he will not try that but concentrate his scattered armies at Raleigh, and I will go straight at him as soon as I get my men reclothed and our wagons reloaded."[54]

Sherman expanded on this theme in a letter to his wife. "Johnston is restored to Supreme Command and will unite the forces hitherto scattered and fight me about Raleigh or Goldsboro. Lee may reinforce him from Richmond, but if he attempts that Grant will pitch in." He concluded, "I can whip Joe Johnston unless his men fight better than they have since I left Savannah." He also wrote to Secretary of War Stanton, telling him that he had ordered the Fayetteville arsenal-armory destroyed.[55]

Sherman was true to his word. After battering down the buildings, the 1st Michigan Engineers burned the debris, destroying a former U. S. Arsenal (now an armory) that had been churning out weapons for the Confederacy since early in the war. The weapon-making machinery was smashed and the magazine was blown up.[56] "The buildings connected with [the armory] were very fine," recounted a horse soldier of the 9th

Michigan Cavalry, "and its destruction will be quite a loss to the Confederacy."[57] Only a few other structures—mostly factories and flour mills—were destroyed, but private homes were left largely unmolested. Unlike during his march across South Carolina, Sherman had chosen to respect the property rights of North Carolina civilians. Considering that the Confederates had skirmished in the streets of Fayetteville, the restraint shown by Sherman and his army was remarkable.[58]

The Northern horse soldiers enjoyed their respite, but they remained uncertain as to the future. "I suppose we will remain here for a few days, when we will march. It is supposed for Raleigh the Capital," recounted Colonel Jordan in a letter to his wife on March 12. "Before leaving here we expect to be all armed with Spencer rifles—7 shooters, and can walk over the Johnnies with ease." Jordan's speculation about receiving new weapons proved correct.[59]

While awaiting orders to move out, Kilpatrick swallowed his pride and penned a note to his arch rival, Wade Hampton, requesting the return of his beloved Spot. "Please give me back my horse," Little Kil pleaded. Hampton had a good chuckle over the missive. "[O]ut of the goodness of his heart, let the man have the horse, to which he was so much attached," wrote Hampton.[60] Kilpatrick later rode "Spot" to the meeting at Bennett Place for his final encounter with Hampton.

Averasboro

After a four-day respite Sherman and his army departed early on March 15. "Moved out before daylight to cross Cape Fear River at Fayetteville," wrote one of Atkins's Hoosiers.[61] The army was headed for Averasboro, where Hardee and Hampton had taken up a strong defensive position astride the Raleigh Plank Road on a narrow finger of land between the Cape Fear and Black rivers. Hardee had chosen the position wisely. Its narrow front would allow him to bring his entire force to bear, but the front was so narrow that it would cramp the superior enemy forces. Hardee right flank was anchored on the steep bank of the Cape Fear River and his left on the swampy bank of Black Creek. His deployment took superb advantage of the many creeks and swamps meandering through the area.[62]

Scrapping almost daily (as they had since January), the opposing cavalry forces skirmished nearly every step of the way to Averasboro.[63]

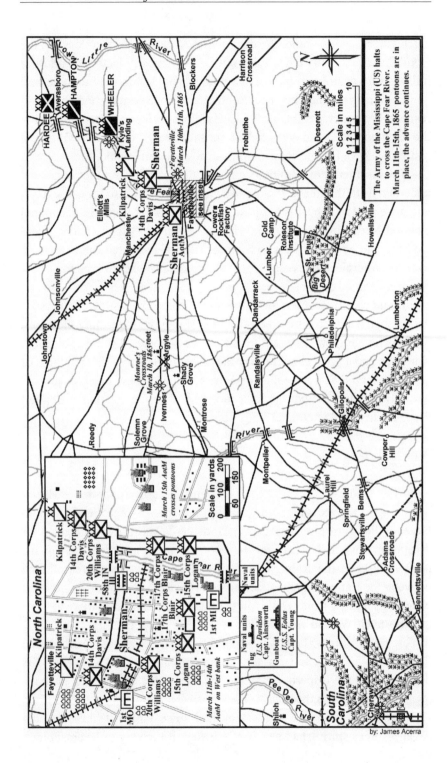

by: James Acerra

On March 15, a 9th Pennsylvania horse soldier noted in his diary, "We left Fayetteville at day lite and crossed the Kapefear river and marched 15 miles and drove the rebels all day, then the 2 brigade charged their breastworks and went 3 miles from their."[64] The blueclad horse soldiers had a trying time of it. "The enemy fought like desperados all day, only drove them three miles during the day," remembered one exhausted Hoosier.[65]

Kilpatrick's cavalry had caught up to the rear of Hardee's column. Colonel Alfred Rhett commanded a brigade of South Carolina infantry in Brig. Gen. William Taliaferro's Division. Rhett threw out skirmishers who promptly engaged the dismounted troopers of the 9th Michigan Cavalry. In a seesaw exchange lasting much of that rainy afternoon, the Michiganders shoved back Rhett's outnumbered advance line of pickets.

While the skirmishers battled, Captain Northrop and three of his Federal scouts, Richard Dowling, William Pitts, and Nelson Minot of the 9th Michigan Cavalry, forayed out behind the enemy lines to reconnoiter, hoping that they could find a way to outflank Hardee's strong position. When the probing Federals discovered that the enemy's skirmish line did not extend all the way to the Cape Fear River, they passed around that flank into the enemy rear. Within a few minutes they spotted Colonel Rhett's main line of battle. Through the rain and fog they could make out several ranking Confederate commanders surrounded by staffers just 100 yards distant. One of the scouts raised his Spencer carbine, but Northrop pushed the gun barrel down. The last thing Northrop wanted to do was alert the Confederates to his presence and focus attention on the unattended right flank.[66]

The men had discovered what they had hoped to find—a way to avoid a direct attack. Worried about being captured by Wheeler's men, Northrop wheeled around and was heading back when he encountered two approaching horsemen. "Where are Gens. Hampton and Taliaferro?" one of them inquired.

Delighted that the two Confederates had not recognized him as a Northern officer, Northrop responded, "They are right back here a short distance on the road." As the two officers rode by Northrop added, "You will have to come with us."

"Do you know who you are talking to?" inquired one of the Southerners. "I am Colonel Rhett." The Southern officer reached for his revolver, but before he could squeeze off a shot one of Northrop's men

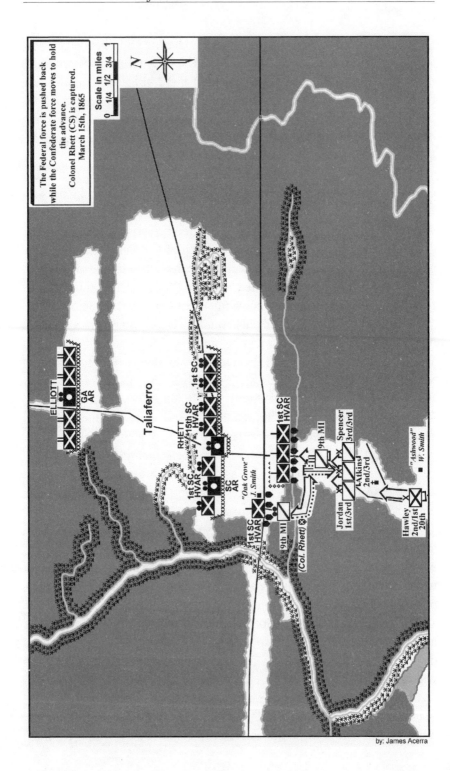

The Federal force is pushed back while the Confederate force moves to hold the advance.
Colonel Rhett (CS) is captured.
March 15th, 1865

Scale in miles
0   1/4   1/2   3/4   1

N

ELLIOTT

GA AR

Taliaferro

RHETT

15th SC HVAR

1st SC

1st SC HVAR

SC AR

"Oak Grove" J. Smith

1st SC HVAR

9th MI

(Col. Rhett)

1st SC HVAR

9th MI

Spencer 3rd/3rd

Atkins 2nd/3rd

Jordan 1st/3rd

"Ashwood" W. Smith

Hawley 2nd/1st 20th

by: James Acerra

pressed the muzzle of his Spencer carbine against Rhett's head. "Well, this is cool," declared the South Carolinian as he dropped his pistol.

Northrop and his little band eluded Wheeler's patrols and brought their prisoners into Kilpatrick's camp. "Hello, Northrop," said the division commander. "What troops are these we are fighting?"

"Taliaferro's Division . . . from Charleston," responded the intrepid young captain. "I have one of the brigade commanders with me."

Thunderstruck, Kilpatrick responded, "The hell you have!"

Northrop confirmed his quarry's identity. "I introduced him to Col. Alfred Rhett," he recalled. With evident delight, Kilpatrick interviewed his new guest.

When Rhett declared that he had been taken in by a "Damned Yankee trick," Kilpatrick snickered. Rhett made quite an impression on the Federals. "Col. Rhett was the best dressed Confederate officer I had ever seen, with patent leather boots reaching to his hips, but was sullen and uncommunicative," declared an eyewitness.[67]

Rhett remained defiant, declaring that "50,000 fresh men [are] ready and waiting to fight."

Kilpatrick shot back, "Yes, and if that is true we will have to hunt the swamps to find the damned cowards." With that, the Yankee sent Rhett to Sherman's headquarters, where the unhappy colonel had an audience with the army commander.[68]

After regaling Sherman with tales of hunting down his own deserters in the swamps, Rhett was returned to Kilpatrick's care the following day. General Atkins, who had found Rhett's appearance so impressive the day before, noted that Rhett was "brought into the room, covered with mud, a sorry-looking picture."[69] When Captain Duncan made his way back to cavalry headquarters later that day, Little Kil learned that after Duncan was captured at Fayetteville on March 11, the Confederates had taken his uniform and accouterments. This infuriated the Federal cavalry commander and he returned the favor by authorizing his men to treat Rhett in a similar fashion. The colonel was compelled to exchange his handsome cavalry boots for a pair of worn, ill-fitting, muddy brogans, before being forced to hobble along on foot with the other Confederate prisoners.[70] "[Rhett] was a dude in style and richly deserved this punishment for his treatment of us," wrote a satisfied Duncan.[71]

The real fighting at Averasboro took place on March 16, when Hardee checked Sherman in a day-long delaying action. The discovery of

Hardee's unprotected right next to the Cape Fear River allowed Sherman's infantry to eventually flank the position and drive away Hardee's dogged first line of battle. Additional fighting prompted Hardee to retire from the field toward Smithfield. Kilpatrick's horse soldiers had opened the battle by attacking the enemy's infantry.

"This action fully demonstrates the fact that Federal cavalry, when properly handled and led by brave, determined officers, are fully equal to rebel infantry," proclaimed Colonel Jordan in his after-action report.[72] Jordan's brigade suffered heavy casualties, especially among the 9th Pennsylvania and 8th Indiana; Jordan received a brevet to brigadier general of volunteers for his handling of his brigade in the heavy fighting.[73]

The fighting did not improve the relationship between Sherman and Little Kil, however. Sherman lost what little respect he may have had for Kilpatrick when the cavalryman displayed what the army commander took for incompetence.

It began when Sherman said, "General Kilpatrick, I want you to move your cavalry to the left and develop the enemy's line."

"How do you propose that I shall do it?" asked the cavalryman.

Astounded by Kilpatrick's response, Sherman shook his head and replied, "Move your men to the left and engage the enemy. Develop their line—make a damn big time—you know how to do it, you know how to do it."

Kilpatrick moved out to obey the order, deploying Spencer's brigade on the left flank of the Federal infantry. It was the last time Little Kil's troopers would play a significant role in any Civil War battle.[74]

As Kilpatrick tangled with Hardee, Sherman's infantry deployed and took over the fight. After a full day of hard fighting the Federals eventually drove Hardee's men from two defensive lines, but were unable to force them from a third. When the combat ended Hardee withdrew unmolested after dark. With the road clear, Sherman and his left wing turned east and headed for Goldsboro.[75] Kilpatrick did a poor job reconnoitering and providing intelligence, incorrectly reporting to Sherman that Hardee was retreating on Smithfield and that Johnston was concentrating his army at Raleigh.[76] Sherman proceeded blithely on.

Bentonville

The opportunity for Joe Johnston to strike Sherman a powerful blow finally arrived. Johnston had formed his so-called Army of the South from essentially four thinned sources: Hardee's infantry corps, remnants of the Army of Tennessee, Robert Hoke's Division, and Hampton's cavalry. Hoke's men, under the command of Braxton Bragg, had been obstructing Schofield's Twenty-Third Corps from the vicinity of Wilmington inland to Smithfield, where Hoke's Division arrived the day before the fighting at Averasboro. The paltry remains of the Army of Tennessee was also gathering there, with more men arriving daily after a long trip from Mississippi. Driven from Averasboro, Hardee's command was also moving to Smithfield. Hampton's cavalry, meanwhile, was divided to shadow the two main columns of Sherman's army.

On March 17, Kilpatrick, supported by a Union infantry division, pressed after Hardee in an effort to convince Johnston that Sherman was moving toward Raleigh in force. His Left Wing, however, turned sharply east and drove toward Goldsboro. Hampton shadowed this wing on the Goldsboro Road and sent a message to Johnston that night: "I think the enemy is moving on Goldsborough." The cavalry leader, who made his headquarters in the Cole house at the junction of the Goldsboro and Smithfield roads, about two miles south of Bentonville, promised Johnston he would remain between Sherman's vanguard, Smithfield, and Goldsboro "until the very last moment." When Johnston asked Hampton for more specific information about Sherman's disposition, Hampton replied with exactly the information "Old Joe" needed, as well as a bold and brilliant idea: coalesce the army near Bentonville while his horsemen disputed the advance of the Federal Left Wing, which was many miles from the Right Wing, roll it up, and destroy it.[77]

On March 19 Johnston arranged his army in a giant sickle formation, with his left and center blocking the Goldsboro Road and his right drawn back to strike a mighty blow. The move caught the marching Federals off-guard—just as Johnston and Hampton hoped it would. So did the the amount of fight left in the Confederates, who fought one of the most aggressive and spirited actions of the war.

Johnston nearly defeated Sherman in detail in a battle that would officially span three days, though the major fighting was conducted on March 19. At one point, General Morgan's Fourteenth Corps infantry division was almost surrounded and had to fight first to the front and then to the rear. Ultimately, command confusion, exhaustion, and numbers began to tell. By evening Johnston had been thrown back and darkness put an end to the fighting. There was less fighting on the following two days, even though Sherman had Johnston's army nearly trapped with a flooded creek behind in his rear. Sherman, however, failed to press for the kill and Johnston wiggled free.

The battle included many interesting elements, including two last grand charges. The gallant infantry of the Army of Tennessee made its last assault of the war at Bentonville. So did Hampton's cavalry, which blunted an attack by Sherman's infantry. His dogged horsemen also repulsed Sherman's tepid pursuit, allowing Johnston's army to slip away yet again.[78] "I have been on the 'go' all the time, and we have had hard work with some hard fighting," recounted a weary Hampton a few days later, describing the battle at Bentonville. "We have injured Sherman a good deal, so that he cannot boast of getting through free. I have captured almost 2000 of his rascals and killed many others."[79]

Bentonville was the last major battle of the Carolinas Campaign, but Kilpatrick's horsemen did not participate in the fighting. Instead, they built barricades and guarded Sherman's left flank against the possibility of Hampton's cavalry attempting mischief in the Federal rear. "We remained in our position till one o clock pm and our brigade advanced 2 miles and built barricades and encamped and the third brigade took our position," reported Cornelius Baker of the 9th Pennsylvania Cavalry on the 19th. The next day he observed, "Shots with the artilary was exchange all day. Our hole line advanced one mile this eavning and had a small skirmish. We are 21 miles from Goaldsborough."[80]

While the fighting raged to the northeast at Bentonville, local blacks ventured out onto the battlefield at Monroe's Crossroads. They found the body of an unburied Confederate soldier lying on the mossy bank of Persimmon Branch. Part of a tent made up his bed, and a collapsible cup lay next to him. His right hand was across his chest, while his left hand rested on the ground by his side. They found a small Bible and a furlough in his breast pocket that bore the name of "William F. Sewell," a private with the 5th Georgia Cavalry. His large black horse, still saddled and carrying all of his accouterments, grazed nearby. Sewell was laid to rest at Longstreet Church a few miles east of Charles Monroe's ravaged farmstead, together with thirty other Confederates killed on March 10. A small marble shaft inscribed "Confederate Soldiers" stands vigil over their graves.[81]

*   *   *

Although the last major battle of the war had been fought in that theater, none of the participants knew it. As far as they were concerned, another battle was always a possibility. Sherman was more than twenty miles from the crucial railroad junction at Goldsboro, and Joe Johnston's small army had plenty of fight left. The two armies continued jockeying for position, and the daily clashes of the opposing cavalry dragged on.

On April 2, Brig. Gen. Charles J. Paine's Division of Alfred Terry's Provisional Corps was attacked by Confederate cavalry and Hampton saw an opportunity for vengeance upon his hated adversary—Sherman. The burning of his beloved estates and the city of Columbia, and the fact that Sherman had publicly and falsely blamed him for it, had raised Hampton to a state of blind fury. He summoned Iron Scout George Shadburne to his headquarters and informed him that "he wanted Sherman" and that Shadburne "must get him for him." Hampton gave Shadburne permission to take as many men as he thought he needed. The scout selected thirty veterans and set off to try his chances.

Shadburne and his command fought their way through one of Kilpatrick's patrols and headed toward Sherman's wagon train. When Shadburne spotted a Federal staff officer, he dashed at him and killed the man. The Confederate took the man's hat and horse and joined the Northern column. He never found the opportunity to nab Sherman, but Shadburne and his intrepid band did capture 100 wagons and about 400 mules and bring them safely into Hampton's lines.[82]

Judson Kilpatrick, meanwhile, was still livid about the indignities visited upon him at Monroe's Crossroads. He was determined to repay the Confederates for his humiliation. The April 9, 1865 surrender of Robert E. Lee's Army of Northern Virginia at Appomattox Court House deprived him of an opportunity to even the score. Lee's surrender convinced Johnston there was no viable reason to prolong the war. Four days later on April 13, Johnston handed Wade Hampton a dispatch to deliver to Sherman under a flag of truce. Hampton didn't know it, but the dispatch asked Sherman for an interview to discuss terms of surrender. Hampton selected Capt. Rawlins Lowndes of his headquarters staff to deliver the message. Lowndes handed off the communication to Kilpatrick, and the cavalry commander forwarded it to Sherman. While awaiting Sherman's response, Lowndes spent most of the day discussing the war with Little Kil and his staff. "They talked about various things, quite amicably, of course, but after awhile the conversation fell upon military matters, and some of them were disposed to chaff Lowndes very much," explained a Confederate veteran who wrote about cavalry matters after the war.

Kilpatrick freely expressed his displeasure at being surprised at Monroe's Crossroads. He even suggested that, had his men been ready to fight, a more favorable outcome would have resulted.

"Well, General," responded Lowndes, who remained unconvinced that the Confederacy had been defeated, "I will make you the following proposition, and I will pledge myself that General Hampton will carry it out in every respect. You, with your staff, take fifteen hundred men, and General Hampton, with his staff, will meet you with a thousand men, all to be armed with the saber alone. The two parties will be drawn up mounted in regimental formations, in opposition to each other, and at a signal to be agreed upon will charge. That will settle the question which are the best men."

Kilpatrick thanked the captain for his idea and indicated that he would consider it. Sherman's response arrived soon thereafter and Lowndes rode off while Kilpatrick stewed.[83] He never got the chance to find out whether his men could best the combined forces of Hampton and Wheeler.

After Sherman's and Johnston's efforts to negotiate a final peace— and not just the surrender of Johnston's army—failed, the Confederates received the same generous terms extended to Lee by Grant. Under these terms, Johnston surrendered to Sherman at the Bennett Place on April 26, 1865. It was on April 17, while negotiations were taking place during the first conference, that Hampton and Kilpatrick nearly came to blows. The pair were ardent enemies, and would despise one another for many years.

Although Johnston surrendered his army at Bennett Place, Hampton vowed to fight on. He proposed to take his cavalry across the Mississippi River and join the Confederate Trans-Mississippi Theater forces. Hampton rode off to find Jefferson Davis, and for several days was away from his troopers, who had no idea where their leader had gone. After consulting with Davis Hampton changed his mind and returned to his command near Hillsborough. He had been gone for three days.

Private J. M. Thomasson served in Company K, 7th Confederate Cavalry, Wheeler's Corps. He watched as Hampton and his staff galloped up. "The General was on his horse—brave and majestic as ever, though the tears were streaming down his cheeks," remembered Thomasson. Removing his hat, Hampton gave an impromptu farewell speech to his dumbstruck troopers. "I have been riding three days and nights trying to get you out of here. But you know there is a higher authority than I am. I never knew until this morning that we were surrendered. I do not know on what terms we were surrendered," he declared. "I advise you to go to Greensboro with [Colonel] Wright and you will find out all about it. I advise you to go home by companies as much as possible. Do not scatter about. I hope you will get home to your families safely and may God be with you."

The burly South Carolinian remained defiant in spite of the gloom cast by the news of the surrender. Certainly he had not lost his fighting spirit. He continued addressing his men:

> There is a day coming when we will meet and fight again. Those that deserted and ran to the woods will come up and fight with us. I ask today if there is one man, or five men, or 50 men who will go with me. I mean single men, not men with families. I will ride by their side and will fight as long as there is a drop of blood in my veins. I will say one thing for this brigade: I never ordered you to dismount from your horses and to take your arms to a trial but you did it. I never ordered you to draw sabers and charge the enemy but you went.

The horsemen were stunned into silence. The war was over? All they could do was watch as Hampton bowed and rode off. "You could have heard a pin drop while he spoke. It was a sad occasion for all of us, but we felt a thrill of pride in our fearless general," recalled Thomasson.[84] Luckily for everyone concerned, Wade Hampton changed his mind about surrendering and wisely laid down his arms. His war, too, was over.[85]

*   *   *

After receiving their paroles, Hampton's horse soldiers started for home. Edward L. Wells, formerly of the Charleston Light Dragoons, headed home to South Carolina. His route led him past Charles Monroe's farm, the scene of the savage fight of March 10. The house had been abandoned. "It was unoccupied by any living thing; the windows were without sashes, the front door broken from its hinges, and all fences and out buildings had disappeared," recalled the cavalryman. Wells walked around the grounds, reliving the horrors of that March morning. Skeletal remains of dead men and animals lay scattered about the property. "The human remains had been interred, but rain and wind, assisted probably by animals, had in many instances partially removed from them the earth, so that the fleshless faces peered up at one, and bony hands stretched forth as if to beckon. The effect was heightened by the faint moonlight," continued Wells. "It was an uncanny place, and the least superstitious would have been likely to have experienced some strange feelings there. The skeleton hands seemed, then, as I said, to beckon." Wells wondered if the upraised hands were not beckoning him back to the late Confederacy that he and his fellow horsemen had served so faithfully.[86]

Joe Wheeler refused to surrender. He bade farewell to most of his command, asked for a few unmarried volunteers to join him, and rode off to serve as part of the escort for Confederate President Jefferson Davis, who had fled Richmond in early April and was trying to reach the Trans-Mississippi Theater.

The North was in a frenzy over the assassination of Abraham Lincoln, and many blamed Davis for that heinous act. Davis was the most wanted man in America, and Federals throughout the South searched for him. Davis, several of his cabinet officers, and his small cavalry escort fled south, evading the large force of Union cavalry assigned to bring the Confederate party to bay.

When Wheeler reached Yorkville, South Carolina in May 1865, he called upon Hampton. "I was shocked at the appearance of my fellow-officer," he wrote. "He was harassed in mind and worn in body; and the story of his march from Greensboro made it plain to us all how sadly our fortunes had fallen."[87] Wheeler eventually surrendered and was imprisoned at Fort Delaware until June 8, 1865, when Secretary of War Stanton ordered he be released from confinement and paroled under the terms of Joe Johnston's surrender agreement[88] Fighting Joe Wheeler was simply Joe Wheeler once more.

The long bitter war of attrition was over. After four years of desperate struggle, the butcher's bill had been paid in full.

Chapter 8

A Critical Assessment

L
ike so many battles, Monroe's Crossroads is fascinating on several levels. The combat clearly demonstrates the power of a well-planned surprise attack, while simultaneously showing the consequences of losing command and control. It also illustrates how unfamiliarity with terrain can cause even the best-planned assault to stumble and ultimately fail. The critical impact the terrain had on the outcome of the fight offers an excellent case study that should not be overlooked. Monroe's Crossroads also offers us a good example of a commander who suffered a tactical defeat, and yet achieved a strategic victory. How a well-planned and well-executed limited objective attack can have far-reaching implications beyond the battlefield itself. Finally, this battle provides an outstanding study of the ingenuity, courage, and intrepidity of the American soldier, irrespective of uniform color. Because of these levels and complexities, there will always be fundamental disagreement as to who got the best of whom in the Battle of Monroe's Crossroads.

By every traditional measure of such things, Wade Hampton lost the battle. Still, he stopped Kilpatrick and kept the road to Fayetteville clear for General Hardee's infantry to use[1] In the Civil War, victories were usually measured by who held the battlefield at the end of the day. At Monroe's Crossroads, the Federals were still occupying the field at the conclusion of the fighting. Kilpatrick had recaptured his headquarters, his field pieces, and his wagons. Hampton had intended to seize Kilpatrick's camp and headquarters, and while he captured them with the initial charges, he was unable to hold them. Kilpatrick reassembled his command, repulsed further charges, recaptured his headquarters, and convinced the enemy by his stubborn defense that further fighting was futile. "This is one of the most remarkable instances in which a partial surprise and defeat, by skill and bravery were turned into a most splendid victory," proclaimed a 9th Pennsylvania cavalryman.[2] By all the traditional measures of the day, Kilpatrick won a tactical victory in the savage fighting at Monroe's Crossroads.

"It is not remarkable that an assault like this was partially successful, when the Rebels are familiar with every foot of the ground, and we strangers in the country," noted one of Sherman's staff officers, though he was wrong about the Rebels' knowledge of the terrain. "But it is the highest honor to our brave men that they so gallantly regained what was lost, and that in the face of thrice their own numbers. The fight cost us fifteen men killed and thirty wounded; but defeat was bravely turned into victory."[3] While this assessment understates the extent of Kilpatrick's losses at Monroe's Crossroads, the conclusion is well-taken.

The victory had been dearly purchased. Kilpatrick admitted to nineteen killed, seventy wounded, and 103 missing, a total of 192 casualties.[4] In reality Little Kil understated his losses, which were probably closer to 250 or more.[5] Because of the shoddy record-keeping that plagued the Confederates at the close of the war, it is impossible to determine precisely the Southern losses at Monroe's Crossroads. One of Wheeler's men, in a letter published in his hometown newspaper, stated that he had it on very good authority that Wheeler's corps had suffered 94 casualties.[6] "The enemy left in our camp upward of 80 killed, including many officers, and a large number of men wounded," claimed Kilpatrick. "We captured 30 prisoners and 150 horses with their equipments."[7] By 1865, the battered Rebel cavalry could ill-afford the heavy losses they incurred at Monroe's Crossroads.

At the same time, the "infernal surprise" unleashed on the Union cavalry camp froze Kilpatrick in place all day on March 10. Kilpatrick was forced to concentrate his scattered brigades to support Spencer's and Way's battered commands, and it also meant that Mitchell's infantry brigade, deprived of cavalry cover, had to stop and wait for mounted support. All of this permitted Hardee's infantry, followed by Hampton's cavalry, with an easy passage to Fayetteville. They were able to cross the Cape Fear River bridge and destroy it at their leisure before the main body of the Federal army arrived. The strategic ramifications, however, were even more dramatic than an easy march to Fayetteville. The cushion Hampton created permitted Hardee and Johnston to select the time and place to coalesce the army and turn on Sherman in an effort to defeat his larger army in detail, first at Averasboro on March 16 and again at Bentonville three days later. By blocking Kilpatrick for a full day, Hampton bought Joe Johnston the time he needed to launch his own surprise upon Sherman's "army group."

Conversely, Judson Kilpatrick was the beneficiary of good fortune that morning. Colonel Spencer had chosen a poor location for his camp site, which was both difficult to defend and did not provide advantageous ground for rallying troops. Kilpatrick compounded Spencer's error by failing to improve the situation. Rather, he made matters worse by failing to deploy an adequate picket screen, enabling Hampton and Wheeler to steal up on the Federal camp undetected. Kilpatrick's men were caught off guard when the Confederates unleashed their surprise attack and suffered heavily as a consequence. Only Kilpatrick's quick rally of his scattered men and their determined fight to retake their camp, coupled with unexpected terrain difficulties for the Rebels, saved his command from disaster.

Monroe's Crossroads exemplifies the paradox that was Judson Kilpatrick. On the one hand, his negligence made possible the surprise of his camp. Had Kilpatrick picketed the approaches to the camp in accordance with sound principles, it is unlikely Hampton and Wheeler could have achieved much surprise at all. This lack of concern for the safety and welfare of his command provides ample evidence of the appropriateness of his *nom-de-guerre*—"Kill-Cavalry." Kilpatrick deserves no credit for leaving the defenseless Alice to her own devices. Only her pluck—and possibly some assistance from Spencer and Way— saved her from capture.

Kilpatrick's conduct that morning well illustrates that Sherman's lack of faith in his cavalry chief (and his firm belief that Kilpatrick was "a hell of damned fool") was well founded. "Hear that Hampton whipped Kilpatrick splendidly," observed an Illinois infantry captain. "Don't think that is any credit to him."[8] Indeed it was not, and everyone in Sherman's army knew it. A few days after the battle, the chief engineer of the Twentieth Corps, who was familiar with Kilpatrick from their time together in the Army of the Potomac, noted in his diary that Kilpatrick's "command is . . . held in contempt by ourselves and the enemy."[9] Kilpatrick realized that his negligence might well have deprived him of the promotion to major general that he had coveted for so long.

Monroe's Crossroads was not the first time Kilpatrick's shoddy dispositions had permitted Wheeler and his horsemen to sneak up on his old West Point classmate's camp undetected. Nor was it the first time the Northern cavalry chieftain had been routed from his bed and forced to flee in a state of undress. Wheeler had approached Kilpatrick's sleeping camp and launched an almost identical attack four months earlier, and with similar results. On November 27, 1864, at Sylvan Grove, Georgia, Wheeler captured Kilpatrick's pickets and charged a sleeping Federal camp at 2:00 a.m. As at Monroe's Crossroads, Kilpatrick was snugly tucked into his bed with Alice when Butler's and Wheeler's surprise attack tore through his camp—just as Hampton had done near Atlee's Station on March 1, 1864.[10]

"We stampeded and came near capturing Kilpatrick twice, but having a fleet horse he escaped bare headed, leaving his hat in our hands," boasted Wheeler the next day.[11] At Sylvan Grove, the Confederates drove the Federals from two positions, captured fifty or so prisoners, a stand of colors, about 100 horses and arms, and all of the camp equipage of the Federals.[12]

"Early in the morning of [November] 28th Kilpatrick himself narrowly escaped capture, having improperly made his quarters for the night at some distance from the body of his command, the Ninth Michigan being with him as a guard," observed Maj. Gen. Jacob D. Cox. Wheeler's troopers got between Kilpatrick and his main body and Little Kil had a difficult time cutting his way to safety. His luck held, though, and he managed to save himself from the consequences of his own folly.[13]

Presumably Kilpatrick would have learned something from his experiences on November 28, but he clearly had not. He had another chance to learn the same lesson at Aiken, South Carolina, on February 11, 1865, but evidently that experience made no impression on him either. In spite of these two episodes, his dispositions remained as shoddy and irresponsible at Monroe's Crossroads as they had been in Georgia and South Carolina. But this time, Kilpatrick's negligence cost him much more than just a few prisoners—it allowed Hardee to escape and Johnston to plan and execute a major attack against one wing of Sherman's army. For an officer who had experienced almost everything the long war had to offer, Kilpatrick's failure to attend to something as basic as posting pickets was unforgivable.

Once Kilpatrick's carelessness had gotten his command into trouble, however, he was at his best. His quick thinking saved him from capture by Captain Bostick's detachment. After he had made his way to the safety of the swamp, Kilpatrick rallied his troops and personally led them in a counterattack that stabilized the battle and eventually drove the enemy from his camp. Having gotten himself into a terrible pickle, Little Kil managed to snatch victory from the jaws of defeat, and he deserves much credit for doing so.

Not surprisingly, both sides claimed victory at Monroe's Crossroads. In his report of the Carolinas Campaign, Kilpatrick crowed, "I . . . was unexpectedly attacked before daylight by the entire rebel cavalry force led by Hampton in person . . . And can proudly boast that without assistance [my men] regained their camp, animals, artillery, and transportation, and drove the enemy in confusion from the ground he had taken by surprise and force of numbers alone."[14] Given the strategic outcome, the Confederates also claimed victory by pointing to the hundreds of prisoners taken, the freeing of Confederate captives, the capture of the camp, the opening of the road to Fayetteville, and the time so dearly purchased and utilized so well by General Johnston at Averasboro and Bentonville.

A Philadelphia newspaper scoffed at the idea that Hampton and his troopers had won a great victory at Monroe's Crossroads. "Wade Hampton's 'victory over Kilpatrick,' the rebel press said would prove a heavy blow to Sherman," reported the editor of the *Philadelphia Public Ledger*. "It is singular that Sherman does not know he was hurt, for he goes right on and says, 'everything moving finely.' We suspect, when the facts turn up, that Hampton's blows will be like Falstaff's, imagination converting those received into those administered."[15] This sarcastic proclamation overstates the case, but it does make a valid point. In the grand scheme of things, the Confederates lacked the numbers to hinder the progress of Sherman's march through the Carolinas. Hampton's battle bought Johnston and the Confederacy one final opportunity that, in the end, failed to alter the course of events.

Although Kilpatrick's characterization of the fight at Monroe's Crossroads as a tactical victory may have saved him from disgrace, it did nothing to improve the cavalry chief's reputation in the eyes of either his men or Sherman. "Kilpatrick is not considered as brilliant as at first," reported Capt. Asbury P. Gatch of the 9th Ohio Cavalry. "He is too risky, with a display of but little judgment."[16] With this single sentence Gatch summarized Judson Kilpatrick's entire tenure as commander of Sherman's cavalry. Sherman never trusted his cavalry leader with an important task again.

Stunned by the magnitude of the surprise Hampton inflicted on Kilpatrick's camp, Sherman lost whatever confidence he retained in Little Kil. All the same, Sherman had no alternative but to depend on the unreliable leader because the only other significant cavalry force available to him, Maj. Gen. George Stoneman's large division based in East Tennessee, departed on a lengthy raid on March 20 that kept it occupied for the rest of the war.[17]

Kilpatrick's actions after March 10 did not increase the value of his stock in anyone's eyes. His bumbling response to Sherman about how to deploy his horse soldiers at Averasboro dumbfounded the army commander. A few days later, Kilpatrick's lack of reconnaissance led to the surprise attack on Slocum's left wing at Bentonville. By this time Sherman was utterly disgusted with his cavalry leader's performance. As a modern scholar described it, "Kilpatrick's poor reconnaissance and rosy prognostications on March 18 [the day before Johnston's attack at Bentonville] caused Generals Sherman and Slocum to ignore the warnings of the foragers, who reported that the Confederates were massing along the Left Wing's front and left flank."[18] Little Kil and his cavalry played no active role in the fighting at Bentonville.

A few days after Monroe's Crossroads, Sherman received a dispatch from Major General Schofield suggesting that Maj. Gen. Philip H. Sheridan and his 10,000 Union cavalrymen from Virginia were riding to Sherman's assistance. "I am delighted that Sheridan is slashing away with his cavalry," replied an elated Sherman. "He will be a disturbing element in the grand and beautiful game of war, and if he reaches me I'll make all of North Carolina howl. I will make him a deed gift of every horse in the state, to be settled for at the day of judgment."[19] Sheridan ignored Grant's orders and never appeared in North Carolina. Had he done so, he may reached Danville by March 12 and could have had a significant impact on Johnston's subsequent actions.

Sheridan had resisted for months any suggestion that he join Sherman, and on March 14 Grant acquiesced to the inevitable. Grant had earlier ordered Sheridan to conduct a raid on the James River canal and the Virginia Central Railroad, and then either return to his winter base at Winchester or ride to join Sherman in North Carolina. Sheridan's intransigence caused the general-in-chief to change his mind. "I am disposed now to bring your cavalry over here and unite it with what we have," wrote Grant. "When you start I want no halt to be made until you make the intended raid, unless rest is necessary; in that case take it before crossing the James."[20] These words were music to Sheridan's ears. He rode as quickly as possible, arriving near Petersburg on March 26. However, Grant still wanted to send Sheridan to reinforce Sherman.

On March 22, Grant informed Sherman that he intended to send Sheridan on a mission to cut the South Side and Danville rail lines, and give the cavalryman the discretion to continue southward and join Sherman in North Carolina.[21] Sheridan, who had a wide insubordinate streak, was unable to work with Maj. Gen. George G. Meade, the commander of the Army of the Potomac. Grant understood this and generally tried to keep the two men apart. Further, Grant believed it would be difficult to drive Lee from Richmond and Petersburg and felt that the cavalry would be more useful to Sherman, who could dispatch Johnston and then, accompanied by Sheridan's horsemen, join Grant to deliver the *coup de grace* to the Army of Northern Virginia. In short, sending Sheridan's cavalry to Sherman made military sense.[22]

In light of Kilpatrick's failure to play any role at Bentonville, the possible arrival of Sheridan came as welcome news to Sherman. The army leader was so eager for Sheridan's support that it was one of the reasons he traveled from Goldsboro to Grant's headquarters to confirm it. On March 27, Sherman reached Grant's headquarters at City Point, Virginia, where he met with President Lincoln, Grant, and Rear Admiral David Dixon Porter to plan the end of the war. Worried that Sherman might prevail upon Grant to send the Union cavalry to North Carolina, Sheridan arrived at City Point that night to argue his case. Sherman informed Sheridan of his plans to finish off Johnston's army, and suggested that Sheridan join him near the Roanoke River after his raid on the railroads.

Sheridan was determined not to go to North Carolina, for he preferred to aid Grant in delivering the *coup de grace* to Lee's army in Virginia. Sheridan argued "that it would be bad policy" for him to help Sherman defeat Johnston, only to have Sherman assist Grant in bringing Lee to bay. "Such a course would give rise to the charge that [Grant's] own forces around Petersburg were not equal to the task, and would seriously affect public opinion in the North," claimed Sheridan. Grant mollified his feisty cavalry chief by telling Sheridan that the plan was merely a contingency should the proposed offensive at Petersburg fail, which somewhat relieved the anxious Sheridan.[23]

Undeterred, Sherman visited Sheridan's tent the next morning to urge him to reconsider; Sheridan once again rebuffed him. It was now clear to Sherman that Grant was unwilling to order Sheridan to join him. Indeed, Lincoln and Grant, for political reasons having to do with a post-Civil War America, wanted Lee to be forced to surrender to Grant's army group, not Sherman's. Therefore, Sherman was not to begin his advance from Goldsboro until April 11. Bitterly disappointed, Sherman would have to continue relying on his own inadequate cavalry force and even more inadequate cavalry commander.[24]

On April 10, the Raleigh newspapers reported that Stoneman's division had come across the mountains from East Tennessee, destroyed the railroad at Salisbury, and was riding toward Greensboro. Sherman had not yet learned of Lee's surrender the previous day, but he did soon thereafter. "I also learned that General Wilson's cavalry corps was 'smashing things' down about Selma and Montgomery, Alabama, and was pushing for Columbus and Macon, Georgia; and I also had reason to expect that General Sheridan would come down from Appomattox to join us at Raleigh with his superb cavalry corps. I needed more cavalry to check Johnston's retreat, so that I could come up to him with my infantry, and therefore had good reason to delay," declared Sherman in his memoirs years after the war.[25] Although he was being diplomatic, Sherman's message was still clear: years after the end of the war he was still seething about Kilpatrick's shoddy performance. Sheridan's unflinching refusal to come to Sherman's aid meant that Sherman had to make do with what he had.

The result of all this was that Sherman kept Little Kil on a short leash until the closing days of the conflict. Not until the final week of the war—more than one month after Monroe's Crossroads—did Sherman finally inform Kilpatrick that "you may act boldly and even rashly now, for this is the time to strike quick and strong. We must get possession of Raleigh before Lee and Johnston have time to confer and make new combinations forced on them by the loss of their capital and the defeat of their principal army about Petersburg."[26] At last unfettered, an elated Kilpatrick responded, "I shall operate boldly and do all the mischief possible."[27]

Hoping to spur Kilpatrick by citing the effectiveness of the large mounted contingent that had cornered Lee's army, Sherman wrote, "General Sheridan has done great service against the retreating infantry, cutting off and capturing whole brigades of infantry, artillery, and wagon trains."[28] The outcome of Sherman's Carolinas Campaign was by this time a foregone conclusion, and there was no risk to turning Kilpatrick loose on the Confederates. Perhaps doing so might help encourage Johnston to surrender, and Little Kil could do no real harm otherwise.

"I look back over the past campaign, so glorious to this army, with feelings of pride and satisfaction," declared Kilpatrick in his report of the Carolinas Campaign. "My entire command, animated by the same spirit, with full confidence in their chiefs, have with skill and energy overcome every obstacle, and have willingly dared every danger that a perfect success might crown our efforts."[29]

George Jenkins, a member of the 1st Alabama Cavalry, felt the same way. He proudly declared, "Our little Third Brigade fought and routed the three rebel divisions of Hampton, Butler, and Hume."[30] His words reflect the general feelings of Kilpatrick's horse soldiers. Little Kil generously praised his brigade commanders for their performance in the campaign. Colonels Spencer and Jordan, and Lt. Col. William Stough, who had assumed command of Way's dismounted troopers after the capture of Kilpatrick's camp, all received brevets as brigadier general of volunteers in recognition of their performance. William Way received a well-deserved promotion to colonel of the 9th Michigan Cavalry in June 1865, not long before his discharge from service.[31]

Colonel Way's dismounted brigade, in particular, earned the respect of Sherman's army for its performance during the war's final months. "During this long campaign we have had much bad, rainy weather. The roads have been very bad and at times almost impassable," recounted a proud Way. "My command were poorly clothed, many of the men being barefooted, but they have borne the hardships, privations and toil of this long and arduous campaign with the fortitude that becomes the true and patriotic soldier, battling for the glorious cause of liberty and the honor of our flag."[32] That these dismounted horsemen, forced to fight with unfamiliar weapons and tactics, kept up with their mounted brethren and performed so well speaks to their effectiveness as "foot cavalry."

In spite of Sherman's obvious misgivings about his cavalry chief, a successful campaign made it easy for the commanding general to be magnanimous. "The cavalry on this march was handled with spirit and skill," wrote Sherman in his endorsement of Kilpatrick's report. "Almost always confronted by a superior force of the enemy, led by rebel generals of high repute—Wade Hampton, Butler, and Wheeler—General Kilpatrick was always willing to attack, but I restrained him as it was important to retain our cavalry strong to cover the flanks of our long wagon trains. In all actions our cavalry fought well." For a commander who had endured several major cavalry failures in his campaigns from Chattanooga to the Carolinas, these were gracious words indeed.[33]

Despite his worries that Hampton's "infernal surprise" would deprive him of his long-awaited promotion to major general, Kilpatrick finally got his wish. On June 19, 1865, Kilpatrick was promoted to captain of artillery in the Regular Army and major general of volunteers.

*   *   *

Wade Hampton, with the assistance of his ranking subordinates, Matthew C. Butler and Joseph Wheeler, had hatched a superb plan to defeat Kilpatrick. One modern historian has described the dawn attack on Kilpatrick's camp as as a brilliant stroke.[34] Although the Confederates enjoyed a decided advantage in manpower, they still lost the battle, tactically speaking. There are many reasons for this.

First, like the Confederates, Kilpatrick's troopers were battle-hardened veterans. The Yankees also had the benefit of seven-shot Spencer carbines, a superior technology that provided them with a significant firepower advantage over the single-shot weapons carried by the Southerners. The routed Federals also had the presence of mind to carry their weapons with them when they fled their camp; they later brought this firepower to bear once they had rallied in the swamp. "The Federals put up a good fight, considering that they were surprised," grudgingly admitted a Confederate veteran.[35]

Second, Wheeler had failed to take into account the swamp along Nicholson Creek. This terrain feature proved to be a major obstacle that hindered two entire divisions for most of the battle. "We were not able to hold the camps on account of the muddy ground," declared a lieutenant of the Jeff Davis Legion, understating both the condition of the ground and the problems it created.[36] The deep swamp prevented nearly half of Wheeler's Corps from entering the fight, negating the substantial Confederate manpower advantage. Rain and darkness had helped hide the swamp, but no systematic reconnaissance of the ground seems to have been conducted during the hours leading up to the dawn assault. The result was that neither Wheeler's combat-tested veterans nor their leaders had a firm understanding of the field's most prominent terrain feature. Thus, when the attack was launched, only Butler's men were available to participate. By the time the Alabamans and Georgians of Allen's Division made their way through the swamp (Wheeler's left-hand division), Kilpatrick's command had rallied and was counterattacking. Butler. Although Kilpatrick had only one-third of his command at Monroe's Crossroads and the Confederates outnumbered him nearly three to one, the swamp equalized the odds and permitted the Federals to carry the day.[37]

Third, the compact area between Charles Monroe's house, the swamp, and Stetson's guns funneled many Confederate horse soldiers into an ever-tightening space. The natural slope of the terrain directed those men away from the Monroe house and toward the swamp, where Butler's and Wheeler's troopers became intermingled and lost unit cohesion. Kilpatrick, on the other hand, employed the swamp as a natural rally point for his routed command, which had nowhere else to go. After he rallied his troops, Kilpatrick turned the tables on the Confederates and used the terrain to his advantage. This battle underscores the crucial role that terrain plays in combat.

Fourth, Butler's failure to commit his entire division to the fight was another factor in the Confederate loss. The capable general decided to hold back Evander Law's South Carolinians to act as provost guards. Planning for prisoners was appropriate, but Butler's decision to hold back an entire brigade was a costly one. Law's men did not enter the fight until after Little Kil had begun to rally his troopers to form an organized resistance. Had Butler committed both of his brigades to the initial attack, it is easy to imagine that the additional horsemen may have tipped the balance in the fighting that raged in the Federal camp. We will never know whether the constricting terrain would have accommodated another brigade of mounted men, but the presence of these veterans would have enabled Butler to bring more weight to bear on the surprised Union defenders, and might have made the initial charge of Wright's brigade even more successful.

Fifth, the units that took part in the fight suffered a disastrous breakdown in command, control, and discipline when they discovered the loot in Kilpatrick's camp. "We were very well satisfied with what we had captured," declared a Georgian.[38] The onrushing Confederates— Wheeler's troopers, in particular—stopped to plunder the Federal camp instead of maintaining the momentum of their attack. Their looting doomed Hampton's plan. Once Stetson got his field pieces into the fight, his blasts of canister killed and wounded many and helped sow chaos among the milling Southerners. Writing in 1913, Pvt. George B. Guild of the consolidated 4th and 8th Tennessee regiments correctly analyzed the outcome of the battle. "My opinion of this affair is: We did very well under the circumstances; but we would have done better had not the men commenced too soon a distribution of the captures, or had the other half of our command succeeded in crossing the swamp."[39]

Not a single member of the Confederate high command accepted responsibility for failing to defeat Kilpatrick at Monroe's Crossroads. Instead, the Confederate commanders engaged in finger-pointing. Butler claimed that Wheeler had failed to support him.[40] Wheeler, in turn, blamed Hampton for not committing Dibrell's Division to the fight sooner. Hampton, meanwhile, denied Wheeler's charges, contending that Butler's failure to carry off Stetson's guns and Wheeler's inability to maintain discipline had doomed the attack.[41] "Terrible consequences sometimes, when jealousy reigns supreme between officers, and patriotism is laid aside for the time," observed Charles M. Calhoun of the 6th South Carolina Cavalry.[42] Regardless of who was to blame, a breakdown in the command structure of Wade Hampton's cavalry corps doomed the battle plan to failure.

Finally, the heavy losses among the division, brigade, and regimental commanders sapped the effectiveness of of Hampton's command. For example, every field grade officer in Hagan's Alabama Brigade, Wheeler's Corps, was killed, wounded, or captured. No outfit can suffer such appalling losses and remain effective.[43] Although Hampton had achieved total surprise and enjoyed initial success, his officer corps was quickly shattered and his command cohesiveness suffered as a result.

For the most part, the Southern cavalry performed admirably at Monroe's Crossroads. The combat was the swan song of the Confederate army's mounted arm. In just over four hours of fighting, Hampton, Wheeler, and Butler demonstrated that the Southern cavalry remained a potent fighting force.

Fighting Joe Wheeler recognized as much. Not long after the surrender he wrote an account of his command's service during the war's final campaign, a much-exaggerated valediction for the Confederate cavalry. "For an entire year my troops had been constantly together, enduring, encountering, triumphing," he proclaimed, exhibiting a rather selective memory in the telling. "During that year the enemy's cavalry had been frequently met and always had our arms been crowned with success. The spirit of my brave men was as buoyant, unbroken, and determined as in the first days of our country's existence. Unity, concord, good-will, devotion to duty and country, and I might add nearly all elements which grow out of continued success, and which I felt would insure success to me in the future, pervaded my command from the highest officer to the youngest trooper."[44]

One of Wheeler's Kentuckians echoed this refrain. "Under Gen. Wheeler, as we followed in the path of desolation left by Sherman's army, we were daily engaged with Gen. Kilpatrick's cavalry, and for eight days were without bread or meat, living on sweet potatoes alone, the only food left from destruction by the Federal troops," wrote trooper Henry Lane Stone. The Kentuckian had served under both Morgan and Wheeler. Stone continued: "The first meat we ate after this fast was some fresh beef, which we found in a camp from which we had just driven the enemy before they had had time to cook and eat it." After Johnston's surrender these hardships finally ended. It was time for both sides to go home.[45]

Monroe's Crossroads was the last major cavalry battle during the Carolinas Campaign. Nearly 6,000 veteran horsemen had taken the field (though not all simultaneously) locked in a fairly tight arena The veterans remembered the desperate fight on Charles Monroe's farm for the rest of their lives. Many proudly recounted their roles in the battle in veterans' publications for years afterward. They re-fought the battle with almost as much zeal as they had shown on that cold and damp March morning, with results that remained just as uncertain as the outcome of the engagement.

Monroe's Crossroads has been largely overlooked and remains little more than a footnote because of the much larger and more important combat at Bentonville nine days later. The location of the battlefield, which is today surrounded by the artillery ranges of modern-day Fort Bragg, limits visitation. Unlike so many other battlefields, few people have the opportunity to walk the grounds and fully understand what happened there.[46]

The fact that the Hampton–Kilpatrick engagement was waged in North Carolina during the war's waning weeks has relegated it to undeserved insignificance. Indeed, even the Battle of Bentonville was almost completely ignored by historians until Mark Bradley's superb account appeared in the mid-1990s—130 years after the battle. Had Monroe's Crossroads been fought in Virginia in 1862, it would would today be a household name.

My hope is that this study rekindles an interest in this long-neglected battle and conveys to its readers a fuller and richer appreciation for the hardships borne by those brave horse soldiers in blue and gray who bore the brunt of the fighting. They deserve to be remembered.

Epilogue

In the years following the Civil War, Wade Hampton, who had demonstrated his military genius on many a battlefield, showed his true greatness. "Wade Hampton was the Moses of his people," proclaimed an admirer, "the God-given instrument to help them free themselves from their enemies."[1] Hampton accepted the Democratic nomination for governor in 1865 and narrowly lost a disputed election to a hand-picked Radical Republican candidate. He vigorously opposed Radical Republican Reconstruction policies, and in particular disputed the harsh punishment meted out to South Carolina, which most Northerners viewed as the cradle of rebellion.

Hampton again ran for governor in 1876 and this time was elected. He espoused equal rights for the freed slaves who comprised the majority of South Carolina's population and an end of the Federal army's occupation of the last three states of the former Confederacy—South Carolina, Louisiana, and Florida—under President Grant. His policies earned Hampton the proud title of "The Savior of South Carolina." President Rutherford B. Hayes withdrew the remaining Federal troops from South Carolina in 1877, marking the official end of Reconstruction in the Palmetto State, as well as Louisiana and Florida. Hampton was re-elected to a second two-year term without opposition in 1878, but resigned in 1879 to take a seat in the United States Senate, which he held for twelve years. His political career was marked not by the pugnacity of his military personality, but by his advocacy of racial inclusiveness. After being defeated for a third Senate term in 1892, Hampton was appointed U.S. railroad commissioner for four years before finally retiring to private life in his beloved home town of Columbia. A handsome monument to Hampton stands in the statuary hall in the Rotunda of the U.S. Capitol, a silent tribute to the esteem in which the old warrior was held.

In 1899, an accidental fire destroyed Hampton's home. He was 82 years old and could not afford to rebuild it. Friends and admirers raised the money to erect a house for the aging warrior-politician and they presented it to him despite the general's protests. Hampton spent his last years of his life in this new home. He died on April 11, 1902. His last words reportedly were, "God bless all my people, black and white." Hampton lay in state in the South Carolina state capitol in Columbia. Some 20,000 mourners followed his casket to the grave site.[2]

After the war, Matthew C. Butler remained Hampton's protégé. As it did to Hampton and so many others, the war financially ruined Butler. "I was twenty-nine years old, with one leg gone, a wife and three children to support, with seventy slaves emancipated, a debt of $15,000, and in my pocket, $1.75 in cash," he recalled many years later.[3] The young lawyer picked himself up by his bootstraps and resumed his practice in his hometown of Edgefield. A lifelong Democrat like Hampton, Butler was elected to the South Carolina General Assembly in 1866, and to the U.S. Senate in 1877, where he served alongside his friend and mentor for twelve years. He served a third term after Hampton left the Senate, but was defeated in his bid for a fourth term, leaving the Senate in March 1895. Butler returned to South Carolina and resumed his law practice until the drums of war began beating again in 1898.

When the United States went to war with Spain, the War Department worried that Southerners would not answer the call to arms. Secretary of War Russell A. Alger had commanded the 5th Michigan Cavalry during the Civil War and remembered Butler as a worthy adversary. Alger offered the 62-year-old Butler a commission as a major general of volunteers, and Butler returned to military service—this time in the blue uniform of the United States Army. He did not see combat. Butler later served as one of the commissioners appointed to supervise the evacuation of Cuba by Spanish forces. With the return of peace, Butler hung up his uniform for the last time, returned to Edgefield, and resumed the practice of law. He died in Washington, D.C. on April 14, 1909.[4]

Fighting Joe Wheeler settled in New Orleans after his release from Fort Delaware. Once he recovered his shattered health he married a wealthy Alabama widow, engaged in several business ventures, and moved into his wife's Alabama home. In 1871, Wheeler and his brother-in-law, Thomas Harrison Jones, were indicted for the murder of an employee in their blacksmith shop in Decatur, Alabama, a man named Dandridge Thompson Galey. Wheeler alleged that Galey had "without any cause . . . commenced to act in a very insubordinate and threatening manner," so he and Jones fired Galey and told him that he would have to vacate the house he was permitted to occupy on the premises. The next day, when Galey and his son came to retrieve their property, they were armed. When things turned sour Jones shot and killed Galey and critically wounded the son. Wheeler and Jones were indicted for these acts.

Wheeler decided to defend himself and his brother-in-law. Calling in favors from his former comrades-in-arms, he arranged for his admission to the Tennessee bar, which then entitled him to admission to the Alabama bar in August 1872. Wheeler's admission to the Alabama bar came on the day his trial began; defending himself against the murder charge was his first case. He was acquitted the next day and then represented Jones, who was also acquitted. "I think they got away with murder," concluded a modern local historian who has carefully evaluated the surviving documents.[5]

Once acquitted, Jones also took up the study of law and the two men established a law firm. Wheeler was a better general and politician than he was an attorney. "Wheeler could do a lot of things politically, but he was not a good lawyer," remarked one of his descendant.[6]

It did not take long for Wheeler, like Hampton and Butler before him, to become involved in Reconstruction-era politics. A Democrat, Wheeler was elected to the U.S. House of Representatives in 1881 and served a single term before losing his reelection bid. When his opponent died in 1883, Wheeler was appointed to complete the term. He held his seat in Congress for seventeen years, chairing the Committee on Expenditures and the Committee on Territories.

Wheeler was one of the earliest, loudest, and most vehement supporters of war against Spain. Like Butler, the 62-year-old former

Rebel general received a major general's commission of U.S. Volunteers during the Spanish-American War. He commanded a cavalry division that included Col. Theodore Roosevelt's renowned "Rough Riders." Wheeler's division saw extensive combat in Cuba, including the famous Battle of Kettle Hill, although the old general was ill that day and Brig. Gen. Samuel S. Summer led the division in his stead. Wheeler was the senior member of the commission that negotiated the surrender of the Spanish Army in Cuba.[7] Having rediscovered his love for the army, Wheeler remained on active duty as a brigadier general in the regular army after the end of the conflict.

During the 1899 Philippine Insurrection, Wheeler commanded the First Brigade, Second Division, Eighth Army Corps, in the Tarlac campaign from July 8, 1899, to January 24, 1900. His commanding officer, Maj. Gen. Arthur MacArthur, found Wheeler to be a "loose cannon on a rolling deck," and sent the former Confederate and his division to the rear. Upon his return to the U.S., Wheeler briefly commanded the Department of the Lakes, headquartered in Chicago. Fighting Joe finally retired on September 10, 1900. He died in Brooklyn, New York, on January 25, 1906, and was buried in Arlington National Cemetery. President Theodore Roosevelt, who had served under Wheeler in Cuba, attended the funeral.[8]

After receiving his brevet to brigadier general of Union volunteers, George E. Spencer resigned his commission in June 1865, writing, "If there was an enemy in arms against the government I was willing to sacrifice every other interest to the public good. I now believe my duty requires me to bestow my entire time and attention to my private affairs." His resignation was accepted, and Spencer moved to Decatur, Alabama, in 1866, where he established a law practice.

In May 1867, Chief Justice Salmon P. Chase appointed Spencer registrar in bankruptcy court for the Fourth District of Alabama, a prized political appointment. His wife, Belle Zilfa, a prolific author, died in Tuscaloosa on August 1, 1867. When Alabama was readmitted for representation the next year, Spencer was elected to the U.S. Senate as a Republican. He was reelected in 1872, serving until March 3, 1879, and chairing the Committee on the District of Columbia and the Committee on Military Affairs.

In 1877, Spencer married a niece of ex-Confederate Maj. Gen. William Wing Loring. When Spencer lost his bid for re-election to a third term, he and his wife settled in Nevada, where he was appointed commissioner of the Union Pacific Railroad and helped to expose postal frauds that led to a reduction in postage rates. He eventually retired to a ranch in Nevada. He died in Washington, D.C. on February 19, 1893, and was buried in Arlington National Cemetery. The city of Spencer, Iowa, was named in his honor.[9]

Unlike his former adversaries in the Battle of Monroe's Crossroads, Judson Kilpatrick did not achieve greatness in other fields of endeavor. Soon after the end of the war he resigned his long-awaited major general's commission and returned to his native New Jersey, hoping that his military notoriety would vault him into the governor's seat. Much to his disappointment, he lost the coveted Republican nomination, in part because of his unsavory reputation as a womanizer. Instead, in November 1865, Kilpatrick was appointed minister to Chile, a safe political backwater where he could no longer embarrass the Republican power brokers who governed the country. He married in Santiago and had several children, one of whom married a Vanderbilt and became the mother of George Vanderbilt. Kilpatrick wrote to Secretary of State William H. Seward in 1867, "I have the honor to report that nothing of political importance has transpired at this capital since my last dispatch." Instead, he enjoyed exotic pursuits such as ostrich hunting on the Argentine pampas.[10] In 1868, President-elect Ulysses S. Grant recalled Kilpatrick to Washington, and did not reappoint him to his post in Chile.

In 1870, the former cavalryman returned to the U.S. and spent several years farming and lecturing, thrilling crowds with his accounts of his Civil War exploits.[11] Kilpatrick also wrote a play that was never staged. Still, he itched for the public spotlight. He made another unsuccessful run for the Republican gubernatorial nomination in New Jersey, after which he again demonstrated his unrelentingly poor judgment by switching parties and siding against Grant in a party insurrection in 1872. The ill-advised move prompted a government investigation of Little Kil's womanizing during the Carolinas Campaign.[12]

Grant's reelection insured that Kilpatrick's political exile would continue for at least another four years. In 1880, when Grant ran for a third term, Kilpatrick cast his lot with James Garfield, another former Union general. Garfield's election resulted in Kilpatrick's reappointment as minister to Chile in 1881. Little Kil returned to Santiago, where he happily resumed his diplomatic duties, involving himself in the War of the Pacific, between Peru, Chile, and Bolivia, much to the State Department's embarrassment.[13]

Kilpatrick had been suffering for many years from Bright's Disease, a painful and debilitating kidney ailment. The disease finally claimed his life on December 4, 1881, at the age of forty-five, just a few months after his benefactor Garfield's assassination. Kilpatrick was buried in the cemetery at West Point not far from the remains of his rival, George A. Custer. His friends and former soldiers raised funds to place a large and impressive monument on his grave. In spite of a lifetime of unbridled ambition and expended energy, greatness eluded Judson Kilpatrick.[14]

When Garfield nominated Kilpatrick for the Chilean post in 1881, the nomination had to be approved by the U.S. Senate. Ironically, his old nemesis, Senator Wade Hampton of South Carolina, placed Judson Kilpatrick's nomination before the Senate, which unanimously approved it.[15] Forgotten were the shame and shock of the "Shirt-tail Skedaddle," and their ugly confrontation at the Bennett Place. For Hampton and Kilpatrick at least, time had healed the wounds of the Civil War.

Appendix A

Order of Battle

Monroe's Crossroads, March 10, 1865

The Military Division of the Mississippi
Maj. Gen. William T. Sherman

Third Cavalry Division
Brig. Gen. Hugh Judson Kilpatrick

Kilpatrick's Scout Company
Capt. Theo Northrop

1st Brigade
Bvt. Brig. Gen. Thomas J. Jordan

3rd Indiana Cavalry Battalion: Capt. Charles U. Patton
8th Indiana Cavalry: Col. Fielder A. Jones
2nd Kentucky Cavalry Maj. Owen Star
3rd Kentucky Cavalry Lt. Col. Robert H. King
9th Pennsylvania Cavalry Lt. Col. David H. Kimmel

2nd Brigade
Bvt. Brig. Gen. Smith D. Atkins

92nd Illinois Mounted Infantry Lt. Col. Matthew van Buskirk
9th Michigan Cavalry Col. George S. Acker
9th Ohio Cavalry Col. William D. Hamilton
10th Ohio Cavalry Col. Thomas W. Sanderson
McLaughlin's Squadron of Ohio Cavalry: Capt. John Dalzell

3rd Brigade
Col. George E. Spencer

1st Alabama Cavalry (U.S.): Maj. Francis L. Cramer (wounded, captured)
5th Kentucky Cavalry: Maj. Christopher T. Cheek
5th Ohio Cavalry: Maj. George H. Rader

4th Provisional Brigade (Dismounted)
Lt. Col. William B. Way

1st Regiment: Maj. Charles A. Appel (captured)
2nd Regiment: Lt. Col. William Stough
3rd Regiment: Capt. John B. Riggs

Horse Artillery

10th Battery, Wisconsin Light Artillery: Capt. Yates V. Beebe

*   *   *

Department of South Carolina, Georgia, and Florida,
including the Army of Tennessee
Gen. Joseph E. Johnston

Cavalry Corps
Lt. Gen. Wade Hampton

Wheeler's Cavalry Corps
Maj. Gen. Joseph Wheeler

Co. G, 1st Alabama Cavalry (headquarters escort)
Lt. James A. Smith

Engineer Troop
Lt. L. C. Anderson

Humes' Division
Brig. Gen. W. Y. C. Humes (wounded)

Harrison's Texas Brigade
Brig. Gen. Thomas Harrison (wounded)

8th Texas Cavalry (Terry's Texas Rangers)
Col. Gustave Cooke (wounded)
11th Texas Cavalry: Capt. C. T. Downing
3rd Arkansas Cavalry: Maj. William H. Blackwell
4th/8th Tennessee Cavalry Consolidated: Col. Baxter Smith*

Ashby's Brigade
Col. Henry M. Ashby

1st/6th Tennessee Cavalry Consolidated: Lt. Col. James H. Lewis
2nd Tennessee Cavalry: Lt. Col. John H. Kuhn
5th Tennessee Cavalry: Col. George W. McKenzie
9th Tennessee Cavalry Battalion: Capt. W. L. Bromley

Dibrell's Division
Brig. Gen. George G. Dibrell

Williams's Brigade
Col. W. C. P. Breckinridge

1st Kentucky Cavalry
2nd Kentucky Cavalry
9th Kentucky Cavalry

Dibrell's Brigade
Col. William S. McLemore

Allison's Squadron (Hamilton's & Shaw's battalions): Col. Robert D. Allison
13th Tennessee Cavalry: Col. Mounce L. Gore

Allen's Division
Brig. Gen. William W. Allen (wounded)

---

* There were two regiments designated as the 4th Tennessee Cavalry. One had served primarily under Nathan Bedford Forrest, and the other had served under Wheeler. The regiment that had served under Wheeler had been consolidated with the small remnant of the 8th Tennessee Cavalry, and should not be confused with the 4th Tennessee Cavalry Regiment that was part of McLemore's Brigade.

Hagan's Alabama Brigade
Col. James Hagan (wounded)

1st Alabama Cavalry: Col. David T. Blakey
3rd Alabama Cavalry: Maj. John D. Farish (wounded)
9th Alabama Cavalry: Capt. S. P. Dobbs
12th Alabama Cavalry: Lt. Col. Marcellus Pointer
51st Alabama Cavalry (Partisan Rangers): Col. Milton L. Kilpatrick
53rd Alabama Cavalry (Partisan Rangers): Col. Moses W. Hannon (wounded)

Anderson's Brigade
Brig. Gen. Robert H. Anderson

3rd Confederate Cavalry: Col. Robert Thompson
5th Georgia Cavalry: Col. Edward Bird
8th Confederate Cavalry: Lt. Col. John S. Prather
10th Confederate Cavalry: Col. William J. Vason

Crews's Brigade
Col. Charles Crews

1st Georgia Cavalry: Col. Samuel W. Davitte
2nd Georgia Cavalry: Capt. George C. Looney
6th Georgia Cavalry: Col. John R. Hart
12th Georgia Cavalry: Col. Issac Avery

Shannon's Special Scouts
Capt. Alexander M. Shannon

Hampton's Cavalry Corps
Lt. Gen. Wade Hampton

Butler's Division
Maj. Gen. Matthew C. Butler

Butler's Brigade
Brig. Gen. Evander M. Law

1st South Carolina Cavalry: Lt. Col. William A. Walker
4th South Carolina Cavalry: Col. B. Huger Rutledge
5th South Carolina Cavalry: Col. Zimmerman Davis

6th South Carolina Cavalry: Lt. Col. Lovick P. Miller
19th South Carolina Battalion: Capt. M. J. Kirk

Young's Brigade
Col. Gilbert J. Wright

Phillips's Legion Cavalry: Maj. W. W. Thomas
Cobb's Georgia Legion Cavalry: Lt. Col. Barrington S. King (killed)
Jeff Davis Legion Cavalry: Col. J. Fred Waring

Horse Artillery

Earle's South Carolina Battery (Furman Light Artillery):
Capt. William E. Earle

Appendix B

Identified Casualties at Monroe's Crossroads

UNION

Spencer's Third Brigade

1st Alabama Cavalry

Killed in Action

Sgt. William C. Boling, Co. K
Pvt. Archie Bowen, Co. D
Pvt. James R. Mize, Co. E
Sgt. Robert F. Vanhoose, Co. C
Pvt. John J. Vines, Co. D

Total: 5

Mortally Wounded

Cpl. Enoch M. Guyse, Co. M

Total: 1

Wounded

Pvt. John Blevins, Co. K
Pvt. James Bradshaw, Co. G
Cpl. James H. Casteel, Co. K
Pvt. George W. Cothern, Co. K
Maj. Francis L. Cramer, Field & Staff
Lt. George W. Emerick, Co. A
Sgt. George J. Hanshew, Co. G
Pvt. Moses J. Hendricks, Co. F
Lt. Joseph H. Hornbeck, Co. K
Lt. George C. Jenkins, Co. M
Capt. John Latty, Co. C
Sgt. Abraham J. Lentz, Co. K
Pvt. William P. Ramey, Co. K
Pvt. Jonathan M. Stewart, Co. K
Pvt. Henry Shelly, Co. D
Pvt. Jesse Walsh, Co. D

Total: 16

Captured

Pvt. David D. Abbott, Co. L
Pvt. James M. Adams, Co. G
Pvt. John M. Albertson, Co. H
Pvt. William R. Baseter, Co. L
Pvt. William T. Batey, Co. C
Pvt. William R. Baxter, Co. F
Cpl. Nathaniel Bice, Co. M
Sgt. John G. Blackwell, Co. M
Lt. Hugh L. Bolton, Co. H
Pvt. Tilmon S. Boyd, Co. K
Pvt. David D. Chastain, Co. A
Pvt. Samuel B. Cottington, Co. I
Pvt. William Doxon
Pvt. John Emerson, Co. C
Pvt. William C. Ernest, Co. A
Pvt. William C. Evins, Co. D
Sgt. Patterson Groves, Co. M
Sgt. Jason Guin, Co. A

Pvt. Jacob J. Guthry, Co. D
Pvt. Richard W. Hall, Co. A
Pvt. Andrew J. Homan, Co. D
Pvt. William D. Homan, Co. D
Pvt. John L. Humphreys, Co. B
Sgt. James W. Jaggers, Co. I
Pvt. John W. Jones, Co. I
Pvt. M. Keith, Co. G
Pvt. William A. Kindrick, Co. M
Pvt. Elisha Lake, Co. B
Pvt. Aaron Livingston, Co. I
Sgt. William Lowry, Co. B
Pvt. Andrew J. McElroy, Co. B
Pvt. John McKnabb, Co. K
Sgt. James P. Medlin, Co. M
Pvt. John G. Moore, Co. M
Pvt. James D. Murphy, Co. B
Pvt. Howell Myers, Co. G
Pvt. George T. Owens, Co. C
Pvt. James Peak, Co. I
Sgt. John Pearson, Co. D
Pvt. Andrew Pearson, Co. D
Pvt. Joel J. Poole, Co. E
Pvt. John W. Richardson, Co. M
Pvt. William J. Rowell, Co. K
Pvt. Micajah Stallings, Co. B
Pvt. William J. Stallings, Co. E (also wounded)
Pvt. Francis M Stancill, Co. I
Pvt. Lemuel L. Stewart, Co. A
Pvt. John Stone, Co. C
Pvt. William Stringfellow, Co. C
Pvt. Christopher Suveal, Co. D
Dr. John G. C. Swaving, Regimental Surgeon
Pvt. Christopher Sweat, Co. D
Pvt. James Sweat, Co. D
Pvt. John J. Taylor, Co. A
Pvt. J. J. Thomas, Co. D
Pvt. William D. Thrasher, Co. K
Pvt. John F. Walker, Co. G
Pvt. Jonathan Walker, Co. I
Pvt. Moses West, Co. B
Pvt. J. White, Co. I

Total: 60

Total Casualties: 82

5th Kentucky Cavalry

Killed

Lt. William Mitchell, regimental adjutant
Saddler John A. Lutarall, Co. C
Pvt. John Bryant, Co. D
Pvt. Joseph F. Riddle, Co. E
Pvt. Nathan H. Wilkeson, Co. C
Pvt. Henry Michaels, Co. C

Total: 6

Wounded

Pvt. William Alvis, Co. K
Pvt. Wilson H. Bartley, Co. K
Pvt. Aaron McClusky, Co. G
Pvt. James L. Melton, Co. D
Pvt. Wilbur Peter, Co. A
Pvt. Samuel F. Reese, Co. I
Pvt. Benjamin F. Rich, Co. D
Pvt. Jesse Whitehouse, Co. A

Total: 8

Captured/Missing

Capt. John D. Smith, Co. C
Lt. John Right, Co. B
Sgt. John F. Woldridge, Co. I
Sgt. John J. Morgan, Co. K
Cpl. Milton Brannam, Co. G
Cpl. James E. Bryant, Co. B
Cpl. Jeremiah S. Ellis, Co. L
Cpl. John I. Emberton, Co. B
Cpl. Nathaniel J. Judd, Co. I

Cpl. Charles W. Moody, Co.
Cpl. Henry Mullins, Co. G
Cpl. James M. B. Park, Co. K
Pvt. Jesse Booker, Co. C
Pvt. Jesse S. Bryant
Pvt. Henry C. Bushong, Co. B
Pvt. Wade Callicotte, Co. I
Pvt. John Cape, Co. I
Pvt. Quintis Coffey
Pvt. Robert Cook, Co. H
Pvt. George W. Crow
Pvt. Haywood Dillahay, Co. G
Pvt. Jacob F. Eller, Co. B
Pvt. Francis M. Elliott, Co. B
Pvt. Francis M. Ellis
Pvt. William Garrett, Co. C
Pvt. John T. Gentry
Pvt. James Greenup, Co. D
Pvt. Fleming M. Harper
Pvt. George W. Jackson, Jr., Co. B
Pvt. John Jackson
Pvt. Martin Jones, Co. B
Pvt. Nathaniel J. Judd
Pvt. Lavin Louis, Co. G
Pvt. Richard M. McMurtry
Pvt. John J. Morgan
Pvt. Granville Mullins
Pvt. John A. Murry, Co. K
Pvt. John W. Page, Co. C
Pvt. Samuel H. Page, Co. K
Pvt. Henry Picker
Pvt. John Short
Pvt. John M. Sims
Pvt. Downan Spear, Co. C
Pvt. John G. Stanton, Co. I
Pvt. Joshua B. Stevens, Co. B
Pvt. Booker Wakefield, Co. H
Pvt. Robert A. Welch, Co. B
Pvt. White W. Westmoreland, Co. C
Pvt. Thomas A. Williams, Co. H
Pvt. Alexander Woldridge, Co. I
Farrier Andrew J. Gannon, Co. C

Farrier Roland T. Norman, Co. K
Hospital Steward Jeremiah Ellis

Total: 53

Total Casualties: 67

5th Ohio Cavalry

Killed

Pvt. John Hulse, Co. D
Pvt. John Hoy, Co. D
Pvt. William Otto, Co. F
Pvt. George Troue, Co. E
Pvt. Thomas William, Co. G

Total: 5

Wounded

Sgt. David H. Walls, quartermaster sergeant

Total: 1

Captured/Missing

Regimental Surgeon David Rannells
Lt. Lee Haldesman, Regimental Adjutant
Lt. Martin Peters, Co. C
Lt. E. H. Shaw, Co. K
Pvt. Thomas Gallagher, Co. D
Pvt. John Harper, Co. H
Pvt. Martin D. Harrell, Co. D
Pvt. Patrick Hinchey, Co. E
Pvt. John Honneck, Co. B
Pvt. Pascal J. Johnson, Co. C
Pvt. Lewis Kittering, Co. L
Pvt. Marquis Lagush, Co. D
Pvt. George B. Luckin, Co. D
Saddler Francis McBride, Co. H

Pvt. Frederick Mestney, Co. L
Pvt. Michael Rudicil, Co. D
Pvt. John Schaffner, Co. B
Pvt. Henry Taylor, Co. L
Pvt. John Walsh, Co. L
Pvt. Thomas Mullen, Co. A
Pvt. Gustave Froelich, Co. A
Pvt. John Leonard, Co. A
Pvt. William Lumley, Co. A
Pvt. John W. Wilson, Co. C

Total: 24

Total Casualties: 30

Kilpatrick's Headquarter's Escort

Company M, 9th Pennsylvania Cavalry

Killed/Mortally Wounded

Pvt. James K. Davis

Total: 1

Missing/Captured

Pvt. O. P. Ball
Pvt. Lafayette Caldwell

Total: 2

Total Casualties: 3

Way's Dismounted Brigade

Killed

Pvt. John Jones (9th Pennsylvania Cavalry)
Cpl. William H. West (9th Pennsylvania Cavalry)
Pvt. John St. Clair (9th Pennsylvania Cavalry)

Pvt. Robert Searlet (9th Pennsylvania Cavalry)
Pvt. Harry Peters (9th Pennsylvania Cavalry)
Pvt. Martin Schneider (9th Michigan Cavalry)
Pvt. Amaziah D. Youngs (9th Michigan Cavalry)
Pvt. John J. Stout (3rd Kentucky Cavalry)

Total: 8

Wounded

Pvt. James Long (10th Ohio Cavalry)
Sgt. John Kemmerly (9th Pennsylvania Cavalry)
Pvt. John Mateen (9th Pennsylvania Cavalry)
Cpl. Christian Stettler (9th Pennsylvania Cavalry)
Pvt. John M. Tarbet (9th Pennsylvania Cavalry)
Pvt. Henry Zerphy (9th Pennsylvania Cavalry)
Pvt. Henry Shelly (8th Indiana Cavalry)

Total: 7

Captured/Missing

Pvt. Daniel Bell (9th Ohio Cavalry)
Pvt. William H. Bondure (9th Ohio Cavalry)
Pvt. Thomas McNamee (9th Ohio Cavalry)
Pvt. James L. Patterson (9th Ohio Cavalry)
Pvt. William Miller (10th Ohio Cavalry)
Pvt. George Snyder (10th Ohio Cavalry)
Pvt. Daniel Whisler (10th Ohio Cavalry)
Pvt. Calvin W. Ballard (10th Ohio Cavalry)
Pvt. John A. Canfield (10th Ohio Cavalry)
Pvt. Thomas Farrell (10th Ohio Cavalry)
Pvt. Walter W. Francis (10th Ohio Cavalry)
Pvt. Walter S. Francis (10th Ohio Cavalry)
Pvt. Schontz Jones (10th Ohio Cavalry)
Pvt. James W. Knapp (10th Ohio Cavalry)
Pvt. Henry McCarty (10th Ohio Cavalry)
Pvt. Hosea H. Meek (10th Ohio Cavalry)
Pvt. Benjamin F. Miley (10th Ohio Cavalry)
Cpl. Oliver Powell (10th Ohio Cavalry)
Pvt. Charles Quinn (10th Ohio Cavalry)

Pvt. Albert Sowers (10th Ohio Cavalry)
Pvt. Clark Hoyt (10th Ohio Cavalry)
Sgt. Carey A. Vaughn (10th Ohio Cavalry)
Pvt. Charles E. Webster (10th Ohio Cavalry)
Pvt. John Onlicker (10th Ohio Cavalry)
Maj. Charles A. Appel (9th Pennsylvania Cavalry)
Pvt. Henry K. Myers (9th Pennsylvania Cavalry)
Pvt. Joseph Jones (9th Pennsylvania Cavalry)
Pvt. Amos Miller (9th Pennsylvania Cavalry)
Pvt. Jacob Metzel (9th Pennsylvania Cavalry)
Pvt. Carnet C. Lathrop (9th Michigan Cavalry)
Pvt. Edwin Bartram (9th Michigan Cavalry)
Sgt. Isaac W. Pierce (9th Michigan Cavalry)
Pvt. William Brown (9th Michigan Cavalry)
Pvt. George Grove (9th Michigan Cavalry)
Pvt. Dan L. Williams (9th Michigan Cavalry)
Bugler Jackson Cleveland (9th Michigan Cavalry)
Bugler Francis Moutau (9th Michigan Cavalry)
Pvt. Peter Vouders (9th Michigan Cavalry)
Pvt. William Woodall (2nd Kentucky Cavalry)
Bugler James W. Lucas (3rd Kentucky Cavalry)

Total: 40

Total Casualties: 55

10th Wisconsin Battery

Killed

Sgt. John Swartz

Total: 1

Missing

10 unidentified members of the battery

Total Casualties: 11

Total Union Casualties: 248

* * *

CONFEDERATE

Wheeler's Corps

Humes's Division

Wounded

Brig. Gen. William Y. C. Humes

Total: 1

Harrison's Texas Brgiade

Wounded

Brig. Gen. Thomas Harrison
Capt. Billy Sayers, Assistant Adjutant General

Total : 2

8th Texas Cavalry

Col. Gustave Cooke

Total: 1

4th/8th Tennessee Cavalry (Consolidated):

Killed

Lt. Joe Massengale, Co. B
Pvt. Arch Roland, Co. C

Total: 2

Wounded

Lt. Col. Paul Anderson

Pvt. Joe Cato, Co. C
Pvt. B. Porter Harrison, Co. I

Total: 3

Total: 5

Hagan's Alabama Brigade

Wounded

Col. James Hagan

Total: 1

3rd Alabama Cavalry

Wounded

Maj. John D. Farish, Commanding regiment
Capt. Joseph Robins

Total: 2

53rd Alabama Cavalry

Wounded

Col. Moses W. Hannon, commanding regiment

Total : 1

Anderson's Brigade

8th Confederate Cavalry

Killed

Reubin D. Newsom

Total: 1

10th Confederate Cavalry

Killed

Lt. William Parker

Total: 1

McLemore's Brigade

4th Tennessee Cavalry

Wounded

Lt. James E. Hogin

Total: 1

Butler's Division

Capt. James Butler (staff officer)
Capt. Nathaniel Butler (staff officer)

Total Casualties: 2

Wright's Brigade

Jeff Davis Legion Cavalry

Wounded

Maj. Ivey F. Lewis, Field and Staff
Total Casualties: 1

Cobb's Legion

Killed

Lt. Col. Barrington S. King, Commanding Regiment

Pvt. Jim Jack

Total: 2

Butler's (Law's) Brigade

4th South Carolina Cavalry

Wounded

Capt. M. C. Dickson

Total: 1

Captured

Pvt. Samuel Quarterman, Co. C

Total: 1

Total Casualties: 2

5th South Carolina Cavalry

Mortally Wounded

Sgt. J. H. Dukes, Co. A
Pvt. D. C. Hill, Co. A

Total: 2

Wounded

Capt. A. H. Caughman, Co. F
Lt. J. P. DeVeaux, Co. D
Pvt. William Teppe, Jr., Co. D
Pvt. D. Lupo, Co. F
Pvt. William Sheal, Co. F
Pvt. D. P. Harmon, Co. F
Pvt. D. C. Eison, Co. K
Pvt. J. T. Stener, Co. K

Total: 8

Missing

Pvt. R. P. McDaniel, Co. K.

Total: 1

Total Casualties: 11

6th South Carolina Cavalry

Killed

Sgt. Sam Cothran, Co. B
Pvt. Tom Sego, Co. B
Pvt. Mat Adams, Co. B
Pvt. Fayette Cogburn, Co. B.

Total: 4

Total Recorded (incomplete) Confederate Casualties: 40

Appendix C

Who was Judson Kilpatrick's Female Companion in March 1865?

Historians have long speculated as to the identity of "Alice," Judson Kilpatrick's female companion at Monroe's Crossroads. Most have concluded that she was Marie Boozer, a noted South Carolina beauty. This appendix will explore the question of whether Kilpatrick's companion really was Marie Boozer.

Marie knew that she was gorgeous and was quite vain about it—never an attractive trait in any person. "Boozer is always on exhibition," noted Mary Chesnut in her diary, "walking, riding, driving—wherever a woman's face can go, there is Boozer."[1]

Born in 1848 in Columbia, South Carolina, the tall blue-eyed blonde beauty was all of seventeen in March 1865. "It seems there was an exceedingly pretty young girl in Columbia when these boys had been there lately, whom some of them had been acquainted with," recalled a South Carolinian. "She dressed very well and drove in a victoria at a time when it was not *comme il faut* to dress well and drive in victorias."[2] Even the gruff William T. Sherman described Marie as beautiful.

Maries's mother, Amelia Feaster, was a Northerner and ardent Unionist. She often stated her political views publicly, which did not sit well with the pro-Confederate Columbians.[3] Mrs. Feaster soon became infamous. "Mrs. Feaster (the mother of the too-famous beauty Boozer), according to Captain James, has left her husband," reported Mrs. Chesnut. "She has had husbands enough. She has been married three times. And yet by all showing did not begin to marry soon enough. Witness the existence of Boozer." The notorious Mrs. Feaster was the subject of *Another Jezebel*, a 1958 novel by Nell S. Graydon. The title makes clear what contemporary Southerners thought of Amelia Feaster.[4]

Unencumbered by her mother's Northern roots, Marie was much more flexible in her loyalties. "Under the Confederate regime and until Sherman entered Columbia Miss Boozer was a good Rebel," noted an early biographer, "but she was too vain and sensible of her attractiveness to allow a matter of patriotism to interfere with her ambition to attract admiration, so she soon numbered her visitors from the ranks of the men whom a short time before she had regarded as enemies."[5] When Columbia fell to Sherman's army, Mrs. Feaster saw a chance for herself and Marie to return to her native Philadelphia, and the two women joined the Union army's march north. Mother and daughter rode in a carriage. Marie was seen conversing with "a gay looking officer," possibly Little Kil.[6]

As a result, many have speculated over the years that Marie Boozer was Alice. "Given the time and places of her appearances there is little doubt that this 'Alice' was Marie," wrote Tom Elmore, an historian from Columbia who has studied Marie Boozer's life in detail and who has described her as the "femme fatale of the Confederacy."[7]

Samuel Martin, who has to date written the only published modern biography of Judson Kilpatrick, also believes that Alice was Marie Boozer, as do Burke Davis and John G. Barrett, two prominent modern Civil War historians and authors. However, none of these historians present evidence to support the claim that Marie Boozer and Alice were the same woman. They rely instead on hearsay accounts that have been passed along for more than a century. So the question remains: was Marie Boozer really Alice?

One eyewitness, Edward L. Wells of the Charleston Light Dragoons, served in Hampton's headquarters escort. Like most of the Dragoons, Wells had seen Marie Boozer during their stay in Columbia and he also knew that Marie and Amelia had subsequently gone north with Sherman's army. On March 9, the day before the Battle of Monroe's Crossroads, rumors flew that Marie was in a carriage following Kilpatrick's headquarters. "Is it she! I know it is!" declared some. "By Jove! Certain?" responded others.[8] The excited soldiers were in for a disappointment.

On the morning of March 10, when Kilpatrick abandoned poor Alice to her fate, Wells got a good look at her when she emerged from Charles Monroe's house. Here is his account:

> About this time, at the entrance-door of the headquarters house, a female skirt, a hat and ribbon and other similar accoutrements of the fair sex appeared, and were at once spied by some of those young fellows who had been found whispering together the night before.

The first duty of the cavalier is to rescue distressed damsels, and so these boys thoroughly believed, and were about delightedly so to do. But, alas! for all human hopes. On nearer inspection this proved to be the wrong damsel, if damsel she could be termed at all, being old, ugly, and perhaps respectable, and she turned out to be a "school-marm" from Vermont, who had availed herself of the assistance of Sherman's army to return to her home. However, she was a woman after all, if she was ugly, and one of those same thoughtless youngsters referred to, quietly dismounted, and, hat in hand, approached her, bowing as deferentially as if it indeed had been the hoped-for fair one, and kindly explained the danger from chance bullets and shells against which the thin weather-boarding of the house would be little better protection than pasteboard. But woman-like, she could not at first be made to comprehend that the horses could not be attached to her vehicle and she drive quietly away to more congenial scenes. However, at length she took in the situation sensibly, and was conducted to a drainage-ditch, in which she lay and was comparatively safe. Fortunately, she was not hurt during the melee, and seemed . . . appreciative of the kindness done her. But it was a sad disappointment to those expectant boys.[9]

Wells was quite emphatic in his assertion that the woman rescued was not noted beauty Marie Boozer. In stark contrast to Wells's account, however, was another penned by an officer of the 3rd Alabama who recalled that the damsel in distress was "a beautiful young Irish woman, in scanty night-dress."[10]

Indisputable documentary evidence exists that Marie Boozer was not present at Monroe's Crossroads. Historian Mark L. Bradley was the first to discover that on March 10, 1865, Marie and her mother were the guests of Maj. Gen. O. O. Howard, who was quite taken with his glamorous young visitor.[11] Howard wrote to his wife that Marie and her mother had lost everything during the burning of Columbia, and that they were heading to Amelia's home town of Philadelphia. An admiring Howard noted that the two women had "completely mastered all the discomforts of military life." The general also noted, "I have mentioned them because we have seen so much of them for the last three weeks and I have learned that [the two women] can campaign."[12] On the basis of Wells's account and Howard's letter to his wife, it is therefore safe to conclude that Marie Boozer was not Kilpatrick's Alice.

Given the scandalous nature of Alice's presence at Kilpatrick's headquarters, her life's details never came to light. She appeared content to maintain her anonymity. The question of Alice's identity remains unanswered.

Appendix D

What was Joseph Wheeler's Rank in March 1865?

"During the spring [of 1865], General Wheeler was appointed by the President *Lieutenant General* of Cavalry, he having held a command which entitled him to that rank continuously for two years and a half, a longer period than any other officer of the Confederate army had retained continuous command of an army corps in the field," proclaimed one of Fighting Joe's staff officers in a brief biography published a few months after the end of the war.[1]

This early biographer was not the only one to claim that Wheeler had been promoted to lieutenant general during the final days of the war. The *Confederate Military History*, a multi-volume encyclopedia of the Confederacy published in 1899, also claims Wheeler "was promoted lieutenant-general, February 28, 1865."[2]

W. C. Dodson chronicled the history of Wheeler's Cavalry Corps. Relying upon a few brief biographies of Wheeler contained in compendia such as the *Dictionary of American Biography*, Dodson declared, "From the above it will be seen that Wheeler was a Lieutenant-General, and that his commission was only fourteen days inferior in date to that of General Hampton." According to Dodson, Wheeler received his promotion on February 28, 1865, less than two weeks after Hampton received his promotion. "Really the reason that Wheeler was not commissioned Lieutenant-General while acting as such in 1863 was owing to it being then the policy of the Administration not to organize the cavalry into army corps," asserted Dodson.[3]

As a result of early works such as these, some modern historians have claimed Wheeler was a lieutenant general. Even the handsome monument erected on the Monroe's Crossroads battlefield by the United States Army in 1981 indicates that Joe Wheeler was a lieutenant general.[4] But was he?

Edward L. Wells of the Charleston Light Dragoons was one of the first to dispute the contention that Wheeler had been promoted to lieutenant general. In his 1899 book *Hampton and His Cavalry in '64*, Wells wrote the following: "Only two officers in the Confederate army attained the commission of Lieutenant-General. These were Hampton and Forrest, ranking in the order stated. Wheeler is frequently referred to in newspapers as a Lieutenant-General, and *Appleton's Cyclopedia of American Biography* states that he was so, but this is a mistake: he was a Major-General [of cavalry]."[5]

Ezra J. Warner, whose magnificent *Generals in Gray* serves as the standard reference work on the general officers of the Confederacy, addressed the question of Wheeler's rank in his introduction:

> It has always been taken for granted, for example, that Major Generals John B. Gordon of Georgia and Joseph Wheeler of Alabama were lieutenant generals, despite the fact that no conclusive evidence exists to support such assumptions. Unofficial lists of Confederate generals usually cite both officers as lieutenant generals...In point of fact, Wheeler's nomination as major general was debated in the Senate for over a year; confirmation was finally voted, 12 to 9, only by Davis's appealing to the distinctly unfriendly Joseph E. Johnston for assistance in persuading certain recalcitrant senators. It is entirely probable that Johnston, who was partial to Wheeler, recommended the latter for promotion; there are indications in the *Official Records* which can be construed to mean that he gave Wheeler assurances of a forthcoming commission at that grade. No evidence of such, however, can be found.[6]

In answering the question of Wheeler's rank in the spring of 1865, Col. Alfred Roman's words are enlightening. In January of that year, Roman wrote a scathing inspection report of Wheeler's corps that has been discussed elsewhere in this book. Some of it bears repeating here. "My honest conviction is that General Wheeler would be a most excellent brigade or division commander," Roman noted, "but I do not consider him the proper man to be placed at the head of a large independent cavalry corps. Under him and in spite of his good discipline and soldierly qualities, no true discipline will ever be perfect in his command nor with the whole efficiency of his corps, the entire fighting capabilities of his men, their dash, their intrepidity, be ever fairly and fully developed. Had I the power to act in the matter," Roman concluded, "I would relieve General Wheeler from his command, not as a rebuke, not as a punishment, for he surely deserves neither, but on higher grounds, that is, for the good of the cause and for his own reputation. We have no time to lose at this juncture of our affairs. If we intend to resist we must do it gloriously, promptly and fear no personal dissatisfaction in the performance of our duties. We have too much at stake to hesitate a moment."[7]

General P. G. T. Beauregard wholeheartedly endorsed his nephew's (Roman's) recommendation, which indirectly led to Wade Hampton's appointment to command the cavalry forces assigned to Joe Johnston's army. Given that fact, it seems unlikely that Wheeler would receive a near-simultaneous promotion in 1865 to lieutenant general.

As Ezra Warner noted, there was considerable resistance to Wheeler's promotion to the lesser rank of major general. The lengthy debate over the propriety of the nomination suggests that the War Child was unpopular with many Confederate politicians. Further, the poor discipline of Wheeler's men during the campaigns in Georgia had endeared him to neither President Davis nor the Confederate Congress. Finally, there is no evidence to suggest that Johnston lobbied for Wheeler in 1865 as he had in 1864. In short, it is unlikely that either Davis or the Confederate Congress would have endorsed a promotion for Wheeler in the spring of 1865. A review of *The Journal of the Confederate Congress* fails to provide any evidence of the presentation of a proposed promotion to lieutenant general to the Senate on Wheeler's behalf.

Late in life, Wade Hampton also weighed in on this question. "Wheeler was never Lt. Genl," he declared to his old friend and subordinate Brig. Gen. Bradley T. Johnson in 1900. "He was under my command when Johnston surrendered. There were 21 Lt. Genls. in all & if you will write to the War Records Office, a list of them will be sent to you. Some of this number held only temporary rank. I think that no commissions were made by the Confederate Govmt. which was sent of the nomination & the confirmation of the Senate."[8] Without confirmation by the Senate, no "promotion" was effective, and there is no record of Wheeler's name being submitted to the Senate for confirmation as a lieutenant general. Just a few months earlier, the aged general proclaimed that Wheeler would "sometimes do the big thing by calling himself Lt. Genl."[9]

An article that appeared in a Charleston, South Carolina, newspaper in 1899 provided the complete list of Confederate officers who achieved the rank of lieutenant general, including their dates of rank. Wheeler's name does not appear on the list. "We have no wish to discredit Gen. Wheeler's services during the Confederate war," proclaimed the newspaper, "and particularly because of his splendid work during the recent war with Spain; but it is a little strange that the War Records office should have discovered no sign of him in the Confederate records of Lieutenant Generals up to within three weeks of the surrender of Lee's army at Appomattox, and within about six weeks of the surrender of the Western army at Greensboro."[10]

A 1904 article that appeared in *The Southern Historical Society Papers* supports this conclusion. The author, responding to representations made in the

Papers that Wheeler was a lieutenant general, recounted a conversation with Wade Hampton regarding the flight of Jefferson Davis at the end of the Civil War. "Gen. Hampton then suggested that with a small escort the President should take Gen. Wheeler to accompany him, as the latter would be useful, being well-known in much of the country through which the party would probably have to pass, and that he (the President) should confer on Wheeler the title of Lieut.-General, in order to increase his prestige and influence with the people of the country. But, the latter part of the proposition the President positively refused to accede to."[11]

Perhaps the best evidence of all that Fighting Joe Wheeler had not received a promotion during that long and unhappy winter is that the cavalryman himself did not sign any of his final reports or routine correspondence as a lieutenant general. As late as April 27, 1865, he signed his correspondence, "J. Wheeler, Major-General."[12] Wheeler's own signature provides the most compelling evidence that he was not promoted to lieutenant general in February 1865.

According to all the pertinent evidence, it appears that Wade Hampton was the only lieutenant general commanding cavalry in Joseph E. Johnston's army in 1865.

Notes

Preface

1. George Ward Nichols, *The Story of the Great March* (New York: Harper & Brothers, 1865), 310.

2. Obviously, a detailed discussion of the momentous events that occurred at Bennett Place goes far beyond the scope of this work. For the best treatment of these events yet written, see Mark L. Bradley, *This Astounding Close: The Road to Bennett Place* (Chapel Hill: University of North Carolina Press, 2000).

3. Diary of J. Frederick Waring, entry for April 17, 1865, J. Frederick Waring Papers, Southern Historical Collection, Wilson Library, University of North Carolina, Chapel Hill.

4. Nichols, *The Story of the Great March,* 310.

5. *Cincinnati Daily Commercial,* April 27, 1865; *New York Herald,* April 27, 1865; and *Philadelphia Inquirer,* April 28, 1865.

6. *Sussex Independent,* January 13, 1882.

7. *Philadelphia Inquirer,* April 28, 1865.

8. David P. Conyngham, *Sherman's March through the South With Sketches and Incidents of the Campaign* (New York: Sheldan & Co., 1865), 365.

9. J. W. Evans, "Reminiscences of J. W. Evans in the War Between the States," included in *Confederate Reminiscences and Letters 1861-1865,* vol. 10 (Atlanta: Georgia Division, United Daughters of the Confederacy, 1999), 22.

10. Memorandum of conversation with Wade Hampton, October 5, 1895, Bradley T. Johnson Papers, Perkins Library, Duke University, Durham, North Carolina.

11. *Cincinnati Daily Commercial,* April 27, 1865; *New York Herald,* April 27, 1865, and *Philadelphia Inquirer,* April 28, 1865; Henry Hitchcock, *Marching With Sherman: Passages From the Letters and Campaign Diaries of Henry Hitchcock,* M. A. DeWolfe Howe, ed. (Lincoln: University of Nebraska Press, 1995), 310; Henry B. McClellan, "The Campaign of 1863—A Reply to Kilpatrick," *The Philadelphia Weekly Times,* February 7, 1880. McClellan, who served as Hampton's able adjutant general, wrote, "During the convention concerning the surrender held at the close of the war, near Greensboro, N.C., by Generals Sherman and Johnston, a conversation occurred between General Kilpatrick and General Wade Hampton which was heard by many officers of both armies. In the conversation various incidents of previous campaigns were discussed. Unable to endure the polished thrusts of Hampton, that prince among gentlemen, General Kilpatrick closed the conversation with an outburst of anger and profanity unworthy of the occasion."

12. Bradley, *This Astounding Close,* 168.

Chapter 1

1. A lengthy discussion of the conduct of Sherman's cavalry during the Atlanta Campaign strays far beyond the scope of this book. See David Evans, *Sherman's Horsemen: Union Cavalry Operations in the Atlanta Campaign* (Bloomington: University of Indiana Press, 1996), for the most detailed analysis of the performance of the Federal cavalry in this critical campaign.

2. Samuel J. Martin, *"Kill-Cavalry:" Sherman's Merchant of Terror—The Life of Union General Hugh Judson Kilpatrick* (Cranbury, N.J.: Associated University Presses, 1996), 15-16.

3. James Harrison Wilson, *Under the Old Flag: Recollections of Military Operations in the War for the Union, the Spanish War, the Boxer Rebellion, Etc.,* 2 vols. (New York: D. Appleton, 1912): 1:370-71.

4. Martin, *Kill-Cavalry,* 17-20. A member of the 9th Pennsylvania Cavalry described Kilpatrick's battle flag. "It is pure red . . . perfectly red with three white stars denoting the number of brigades in our division. Above the flag float two white streamers about three feet in length, one of them bearing the inscription in letters of gold—'Kilpatrick's Cavalry,' the other 'Alice.'" This veteran noted that "The rebels hate the flag infernally. They look upon it with horror; and well they may. For wherever it waves, the cavalry make their mark." Diary of William

W. Pritchard, entry for June 2, 1865, Civil War Miscellaneous Collection, United States Army Military History Institute, Carlisle, Pennsylvania.

5. G. Wayne King, "General Judson Kilpatrick," *New Jersey History*, vol. XCI, no. 1 (Spring 1973), 35-38.

6. For a detailed discussion of Elon Farnsworth's charge and death, see Eric J. Wittenberg, *Gettysburg's Forgotten Cavalry Actions* (Gettysburg, Pa.: Thomas Publications, 1998).

7. Martin, *Kill-Cavalry,* 127-28.

8. For a detailed treatment of the Kilpatrick-Dahlgren Raid, see, Virgil Carrington Jones, *Eight Hours Before Richmond* (New York: Holt, 1957).

9. *Detroit Free Press,* March 26, 1864.

10. King, "General Judson Kilpatrick," 43.

11. James H. Kidd, *Personal Recollections of a Cavalryman in Custer's Michigan Brigade* (Ionia, Mich.: Sentinel Publishing Co., 1908), 164-65.

12. James A. Connelly, *Three Years in Army of the Cumberland: The Letters and Diary of Major James A. Connelly,* Paul M. Angle, ed. (Bloomington: University of Indiana Press, 1959), 348.

13. George R. Agassiz, ed., *Meade's Headquarters 1863-1865: Letters of Colonel Theodore Lyman From the Wilderness to Appomattox* (Boston: The Atlantic Monthly Press, 1922), 76.

14. Edward G. Longacre, "Judson Kilpatrick," *Civil War Times Illustrated* 10 (April 1971), 25, hereafter referred to as *CWTI.*

15. Charles Francis Adams, *A Cycle of Adams Letters, 1861-1865,* Worthington C. Ford, ed., 2 vols. (Boston: Houghton-Mifflin, 1920), 2:44-45.

16. Longacre, "Judson Kilpatrick," 25.

17. Henry C. Meyer, *Civil War Experiences Under Bayard, Gregg, Kilpatrick, Custer, Raulston, and Newbury, 1862, 1863, 1864* (New York: Knickerbocker Press, 1911), 97.

18. Charles S. Wainwright, *A Diary of Battle: The Personal Journals of Colonel Charles S. Wainwright, 1861-1865,* Allan Nevins, ed. (New York: Harcourt, Brace & World, 1962), 265.

19. Oliver Otis Howard, *Autobiography of Oliver Otis Howard, Major General, United States Army,* 2 vols. (New York: Baker & Taylor Co., 1907), 2:29.

20. Affidavit of Dr. R. Blacknall, August 8, 1872, RG 107, Records of the Office of the Secretary of War, "Statements dated 1872 concerning Gen. H. Judson Kilpatrick's affair with a woman during the Civil War," included in "Letters, telegrams, reports, and other records concerning the loyalty of Army Officers, War Department employees, and citizens during the Civil War, 1861-1872," Box 2.

21. Statement of Mrs. James Dick, August 10, 1872, "Statements dated 1872."

22. Statement of Edmund Hill, August 9, 1872, "Statements dated 1872."

23. Statement of Mrs. James Dick, August 10, 1872, "Statements dated 1872."

24. Statement of James H. Miller , August 6, 1872, "Statements dated 1872."

25. Edward L. Wells, *A Sketch of the Charleston Light Dragoons, From the Earliest Formation of the Corps* (Charleston, S.C.: Lucas, Richardson & Co., 1888), 90.

26. *Ibid.*

27. James H. Miller Statement. Many historians have speculated that "Alice" was actually Marie Boozer of Columbia, South Carolina, reputedly the most beautiful woman in the South. While it is true that Marie Boozer and her mother were traveling north with the Union army, they accompanied Maj. Gen. Oliver O. Howard's headquarters. See O. O. Howard to his wife, March 12, 1865, O. O. Howard Papers, Special Collections, Bowdoin College, Brunswick, Maine. The subject of the identity of Kilpatrick's female companion is addressed at some length in Appendix C of this book.

28. H. C. Reynolds to Thomas M. Owen, September 17, 1913, Henry Clay Reynolds Papers, LPR 61, Alabama Department of Archives & History, Montgomery, Alabama.

29. *Memorial Addresses of the Life and Character of Robert M. A. Hawk, Delivered in the House of Representatives and in the Senate, Forty-Seventh Congress* (Washington, D.C.: U.S. Government Printing Office, 1883), 9.

30. Sherman, *Memoirs,* 2:253, 259-261

31. Sokolosky, *The Role of Union Logistics,* 9; Ulysses S. Grant, *Personal Memoirs of Ulysses S. Grant,* 2 vols. (New York: Charles Webster and Company, 1885), 2:529.

32. Sherman, *Memoirs*, 2:224-225; Bradley, *Last Stand*, 2.

33. Sherman, *Memoirs*, 2:238.

34. Sherman, Memoirs, 2:263 and *The War of the Rebellion: A Compilation of the Official Records of the Union and Confederate Armies*, 128 vols. (Washington, D.C.: U.S. Government Printing Office, 1889-1904), Series 1, 47, part 1, 136. Hereinafter referred to as *OR*. Unless otherwise noted, all subsequent references are to Series 1.

35. Bradley, *Last Stand*, 2-4; Sherman, *Memoirs*, 2:225.

36. Sherman, *Memoirs*, 2:272-274; Bradley, *Last Stand*, 3-4.

37. John Reed, "The Action at Aiken, S.C.," *National Tribune*, August 30, 1888.

38. Committee of the Regiment, *Ninety-Second Illinois Volunteers* (Freeport, Ill.: Journal Steam Publishing House and Bookbindery, 1875), 215.

39. Wilbur F. Hinman, *The Story of the Sherman Brigade, the Camp, the March, the Bivouac, the Battle, and How the Boys Lived and Died During Four Years of Active Field Service* (Alliance, Ohio: privately published, 1897), 911.

40. Reed, "The Action at Aiken, S.C."

41. *Ibid.*

42. *Ninety-Second Illinois Volunteers*, 218.

43. D. B. Morgan, "Incidents of the Fighting at Aiken, S.C.," *Confederate Veteran* 32 (1924): 300-301; Tom Elmore, "Head to Head," *CWTI,* 40 (Feb 2001): 44-52 and 54-55; and John G. Barrett, *Sherman's March Through the Carolinas* (Chapel Hill: University of North Carolina Press, 1956), 56-57.

44. *OR* 47, pt. 2, 450.

45. Connelly, *Three Years in Army of the Cumberland*, 349.

46. *OR* 46, pt. 1, 47-48.

47. Barrett, *Sherman's March*, 91; and Sherman, *Memoirs*, 2:281.

48. *OR* 46, pt. 2, 606. Grant had been begging Sheridan to come to Petersburg since November 1864, after Sheridan's victory at Cedar Creek on October 19, 1864, but he had never ordered him to do so.

49. *Ibid.*, 701.

50. For a detailed discussion of Sheridan's insubordination, see Eric J. Wittenberg, *Little Phil: A Critical Assessment of the Civil War Generalship of Philip H. Sheridan* (Dulles, Va.: Brassey's, 2002), 97-100.

51. Sherman, *Memoirs*, 2:280-8; and Barrett, *Sherman's March*, 89-90. For a more detailed account of the burning of Columbia, see Marion Brunson Lucas, *Sherman and the Burning of Columbia* (College Station, Texas: Texas A&M University Press, 1976).

52. Bradley, *Last Stand*, 78; Barrett, *Sherman's March*, 122.

53. Sherman, *Memoirs,* 2:292-93.

54. Samuel P. Bates, *Martial Deeds of Pennsylvania* (Philadelphia: T. H. Davis & Co., 1875), 704-5.

55. *Ibid.*, 705.

56. *Ibid.*, 707.

57. John W. Rowell, *Yankee Cavalrymen: Through the Civil War With the Ninth Pennsylvania Cavalry* (Knoxville: University of Tennessee Press, 1971), 21; Roger D. Hunt and Jack R. Brown, *Brevet Brigadier Generals in Blue* (Gaithersburg, Md.: Olde Soldier Books, 1989), 322; Joseph G. Vale, *Minty and the Cavalry: A History of Cavalry Campaigns in the Western Armies* (Harrisburg, Pa.: E. K. Meyers, 1886), 543.

58. For more detail on the critical role played by the Lightning Brigade at Chickamauga, see Richard A. Baumgartner, *Blue Lightning: Wilder's Mounted Infantry Brigade in the Battle of Chickamauga* (Huntington, W.V.: Blue Acorn Press, 1999).

59. Hunt and Long, *Brevet Brigadier Generals in Blue*, 19.

60. Claire E. Swordberg, ed., *Three Years With the 92nd Illinois: The Civil War Diary of John M. King* (Mechanicsburg, Pa.: Stackpole Books, 1999), 8-9.

61. Hunt and Long, *Brevet Brigadier Generals in Blue*, 575; Glenda McWhirter Todd, *First Alabama Cavalry USA: Homage to Patriotism* (Bowie, Md.: Heritage Books, 1999), 9-13 and 355.

62. *OR* 44, 504-5.

63. For more on the pursuit and capture of John Hunt Morgan and his raiders, see Lester V. Horwitz, *The Longest Raid of the Civil War* (Cincinnati: Farmcourt Publishing, 1999).

64. William B. Way service records, RG 94, The National Archives, Washington, D.C.; John Robertson, comp., *Michigan in the War* (Lansing: W. S. George & Co., 1882), 705-15.

65. "Death of Civil War Veteran on Sunday," *Wantage Recorder*, February 1, 1918.

66. Interestingly, Northrop's term of service ended in the fall of 1864, and he was ordered to return to his regiment, the 2nd New York Cavalry, in order to be mustered out of service, in part because there were too few men left in his company to keep him in the service. It required the intervention of Kilpatrick and army headquarters to keep Northrop in service. See Special Field Orders No, 267, copy included in Northrop's service records file, RG 393, The National Archives, Washington, D.C.

67. "Death of Capt. Northrop," *Sussex Independent*, February 1, 1918, and *The Sussex Register*, January 31, 1918.

68. Theodore F. Northrop to the Adjutant General of the Army, March 12, 1917, RG 94, Records of the Adjutant General's Office 1780-1917, Theodore F. Northrop, Captain of Volunteers File, File No. 1674 vs. 1676, Box 1200, National Archives, Washington, D.C.

69. Meyer, *Civil War Experiences*, 102.

70. Theodore F. Northrop, "Capture of Gen. Rhett," *National Tribune*, January 18, 1906. Northrop was mistaken; Rhett was never a general.

71. T. E. Camburn, "Capture of Col. Rhett," *National Tribune*, August 23, 1906.

72. Theodore F. Northrop service and pension records, RG 94, National Archives, Washington, D.C.

73. James Miller, "With Sherman Through the Carolinas," *Civil War Times, Illustrated*, 8, No. 6 (Oct. 1969), 37.

74. These weapons were a variety of calibers, ranging from .52 caliber to .57 caliber.

75. Douglas D. Scott and William J. Hunt, Jr., *The Civil War Battle of Monroe's Crossroads: A Historical Archaeological Perspective* (Fort Bragg, N.C.: U. S. Army, 1998), 76-97. The Sharps was the most popular of the breech-loading carbines utilized by either side during the Civil War. It fired a .52 caliber bullet.

Chapter 2

1. John P. Dyer, *From Shiloh to San Juan: The Life of "Fightin' Joe" Wheeler* (Baton Rouge: Louisiana State University Press, 1961), 1-15.

2. *Ibid.,* 18-57.

3. Joseph Wheeler, *A Revised System of Cavalry Tactics, for the Use of the Cavalry and Mounted Infantry, C. S. A.* (Mobile, Ala.: S. H. Goetzel & Co., 1863).

4. Evans, *Sherman's Horsemen,* 242.

5. For a detailed study of Wheeler's negligence leading up to the Battle of Chickamauga, see, Peter Cozzens, *This Terrible Sound: The Battle of Chickamauga* (Urbana: University of Illinois Press, 1992).

6. "A Staff Officer," *Synopsis of the Military Career of Gen. Joseph Wheeler, Commander of the Cavalry Corps, Army of the West* (New York: n.p., 1865), 34.

7. J. A. Wyeth, "Gen. Joseph Wheeler," *Confederate Veteran* 6 (1898), 361.

8. "A Staff Officer," *Synopsis of the Military Career,* 34.

9. T. C. DeLeon, *Joseph Wheeler; the Man, the Statesman, the Soldier, Seen in Semi-Biographical Sketches* (Atlanta: Byrd Printing, 1899), 120, 131.

10. "A Staff Officer," *Synopsis of the Military Career,* 35.

11. Thomas L. Connelly, *Autumn of Glory: The Army of Tennessee, 1862-1865* (Baton Rouge: Louisiana State University Press, 1971), 316.

12. *Atlanta Southern Confederacy,* July 5, 1864.

13. There is some dispute about Wheeler's rank during the winter of 1865. Wheeler and many of his supporters claimed that Wheeler had received a promotion to lieutenant general that winter. The record does not support this conclusion. This controversy will be explored at length in Appendix D.

14. Jacqueline Glass Campbell, *When Sherman Marched North from the Sea: Resistance on the Confederate Home Front* (Chapel Hill: University of North Carolina Press, 2003), 10.

15. "Outrages of Wheeler's Command," *Charleston Mercury,* January 14, 1865.

16. Dyer, *From Shiloh to San Juan,* 165.

17. Harold S. Wilson, *Confederate Industry: Manufacturers and Quartermasters in the Civil War* (Jackson: University Press of Mississippi, 2002), 212-13.

18. Charles M. Calhoun, "Credit to Wheeler Claimed by Others," *Confederate Veteran* 20 (1912), 82.

19. Alfred Roman to Col. G. W. Brent, January 22, 1865, Papers of Alfred Roman, Manuscripts Division, Library of Congress, Washington, D. C.

20. *OR* 47, pt. 2, 1165.

21. The three full-length biographies of Wade Hampton are Manly Wade Wellman, *Giant in Gray: A Biography of Wade Hampton of South Carolina* (New York: Charles Scribner's Sons, 1949), Edward G. Longacre, *Gentleman and Soldier: A Biography of Wade Hampton III* (Nashville, Tenn.: Rutledge Hill, 2003), and Walter Brian Cisco, *Wade Hampton: Confederate Warrior, Conservative Statesman* (Dulles, VA,: Potomac Books, 2004).

22. McClellan, "The Campaign of 1863."

23. For a detailed discussion of the cavalry fight on East Cavalry Field, see Eric J. Wittenberg, *Protecting the Flank: The Battles for Brinkerhoff's Ridge and East Cavalry Field, July 2-3, 1863* (Celina, Ohio: Ironclad Publishing, 2002).

24. James G. Holmes, "The Fighting Qualities of Generals Hampton, Butler, and Others Related by Adjutant-General Holmes of Charleston," *The Sunny South,* June 13, 1896.

25. Edward L. Wells, *Hampton and His Cavalry in '64* (Richmond, VA.: B. F. Johnson Co., 1899), 76.

26. Theophilus F. Rodenbough, "Some Cavalry Leaders," in *The Photographic History of the Civil War,* vol. 10, ed. Francis Trevelyan Miller (New York: The Review of Reviews Co., 1911), 2:275-276.

27. U. R. Brooks, *Stories of the Confederacy* (Columbia, S. C.: The State Co., 1912), 367.

28. Thomas T. Munford, "A Fine Tribute to Hampton," *The State,* February 18, 1891.

29. *OR.*36, pt. 2, 1001.

30. Douglas Southall Freeman, ed., *Lee's Dispatches* (New York: G. P. Putnam's Sons, 1915), 268.

31. Tammy Galloway, ed., *Dear Old Roswell: The Civil War Letters of the King Family of Roswell, Georgia* (Macon, Ga.: Mercer University Press, 2003), 109.

32. Leonidas B. Giles, *Terry's Texas Rangers* (Austin: The Pemberton Press, 1967), 94.

33. Mamie Yeary, ed., *Reminiscences of the Boys in Gray, 1861-1865* (Dallas, Texas: Wilkinson Printing Co., 1912), 11.

34. Douglas Southall Freeman, *Lee's Lieutenants: A Study in Command,* 3 vols. (New York: Charles Scribner's Sons, 1942-44), 3:679.

35. Freeman, *Lee's Dispatches,* 317.

36. Wade Hampton, Narrative of Service 1863-1865, Wade Hampton Papers, South Caroliniana Library, University of South Carolina, Columbia, South Carolina, 159.

37. Charles E. Cauthen, ed., *Family Letters of the Three Wade Hamptons, 1782-1901* (Columbia: University of South Carolina Press, 1953), 113.

38. Freeman, *Lee's Lieutenants,* 3:679.

39. Wade Hampton to Louis T. Wigfall, January 20, 1865, Wigfall Family Papers, Library of Congress, Washington, D. C.

40. Dunbar Rowland, ed., *Jefferson Davis, Constitutionalist: His Letters, Papers, and Speeches,* 10 vols. (Jackson, Miss.: Mississippi Department of Archives and History, 1923): 6:480.

41. Wade Hampton to Edward L. Wells, April 9, 1900, Edward L. Wells Correspondence, Charleston Library Society, Charleston, South Carolina.

42. Dyer, *From Shiloh to San Juan,* 172.

43. John W. DuBose, "The Fayetteville Road Fight," *Confederate Veteran* 20 (1912), 84.

44. "An Interesting Letter," *Macon Daily Telegraph,* April 6, 1865.

45. William C. Dodson, *Campaigns of Wheeler and His Cavalry, 1862-1865* (Atlanta: Hudgins Publishing Co., 1899), 334-37. Emphasis is in the original.

46. Mary Boykin Chesnut, *A Diary from Dixie,* edited by Ben Ames Williams (Boston: Houghton-Mifflin Co., 1949), 475. Hampton apparently carried a grudge against Lee for the failure to place him in command of the Army of Northern Virginia's Cavalry Corps immediately upon the death of Jeb Stuart.

47. Edward G. Longacre, *Gentleman and Soldier: A Biography of Wade Hampton III* (Nashville, Tenn.: Rutledge Hill, 2003), 226-28.

48. Wade Hampton to Louis T. Wigfall, January 20, 1865, Louis T. Wigfall Papers, Manuscripts Division, Library of Congress, Washington, D. C.

49. *OR* 47, pt. 1, 21; William T. Sherman, *Memoirs of General William T. Sherman,* 2 vols. (New York: Charles Webster & Co., 1875), 2:287.

50. Campbell, *When Sherman Marched North,* 45.

51. Galloway, *Dear Old Roswell,* 116.

52. *OR* 47, pt. 2, 533.

53. *Ibid.,* 544.

54. *Ibid.,* pt. 1, 860.

55. *Ibid.*

56. Daniel E. Huger Smith, et al., eds., *Mason Smith Family Letters 1960-1865* (Columbia: University of South Carolina Press, 1950), 201.

57. Daniel Oakey, "Marching Through Georgia and the Carolinas," included in *Battles and Leaders of the Civil War,* Robert U. Johnson and Clarence C. Buel, eds. (New York: The Century Co., 1888), 4:678.

58. *OR* 47, pt. 2, 546.

59. *Ibid.,* 547. Troopers of the 8th Texas Cavalry, who perpetrated these killings, were armed with Spencer carbines, probably captured from the Federals.

60. *Ibid.,* 596-97.

61. Ezra J. Warner, *Generals in Gray: Lives of the Confederate Commanders* (Baton Rouge: Louisiana State University Press, 1959), 144-45; Clement A. Evans, ed., *Confederate Military History: A Library of Confederate States History, Written by Distinguished Men of the South,* 12 vols. (Atlanta: Confederate Publishing Co., 1899): 8:313-14 (hereafter referred to as "CMH"); Richard M. McMurry, *Virginia Military Institute Alumni in the Civil War: In Bello Praesidium* (Lynchburg, Va.: H. E. Howard Co., 1999), 149. Humes was a VMI classmate of Brig. Gen. Alfred J. Vaughan, who commanded a brigade of Tennessee infantry in the Army of Tennessee. Humes was apparently nominated for a commission as major general in late 1864 or early 1865, but it is unlikely the promotion was ever approved by the Confederate Senate. If it was, word did not reach Humes prior to the Battle of Monroe's Crossroads.

62. *Ibid.,* 126-7; *CMH,* 11: 239-40.

63. Roman to Brent, January 22, 1865. There were actually two different regiments designated as the 4th Tennessee Cavalry. One regiment had been raised by Nathan Bedford Forrest, and was part of McLemore's Brigade. The other 4th Tennessee was part of Wheeler's command and was the regiment that served in Harrison's Brigade, and which was consolidated with the small remnant of the 8th Tennessee Cavalry. The reader should be careful not to confuse these two regiments.

64. James P. Coffin, "Col. Henry M. Ashby," *Confederate Veteran* 14 (1906), 121; "Henry Ashby's 2nd Tennessee Cavalry in the Confederate Heartland," by James L. Mohon, in *Civil War Regiments: A Journal of the American Civil War,* vol. 4, No. 1 (1994), 1-43.

65. *CMH,* 7:385-86.

66. William B. Jones, "The Late Maj. Gen. William Wirt Allen," *Confederate Veteran* 2 (1894), 334.

67. Bruce S. Allardice, *More Generals in Gray* (Baton Rouge: Louisiana State University Press, 1995), 111-13; *CMH,* 7:415-16. There is some dispute over whether Hagan received a promotion to brigadier general in the waning days of the war, and there is some evidence to indicate that he did. For the purposes of this work Hagan will be considered a colonel.

68. Warner, *Generals in Gray,* 9-10; *CMH,* 6:392-94.

69. Allardice, in *More Generals in Gray,* 66-67, claims Crews suffered a severe wound at Monroe's Crossroads, but there is no evidence to support this assertion; John Randolph Poole, *Cracker Cavaliers: The 2nd Georgia Cavalry Under Wheeler and Forrest* (Macon, Ga.: Mercer University Press, 2000), 13, 182.

70. Warner, *Generals in Gray,* 72-3; *CMH,* 8:305-7; Roman to Brent, January 22, 1865.

71. "Col. W. C. P. Breckinridge," *Confederate Veteran* 13 (1905): 84.

72. James C. Klotter, *The Breckinridges of Kentucky, 1760-1981* (Lexington: University of Kentucky Press, 1986), 140.

73. "Meteoric War Record of Colonel W. C. P. Breckinridge, in two parts," *The Sunny South,* October 12, 1901.

74. Klotter, *The Breckinridges of Kentucky,* 141.

75. *Ibid.,* viii.

76. "Meteoric War Record of Colonel W C P Breckinridge."

77. Russell Mann, "Ninth Kentucky Cavalry, C.S.A.," *Confederate Veteran* 17 (1909), 233.

78. Milford Overley, "Williams's Kentucky Brigade, C.S.A.," *Confederate Veteran* 13 (1905), 460.

79. Klotter, *The Breckinridges of Kentucky, 1760-1981,* 143; Bennett H. Young, *Confederate Wizards of the Saddle* (Boston: Chapple Publishing Co., 1914), 69-70.

80. *History of Tennessee with an Historical and Biographical Sketch of Maury, Williamson, Rutherford, Wilson, Bedford, and Marshall Counties* (Nashville: The Goodspeed Publishing Co., 1886), 996-97; Michael Cotten, *The Williamson County Cavalry: A History of Company F, Fourth Tennessee Cavalry Regiment, CSA* (Goodlettsville, Tenn.: privately published, 1994), 3-4.

81. Nathan Bedford Forrest to James A. Seddon, August 30, 1863, Kevin D. McLemore Collection, Fort Campbell, Kentucky.

82. At the 1863 Battle of Thompson's Station, his canteen was shot through, and he mistook the warm water dribbling down his side for blood. See Diary of Bethenia McLemore, Kevin D. McLemore Collection, at 106-107.

83. B. L. Ridley, "Chat With Col. W. S. McLemore," *Confederate Veteran* 8 (1900), 262-63; John E. Fisher, *They Rode with Forrest and Wheeler: A*

Chronicle of Five Tennessee Brothers' Service in the Confederate Western Cavalry (Jefferson, N.C.: McFarland, 1995), 51.

84. Edward Laight Wells, "A Morning Call on Kilpatrick," *Southern Historical Society Papers* 12 (March 1884), 127.

85. Ulysses R. Brooks, *Butler and His Cavalry in the War of Secession, 1861-1865* (Columbia, S. C.: The State Co., 1909), 254.

86. Warner, *Generals in Gray,* 40-1. For a full-length biography of Butler, see Samuel J. Martin, *Southern Hero: Matthew Calbraith Butler—Confederate General, Hampton Red Shirt, and U. S. Senator* (Mechanicsburg, Pa.: Stackpole, 2001).

87. J. W. Ward, "General M. C. Butler of South Carolina," *Confederate Veteran* 3 (1895), 42.

88. J. Russell Wright, "Battle of Trevilian," *Recollections and Reminiscences 1861-1865,* vol. 6 (Charleston: South Carolina Division of the United Daughters of the Confederacy, 1995), 372; Wells, "A Morning Call on Kilpatrick," 127.

89. Holmes, "The Fighting Qualities."

90. Ward, "General M. C. Butler of South Carolina," 42.

91. Warner, *Generals in Gray,* 174-75; *CMH,* 7:422-24.

92. "General E. M. Law at Gettysburg," *Confederate Veteran* 30 (1922), 50.

93. "The Surprise of Kilpatrick's Camp as I Saw It," J. J. Bunch, included in *Confederate Veteran* Papers, Box 1, Perkins Library, Duke University, Durham, North Carolina.

94. Allardice, *More Generals in Gray,* 239-40; William J. Northern, *Men of Mark in Georgia,* 6 vols. (Atlanta: A. B. Caldwell, 1907-1912), 3:351-52.

95. "Unveiling of Confederate Monument at Montgomery, AL: Major Falkner's Words," *Charleston Sunday News,* November 20, 1898. For a detailed description of the weaponry carried by Wheeler's Corps, see Wayne R. Austerman, "C. S. Cavalry Arms—1865," *North South Trader,* vol. XII, No. 2 (Jan.-Feb. 1985), 22-27.

96. Roman to Brent, January 22, 1865. In fact, the Confederates tended to prefer captured Yankee ordnance to their own weapons. This made supplying ammunition to these captured weapons difficult at best.

97. Butler himself often referred to his command as mounted infantry, and not as cavalry.

98. Dodson, *Campaigns of Wheeler and His Cavalry,* 408-420.

99. Roman to Brent, January 22, 1865. Colonel Roman speculated that this was part of the reason for the poor discipline in Wheeler's command.

Chapter 3

1. Joseph E. Johnston, "My Negotiations with General Sherman," *B & L*: 653; Jefferson Davis, *The Rise and Fall of the Confederate Government*, 2 vols. (New York: D. Appleton & Co., 1881), 2:631.

2. Henry W. Grady, "An Interview with General Longstreet," included in Peter Cozzens, ed., *Battles & Leaders of the Civil War*, vol. 5 (Urbana, Ill.: University of Illinois Press, 2002), 691. (Hereafter referred to as *B & L*.)

3. Stephen R. Mallory, "The Last Days of the Confederate Government," *B & L*: 677.

4. Raleigh *Daily Confederate*, March 9, 1865.

5. William Collin Stevens to Dear Ones at Home, March 12, 1865, William Collin Stevens Papers, Bentley Historical Library, University of Michigan, Ann Arbor.

6. Raleigh *North Carolina Standard*, March 1, 1865.

7. Joseph E. Johnston, *Narrative of Military Operations, Directed During the Late War Between the States* (New York: D. Appleton and Co., 1874), 372.

8. Raleigh *Daily Confederate*, March 2, 1865.

9. William T. Sherman, *Memoirs of General William T. Sherman*, 2 vols. (New York: Charles Webster & Co., 1875), 2:725.

10. Mrs. J. H. Anderson, "Confederate Arsenal at Fayetteville, N.C.," *Confederate Veteran* 36 (1928), 223. The Confederates captured the United States arsenal in Fayetteville when North Carolina seceded in 1861. 37,000 stand of arms fell into the hands of the Confederate government at that time. Heavy equipment was shipped to Fayetteville from the large Federal armory at Harpers Ferry and installed in the North Carolina arsenal, which was then put to work manufacturing arms for the Confederacy, and it remained in service until Fayetteville was recaptured by Sherman's army. John G. Barrett, *The Civil War in North Carolina* (Chapel Hill: University of North Carolina Press, 1963), 27.

11. *OR* 47, pt. 1, 22-24. Wilmington was the last open seaport in the Confederacy. The fall of Wilmington made Confederate defeat in the Civil War inevitable. For a superb and comprehensive treatment of the Wilmington Campaign, see Chris E. Fonvielle, Jr., *The Wilmington Campaign: Last Departing Rays of Hope* (Mechanicsburg, Pa.: Stackpole Books, 2001).

12. Sherman, *Memoirs*, 2:275.

13. Barrett, *The Civil War in North Carolina*, 39.

14. *Ibid.*

15. *OR* 47, pt. 3, 1297.

16. Fayetteville *Daily Telegraph*, March 1, 1865.

17. Johnston, *Narrative of Military Operations*, 377.

18. See, for example, the diary of Union soldier William Schaum, who noted on March 4, "The cavalry fought our foragers all along today. There were several our boys in the Regt. captured." William Schaum diary, entry for March 4, 1865, William Schaum Papers, Perkins Library, Duke University, Durham, N.C.

19. Wells, "A Morning Call on Kilpatrick," 124.

20. *OR* 47, pt. 3, 1314.

21. Galloway, *Dear Old Roswell*, 115.

22. Johnston, *Narrative of Military Operations*, 380.

23. *OR* 47, pt. 3, 692.

24. Hinman, *The Story of the Sherman Brigade,* 916.

25. Bradley, *Last Stand in the Carolinas*, 58-66.

26. *OR* 47, pt. 3, 670.

27. Rowell, *Yankee Cavalrymen*, 229-30.

28. *OR* 47, pt. 1, 894-95.

29. *Ibid.*, pt. 3, 671.

30. *Ibid.*, pt. 1, 904.

31. *Ibid.*, pt. 3, 1317.

32. *Ibid.*, 1318.

33. *Ibid.*, pt. 1, 682.

34. Rowell, *Yankee Cavalrymen*, 230.

35. *Ibid.*, 231.

36. *OR* 47, pt. 1, 876.

37. C. G. Rogers diary, entry for March 4, 1865, Schoff Diaries and Journals, W. L. Clements Library of the University of Michigan, Ann Arbor, Mich.

38. *Ninety-Second Illinois Volunteers*, 221.

39. "The Yankees in Anson," *The Argus*, March 30, 1865.

40. *Ibid.*

41. Donald E. Reynolds and Max H. Kele, "A Yank in the Carolinas Campaign: The Diary of James W. Chapin, Eighth Indiana Cavalry," *North Carolina Historical Review*, 46, no. 1 (Winter 1969), 51.

42. *OR* 47, pt. 1, 1125.

43. *Ibid.*, 885.

44. *Ibid.*, 1125.

45. *Ninety-Second Illinois Volunteers*, 222.

46. Smith D. Atkins, "Gen. Sherman's March Through the Carolinas," *The State*, June 21, 1908.

47. *OR* 47, pt. 1, 904.

48. *Ibid.*, 878.

49. *Ibid.*, 1125.

50. *Ibid.*, 868.

51. Diary of Jesse R. Sparkman, entry for March 4, 1865, Tennessee State Library and Archives, Nashville, Tennessee.

52. Diary of Williamson D. Ward, entry for March 5, 1865, Williamson D. Ward Papers, Indiana Historical Society, Indianapolis, Ind.

53. *Ninety-Second Illinois Volunteers*, 222.

54. Reynolds and Kele, "A Yank in the Carolinas Campaign," 52.

55. *OR* 47, pt. 1, 867.

56. *Ibid.*, 885-86.

57. Frank Smith, "A Maine Boy in the Tenth Ohio Cavalry," *Maine Bugle* Campaign IV (1897), 21.

58. *The Argus*, March 9, 1865.

59. *Ibid.*

60. *Ibid.*

61. *Cincinnati Daily Commercial*, March 22, 1865.

62. James Pike, *The Scout and Ranger, Being the Personal Adventures of Corporal Pike, of the Fourth Ohio Cavalry* (Cincinnati: J. R. Hawley & Co., 1865), 383.

63. Thomas Atkinson to Cornelia P. Spencer, January 30, 1866, D. L. Swain Papers, Southern Historical Collections, Wilson Library, University of North Carolina, Chapel Hill, N.C.

64. Wilson Angley, Michael Hill, and Jerry L. Cross. *Sherman's March Through North Carolina: A Chronology* (Raleigh: North Carolina Division of Archives & History, 1996), 7.

65. "Our Trip With the Yankee Raiders," *The Argus*, March 30, 1865.

66. G. C. Rogers diary, entry for March 5, 1865.

67. John R. Kennedy, "The Mills of the Gods," *Confederate Veteran* 32 (1924), 126.

68. *Ninety-Second Illinois Volunteers*, 223.

69. Hinman, *The Story of the Sherman Brigade*, 917.

70. *OR* 47, pt. 3, 1326-27.

71. William Douglas Hamilton, *Recollections of a Cavalryman After Fifty Years* (Columbus: F. J. Heer Printing Co., 1915), 195-96.

72. Charles M. Calhoun, *Liberty Dethroned: A Concise History of Some of the Most Startling Events Before, During, and Since the Civil War* (Greenwood, S.C.: n. p. 1903), 176-7.

73. Waring diary, entry for March 5, 1865.

74. *OR* 47, pt. 3, 1329.

75. Sparkman diary, entries for March 5 and 6, 1865.

76. *OR* 47, pt. 3, 1330.

77. *Ibid.*, 1335.

78. Ward diary, entry for March 6, 1865.

79. *Ninety-Second Illinois Volunteers*, 223.

80. *OR* 47, pt. 1, 867.

81. *Ibid.*, 897.

82. William W. Pritchard Diary, entry for March 7, 1865, Civil War Miscellaneous Collection, United States Army Military History Institute ("USAMHI"), Carlisle, Pennsylvania.

83. Schaum diary, entry for March 6, 1865.

84. William W. Gordon Memoirs, J. F. Waring Papers, Georgia Historical Society, Savannah, Georgia.

85. John W. DuBose, *General Joseph Wheeler and the Army of Tennessee* (New York: Neale Publishing Co., 1912), 444.; E. H. McKnight, "Scouting With General Wheeler," *Confederate Veteran* 19 (1911), 72.

86. Ed Kennedy, "Scouting With Wheeler," *Confederate Veteran* 36 (1918), 344.

87. *Ibid.*

88. DuBose, *General Joseph Wheeler and the Army of Tennessee*, 444.

89. Dockery's name appears as "General Dockery" in the Official Records, although there is no evidence that he actually held a general's commission. Nevertheless, he is listed as such in an appendix that appears in Allardice, *More Generals in Gray*, 246.

90. G. C. Rogers diary, entry for March 7, 1865.

91. *OR* 47, pt. 3, 1339.

92. Charlotte *Western Democrat*, March 7, 1865.

93. Shannon was one of seven voters against secession in Karnes County, Texas. *The New Handbook of Texas*, 6 vols. (Austin: The Texas State Historical Assoc., 1996), 5:992.

94. B. B. Sandiford, "Col. A. M. Shannon," *Confederate Veteran* 15 (1907), 84. There is some dispute about what Shannon's rank was in March 1865. The obituary that appeared in *Confederate Veteran* years after the end of the war indicates that Shannon received a promotion to colonel in February 1865, but this is unsubstantiated. Michael Shannon, a descendant of the captain, provided me with some post-war correspondence from Wheeler to Shannon wherein Wheeler called him "colonel." That, of course, is insufficient evidence of promotion, and may reflect the honorary title of "colonel" claimed by many Civil War veterans. Joseph Wheeler to Alexander M. Shannon, November 5 and 21, 1898, Michael Shannon Collection, Houston, Texas. Alexander Shannon himself signed a report as "captain" as late as April 1865. Given that, the author

will treat Shannon as having been a captain at the time of the Battle of Monroe's Crossroads.

95. Paul R. Scott, "Shannon's Scouts: Combat Reconnaissance Detachment of Terry's Texas Rangers," *Military History of Texas and the Southwest*, 15 (1979), 6.

96. H. W. Graber, *The Life Record of H. W. Graber: A Terry Texas Ranger 1861-1865* (privately published, 1918), 238.

97. Paul R. Scott, ed., "'With Tears in Their Eyes': On the Road to the Sea: Shannon's Scouts," *CWTI*, 21 (January 1983), 29.

98. Scott, *"Shannon's Scouts,"* 13-14.

99. David Nevin and the Editors of Time-Life Books, *Sherman's March: Atlanta to the Sea* (Alexandria, Va.: Time-Life Books, 1986), 55.

100. McKnight, "Scouting With General Wheeler," 72.

101. Ward diary, entry for March 7, 1865.

102. *OR* 47, pt. 1, 1130; E. H. McKnight, "Scouting with General Wheeler," *Confederate Veteran* 19 (1911), 72.

103. Kennedy, "Scouting with Wheeler," 344.

104. Hinman, *The Story of the Sherman Brigade*, 918.

105. *OR* 47, pt. 1, 867.

106. Waring diary, entry for March 7, 1865.

107. Hinman, *The Story of the Sherman Brigade*, 918.

108. Ulysses R. Brooks, *Butler and His Cavalry in the War of Secession, 1861-1865* (Columbia, S. C.: The State Co., 1909), 424.

109. James Moore, M. D., *Kilpatrick and Our Cavalry: Comprising a Sketch of the Life of General Kilpatrick, With an Account of the Cavalry Raids, Engagements, and Operations Under His Command, From the Beginning of the Rebellion to the Surrender of Johnston* (New York: W. J. Widdleton, 1865), 227.

110. *OR* 47, pt. 3, 721.

111. Nixon B. Stewart, *Dan McCook's Regiment: 52nd O.V.I.: A History of the Regiment, Its Campaigns and Battles from 1862 to 1865* (Alliance, Ohio: Review Print, 1900), 157.

112. Waring diary, entry for March 8, 1865.

113. *OR* 47, pt. 1, 1111-12.

114. *Ibid.*, pt. 3, 1338.

115. Bradley, *Last Stand in the Carolinas*, 75-76.

116. *OR* 47, pt. 1, 1348.

117. *Ibid.*, 1349.

118. DuBose, *General Joseph Wheeler*, 445.

119. *OR* 47, pt. 1, 1130.

120. Sparkman diary, entry for March 8, 1865.

121. Calhoun, *Liberty Dethroned*, 178.

122. The common practice for columns of cavalry on campaign was for units to take turns leading the advance and bringing up the rear. The lead brigade on one day dropped back the next, and so on. That way, no single unit was stuck at the rear of the column for more than a day at a time. The rear of a lengthy column of cavalry was not a particularly pleasant place to be. For a detailed description of this process, see Karla Jean Husby, comp., and Eric J. Wittenberg, ed., *Under Custer's Command: The Civil War Journal of James Henry Avery* (Dulles, Va.: Brassey's, 2000), 84.

123. Ward diary, entry for March 8, 1865.

124. Quoted in Kenneth Belew, *Cavalry Clash in the Sandhills: The Battle of Monroe's Crossroads, North Carolina* (Fort Bragg, N.C.: U. S. Army, 1997), 30.

125. *Ibid.*, 30-31.

126. William S. Thompson diary, entry for March 8, 1865, William S. Thompson diary for 1864 and 1865, Indiana Historical Society Library, Indianapolis, Ind.

127. Hinman, *The Story of the Sherman Brigade*, 918.

128. George E. Carter, ed., *The Story of Joshua D. Breyfogle, Private, 4th Ohio Infantry (10th Ohio Cavalry) and the Civil War* (Lewiston, N. Y.: The Edward Mellen Press, 2001), 326.

129. *OR* 47, pt. 1, 874.

130. Quoted in Belew, *Cavalry Clash in the Sandhills*, 31.

131. Emma G. B. Robertson and Thomas C. Robertson, *History of Aberdeen* (Aberdeen, N.C.: Malcolm Blue Historical Society, 1976), 31.

132. *OR* 47, pt. 1, 867.

133. Ward diary, entry for March 8, 1865.

134. Hinman, *The Story of the Sherman Brigade*, 918.

135. Warren McCain, *A Soldier's Diary; or, The History of Company L, Third Indiana Cavalry* (Indianapolis: William A. Patton, 1885), 49.

136. *OR* 47, pt. 1, 904.

137. *Ibid.*, 867.

138. Reynolds and Kele, "A Yank in the Carolinas Campaign," 52. Adjutant Chapin referred to the famed Revolutionary War partisan leader, Brig. Gen. Francis Marion, known as "The Swamp Fox" for his ability to strike blows against the British and then disappear into the deep swamps, forests, and savannas of South Carolina.

139. Hinman, *The Story of the Sherman Brigade*, 918.

140. *OR* 37, pt. 1, 861.

141. *Ibid.*, 867.

142. Scott, "Shannon's Scouts," 14.

143. John W. DuBose, "The Fayetteville (N.C.) Road Fight," *Confederate Veteran* 20 (1912), 85; Reynolds to Owen, September 17, 1913.

144. There is some dispute about whether the war-time Morganton Road ran to the north or the south of the Monroe house. The battle descriptions indicate that Morganton Road passed to the north of the Monroe house, but 1919 topographical maps suggest that the road ran well to the south of the house—in fact, south of Green Springs Swamp. It appears that the road was moved some time after 1865. The U. S. Army moved it again during World War II. Charles Heath, a staff historian employed at Fort Bragg, writes, "Logistically, the current route makes more sense, as it now passes over high ground north of Nicholson Creek. To make a long story short, this is a puzzle, but there does not seem to be any way, at least based on the primary source accounts of the battle, that Morganton Road passed to the south of Green Springs Swamp in 1865." Charles Heath to the author, November 4, 2003. For purposes of this book, I will assume that the Morganton Road passed to the north of the Monroe house, and not to the south. All maps will depict it passing to the north of the Morganton Road.

145. "Drama at the Crossroads: The Battle at Monroe's Crossroads," *Fayetteville Observer*, October 8, 1961; Scott and Hunt, *The Civil War Battle at Monroe's Crossroads*, 14-15.

146. Theodore F. Northrop, "A Federal on the Fight at Fayetteville," *Confederate Veteran* 21 (1913), 477.

147. Northrop to Adjutant General of the Army, March 12, 1917.

148. Belew, *Cavalry Clash in the Sand Hills*, 33.

149. *OR* 47, pt. 1, 861.

150. See, e.g,, Napoleon Bonaparte, *Napoleon's Art of War*, Lt. Gen. Sir G. C. D'Aguilar, trans. (New York: Barnes & Noble, 1995), Maxim XXXIV, 52.

151. *OR* 47, pt. 1, 861.

152. *Ibid.*, 867.

153. Cavalryman, "Campaign Through the Carolinas," *National Tribune*, May 5, 1892.

154. *Ninety-Second Illinois Volunteers*, 223.

155. Diary of Josiah D. Wilson, entry for March 9, 1865, E. A. Wilson Collection, Houston, Texas.

156. Included in Timothy Daiss, *In the Saddle: Exploits of the 5th Georgia Cavalry During the Civil War* (Atglen, Pa.: Schiffer Publishing, 1999), 93.

157. Excessive Rain Statistics for March 1865, National Climactic Data Center, Asheville, N.C.

158. Brooks, *Butler and His Cavalry*, 424.

159. Matthew C. Butler to Edward L. Wells, March 27, 1900, Wells Correspondence.

160. J. A. Jones, "Report by Joseph A. Jones, Birmingham, Ala., Company E, 51st Alabama Partisan Rangers," *Confederate Veteran* 19 (1911), 434; E. W. Watkins, "Another Account," *Confederate Veteran* 20 (1912), 84.

161. Sparkman diary, entry for March 9, 1865.

162. Fayetteville *Daily Telegraph*, March 9, 1865. The presence of a large Union force in the area put the paper out of business. Sherman burned it to the ground on March 12, when he also destroyed the large Confederate arsenal/armory located in Fayetteville.

Chapter 4

1. *OR* 47, pt. 1, 904.

2. Robertson and Robertson, *History of Aberdeen,* 31. The Malcolm Blue farm still stands, and now is a small museum near the town of Aberdeen, and not too distant from Pinehurst, in North Carolina's golf Mecca. The museum features a small exhibit on the Battle of Monroe's Crossroads.

3. *Ibid.*; Manly Wade Wellman, *The Story of Moore County: Two Centuries of a North Carolina Region* (Southern Pines, N.C.: Moore County Historical Assoc., 1974), 75.

4. *OR* 47, pt. 1, 894.

5. *Ibid.,* 883.

6. W. H. Morris, "The Other Side at Fayetteville," *Confederate Veteran* 20 (1912), 83.

7. Ward diary, entry for March 9, 1865.

8. *OR* 47, pt. 1, 867.

9. Ward diary, entry for March 9, 1865.

10. *OR* 47, pt. 1, 904; Scott and Hunt, *The Civil War Battle at Monroe's Crossroads,* 17.

11. *Ibid.,* 900.

12. Scott and Hunt, *The Civil War Battle at Monroe's Crossroads*, 17; James B. Legg to the author, January 14, 2004. Scott and Hunt concluded that Stetson's guns had been unlimbered on a low plateau about fifty yards to the south of the Monroe house based on finding a large quantity of friction primers on the plateau when they performed their archaeological survey of the site. As a result, the modern interpretations of the Battle of Monroe's Crossroads put Stetson's guns on that plateau, approximately fifty yards to the south of the Monroe home site. However, Legg is an archaeologist who has studied the ground at Monroe's Crossroads. His detective work suggests that the friction

primers that were discovered on the plateau south of the site of the Monroe house were all unfired/unused, and were left when a primer box was dropped, perhaps by Stetson's retreating gunners. Legg found used/fired friction tubes and wires on Blue's Rosin Road, adjacent to the Monroe house site, and also evidence of exploded projectiles there, including Hotchkiss canister, shell, and case, all radiating out from the position hear the house, perhaps directed at the Confederate center. This detritus could not have come from the plateau to the south of the Monroe home site, as suggested by Scott and Hunt. Legg to the author, February 12, 2004. Kilpatrick himself placed the guns about twenty feet from the house: "We retook the artillery, turned it upon the enemy about our headquarters, not twenty steps distant, and finally forced him out of the camp with great slaughter." *OR* 47, pt. 1, 863. This interpretation varies from the commonly accepted interpretation, but is credible.

13. Sun Tzu, *The Art of War,* Samuel B. Griffith, trans. (London: Oxford University Press, 1963), 114.

14. Dennis Hart Mahan, Advanced-Guard, Outpost, and Detachment Service of Troops, with the Essential Principles of Strategy, and Grand Tactics (New York: John Wiley, 1863), 83.

15. *Ibid.,* 85.

16. *Instructions for Officers and Non-Commissioned Officers On Outpost and Patrol Duty, and Troops in Campaign* (Washington, D.C.: Government Printing Office, 1863), 55-6.

17. *OR* 47, pt. 1, 894. Spencer claimed that "In obedience to instructions we picketed carefully the country in the direction of Fayetteville, leaving Lieutenant-Colonel Way, whose command was immediately in the rear of my brigade, to picket the rear." This misunderstanding meant that Spencer was relying on Way to cover his front, but Way did not know that he was expected to do so. This left Spencer's front entirely unprotected. Spencer committed an error that would cost his command dearly.

18. Matthew C. Butler to Edward L. Wells, March 27, 1900, Wells Correspondence.

19. Watkins, "Another Account," 84.

20. Reynolds to Owen, September 17, 1913.

21. *OR* 47, pt. 1, 1125.

22. Calhoun, *Liberty Dethroned,* 178.

23. Wells, *Hampton and his Cavalry in '64,* 397.

24. Butler to Wells, March 27, 1900.

25. U. R. Brooks, "More on Fight at Fayetteville," *Confederate Veteran* 19 (1911), 453.

26. *OR* 47, pt. 1, 861. Kilpatrick claimed that he "actually rode through one of General Hampton's divisions of cavalry, which by 11 o'clock had flanked General Atkins and was encamped within three miles of General Spencer. My escort of 15 men and 1 officer was captured, but I escaped with my staff."

27. Sun Tzu, *The Art of War,* 134.

28. Brooks, *Butler and His Cavalry,* 417.

29. Butler to Wells, March 27, 1900, Wade Hampton to Edward L. Wells, March 28, 1900, Wells Correspondence.

30. Hampton to Wells, April 4, 1900, and April 8, 1900, Wells Correspondence; *OR* 47, pt. 1, 1130.

31. Wells, "A Morning Call on Kilpatrick," 126.

32. Butler to Wells, March 27, 1900.

33. Calhoun, "Credit to Wheeler Claimed by Others," 83.

34. Wells, *Hampton and His Cavalry in '64,* 400.

35. Calhoun, *Liberty Dethroned,* 179.

36. Dodson, *Campaigns of Wheeler and His Cavalry,* 344.

37. W. G. Allen, "About the Fight at Fayetteville, N.C.," *Confederate Veteran* 19 (1911), 433.

38. W. M. Lomax, "At Monroe's Crossroads," *National Tribune,* July 6, 1899.

39. A. B. Straw, "Kilpatrick's Version," *The National Tribune,* October 4, 1900.

40. George Ward Nichols, *The Story of the Great March* (New York: Harper & Brothers, 1865), 247.

41. "Drama at the Crossroads," *Fayetteville Observer,* October 8, 1961.

42. John W. DuBose, "The Fayetteville Road Fight," *Confederate Veteran* 20 (1912), 85.

43. Hugh H. Scott, "'Fighting Kilpatrick's Escape," *Confederate Veteran* 12 (1904), 588; Scott, "Shannon's Scouts," 17.

44. "Unveiling of the Confederate Monument at Montgomery, Ala.: Major Falkner's Words," *Charleston Sunday News,* November 20, 1898.

45. Watkins, "Another Account," 84.

46. J. C. Witcher, "Shannon's Scouts—Kilpatrick," *Confederate Veteran* 14 (1906), 511.

47. DuBose, "The Fayetteville Road Fight," 85.

48. *Ibid.*

49. Natt Holman, "Participant in Battle of Fayetteville, N.C.," *Confederate Veteran* 19 (1911), 544.

50. William W. Gordon Reminiscences, Gordon Family Papers, Georgia Historical Society, Savannah, GA.

51. J. A. Jones, "Report by Joseph A. Jones, Birmingham, Ala., Company E, 51st Alabama Partisan Rangers," *Confederate Veteran* 19 (1911), 434.

52. Posey Hamilton, "The Effort to Capture Kilpatrick," *Confederate Veteran* 29 (1921), 329.

53. C. G. Rogers diary, entry for March 10, 1865.

54. John C. Oeffinger, ed., *A Soldier's General: The Civil War Letters of Major General Lafayette McLaws* (Chapel Hill: University of North Carolina Press, 2002), 262. McLaws, who commanded one of Hardee's divisions, wrote, "Met Hampton's Scout (Col. Henry M. Ashby of the 2nd Tennessee Cavalry) who reported the enemy in force on our right five miles, having crossed at bridge & moving with whole force on Fayetteville. . . . Squadron of enemys cavalry about one & half miles in my rear."

55. Ansen L. Harmon, "Woods Full of Johnnies: A 10th Ohio Cav. Comrade Gives Credit to the 1st Ala. Cav.," *National Tribune*, January 24, 1901.

56. "Cavalryman," "Campaign Through the Carolinas."

57. *Ninety-Second Illinois Volunteers*, 223.

58. *OR* 47, pt. 1, 889.

59. "Cavalryman," "Campaign Through the Carolinas."

60. Harmen, "Woods Full of Johnnies."

61. Carter, *The Story of Joshua D. Breyfogle*, 326.

62. *OR* 47, pt. 1, 889.

63. "Cavalryman," "Campaign Through the Carolinas."

64. *Ninety-Second Illinois Volunteers*, 224-25.

65. Reynolds and Kele, "A Yank in the Carolinas Campaign," 52-53.

66. *OR* 47, pt. 1, 867.

67. *Ibid.*, 861.

Chapter 5

1. Diary of William W. Gordon, entry for March 10, 1865, Gordon Family Papers, Southern Historical Collections, Wilson Library, University of North Carolina, Chapel Hill.

2. Wells, *Hampton and His Cavalry in '64*, 404.

3. Wells, "A Morning Call on Kilpatrick," 126.

4. Jones, "Report by Joseph A. Jones," 434.

5. Scott, "Fighting Kilpatrick's Escape," 588.

6. Wells, "A Morning Call on Kilpatrick," 126.

7. S. W. Bailey, "Gen. Wade Hampton's Charge into Kilpatrick's Camp in 1865," *Atlanta Journal*, March 8, 1902.

8. Calhoun, *Liberty Dethroned,* 131; Wells, *Hampton and His Cavalry in '64,* 404.

9. Wiley C. Howard, *Sketch of the Cobb Legion Cavalry and Some Incidents and Scenes Remembered* (Atlanta, Ga.: privately published, 1901), 12.

10. Waring diary, entry for March 10, 1865.

11. Reid, *Ohio in the War,* 2:787.

12. Wells, "A Morning Call on Kilpatrick," 127.

13. Wells, *Hampton and His Cavalry in '64,* 405.

14. Bailey, "Gen. Wade Hampton's Charge."

15. N. A. Hood, "History of the Surprise of Kilpatrick," *Confederate Veteran* 14 (1906), 176.

16. Gordon diary, entry for March 10, 1865.

17. George B. Guild, *A Brief Narrative of the Fourth Tennessee Cavalry Regiment* (Nashville: n. p., 1913), 123.

18. W. H. Davis, "Kilpatrick's Spotted Horse," *Confederate Veteran* 14 (1906), 62.

19. W. G. Caruthers, "More About Kilpatrick's Horses," *Confederate Veteran* 13 (1905), 456.

20. Wilbur F. Mims, *War History of the Prattville Dragoons* (n.p., n.d.), 14.

21. Hamilton, "The Effort to Capture Kilpatrick," 329.

22. DuBose, "The Fayetteville (N.C.) Road Fight," 85.

23. J. W. Inzer, "How Kilpatrick Lost Pistols and Holsters," *Confederate Veteran* 12 (1904), 177.

24. Daiss, *In the Saddle,* 93.

25. Gordon Reminiscences, 2-3.

26. J. W. DuBose to U. R. Brooks, August 9, 1911, U. R. Brooks Papers, Perkins Library, Duke University, Durham, N.C.

27. Calhoun, *Liberty Dethroned,* 130.

28. Gary R. Baker, *Cadets in Gray: The Story of the Cadets of the South Carolina Military Academy and the Cadet Rangers in the Civil War* (Columbia: Palmetto Bookworks, 1989), 171. Moses was one of a number of Southern Jews who faithfully served the Confederacy. For more on the role played by Southern Jews, see, Robert N. Rosen, *The Jewish Confederates* (Columbia: University of South Carolina Press, 2000).

29. *Ibid.*

30. Hamilton, "The Effort to Capture Kilpatrick," 329.

31. John Latta, "Kilpatrick's Surprise: How a Captain Saved the Brigade," *National Tribune*, April 1, 1886.

32. "Drama at the Crossroads," *Fayetteville Observer*, October 8, 1961.

33. *OR* 47, pt. 1, 901.

34. *Ibid.*, 899.

35. T. W. Fanning, *The Hairbreadth Escapes and Humorous Adventures of a Volunteer in the Cavalry Service* (Cincinnati: P. C. Browne, 1865), 158.

36. *OR* 47, pt. 1, 894.

37. Watkins, "Another Account," 84.

38. Bailey, "Gen. Wade Hampton's Charge."

39. Wells, "A Morning Call on Kilpatrick," 128-29.

40. Straw, "Kilpatrick's Version."

41. M. C. Butler to E. L. Wells, March 27, 1900, Wells Correspondence; Brooks, *Butler and His Cavalry*, 446.

42. *OR* 47, pt. 1, 861.

43. Brooks, *Butler and His Cavalry*, 446-47. Kilpatrick later claimed that he had already awakened that morning, and that he had come out onto the porch of the house to supervise the feeding of his horses while clad in his nightshirt and slippers. He claimed that this was his habit. However, such a habit would be very uncommon among officers of high rank, who had orderlies to perform that sort of duty. One of Wheeler's men correctly observed that he presumed Kilpatrick to be the only example from Joshua to the Nineteenth Century of a major general who would walk partially dressed out of a warm room in cold weather to see that his horses were fed. DuBose to Brooks, February 12, 1908. William Small, *Campfire Talk on the Life and Military Services of Maj. Gen. Judson Kilpatrick* (G.A.R., Dept. of the Potomac, John A. Rawlins Post No. 1, 1887), 23.

44. William P. Carlin, "Military Memoirs," *National Tribune*, July 30, 1885.

45. Matthew C. Butler, "Kilpatrick Almost Caught: How a Federal Major Gen. Escaped En Dishabille," *Charleston News & Courier*, November 7, 1897.

46. Straw, "Kilpatrick's Version."

47. *OR* 47, pt. 1, 861.

48. Wells, "A Morning Call on Kilpatrick," 127.

49. Inzer, "How Kilpatrick Lost Pistols and Holsters," 177.

50. *Ibid.*; Hood, "History of the Surprise of Kilpatrick," 176-77.

51. The officer's name was Capt. John Ahrens, of Co. G, 11th South Carolina Infantry. Ahrens kept the saber until 1911, when he presented it to Ulysses R. Brooks, one of Butler's couriers, saying that he thought that Brooks, one of the first to reach Kilpatrick's headquarters that fateful morning, ought to have it. "A day or two after the fight in which General Kilpatrick's headquarters were captured," recalled Brooks, Kilpatrick "sent to General Hampton a note asking him if he would be so kind and gracious as to return to him his horse. The sword was not mentioned, as it was useless to ask for it." Ulysses R. Brooks, *Stories of the Confederacy* (Columbia, S.C.: The State Co., 1912), 66.

52. D. A. K. McDowell, et al., "The Kilpatrick Spotted Horse Affair," *Confederate Veteran* 14 (1906), 309; Natt Holman, "Participant in Battle of Fayetteville, N.C.," *Confederate Veteran* 19 (1911), 544. There is some dispute over what happened to the so-called "spotted horse." Wheeler wrote later that Shannon's Scouts had presented the horse to him as a gift, and that he rode him for the rest of the war. Witcher, "Shannon's Scouts—Kilpatrick," 512.

53. Caruthers, "More About Kilpatrick's Horses," 456.

54. Holmes, "The Fighting Qualities."

55. DuBose, "The Fayetteville (N.C.) Road Fight," 84.

56. "We had quite a number of Confederate prisoners that had been picked up from time to time on the march. Their lot was not a very happy one, and I was glad when they were released" recalled Capt. Theodore F. Northrop, Kilpatrick's chief of scouts. "We called their camp the 'bull pen,' and at times it was not much better than one." Northrop, "A Federal on the Fight at Fayetteville," 477.

57. Brooks, *Butler and His Cavalry*, 425.

58. Kennedy, "The Mills of the Gods," 126.

59. Calhoun, "Credit to Wheeler Claimed by Others," 83.

60. Wells, "A Morning Call on Kilpatrick," 128.

61. Brooks, *Butler and His Cavalry*, 445.

62. *Ibid.*, 434-35. Brooks concluded his parable by saying, "Moral: Be kind to those in your power, for we know not what a day will bring forth." This was good advice then, and it remains so today.

63. *Ibid.*, 426.

64. *Ibid.*, 446.

65. Robert E. L. Krick, *Staff Officers in Gray: A Biographical Register of the Staff Officers in the Army of Northern Virginia* (Chapel Hill: University of North Carolina Press, 2003), 88. Young Nat Butler was described as "one of the handsomest men boys in the Army."

66. Brooks, *Butler and His Cavalry*, 427, and Butler, "Kilpatrick Almost Caught."

67. Wells, *Hampton and His Cavalry in '64*, 410.

68. Brooks, *Butler and His Cavalry*, 427.

69. Calhoun, *Liberty Dethroned*, 131.

70. George Shuman to My Dearest Jennie, March 28, 1865, Harrisburg CWRT Collection, United States Army Military History Institute, Carlisle, Pa.

71. Wells, "A Morning Call on Kilpatrick," 127.

72. Hamilton, "The Effort to Capture Kilpatrick," 329.

73. DuBose, "The Fayetteville (N.C.) Road Fight," 86.

74. Dodson, *Campaigns of Wheeler and His Cavalry*, 345.

75. *OR* 47, pt. 1, 894.

76. *Ninety-Second Illinois Volunteers*, 227.

77. Carlin, "Military Memoirs," *Delaware Gazette*, March 24, 1865; Pritchard diary, entry for March 11, 1865.

78. Butler to Wells, March 27, 1900.

79. Nichols, *The Story of the Great March*, 248.

80. *OR* 47, pt. 1, 861.

81. George C. Jenkins, "Kilpatrick's Capture," *National Tribune*, October 15, 1885.

82. *OR* 47, pt. 1, 1130.

83. Wells, "A Morning Call on Kilpatrick," 128.

84. *OR* 47, pt. 1, 904.

85. *Ibid.*, 899. It appears that Way's men fled in a helter-skelter rout, every man for himself.

86. William Collin Stevens to My Dear Sister, March 14, 1865, Stevens Letters.

87. Whitelaw Reid, *Ohio in the War; Her Statement, Generals and Soldiers* (Columbus, Ohio, Eclectic Publishing Co., 1893), 1:984; Hunt and Long, *Brevet Brigadier Generals in Blue*, 592.

88. Lomax, "At Monroe's Crossroads."

89. *OR* 47, pt. 1, 897."

90. Scott and Hunt, *The Civil War Battle at Monroe's Crossroads*, 113.

91. *Ibid.*, 110.

92. Calhoun, "Credit to Wheeler Claimed for Others," 83.

93. Calhoun, *Liberty Dethroned*, 131.

94. Watkins, "Another Account," 84.

95. *OR* 47, pt. 1, 861.

96. Butler, "Kilpatrick Almost Caught."

97. Butler to Wells, March 27, 1900.

98. U. R. Brooks, "More on Fight at Fayetteville," *Confederate Veteran* 19 (1911), 453.

99. Brooks, *Butler and His Cavalry*, 445. Hampton later told Edward L. Wells of the 4th South Carolina Cavalry that he believed that the desire to plunder Kilpatrick's camp, and not the swamp, prevented Wheeler from coming to Butler's aid in a timely fashion. Hampton to Wells, April 3, 1900, Wells Correspondence.

Chapter 6

1. Carter, *The Story of Joshua D. Breyfogle*, 326.

2. Carlin, "Military Memoirs"; Small, *Campfire Talk*, 23.

3. T. W. Fanning, *The Hairbreadth Escapes and Humorous Adventures of A Volunteer in the Cavalry Service By One of Them* (Cincinnati: P. C. Browne, 1865), 158.

4. Northrop to Adjutant General of the Army, March 12, 1917.

5. Northrop, "A Federal on the Fight at Fayetteville," 477.

6. Northrop to Adjutant General of the Army, March 12, 1917.

7. Northrop, "A Federal on the Fight at Fayetteville," 477.

8. Sussex Independent, February 1, 1918. He also nominated himself for a Medal of Honor in 1917. The application was rejected. "The Medal of Honor is not awarded to an officer for leading his command in battle whatever measure of gallantry he displayed and that as no specific act of individual gallantry is shown by the reason to have been performed by Mr. Northrop his case does not come within the provisions of the Act of Congress approved March 3, 1863, and, consequently, a Medal of Honor could not be awarded to him," wrote the Adjutant General of the Army. He concluded, "While the conduct of Captain Northrop at the Battle of Monroe Cross Roads, North Carolina, March 10, 1865, was no doubt highly gallant and meritorious, in view of the practice of the Department and approved decisions heretofore made in cases of this kind, a Medal of Honor cannot be awarded to him. It is regretted that favorable action cannot be taken on his application." H. P. McCain to the Assistant Secretary of War, March 31, 1917, RG 94, Records of the Adjutant General's Office 1780-1917, Theodore F. Northrop, Captain of Volunteers File, File No. 1674 vs. 1676, Box 1200, National Archives, Washington, D.C.

9. Hamilton, "The Effort to Capture Kilpatrick," 329.

10. George C. Jenkins, "Kilpatrick's Capture," *The National Tribune*, October 15, 1885.

11. *OR* 47, pt. 1, 899.

12. *Ibid.*, 44, 370.

13. *Ibid.*, 47, pt. 1, 895.

14. *Ibid.*, 899.

15. *Charleston Courier*, March 30, 1865.

16. Zimmerman Davis to Edward L. Wells, June 10, 1898, Wells Correspondence.

17. Brooks, *Butler and His Cavalry*, 434. The mortally wounded man was actually Sgt. John Swartz, not Lieutenant Stetson.

18. Holmes, "The Fighting Qualities."

19. Baker, *Cadets in Gray*, 170-71.

20. Hood, "History of the Surprise of Kilpatrick," 176-77.

21. "An Interesting Letter."

22. *OR* 47, pt. 1, 861; Hamilton, "The Effort to Capture Kilpatrick," 329.

23. Hamilton, *Recollections of a Cavalryman*, 199.

24. J. H. Gardner, "Alabama's Sons Fought," *The National Tribune*, August 13, 1896.

25. Atkins, "Gen. Sherman's March Through the Carolinas."

26. Thompson diary, entry for March 10, 1865.

27. Daiss, *In the Saddle: Exploits of the 5th Georgia Cavalry*, 94.

28. *Ibid.*

29. Reynolds to Owen, September 17, 1913.

30. Wells, "A Morning Call on Kilpatrick," 129.

31. Calhoun, *Liberty Dethroned*, 183.

32. Krick, *Lee's Colonels*, 223; Bruce S. Allardice to the author, January 24, 2003.

33. Galloway, *Dear Old Roswell*, 121.

34. Howard, *Sketch of the Cobb Legion Cavalry*, 14.

35. Bailey, "Gen. Hampton's Charge."

36. *Ibid.* Lieutenant Wiley C. Howard survived Monroe's Crossroads and lived until 1930, when he died in Clarke Country, Georgia, at the age of 92.

37. Galloway, *Dear Old Roswell*, 122.

38. Howard, *Sketch of the Cobb Legion Cavalry*, 14.

39. Bailey, "Gen. Hampton's Charge."

40. Brooks, *Butler and His Cavalry*, 445.

41. Fanning, *The Hairbreadth Escapes*, 159.

42. *OR* 47, pt. 1, 862.

43. Jenkins, "Kilpatrick's Capture."

44. Shuman to Jennie, June 9, 1865.

45. *OR* 47, pt. 1, 900.

46. Statement of James H. Miller, August 6, 1872, "Statements dated 1872."

47. *OR* 47, pt. 1, 862.

48. Guild, *Fourth Tennessee Cavalry Regiment*, 124.

49. Mims, *War History of the Prattville Dragoons*, 14.

50. Reynolds to Owen, September 17, 1913.

51. *OR* 47, pt. 1, 1130.

52. Dodson, *Campaigns of Wheeler and His Cavalry*, 345.

53. *Ninety-Second Illinois Volunteers*, 228. The historian of the 92nd Illinois Mounted Infantry claimed, "when the Rebels saw that column of dismounted men, under Colonel Stough, with their long Springfield muskets and bright bayonets gleaming in the morning sunlight, they mistook it for the Fourteenth Corps of infantry, and, setting up the cry, plainly heard by the Union

officers in the second story of the house, 'The Fourteenth Corps! The Fourteenth Corps!' the Rebels hastily beat a retreat."

54. Dodson, *Campaigns of Wheeler and His Cavalry*, 345-46.

55. Wells, *Hampton and His Cavalry in '64*, 415.

56. *OR* 47, pt. 1, 524.

57. *Ibid.*, 510.

58. Stewart, *Dan McCook's Regiment*, 157.

59. Wells, "A Morning Call on Kilpatrick," 129.

60. John Berrien Lindsley, ed., *The Military Annals of Tennessee, Confederate. First Series: Embracing a Review of Military Operations with Regimental Histories and Memorial Rolls, Compiled From Original and Official Sources* (Nashville: J. M. Lindsley & Co., 1886), 675.

61. Berrien, *Military Annals of Tennessee*, 675.

62. Dodson, *Campaigns of Wheeler's Cavalry*, 346.

63. Leroy M. Nutt, "History of Hamilton's and Shaw's 4th Battalion Tennessee Cavalry," unpublished manuscript, Leroy M. Nutt Papers, Southern Historical Collection, University of North Carolina, Chapel Hill, N.C., at 12.

64. Stewart, *Dan McCook's Regiment*, 157.

65. Fanning, *The Hairbreadth Escapes*, 159. Some accounts of the battle credit Alice with saving the flag by snatching it in the opening minutes of the battle and then tucking it under her clothing in order to protect it from capture. This account cannot be verified. Captain Miller's account about retrieving the standard from a wounded soldier is a much more credible account, and is the one accepted for purposes of this book.

66. John A. Oates, *The Story of Fayetteville and the Upper Cape Fear* (Charlotte, N.C.: The Dowd Press, 1950), 419.

67. Josiah D. Wilson diary, entry for March 10, 1865, E. D. Wilson Collection, Houston, Tx.

68. W. C. Leonard, "A Surprise and a Rally," *The National Tribune*, August 2, 1900.

69. Waring diary, entry for March 10, 1865.

70. *Ninety-Second Illinois Volunteers*, 228.

71. Hunt and Brown, *Brevet Brigadier Generals in Blue*, 592; Reid, Ohio in the War, 1:984.

72. *OR* 47, pt. 1, 894.

73. March 1865 return of Capt. Yates Beebe, RG 94, National Archives, Washington, D.C.

74. *OR* 47, pt. 1, 862.

75. *Cincinnati Daily Commercial*, March 22, 1865.

76. *Delaware Gazette*, March 24, 1865.

77. Hamilton, "The Effort to Capture Kilpatrick," 329.

78. Burch, "The Surprise of Kilpatrick's Camp."

79. Gordon Reminiscences, 4.

80. *OR* 47, pt. 1, pp. 862, 895.

81. Dodson, *Campaigns of Wheeler's Cavalry*, 346.

82. Thompson diary, entry for March 10, 1865; *OR* 47, pt. 1, 899.

83. Calhoun, *Liberty Dethroned*, 183.

84. Butler to Wells, March 27, 1900.

85. Hamilton, *Recollections of a Cavalryman*, 198-99.

86. *OR* 47, pt. 1, 889.

87. Carter, *The Story of Joshua D. Breyfogle*, 326.

88. *Ninety-Second Illinois Volunteers*, 226.

89. Reynolds and Kele, "A Yank in the Carolinas Campaign," 53.

90. Thompson diary, entry for March 10, 1865.

91. *OR* 47, pt. 1, 867.

92. *Ibid.*, 524.

93. Bradley, *Last Stand in the Carolinas*, 100.

94. *OR* 47, pt. 1, 764.

95. William H. Seaman, "The Battle of Bentonville, N.C.," *The National Tribune*, August 20, 1885.

96. Wilson diary, entry for March 10, 1865.

97. *OR* 47, pt. 1, 510.

98. Affidavit of Neil S. Blue, included in North Carolina Clippings File, Southern Historical Collections, Wilson Library, University of North Carolina, Chapel Hill, N.C.; Robertson and Robertson, *History of Aberdeen*, 33.

99. Burke Davis, *Sherman's March* (New York: Random House, 1980), 214.

100. Schaum diary, entry for March 10, 1865.

101. *Ninety-Second Illinois Volunteers*, 228; Ward diary, entry for March 10, 1865.

102. Rogers diary, entry for March 10, 1865. This Georgia officer claimed that Hampton captured 461 men in the fighting at Monroe's Crossroads, surely an inflated number.

103. Gordon Reminiscences, 4.

104. Moore, *Kilpatrick and His Cavalry*, 488.

105. Sparkman diary, entry for March 11, 1865.

106. John C. Oeffinger, ed., *A Soldier's General: The Civil War Letters of Major General Lafayette McLaws* (Chapel Hill: University of North Carolina Press, 2002), 263.

107. *War Days in Fayetteville, North Carolina: Reminiscences of 1861 to 1865*, J. E. B. Stuart Chapter, United Daughters of the Confederacy (Fayetteville, N.C.: Judge Printing Co., 1910), 46-47.

108. *Ibid.*, 42.

109. *OR* 47, pt. 1, 1045.

Chapter 7

1. Johnston, *Narrative of Military Operations*, 381.

2. Nathaniel Cheairs Hughes, *General William J. Hardee: Old Reliable* (Wilmington, N.C.: Broadfoot Publishing Co., 1987), 281.

3. Wade Hampton to Edward L. Wells, December 20, 1892, Wells Correspondence.

4. *OR* 47, pt. 2, 763; Bradley, *Last Stand*, 80.

5. George W. Pepper, *Personal Recollections of Sherman's Campaigns in Georgia and the Carolinas* (Zanesville, Ohio: Hugh Dunne, 1866), 257 and 259.

6. William H. Duncan, "With the Army of the Tennessee Through the Carolinas," *Glimpses of the Nation's Struggle*, Military Order of the Loyal Legion of the United States, Minnesota Commandery, Fourth Series (Saint Paul: H. L. Collins Co., 1898), 517. According to one source, three decades later Hampton, who was a United States Railway Commissioner was called upon by a stranger in Denver, Colorado. The man told him he was the spy David Day, the man captured while dressed in Confederate uniform. Hampton supposedly congratulated Day and said, "I'm glad the hanging did not come off." Day answered, "So am I!", to which both men had a good laugh. Arthur Peronneau Ford, *Life in the Confederate Army: Being Personal Experiences of a Private Soldier in the Confederate Army* (Neale Company, 1905), 47.

7. *Ibid.*, 518.

8. *OR* 47, pt. 1, 203.

9. E. Collins, "The First to Enter Fayetteville," National Tribune, May 13, 1886.

10. Hampton to Wells, December 20, 1892.

11. Edward L. Wells, "Hampton at Fayetteville," *Southern Historical Society Papers* 13 (1885), 144-46.

12. Edward L. Wells to Wade Hampton, February 8, 1893, Wells Correspondence. Hampton roundly praised the dragoons to their commanding officer. "Lieutenant, I commend to you Privates Wells, Bellinger and Fishburn, of your company, who, with Private Scott and one member of Wheeler's command, whose name I regret I do not remember, acted with conspicuous gallantry in charging and driving from the town of Fayetteville that portion of the

enemy's cavalry that had entered before it had been evacuated by my troops. Their conduct on this occasion reflects high credit on them as soldiers," wrote the lieutenant general on March 19, 1865. Scott, "'Fighting' Kilpatrick's Escape."

13. Wells, "Hampton at Fayetteville," 146.

14. Collins, "The First to Enter Fayetteville."

15. Hampton to Wells, December 20, 1892. Hampton's account of these events was corroborated by Arthur P. Ford, who was one of Hardee's infantrymen. See Arthur P. Ford, *Life in the Confederate Army: Being Personal Experiences of a Private Soldier in the Confederate Army* (New York: Neale Publishing Co., 1905), 46-7. Captain Duncan painted a very different picture of the death of one Federal. "Just then in the field to our left, was one of our infantry boys who had followed us into town," recalled Duncan. "He was passing back towards our lines; General Hampton called to him to halt; he either did not hear or was indifferent. I thought from where I was that he had been wounded in the right breast. General Hampton left me with one of his staff to receive my arms, and rode over to this young man and cut him down with his saber. The man did not offer to shoot or show any resistance. I denounced it then as murder, and so reported on my return to our army after my escape, to Colonel L. M. Dayton, adjutant-general, at Sherman's headquarters, and at our own headquarters." Duncan, "With the Army of the Tennessee," 520. Maj. Gen. Lafayette McLaws, who commanded one of Hardee's infantry divisions, also expressed doubt about the veracity of Hampton's claims to have cut down two Federals in the streets of Fayetteville. "Report says [Hampton] killed two with his own hand," wrote McLaws in his order book, "but the chivalry have fallen so deep into the pit of 'want of chivalry' that they are constantly inventing Munchauseus as to the prowess of those from the state, or defaming others in order that thereby they may appear elevated by their contrast." Oeffinger, *A Soldier's General*, 263-64. It does not appear, though, that McLaws had personal knowledge of these events, and that he was simply expressing his frustration with the performance of the Confederate cavalry.

16. Scott, "Sketches."

17. Collins, "The First to Enter Fayetteville."

18. Duncan, "With the Army of the Tennessee," 519-20.

19. Hampton to Wells, December 20, 1892.

20. Duncan, "With the Army of the Tennessee," 520-21.

21. *Ibid.*, 521.

22. "Colonel Dave Day," *Rocky Mountain News*, September 8, 1905.

23. Andrew Hickenlooper to Daniel S. Lamont, Secretary of War, April 19, 1893, Case of David F. Day, Late of Company D, 57th Ohio Infantry.

Application for the Medal of Honor, RG —, General Correspondence of the Office of the Adjutant General, R&P #402,695, National Archives, Washington, D.C.

24. David F. Day to Daniel S. Lamont, December 3, 1894, *Case of David F. Day.*

25. In 1895, Day was awarded the Medal of Honor for "gallantry in the charge of a 'volunteer storming party' on May 22, 1863" at Vicksburg. After the war, he became an Indian agent in the West. 1907 AGO Records, Entry No. 1243619, National Archives, Washington, D.C. For a description of the events that led to Day's being awarded the Medal of Honor, see W. F. Beyer and O. F. Keydel, *Deeds of Valor*, 2 vols. (Detroit: The Perrien-Keydel Co., 1905), 1:190-197. He settled in Durango, Colorado, where he published an unusual and irreverent newspaper known for lampooning politicians and prominent local citizens that had the unlikely title of *The Solid Muldoon*, named after a prizefighter admired by Day. At one time, Day had 42 different libel suits pending against him for some of the outrageous things that he wrote in the paper. He eventually left *The Solid Muldoon* to found a competing paper, *The Durango Democrat*. He became famous for the saying, "No man's property or life is safe while the legislature is in session."

26. Hampton intended to hang the unfortunate Day the next morning, but the spy's timely escape saved his life. Day, Duncan, and several others made quite a daring escape that was documented by Duncan. See Duncan, "With the Army of the Tennessee," 525-26. In 1891, Hampton and Day met again. "Last year when I was in Denver, he called to see me & spoke of having been in the Fayetteville fight & when I told him of the man in gray whom I had intended to hang he said that he was that man. I told him that I was glad I did not hang him, but that I certainly should have done so before his escape," recounted Hampton in a letter to Edward L. Wells. Hampton to Wells, December 20, 1892. See, also, "The Unterrified of Durango Met Wade Hampton Once," undated newspaper article from *The State* (Columbia, S.C.), included in the U. R. Brooks Papers, Perkins Library, Duke University, Durham, N.C., wherein the following exchange between Hampton and Day was recorded at the meeting that Hampton described in his 1892 letter to Wells: "'I had a legal right to kill you, but I am glad that I did not,' remarked the general. 'I am glad you did not,' replied Dave."

27. Day to Lamont, December 3, 1894, Case of David F. Day. In a postwar newspaper account, Day claimed the Union force had faced nearly 3,700 Confederates at Fayetteville on March 11, 1865. He wrote, "Count up the loss of the Scout's charge at Fayetville [sic] North Carolina. Sixty-eight in—fourteen out without a scratch. The 'Fighting Fourteenth.'" *Durango Democrat*, August 22, 1907.

28. Oeffinger, *A Soldier's General*, 263.

29. "The Unterrified of Durango Met Wade Hampton Once."

30. *War Days in Fayetteville*, 48.

31. Oates, *The Story of Fayetteville*, 419.

32. Guild, *Fourth Regiment Tennessee Cavalry*, 126.

33. Gordon memoir, 7-8.

34. Waring diary, entry for March 11, 1865.

35. Wells, "Hampton at Fayetteville," 148.

36. Carter, *The Story of Joshua D. Breyfogle*, 327.

37. John Herr to his sister, March 14, 1865, John Herr Papers, Perkins Library, Duke University, Durham, N.C.

38. *Richmond Dispatch*, March 22, 1865.

39. William B. Styple, ed., *Writing and Fighting the Civil War: Soldier Correspondence to the New York Sunday Mercury* (Kearny, N.J.: Belle Grove Publishing, 2000), 344.

40. Stewart, *Dan McCook's Regiment*, 158.

41. Pritchard diary, entry for March 11, 1865.

42. J. W. DuBose to U. R. Brooks, August 19, 1911, U. R. Brooks Papers, Perkins Library, Duke University, Durham, N.C.

43. Waring diary, entry for March 12, 1865.

44. "Cavalryman," "Campaign Through the Carolinas."

45. William H. Brown to his wife, March 12, 1865, CWTI Collection, USAMHI.

46. Carter, *The Story of Joshua D. Breyfogle*, 327.

47. Asbury P. Gatch to his wife, March 14, 1865, Asbury P. Gatch letters, Ohio Historical Society, Columbus, Ohio.

48. Stevens to his wife, March 12, 1865.

49. "Cavalryman," "Campaign Through the Carolinas."

50. *OR* 47, pt. 2, 787.

51. Statement of James H. Miller , August 6, 1872, "Statements dated 1872."

52. *OR* 47, pt. 2, 788-89. Interestingly, the Union commander considered Monroe's Crossroads to be a defeat. On March 16, Grant sent a dispatch to Assistant Secretary of War C. A. Dana. Sherman, reported Grant, "says nothing about Kilpatrick's defeat by Hampton, but the officer who brings his letter says that before daylight on the 10th Hampton got two brigades in rear of Kilpatrick's headquarters, and surprised and captured all the staff but two officers. Kilpatrick escaped, formed his men, and defeated the enemy with great loss, recapturing about all that he had lost. Hampton lost eighty-six, left dead on the field." *Ibid.*, pt. 2, 788.

53. *Ibid.*, pt. 1, 1053.

54. *Ibid.*, pt. 2, 794-95.

55. Brooks D. Simpson and Jean V. Berlin, eds., *Sherman's Civil War: Selected Correspondence of William T. Sherman, 1860-1865* (Chapel Hill: University of North Carolina Press, 1999), 823-25.

56. Henry C. Hackett, "The Fayetteville Arsenal," *The National Tribune*, May 18, 1916.

57. Stevens to his sister, March 14, 1865.

58. "Cavalryman," "Campaign Through the Carolinas."

59. Thomas J. Jordan to his wife, March 12, 1865, Thomas J. Jordan Civil War Letters 1861-1866, Pennsylvania Historical Society, Philadelphia, Pa.

60. Wade Hampton Manning to U. R. Brooks, June 26, 1908, included in "Keeping History Straight: Gen. M. C. Butler Denies the Statements of Gen. Smith D. Atkins Before Loyal Legion in Chicago, the Address Being Reprinted in The State Last Sunday," *The State*, June 28, 1908. Manning was a member of the Charleston Light Dragoons, and had served as one of Hampton's couriers for most of the war.

61. Reynolds and Kele, "A Yank in the Carolinas Campaign," 54.

62. Hughes, *William J. Hardee*, 282.

63. Sparkman diary, entries for March 12-16, 1865.

64. Rowell, *Yankee Cavalrymen*, 236-37.

65. Thompson diary, entry for March 15, 1865.

66. *Ninety-Second Illinois Volunteers*, 229.

67. Atkins, "Gen. Sherman's March Through the Carolinas."

68. Theodore F. Northrop, "The Capture of Col. Rhett. The Captor Tells the Story of Its Occurrence," *The National Tribune*, December 7, 1911; Theodore F. Northrop, "Capture of Gen. Rhett," *The National Tribune*, January 18, 1906; Theodore F. Northrop, "Gen. Rhett's Capture. As told by the One Who Took Him to Sherman," *The National Tribune*, April 23, 1891.

69. Atkins, "Gen. Sherman's March Through the Carolinas."

70. Northrop, "Capture of Gen. Rhett."

71. Duncan, "With the Army of the Tennessee," 529.

72. *OR* 47, pt. 1, 869.

73. *Ibid.*; Rowell, *Yankee Cavalrymen*, 235.

74. Samuel Toombs, *Reminiscences of the War, Comprising a Detailed Account of the Experiences of the Thirteenth Regiment New Jersey Volunteers* (Orange, N.J.: Printed at the Journal Office, 1878), 212-13.

75. *Ninety-Second Illinois Volunteers*, 231.

76. *OR* 47, pt. 1, 172.

77. General Hardee's sixteen-year-old son Willie, who had just been sworn into the 8th Texas Cavalry, received a mortal wound in this charge. Obviously, the details of the fights at Averasboro and Bentonville go far beyond the scope of this book. For the best and most detailed study of these two important infantry battles, see Bradley, *Last Stand in the Carolinas*. See, also, Nathaniel Chears Hughes, *Bentonville: The Final Battle of Sherman and Johnston* (Chapel Hill: University of North Carolina Press, 1996).

78. Cauthen, *Family Letters of the Three Wade Hamptons*, 114.

79. Rowell, *Yankee Cavalrymen*, 243.

80. "Drama at the Crossroads," *Fayetteville Observer*, October 8, 1961.

81. Johnson, Memorandum of Conversation with General Hampton.

82. Wells, *Hampton and His Cavalry in '64*, 421-23.

83. J. M. Thomasson, "Hampton's Farewell to His Gallant Men," *The State*, May 11, 1908.

84. Wellman, *Giant in Gray*, 180-89.

85. Wells, "A Morning Call on Kilpatrick," 130.

86. Dyer, *From Shiloh to San Juan*, 180-81.

87. Dodson, *Campaigns of Wheeler and His Cavalry*, 358-62.

Chapter 8

1. Johnston, *Narrative of Military Operations*, 381.

2. Moore, *Kilpatrick and Our Cavalry*, 229.

3. Nichols, *The Story of the Great March*, 248.

4. *OR* 47, pt. 1, 862.

5. See Appendix B to this book for a complete listing of all known Union casualties at Monroe's Crossroads, compiled from regimental rosters and muster rolls at the National Archives.

6. "An Interesting Letter."

7. *OR* 47, pt. 1, 862.

8. Davis, *Sherman's March*, 214.

9. Diary of Robert Morris McDowell, entry for March 15, 1865, Chemung County Historical Society, Elmira, N.Y.

10. Davis, *Sherman's March*, 82.

11. *OR* 44, 910.

12. Dodson, *Campaigns of Wheeler and His Cavalry*, 289; W. H. Davis, "Cavalry Service Under Gen. Wheeler," *Confederate Veteran* 11 (1903), 353-54. Davis's account provides an interesting study in how the passage of years blurs memories. Davis confuses the action at Sylvan Grove of November 27 with Monroe's Crossroads; he attributes the capture of Kilpatrick's spotted

horse to the November 27 fight and not to the battle of March 10, 1865. Nevertheless, it contains a good account of the engagement.

13. Jacob D. Cox, *The March to the Sea, Franklin, and Nashville* (New York: Charles Scribner's Sons, 1883), 33.

14. *OR* 47, pt. 1, 862.

15. *Philadelphia Public Ledger*, March 15, 1865.

16. Gatch to his wife, March 14, 1865, Gatch letters.

17. Discussion of the March 1865 Stoneman Raid through eastern Tennessee and western North Carolina goes far beyond the scope of this book. For readers interested in learning more about the war's last major mounted raid see Chris J. Hartley, "'Like an Avalanche': George Stoneman's 1865 Cavalry Raid," *Civil War Regiments*, vol. 6, No. 1 (1998): 74-92.

18. Bradley, *Last Stand in the Carolinas*, 304.

19. *OR* 47, pt. 2, 803, 867.

20. *Ibid.*, 46, pt. 2, 980. Grant was well aware of Kilpatrick's shortcomings, and he also knew well Sherman's desire to have a more reliable cavalry commander. Grant was relieved to hear that Kilpatrick's command was not wiped out by Hampton's sneak attack on the sleeping camp. A staff officer named S. H. Byers left a fascinating insight into Grant's reaction to learning the news of the fight at Monroe's Crossroads. Byers carried Sherman's dispatch to Grant:

> He [U.S. Grant] hurried them through again, rose to his feet, and for a moment paced the little room; then suddenly opening the door he called General Ord, who was in the adjoining room, to come in and hear the good news from Sherman. Bad news of some misfortune to Sherman's army had been telegraphed to Richmond by Wade Hampton, of the enemy's army, the day before. The reports had come through the lines to Grant in most exaggerated form. "Glorious!' cried Ord, "glorious! I was beginning to have my fears, but —"
>
> "Not a bit! Not a bit!" replied Grant. "I knew him. I knew my man. I expected him to do just this, and he has done it."
>
> I was then questioned as to many a detail of Sherman's last movements. "We have been in perfect ignorance," said Grant, "of all these things; you have brought me the first authentic news. How about Kilpatrick?" And I told him how, a few nights before, this officer had been surprised in bed and his staff all captured; how he fled to the swamp, rallied his men, and returning, chased Wade Hampton completely from the road. Grant and Ord both laughed heartily. "And this then was the disaster to Sherman's army of

which the rebels had been boasting so loudly. I expected just exactly as much," said Grant.

However, Grant refused to give Sheridan a direct order, or to punish Sheridan for his insubordination, so nothing came of it. S. H. M. Byers, "Some Recollections of Grant," *Philadelphia Weekly Times*, October 27, 1877.

21. *Ibid.*, 47, pt. 2, 948-49.

22. For a more detailed examination of this episode, see Edward G. Longacre, *The Cavalry at Appomattox: A Tactical Study of Mounted Operations during the Civil War's Climactic Campaign, March 27-April 9, 1865* (Mechanicsburg, Pa.: Stackpole Books, 2003), 37-40.

23. Philip H. Sheridan, *Personal Memoirs of Philip H. Sheridan*, 2 vols. (New York: Charles Webster & Co., 1888), 2:126-29.

24. *Ibid.*, *OR* 47, pt. 2, 135. On April 22, nearly two weeks after the surrender of Lee's Army of Northern Virginia, Grant again ordered Sheridan to march to North Carolina with his cavalry. No longer able to claim being with the Army of the Potomac as an excuse for not going to Sherman's assistance, Sheridan lollygagged instead of promptly moving out. He began his leisurely march on April 24, and had only made it as far as Danville, Virginia by April 26, when Grant ordered Sheridan to return to Petersburg because Johnston had surrendered to Sherman and there was no longer any reason for Sheridan to march to North Carolina. Not even direct orders from the lieutenant general commanding the armies of the United States could get Sheridan to do something that the little Irishman clearly did not want to do. *OR* 46, pt. 3, 888-89. For more on the Danville expedition, see Christopher Calkins, *The Danville Expedition of May and June 1865* (Danville, Va.: Blue & Gray Education Society, 1998), 6-17.

25. Sherman, *Memoirs*, 833.

26. *OR* 47, pt. 3, 123.

27. *Ibid.*, 133.

28. *Ibid.*

29. *Ibid.*, pt. 1, 863.

30. George C. Jenkins, "Report of Co. M, 1st Ala. Cav.," National Tribune, February 21, 1889.

31. *Record of Service of Michigan Volunteers in the Civil War 1861-1865*, 46 vols. (Kalamazoo: Ihling Bros. & Everard, n.d), 29:106.

32. *OR* 47, pt. 1, 905.

33. *Ibid.*, 863.

34. Mrs. John H. Anderson, "Last Days of the Confederacy in North Carolina," *Confederate Veteran* 39 (1931), 21.

35. Robert Herriott, "Fighting to the End," *Confederate Veteran* 31 (1923), 167.

36. Diary of Jesse Roderick Sparkman, entry for March 10, 1865, Fredericksburg/Spotsylvania National Military Park, Fredericksburg, Va.

37. Moore, *Kilpatrick and His Cavalry*, 230.

38. "Letter from Cobb's Legion."

39. Guild, *Fourth Tennessee Cavalry Regiment*, 124.

40. Brooks, *Butler and His Cavalry*, 445.

41. Dodson, *Campaigns of Wheeler and His Cavalry*, 345-46; Hampton to Wells, March 25, 1900 and April 8, 1900.

42. Calhoun, *Liberty Dethroned*, 186.

43. "An Interesting Letter."

44. *OR* 47, pt. 1, 1132.

45. Henry Lane Stone, *"Morgan's Men": A Narrative of Personal Experiences* (Louisville, Ky.: George B. Easton Camp, United Confederate Veterans, 1919), 21.

46. Fortunately, the United States Army regularly uses the Monroe's Crossroads battlefield for staff rides and other teaching exercises, so modern military professionals can learn its lessons and apply them to problems facing today's Army.

Epilogue

1. Mrs. Julia Porcher Wickham, "Wade Hampton, the Cavalry Leader, and His Times," *Confederate Veteran* 36 (1928), 448.

2. Wellman, *Giant in Gray,* 193-334.

3. Martin, *Southern Hero,* 164.

4. *Ibid.,* 165-310.

5. Deangelo McDaniel, "On Trial for Killing: Wheeler, Jones Beat Murder Rap," *The Decatur Daily News,* December 10, 2003. This episode has been largely overlooked for years, but Wheeler's papers at the Alabama Department of Archives and History provide enough clues to enable an interested person to piece together the clues.

6. *Ibid.*

7. Wheeler wrote a well-respected account of his service in Cuba during the Spanish-American War. See Joseph Wheeler, *The Santiago Campaign* (Boston: Lamson, Wolf & Co., 1898). A recent study suggests that Alger's decision to grant Wheeler a commission not only helped to heal the lingering wounds of the Civil War, but also brought a faster end to the Spanish-American War. See

Anders M. Kinney, *Joseph Wheeler: Uniting the Blue and the Gray* (Lincoln, Neb.: Writers Club Press, 2002).

8. Dyer, *From Shiloh to San Juan*, 188-259; Mrs. C. W. McMahon, "General Joseph Wheeler," *Confederate Veteran* 33 (1925), 455. Robert E. Lee's nephew, Fitzhugh Lee, had also served as a major general of cavalry in the Confederate army. Lee likewise accepted a major general's commission and served in the Spanish-American War. The War Department's strategy of employing former Confederate cavalry commanders proved both militarily and politically successful.

9. *Biographical Directory of the United States Congress 1774-1989* (Washington, D.C.: U.S. Government Printing Office, 1989), 1852; Sarah Van V. Woolfolk, "George E. Spencer: A Carpetbagger in Alabama," *Alabama Review* 19 (January 1966), 41-52; and James Grant Wilson and John Fiske, eds., *Appleton's Cyclopedia of American Biography*, 6 vols. (New York: D. Appleton & Co., 1887-1889).

10. "Ostrich Hunting," *Harper's Weekly*, August 22, 1868. An entire regiment of Argentine cavalry accompanied the former horse soldier on his ostrich hunt.

11. Kilpatrick became one of the most popular lecturers in the United States. "Personal," *Harper's Weekly*, December 9, 1876.

12. A number of North Carolinians and a former officer of the 5th Ohio Cavalry gave statements describing Kilpatrick's conduct with Charley, Molly, and Alice during the 1865 Carolinas Campaign. Capt. Robert Miller of the 5th Ohio gave his statement with some trepidation. Miller's attorney wrote, "In consideration of these facts Capt. Miller requests that those into whose hands the affidavit may fall will use his statement only when found necessary to protect the administration from false charges made by him in the ensuing campaign in his advocacy of the Greeley movement." A. W. Shaffer to J. N. Beach, August 6, 1872, "Statements Dated 1872."

13. "The South American Affair," *Harper's Weekly*, December 24, 1881.

14. Martin, *Kill-Cavalry*, 237-263.

15. *Sussex Independent*, February 1, 1918.

Appendix C

1. C. Vann Woodward, ed., *Mark Chesnut's Civil War* (New Haven: Yale University Press, 1981): 695.

2. Wells, *Hampton and His Cavalry in '64*, 402.

3. Marie's mother had been married several times, and Marie carried her father's last name, which was different from that of Amelia by 1865. See "Living Descendant's Letter Sheds Light," *The State*, November 1, 1959.

4. Woodward, *Mary Chesnut's Civil War*, 695.

5. R. DeT. Lawrence, "The Muchly Married Miss Mary Boozer," *Confederate Veteran* 29 (1921): 23.

6. Tom Elmore, "Mary Boozer: The Confederacy's Femme Fatale," unpublished manuscript, Columbia, S.C., 2002: 1-6.

7. *Ibid.*, 8

8. Wells, *Hampton and His Cavalry in '64*, 401.

9. *Ibid.*, 408-10.

10. DuBose, *General Joseph Wheeler*, 449.

11. Bradley, *Last Stand in the Carolinas*, 475, n. 23.

12. Howard to his wife, March 12, 1865, Howard Papers, Bowdoin College, Brunswick, Me.

Appendix D

1. "A Staff Officer," *Synopsis of the Military Career of General Joseph Wheeler*, 32.

2. *CMH*, 1:708.

3. Dodson, *Campaigns of Wheeler and His Cavalry*, 339.

4. The monument also incorrectly identifies Dibrell as a brigade commander, and omits one of Wheeler's brigades.

5. Wells, *Hampton and His Cavalry in '64*, 151.

6. Warner, *Generals in Gray*, xvii.

7. Alfred Roman to Col. G. W. Brent, January 22, 1865, Papers of Alfred Roman, Manuscripts Division, Library of Congress, Washington, D.C.

8. Wade Hampton to Bradley T. Johnson, September 21, 1900, Johnson Papers.

9. Hampton to Johnson, December 28, 1899, Johnson Papers.

10. "Lieutenant Generals C.S.A.," *The News and Courier*, February 24, 1899.

11. "Joseph Wheeler," *The Southern Historical Society Papers* 32 (December-January 1904), 42.

12. *OR* 47, pt. 1, 1129.

Bibliography

PRIMARY SOURCES

Newspapers:

Atlanta Journal
Atlanta Southern Confederacy
Carolina Watchman (Salisbury, N.C.)
Charleston Daily Courier
Charleston Mercury
Charleston News & Courier
Charleston Sunday News
Cincinnati Daily Commercial
Daily Confederate (Raleigh, N.C.)
Daily Constitutionalist (Augusta, Ga.)
Daily Journal and Messenger (Macon, Ga.)
Delaware Gazette (Delaware, Ohio)
Detroit Free Press
Durango Democrat
Edgefield (S.C.) Advertiser
Fayetteville Daily Telegraph
Fayetteville Observer
Galveston Weekly News
Harper's Weekly
Macon Daily Telegraph (Macon, Ga.)
National Tribune (Washington, D.C.)
New Bern Times

New York Herald
New York Times
North Carolina Standard (Raleigh, N.C.)
Philadelphia Inquirer
Philadelphia Public Ledger
Raleigh Weekly Conservative
Richmond Dispatch
Richmond Examiner
Rocky Mountain News
The Argus (Wadesboro, N.C.)
The Decatur Daily
The Philadelphia Weekly Times
The State (Columbia, S.C.)
The Sunny South (Atlanta, Ga.)
Sussex Independent
The Sussex Register
Wantage Recorder
Western Democrat (Charlotte, N.C.)
Wilmington Journal

Unpublished Manuscripts

Alabama Department of Archives and History, Birmingham, Ala.:
    George Knox Miller memoir of service in Eighth Confederate
        Cavalry, 1861-1865
    Henry Clay Reynolds Papers
    Joseph Wheeler Papers

Bentley Historical Library, University of Michigan, Ann Arbor, Michigan:
    William Wallace Cook Papers
    William Collin Stevens Papers
    Edward Michael Watson Papers

Special Collections, The Library, Bowdoin College, Brunswick, Maine:
    O. O. Howard Papers

Charleston Library Society, Charleston, South Carolina:
    Edward L. Wells Correspondence
    Edward L. Wells Memoirs

Chemung County Historical Society, Elmira, New York:

Robert Morris McDowell Diary

W. L. Clements Library of the University of Michigan, Ann Arbor:
Schoff Diaries and Journals
C. G. Rogers Diary for 1865

Fredericksburg-Spotsylvania National Military Park, Fredericksburg, VA:
Jesse Roderick Sparkman Diary

Georgia Historical Society, Savannah, Ga.:
J. Frederick Waring Papers
William Washington Gordon Reminiscences

Manuscripts Division, Library of Congress, Washington, D.C.:
P. G. T. Beauregard Papers
John M. Schofield Papers
Louis T. Wigfall Papers

Kevin D. McLemore Collection, Fort Campbell, Kentucky:
Bethenia McLemore Diary
William S. McLemore Service Records

National Archives, Washington, D.C.:
RG 94, Office of the Adjutant General; Volunteer Organizations of
the Civil War, Various Regimental Returns for March 1865
RG 94, Service and Pension Records of Civil War Soldiers
RG 94, Records of the Adjutant General's Office 1780-1917,
Theodore F. Northrop, Captain of Volunteers File, File No. 1674 vs
1676, Box 1200
RG 107, Records of the Office of the Secretary of War, "Statements
dated 1872 concerning Gen. H. Judson Kilpatrick's affair with
a woman during the Civil War," included in "Letters, telegrams,
reports, and other records concerning the loyalty of Army Officers,
War Department employees, and citizens during the Civil War,
1861-1872," Box 2

National Climactic Data Center, Asheville, North Carolina:
Excessive Precipitation Records for the Winter and Spring of 1865

North Carolina State Archives, Raleigh, North Carolina:
Historic Sites Sections Files for Monroe's Crossroads

Mrs. J. W. McLaughlin Papers, P. C. 1443

Ohio Historical Society, Columbus, Ohio:
   Asbury P. Gatch Papers
   William M. Heath Diary for 1865

Pennsylvania Historical Society, Philadelphia, Pennsylvania:
   Thomas J. Jordan Civil War Letters, 1861-1866

Perkins Library, Duke University, Durham, North Carolina:
   U. R. Brooks Papers
   Confederate Veteran Papers
   John Herr Papers
   Bradley T. Johnson Papers
   William Schaum Diary for 1865

Michael Shannon Collection, Houston, Texas:
   Alexander M. Shannon Papers

Smith Memorial Library, Indiana Historical Society, Indianapolis, Indiana:
   James S. Thompson Diary for 1864 and 1865
   Williamson D. Ward Diary for 1865

South Caroliniana Library, University of South Carolina, Columbia, SC:
   Zimmerman Davis Papers
   Wade Hampton Papers
   Civil War Letters of H. Lide Law
   Henry Minor Memoirs

Southern Historical Collections, Wilson Library, University of North Carolina, Chapel Hill:
   Matthew C. Butler Letters
   Gordon Family Papers
   O. P. Hargis Reminiscences
   Lafayette McLaws Papers
   North Carolina Clippings Files
   Leroy M. Nutt Papers
   Wilbur S. Nye, "The Battle That Was Fought on the Fort Bragg
       Reservation" (unpublished manuscript)
   D. L. Swain Papers
   Joseph F. Waring Papers

Tennessee State Library and Archives, Nashville, Tennessee:
    Jesse Roderick Sparkman Diary, Memoirs and Diaries Collection

United States Army Military History Institute, Carlisle, Pennsylvania:
    Civil War Miscellaneous Collection
    William W. Pritchard Diary for 1865
    Civil War Times Illustrated Collection
    William H. Brown Correspondence, September 14, 1862-June 4,
        1865
    Harrisburg CWRT Collection
    George Shuman Letters May 31, 1863-July 9, 1865

Virginia Historical Society, Richmond, Virginia:
    Henry B. McClellan Papers

E. D. Wilson Collection, Houston, Texas:
    Josiah D. Wilson Diary

Eric J. Wittenberg Collection, Columbus, Ohio:
    Miscellaneous correspondence

Woodruff Library, Emory University, Atlanta, Ga.:
    John Ash Papers

Published Primary Sources

"Achievements of the Thirty Rangers." *Galveston Weekly News*, March 8, 1865.

Adams, Charles Francis. *A Cycle of Adams Letters, 1861-1865*. Edited by Worthington C. Ford. 2 vols. Boston: Houghton-Mifflin, 1920.

Agassiz, George R., ed. *Meade's Headquarters 1863-1865: Letters of Colonel Theodore Lyman From the Wilderness to Appomattox*. Boston: The Atlantic Monthly Press, 1922.

Allen, W. G. "About the Fight at Fayetteville, N.C." *Confederate Veteran* 19 (1911): 433-34.

"An Interesting Letter." *Macon Daily Telegraph*, April 6, 1865.

Anderson, Mrs. J. H. "Confederate Arsenal at Fayetteville, N.C." *Confederate Veteran* 36 (1928): 223.

Atkins, Smith D. "Gen. Sherman's March Through the Carolinas." *The State*, June 21, 1908.

Bailey, S. W. "Gen. Hampton's Charge into Kilpatrick's Camp in 1865," *Atlanta Journal*, March 8, 1902.

Bennett, L. G. and W. M. Haigh. *History of the Thirty-Sixth Regiment Illinois Volunteers, During the War of the Rebellion*. Aurora, Ill.: Knickerbocker & Hodder, 1876.

Bennett, S. "Another Brief Report." *Confederate Veteran* 19 (1911): 434.

Blackburn, J. K. P. "Reminiscences of the Terry Rangers." *The Southwestern Historical Quarterly* 22 (September and December 1968): 308-336 and 451-479.

"Bombardment of Valparaiso." *Harper's Weekly*, May 19, 1866.

Bonaparte, Napoleon. *Napoleon's Art of War*. Translated by Lt. Gen. Sir. G. C. D'Aguilar. New York: Barnes & Noble, 1995.

Bowman, Col. S. M. and Lt. Col. R. B. Irwin. *Sherman and His Campaigns: A Military Biography*. New York: Charles B. Richardson, 1865.

Brooks, Ulysses R. *Butler and His Cavalry in the War of Secession, 1861-1865*. Columbia, S.C.: The State Co., 1909.

——. "More on Fight at Fayetteville." *Confederate Veteran* 19 (1911): 453.

——. "Some Pages of Heretofore Unwritten History." *The State*, September 10, 1895.

——. *Stories of the Confederacy*. Columbia, S.C.: The State Co., 1912.

Butler, Matthew C. "Kilpatrick Almost Caught: How a Federal Major Gen. Escaped En Dishabille." *Charleston News & Courier*, November 7, 1897.

Calhoun, Charles M. "Credit to Wheeler Claimed by Others." *Confederate Veteran* 20 (1912): 82-83.

——. *Liberty Dethroned: A Concise History of Some of the Most Startling Events Before, During, and Since the Civil War*. Greenwood, S.C.: n.p., 1903.

Camburn, T. E. "Capture of Col. Rhett." *National Tribune*, August 23, 1906.

Carlin, William P. "Military Memoirs." *National Tribune*, July 23, 30 and August 6, 1885.

Carter, George E., ed. *The Story of Joshua D. Breyfogle, Private, 4th Ohio Infantry (10th Ohio Cavalry) and the Civil War*. Lewiston, N. Y.: The Edward Mellen Press, 2001.

Caruthers, W. G. "More About Kilpatrick's Horses." *Confederate Veteran* 13 (1905): 456.

Cavalryman. "Campaign Through the Carolinas." *National Tribune*, April 28, May 5, May 12, 1892.

Cauthen, Charles E., ed. *Family Letters of the Three Wade Hamptons, 1782-1901*. Columbia: University of South Carolina Press, 1953.

Chesnut, Mary Boykin. *A Diary from Dixie*. Edited by Ben Ames Williams. Boston: Houghton-Mifflin Co., 1949.

Coffin, James P. "Col. Henry M. Ashby." *Confederate Veteran* 14 (1906): 121.

Collins, E. "The First to Enter Fayetteville." *The National Tribune*, May 13, 1886.

"Col. Jo. Robbins, 3rd Alabama Cavalry." *Confederate Veteran* 2 (1899): 77.

"Col. W. C. P. Breckinridge." *Confederate Veteran* 13 (1905): 84.

Committee of the Regiment. *Ninety-Second Illinois Volunteers*. Freeport, Ill.: Journal Steam Publishing House and Bookbindery, 1875.

Connelly, James A. *Three Years in Army of the Cumberland: The Letters and Diary of Major James A. Connelly*. Edited by Paul M. Angle. Bloomington: University of Indiana Press, 1959.

Conyngham, David P. *Sherman's March through the South With Sketches and Incidents of the Campaign*. New York: Sheldan & Co., 1865.

Cox, Jacob D. *The March to the Sea, Franklin, and Nashville*. New York: Charles Scribner's Sons, 1883.

Davis, Jefferson. *The Rise and Fall of the Confederate Government*. 2 vols. New York: D. Appleton & Co., 1881.

Davis W. H. "Cavalry Service Under Gen. Wheeler." *Confederate Veteran* 11 (1903): 353-54.

———. "Kilpatrick's Spotted Horse." *Confederate Veteran* 14 (1906): 62.

Davis, Zimmerman. "Letter to the Editor." *Edgefield Advertiser*, May 12, 1865.

"Death of Capt. Northrop." *Sussex Independent*, February 1, 1918.

"Death of Civil War Veteran on Sunday." *Wantage Recorder*, February 1, 1918.

Dodson, William C. *Campaigns of Wheeler and His Cavalry, 1862-1865*. Atlanta: Hudgins Publishing Co., 1899.

Du Bose, John W. "The Effort to Capture Kilpatrick." *Confederate Veteran* 29 (1921): 329.

———. "The Fayetteville Road Fight." *Confederate Veteran* 20 (1912): 84-86.

———. *General Joseph Wheeler and the Army of Tennessee*. New York: Neale Publishing Co., 1912.

Duncan, William H. "With the Army of the Tennessee Through the Carolinas." *Glimpses of the Nation's Struggle*. Military Order of the Loyal Legion of the United States, Minnesota Commandery. Fourth Series. Saint Paul: H. L. Collins Co., 1898: 517-529.

Evans, J. W. "Reminiscences of J. W. Evans in the War Between the States." Included in *Confederate Reminiscences and Letters 1861-1865*. Vol. 10. Atlanta: Ga. Division, United Daughters of the Confederacy, 1999: 19-23.

Fallis, Leroy S. "Kilpatrick Surprised: Comrade Fallis Tells the Story of Montrose Crossroads as He Understands It." *National Tribune*, December 27, 1900.

Fanning, T. W. *The Hairbreadth Escapes and Humorous Adventures of A Volunteer in the Cavalry Service By One of Them*. Cincinnati: P. C. Browne, 1865.

Fletcher, William A. *Rebel Private, Front and Rear: Memoirs of a Confederate Soldier*. New York: Dutton, 1995.

Ford, Arthur P. *Life in the Confederate Army: Being Personal Experiences of a Private Soldier in the Confederate Army*. New York: Neale Publishing Co., 1905.

Freeman, Douglas Southall, ed. *Lee's Dispatches*. New York: G. P. Putnam's Sons, 1915.

"From Wheeler's Command." *Macon Daily Telegraph*, February 14, 1865.

Galloway, Tammy, ed. *Dear Old Roswell: The Civil War Letters of the King Family of Roswell, Georgia*. Macon, Ga.: Mercer University Press, 2003.

Gardner, J. H. "Alabama's Sons Fought: Comrade Gardner Has Something to Say About Comrade Wentz's Story." *National Tribune*, August 13, 1896.

"General E. M. Law at Gettysburg." *Confederate Veteran* 30 (1922): 50-51.

"General Kilpatrick's Operations." *Harper's Weekly*, April 1, 1865.

Giles, Leonidas B. *Terry's Texas Rangers*. Austin: The Pemberton Press, 1967.

Graber, H. W. *The Life Record of H. W. Graber: A Terry Texas Ranger 1861-1865*. Privately published, 1918.

Grady, Henry W. "An Interview with General Longstreet." Included in *Battles & Leaders of the Civil War*. Vol. 5. Edited by Peter Cozzens. Urbana, Ill.: Univesity of Illinois Press, 2002: 686-96.

Grant, Ulysses S. *Personal Memoirs of U. S. Grant*. New York: Charles Webster & Co., 1885.

Guild, George B. *A Brief Narrative of the Fourth Tennessee Cavalry Regiment*. Nashville: n.p., 1913.

Hackett, Henry C. "The Fayetteville Arsenal." *National Tribune*, May 18, 1916.

Halliburton, Lloyd, ed. *Saddle Soldiers: The Civil War Correspondence of General William Stokes of the 4th South Carolina Cavalry*. Orangeburg, S.C.: Sandlapper Publishing, 1993.

Hamilton, Posey. "The Effort to Capture Kilpatrick." *Confederate Veteran* 29 (1921): 329.

Hamilton, William Douglas. *Recollections of a Cavalryman After Fifty Years*. Columbus, Ohio: F. J. Heer Printing Co., 1915.

Hampton, Wade. "The Battle of Bentonville." Included in Robert U. Johnson and Clarence C. Buel, eds. *Battles and Leaders of the Civil War*. 4 vols. New York: Century Publishing Co., 1884-1889. 4:700-705.

Hancock, Richard R. *Hancock's Diary: or, A History of the Second Tennessee Confederate Cavalry*. Nashville, Tenn.: Brandon Printing Co., 1887.

Harcourt, A. P. "Terry's Texas Rangers." *The Southern Bivouac*, Vol. 1, No. 8 (Old Series, November 1882), 89-97.

Harmon, Ansen L. "Woods Full of Johnnies: A 10th Ohio Cav. Comrade Gives Credit to the 1st Ala. Cav." *National Tribune*, January 24, 1901.

Harwell, Richard and Philip N. Racine, eds. *The Fiery Trail: A Union Officer's Account of Sherman's Last Campaigns*. Knoxville: University of Tennessee Press, 1986.

Hawthorne, J. J. "Active Service with the Third Alabama Cavalry." *Confederate Veteran* 34 (1926): 334-336.

Herriott, Robert. "Fighting to the End." *Confederate Veteran* 31 (1923): 167-168.

Hibbets, Jeff J. "Fayetteville, N.C." *National Tribune*, June 11, 1885.

Hinman, Wilbur F. *The Story of the Sherman Brigade, the Camp, the March, the Bivouac, the Battle, and How the Boys Lived and Died During Four Years of Active Field Service*. Alliance, Ohio: privately published, 1897.

Hitchcock, Henry. *Marching With Sherman: Passages From the Letters and Campaign Diaries of Henry Hitchcock*. Edited by M. A. DeWolfe Howe. Lincoln: University of Nebraska Press, 1995.

Holman, Natt. "Muster Roll of Company F, Eighth Texas." *Confederate Veteran* 19 (1911): 574-5.

———. "Participant in Battle of Fayetteville, N.C." *Confederate Veteran* 19 (1911): 544.

Holmes, James G. "The Fighting Qualities of Generals Hampton, Butler, and Others Related by Adjutant-General Holmes of Charleston." *The Sunny South*, June 13, 1896.

"Home and Foreign Gossip." *Harper's Weekly*, November 5, 1870.

Hood, N. A. "History of the Surprise of Kilpatrick." *Confederate Veteran* 14 (1906): 176-77.

Howard, Oliver Otis. *Autobiography of Oliver Otis Howard, Major General United States Army*. 2 vols. New York: Baker & Taylor Co., 1907.

Howard, Wiley C. *Sketch of the Cobb Legion Cavalry and Some Incidents and Scenes Remembered*. Atlanta, Ga.: privately published, 1901.

Husby, Karla Jean, comp., and edited by Eric J. Wittenberg. *Under Custer's Command: The Civil War Journal of James Henry Avery*. Dulles, Va.: Brassey's, 2000.

Instructions for Officers and Non-Commissioned Officers On Outpost and Patrol Duty, and Troops in Campaign. Washington, D.C.: Government Printing Office, 1863.

Inzer, J. W. "How Kilpatrick Lost Pistols and Holsters." *Confederate Veteran* 12 (1904): 177.

Jenkins, A. E. "Kilpatrick's Spotted Horse." *Confederate Veteran* 13 (1905): 315.

Jenkins, George C. "Kilpatrick's Capture." *National Tribune*, October 15, 1885.

———. "Report of Co. M, 1st Ala. Càv." *National Tribune*, February 21, 1889.

Johnston, Joseph E. "My Negotiations with General Sherman." Included in *Battles & Leaders of the Civil War*. Vol. 5. Edited by Peter Cozzens. Urbana, Ill.: University of Illinois Press, 2002: 653-664.

———. *Narrative of Military Operations, Directed, During the Late War Between the States*. New York: D. Appleton and Co., 1874.

Jones, J. A. "Report by Joseph A. Jones, Birmingham, Ala., Company E, 51st Alabama Partisan Rangers." *Confederate Veteran* 19 (1911): 434.

Jones, William B. "The Late Maj. Gen. William Wirt Allen." *Confederate Veteran* 2 (1894): 324.

"Joseph Wheeler." *Southern Historical Society Papers* 32 (January-December 1904): 41-42.

"Keeping History Straight: Gen. M. C. Butler Denies the Statements of Gen. Smith D. Atkins Before Loyal Legion in Chicago, the Address Being Reprinted in The State Last Sunday." *The State*, June 28, 1908.

Kennedy, Ed. "Scouting with Wheeler." *Confederate Veteran* 36 (1918): 344.

Kennedy, John R. "The Mills of the Gods." *Confederate Veteran* 32 (1924): 126.

Kidd, James H. *Personal Recollections of a Cavalryman in Custer's Michigan Brigade*. Ionia, Mich.: Sentinel Publishing Co., 1908.

Kyle, Anne K. "Incidents of Hospital Life." *War Days of Fayetteville, N.C.* Fayetteville, N.C.: Judge Printing Co., 1910: 35-45.

La Bree, Benjamin, ed. *Camp Fires of the Confederacy*. Louisville, Ky.: Courier-Journal Job Printing Co., 1898.

Latta, John. "Kilpatrick's Surprise: How a Captain Saved the Brigade." *National Tribune*, April 1, 1886.

Lawrence, R. DeT. "The Muchly Married Miss Mary Boozer." *Confederate Veteran* 29 (1921): 23.

Leonard, W. C. "A Surprise and a Rally." *National Tribune*, August 2, 1900.

"Letter from Cobb's Legion." *Daily Constitutionalist*, April 19, 1865.

"Lieutenant Generals C. S. A." *The News and Courier*, February 24, 1899.

Lindsley, John Berrien, ed. *The Military Annals of Tennessee, Confederate. First Series: Embracing a Review of Military Operations with Regimental Histories and Memorial Rolls, Compiled From Original and Official Sources*. Nashville: J. M. Lindsley & Co., 1886.

Lomax, W. M. "At Monroe's Crossroads." *National Tribune*, July 6, 1899.

"M. C. Butler: Beautiful Tribute From Veterans of Washington City." *The State*, June 21, 1909.

Mahan, Dennis Hart. *Advanced-Guard, Outpost, and Detachment Service of Troops, with the Essential Principles of Strategy, and Grand Tactics*. New York: John Wiley, 1863.

Mallory, Stephen R. "The Last Days of the Confederate Government." Included in *Battles & Leaders of the Civil War*. Vol. 5. Edited by Peter Cozzens. Urbana, Ill.: University of Illinois Press, 2002: 665-685.

Mann, Russell. "Ninth Kentucky Cavalry, C.S.A." *Confederate Veteran* 17 (1909): 233.

Manning, Wade Hampton. "Career of Wade Hampton." *The State*, April 16, 1911.

McCain, Warren. *A Soldier's Diary; or, The History of Company L, Third Indiana Cavalry*. Indianapolis: William A. Patton, 1885.

McClellan, Henry B. "The Campaign of 1863—A Reply to Kilpatrick." *The Philadelphia Weekly Times*, February 7, 1880.

McDowell, D. A. K, et al. "The Kilpatrick Spotted Horse Affair." *Confederate Veteran* 14 (1906): 309.

McKnight, E. H. "Scouting With General Wheeler." *Confederate Veteran* 19 (1911): 72.

Memorial Addresses of the Life and Character of Robert M. A. Hawk, Delivered in the House of Representatives and in the Senate, Forty-Seventh Congress. Washington, D.C.: U.S. Government Printing Office, 1883.

"Meteoric War Record of Colonel W C P Breckinridge, in two parts." *The Sunny South*, October 12 and 19, 1901.

Meyer, Henry C. *Civil War Experiences Under Bayard, Gregg, Kilpatrick, Custer, Raulston, and Newberry, 1862, 1863, 1864*. New York: Knickerbocker Press, 1911.

Miller, James. "With Sherman Through the Carolinas." *Civil War Times Illustrated* Vol. VIII, No. 6 (Oct. 1969): 35-37, 40-44.

Mims, Wilbur F. *War History of the Prattville Dragoons*. n.p., n.d.

Moore, Frank, ed. *The Rebellion Record*. 11 vols. New York: G. P. Putnam, 1861-1868.

Moore, James, M. D. *Kilpatrick and Our Cavalry: Comprising a Sketch of the Life of General Kilpatrick, With an Account of the Cavalry Raids, Engagements, and Operations Under His Command, From the Beginning of the Rebellion to the Surrender of Johnston*. New York: W. J. Widdleton, 1865.

Morgan, D. B. "Incidents of the Fighting at Aiken, S.C." *Confederate Veteran* 32 (1924): 300-301.

Morris, W. H. "The Other Side at Fayetteville." *Confederate Veteran* 20 (1912): 83-84.

Munford, Thomas T. "A Fine Tribute to Hampton." *The State*, February 18, 1891.

Nichols, George Ward. "Captain Duncan." *Harper's Weekly* (December 8, 1866): 773-774.

———. *The Story of the Great March*. New York: Harper & Brothers, 1865.

Northrop, Theodore F. "A Federal on the Fight at Fayetteville." *Confederate Veteran* 21 (1913): 477.

———. "Capture of Gen. Rhett." *National Tribune*, January 18, 1906.

———. "Gen. Rhett's Capture. As told by the One Who Took Him to Sherman." *National Tribune*, April 23, 1891.

———. "Incidents of Sherman's March in North Carolina." *Confederate Veteran* 21 (1913): 477.

———. "Other Side of the Fayetteville Road Fight." *Confederate Veteran* 20 (1912): 423.

———. "The Capture of Col. Rhett. The Captor Tells the Story of Its Occurrence." *National Tribune*, December 7, 1911.

Oakey, Daniel. "Marching Through Georgia and the Carolinas." Included in *Battles and Leaders of the Civil War*, Robert U. Johnson and Clarence C. Buel, eds. 4 vols. New York: The Century Co., 1888. 4:671-679.

Oeffinger, John C., ed. *A Soldier's General: The Civil War Letters of Major General Lafayette McLaws*. Chapel Hill: University of North Carolina Press, 2002.

"Ostrich Hunting." *Harper's Weekly*, August 22, 1868.

"Our Trip With the Yankee Raiders." *The Argus*, March 30, 1865.

"Outrages of Wheeler's Command." *Charleston Mercury*, January 14, 1865.

Overley, Milford. "Williams's Kentucky Brigade, C.S.A." *Confederate Veteran* 13 (1905): 460-62.

Payne, Edwin H. *History of the Thirty-Fourth Regiment of Illinois Volunteer Cavalry*. Clinton, Iowa.: Allen Printing Co., 1903.

Pepper, George Whitefield. *Personal Recollections of Sherman's Campaigns in Georgia and the Carolinas*. Zanesville, Ohio: H. Dunne, 1866.

"Personal." *Harper's Weekly*, December 9, 1876.

Pike, James. *The Scout and Ranger, Being the Personal Adventures of Corporal Pike, of the Fourth Ohio Cavalry*. Cincinnati: J. R. Hawley & Co., 1865.

Quaife, Milo M., ed. *From the Cannon's Mouth: The Civil War Letters of General Alpheus S. Williams*. Detroit: Wayne State University, 1959.

Record of Service of Michigan Volunteers in the Civil War 1861-1865. Vol. 29: Ninth Michigan Cavalry. 46 vols. Kalamazoo: Ihling Bros. & Everard, n.d.

Reed, John. "The Action at Aiken, S.C." *National Tribune*, August 30, 1888.

Reneau, T. W. "Montrose Crossroads." *National Tribune*, September 6, 1900.

Report of the Adjutant General of the State of Kentucky. Frankfort: Kentucky Yeoman Office, 1866.

Reynolds, Donald E. and Kele, Max H. "A Yank in the Carolinas Campaign: The Diary of James W. Chapin, Eighth Indiana Cavalry." *North Carolina Historical Review*, vol. 46, no. 1 (Winter 1969): 42-57.

Ridley, B. L. "Chat With Col. W. S. McLemore." *Confederate Veteran* 8 (1900): 262-64.

Rodenbough, Theophilus F. "Some Cavalry Leaders." In *Miller's Photographic History of the Civil War* vol. 4. New York: Review of Reviews Co., 1911: 262-88.

Roster and List of Engagements 10th Ohio Volunteer Cavalry, Organized October 1, 1862 at Camp Cleveland, Ohio. Hebron, Ohio: privately published, 1919.

Rowland, Dunbar, ed. *Jefferson Davis, Constitutionalist: His Letters, Papers, and Speeches*. 10 vols. Jackson, Miss.: Mississippi Department of Archives and History, 1923.

Sandiford, B. B. "Col. A. M. Shannon." *Confederate Veteran* 15 (1907), 84-5.

Scott, Hugh H. "Fighting Kilpatrick's Escape." *Confederate Veteran* 12 (1904): 588.

Scott, Paul, ed. "'With Tears in Their Eyes': One the Road to the Sea: Shannon's Scouts." *Civil War Times Illustrated* Vol. XXI, No. 9 (January 1983): 26-29.

Seaman, William H. "The Battle of Bentonville, N.C." *The National Tribune*, August 20, 1885.

Sheridan, Philip H. *Personal Memoirs of Philip H. Sheridan*. 2 vols. New York: Charles Webster & Co., 1888.

Sherman, William T. *Memoirs of General William T. Sherman*. 2 vols. New York: Charles Webster & Co., 1875.

Simpson, Brooks D. and Jean V. Berlin, eds. *Sherman's Civil War: Selected Correspondence of William T. Sherman, 1860-1865*. Chapel Hill: University of North Carolina Press, 1999.

Small, William. *Campfire Talk on the Life and Military Services of Maj. Gen. Judson Kilpatrick*. G.A.R., Dept. of the Potomac, John A. Rawlins Post No. 1, 1887.

Smith, Daniel E. Huger, et al., eds. *Mason Smith Family Letters 1960-1865*. Columbia: University of South Carolina Press, 1950.

Smith, Frank. "A Maine Boy in the Tenth Ohio Cavalry." *Maine Bugle* Campaign IV (1897): 19-21.

"Spain and Chile." *Harper's Weekly*, December 9, 1865.

Stewart, Nixon B. *Dan McCook's Regiment: 52nd O.V.I.: A History of the Regiment, Its Campaigns and Battles from 1862 to 1865*. Alliance, Ohio: Review Print, 1900.

Stone, Henry Lane. *"Morgan's Men": A Narrative of Personal Experiences*. Louisville, Ky.: George B. Easton Camp, United Confederate Veterans, 1919.

Straw, A. B. "Kilpatrick's Version." *National Tribune*, October 4, 1900.

Styple, William B., ed. *Writing and Fighting the Civil War: Soldier Correspondence to the New York Sunday Mercury*. Kearny, N.J.: Belle Grove Publishing, 2000.

Sun Tzu. *The Art of War*. Translated by Samuel B. Griffith. London: Oxford University Press, 1963.

Supplement to the Official Records of the Union and Confederate Armies, Reports, Addendum, Series 1, vol. 7. Wilmington, N.C.: Broadfoot Publishing Co., 1997.

Swan, J. W. "Kilpatrick's Cavalry. A Boy's Experiences at the Front." *National Tribune*, April 6, 1905.

Swordberg, Claire E., ed. *Three Years With the 92nd Illinois: The Civil War Diary of John M. King*. Mechanicsburg, Pa.: Stackpole Books, 1999.

"The Last Roll Call: Col. M. C. Dickson." *Confederate Veteran* 14 (1906): 516.

The War of the Rebellion: A Compilation of the Official Records of the Union and Confederate Armies, 70 vols. in 4 series. Washington, D.C.: U.S. Government Printing Office, 1889-1904.

"The Yankees in Anson." *The Argus*, March 30, 1865.

Thomasson, J. M. "Hampton's Farewell to His Gallant Men." *The State*, May 11, 1908.

Tomlinson, Helyn W., ed. *"Dear Friends": The Civil War Letters and Diary of Charles Edwin Cort*. n.p. 1962.

Samuel Toombs. *Reminiscences of the War, Comprising a Detailed Account of the Experiences of the Thirteenth Regiment New Jersey Volunteers*. Orange, N.J.: Printed at the Journal Office, 1878.

"Unveiling of Confederate Monument at Montgomery, Alabama: Major Falkner's Words." *Charleston Sunday News*, November 20, 1898.

Vale, Joseph G. *Minty and the Cavalry: A History of Cavalry Campaigns in the Western Armies*. Harrisburg, Pa.: E. K. Meyers, 1886.

"Wade Hampton." *Harper's Weekly*, November 11, 1865.

Wainwright, Charles S. *A Diary of Battle: The Personal Journals of Colonel Charles S. Wainwright, 1861-1865*. ed., Allan Nevins. New York: Harcourt, Brace & World, 1962.

Ward, J. W. "General M. C. Butler of South Carolina." *Confederate Veteran* 3 (1895): 42.

Watkins, E. W. "Another Account." *Confederate Veteran* 20 (1912): 84.

Wells, Edward L. "Hampton at Fayetteville." *Southern Historical Society Papers* 13 (1885): 144-48.

———. "A Morning Call on Kilpatrick." *Southern Historical Society Papers* 12 (1884): 123-30.

———. *A Sketch of the Charleston Light Dragoons, From the Earliest Formation of the Corps*. Charleston, S.C.: Lucas, Richardson & Co., 1888.

———. *Hampton and His Cavalry in '64*. Richmond, Va.: B. F. Johnson Co., 1899.

Wheeler, Joseph. *A Revised System of Cavalry Tactics, for the Use of the Cavalry and Mounted Infantry, C.S.A.* Mobile, Ala.: S. H. Goetzel & Co., 1863.

———. "An Effort to Rescue Jefferson Davis." *Century Magazine* 56 (1898): 85-91.

———. *The Santiago Campaign*. Boston: Lamson, Wolf & Co., 1898.

Widney, Lyman S. "From the Sea to the Grand Review." *National Tribune*, August 13, 20, 27 and September 3, 1903.

Wilson, James Harrison. *Under the Old Flag: Recollections of Military Operations in the War for the Union, the Spanish War, the Boxer Rebellion, Etc.* 2 vols. New York: D. Appleton, 1912.

Witcher, J. C. "Shannon's Scouts–Kilpatrick." *Confederate Veteran* 14 (1906): 511-12.

"With Hampton in Battle: A Brilliant Cavalry Charge at Fayetteville." *The Sunny South*, December 5, 1897.

Woodward, C. Vann, ed. *Mary Chesnut's Civil War*. New Haven: Yale University Press, 1981.

Wright, J. Russell. "Battle of Trevilian." *Recollections and Reminiscences 1861-1865*. Vol. 6. Charleston: South Carolina Division of the United Daughters of the Confederacy, 1995: 127-28.

Wyeth, J. A. "Gen. Joseph Wheeler." *Confederate Veteran* 6 (1898): 361.

Yeary, Mamie, ed. *Reminiscences of the Boys in Gray, 1861-1865*. Dallas, Texas: Wilkinson Printing Co., 1912.

SECONDARY SOURCES

Articles

Anderson, Mrs. John H. "Last Days of the Confederacy in North Carolina." *Confederate Veteran* 39 (1931): 20-24.

Austerman, Wayne R. "C. S. Cavalry Arms—1865." *North South Trader* Vol. XII, No. 2 (Jan.-Feb. 1985): 22-27.

"Drama at the Crossroads: The Battle at Monroe's Crossroads." *Fayetteville Observer*, October 8, 1961.

Dyer, J. P. "Some Aspects of Cavalry Operations in the Army of Tennessee." *The Journal of Southern History* Vol. 8, No. 2 (May 1942): 210-225.

Elmore, Tom. "Head to Head." *Civil War Times Illustrated* Vol. 40 (Feb 2001): 44-52 & 54-55.

———. "The Burning of Columbia, South Carolina, February 17, 1865." *Blue & Gray* Vol. XXI, No. 3 (Winter 2004): 6-27.

Halsey, Ashley. "Last Duel of the Confederacy." *Civil War Times Illustrated* Vol. 1 (Nov. 1962): 7-8, 31.

Hartley, Chris J. "'Like an Avalanche': George Stoneman's 1865 Cavalry Raid." *Civil War Regiments* Vol. 6, No. 1 (1998): 74-92.

King, G. Wayne. "General Judson Kilpatrick." *New Jersey History* 91 (Spring 1973): 35-52.

"Living Descendant's Letter Sheds Light." *The State*, November 1, 1959.

Longacre, Edward G. "Judson Kilpatrick." *Civil War Times Illustrated* (April 1971): 25-33.

Mangum, William P., II. "Kill Cavalry's Nasty Surprise." *America's Civil War* 9 (Nov 1996): 42-48.

McMahon, MrS.C. W. "General Joseph Wheeler." *Confederate Veteran* 33 (1925): 454-455.

Nye, Wilbur S. "The Battle That Was Fought on the Fort Bragg Reservation." *Field Artillery Journal* 22 (Jan./Feb. 1932): 67-92.–

———. "Kilpatrick Caught in His Underwear." *Civil War Times Illustrated* (April 1961): 17-19.

Scott, Paul R. "Shannon's Scouts: Combat Reconnaissance Detachment of Terry's Texas Rangers." *Military History of Texas and the Southwest* 15 (1979): 5-23.

Wickham, Mrs. Julia Porcher. "Wade Hampton, the Cavalry Leader, and His Times." *Confederate Veteran* 36 (1928): 448-450.

Wittenberg, Eric J. "Giant in Gray." *North & South*, Vol. 6, No. 6 (September 2003): 82-86.

Woolfolk, Sarah Van V. "George E. Spencer: A Carpetbagger in Alabama." *Alabama Review* 19 (January 1966): 41-52.

Books

"A Staff Officer." *Synopsis of the Military Career of Gen. Joseph Wheeler, Commander of the Cavalry Corps, Army of the West.* New York: n.p., 1865.

Allardice, Bruce S. *More Generals in Gray.* Baton Rouge: Louisiana State University Press, 1995.

Angley, Wilson, Michael Hill, and Jerry L. Cross. *Sherman's March Through North Carolina: A Chronology.* Raleigh: North Carolina Division of Archives & History, 1996.

Bailey, Anne J. *War and Ruin: William T. Sherman and the Savannah Campaign*. Wilmington, Del.: Scholarly Resources, 2003.

Baker, Gary R. *Cadets in Gray: The Story of the Cadets of the South Carolina Military Academy and the Cadet Rangers in the Civil War*. Columbia: Palmetto Bookworks, 1989.

Barrett, John G. *The Civil War in North Carolina*. Chapel Hill: University of North Carolina Press, 1963.

———. *Sherman's March Through the Carolinas*. Chapel Hill: University of North Carolina Press, 1956.

Bates, Samuel P. *History of Pennsylvania Volunteers, 1861-5*. 5 vols. Harrisburg: B. Singerly, State Printer, 1869-71.

———. *Martial Deeds of Pennsylvania*. Philadelphia: T. H. Davis & Co., 1875.

Baumgartner, Richard A. *Blue Lightning: Wilder's Mounted Infantry Brigade in the Battle of Chickamauga*. Huntington, W.V.: Blue Acorn Press, 1997.

Belew, Kenneth. *Cavalry Clash in the Sandhills: The Battle of Monroe's Crossroads, North Carolina*. Fort Bragg, N.C.: U.S. Army, 1997.

Beyer, W. F. and O. F. Keydel. *Deeds of Valor*. 2 vols. Detroit: The Perrien-Keydel Co., 1905.

Biographical Directory of the United States Congress 1774-1989. Washington, D.C.: U.S. Government Printing Office, 1989.

Boyko, Beverly A. and William H. Kern, eds. *Cemeteries of Fort Bragg, Camp Mackall, and Pope Air Force Base, North Carolina*. 4th ed. Fort Bragg, N.C.: United States Army, 2002.

Boylston, Raymond P., Jr. *Butler's Brigade: That Fighting Brigade from South Carolina*. Raleigh, N.C.: Jarrett Press and Publications, 2000.

Bradley, Mark L. *Last Stand in the Carolinas: The Battle of Bentonville*. Campbell, Cal.: Savas Woodbury, 1996.

———. *Old Reliable's Finest Hour: The Battle of Averasboro, North Carolina, March 15-16, 1865*. Columbus, Ohio: Blue & Gray Magazine, 2002.

———. *This Astounding Close: The Road to Bennett Place*. Chapel Hill: University of North Carolina Press, 2000.

Broadwater, Robert, ed. *Battle of Despair: Bentonville and the North Carolina Campaign*. Macon, Ga.: Mercer University Press, 2004.

Bush, Bryan S. *Terry's Texas Rangers: History of the Eighth Texas Cavalry*. Paducah, Ky.: Turner Publishing Co., 2002.

Calkins, Christopher. *The Danville Expedition of May and June 1865*. Danville, Va.: Blue & Gray Education Society, 1998.

Campbell, Jacqueline Glass. *When Sherman Marched North from the Sea: Resistance on the Confederate Home Front*. Chapel Hill: University of North Carolina Press, 2003.

Carter, Samuel, III. *The Last Cavaliers: Confederate and Union Cavalry in the Civil War*. New York: St. Martin's Press, 1979.

Cisco, Walter Brian. *Wade Hampton: Confederate Warrior, Conservative Statesman*. Dulles, Va.: Potomac Books, 2004.

Coates, Earl J. and Dean S. Thomas. *An Introduction to Civil War Small Arms*. Gettysburg, Pa.: Thomas Publications, 1990.

Collier, Calvin L. *The War Child's Children: The Story of the Third Regiment, Arkansas Cavalry, Confederate States Army*. Little Rock, Ark.: Pioneer Press, 1965.

Connelly, Thomas L. *Autumn of Glory: The Army of Tennessee, 1862-1865*. Baton Rouge: Louisiana State University Press, 1971.

Cook, Harvey T. *Sherman's March Through South Carolina in 1865*. Greenville, S.C.: n.p., 1938.

Cotten, Michael. *The Williamson County Cavalry: A History of Company F, Fourth Tennessee Cavalry Regiment, CSA*. Goodlettsville, Tenn.: privately published, 1994.

Cozzens, Peter. *This Terrible Sound: The Battle of Chickamauga*. Urbana: University of Illinois Press, 1992.

Cutrer, Thomas W., ed. *Terry Texas Ranger Trilogy*. Austin: State House Press, 1996.

Daiss, Timothy. *In the Saddle: Exploits of the 5th Georgia Cavalry During the Civil War*. Atglen, Pa.: Schiffer Publishing, 1999.

Davis, Burke. *Sherman's March*. New York: Random House, 1980.

DeLeon, T. C. *Joseph Wheeler; the Man, the Statesman, the Soldier, Seen in Semi-Biographical Sketches*. Atlanta: Byrd Printing, 1899.

Drake, Edwin L. *Chronological Summary of Battles and Engagements of the Western Armies of the Confederate States*. Nashville: Tavel, Eastman & Howell, 1879.

Dyer, John P. *Fightin' Joe Wheeler*. Baton Rouge: Louisiana State University Press, 1941.

Elmore, Tom. "Mary Boozer: The Confederacy's Femme Fatale," unpublished manuscript, Columbia, S.C., 2002.

Evans, Clement A., ed. *Confederate Military History: A Library of Confederate States History, Written by Distinguished Men of the South*. 12 vols. Atlanta: Confederate Publishing Co., 1899.

Evans, David. *Sherman's Horsemen: Union Cavalry Operations in the Atlanta Campaign*. Bloomington: Indiana University Press, 1996.

Fisher, John E. *They Rode with Forrest and Wheeler: A Chronicle of Five Tennessee Brothers' Service in the Confederate Western Cavalry*. Jefferson, N.C.: McFarland, 1995.

Fitzhugh, Lester. *Terry's Texas Rangers*. Houston: Civil War Roundtable, 1958.

Fonvielle, Chris E., Jr. *The Wilmington Campaign: Last Departing Rays of Hope*. Mechanicsburg, Pa.: Stackpole Books, 2001.

Foote, Shelby. *The Civil War*. 3 vols. New York: Vintage Books, 1963.

Freeman, Douglas Southall. *Lee's Lieutenants: A Study in Command*. 3 vols. New York: Charles Scribner's Sons, 1942-44.

Gibson, John M. *Those 163 Days: A Southern Account of Sherman's March from Atlanta to Raleigh*. New York: Van Rees Press, 1961.

Glatthaar, Joseph T. *The March to the Sea and Beyond: Sherman's Troops in the Savannah and Carolinas Campaigns*. New York: New York University Press, 1985.

Govan, Gilbert E. and James W. Livingood. *A Different Valor: The Story of General Joseph E. Johnston, C.S.A.* Indianapolis: Bobbs-Merrill, 1956.

Heitman, Francis B. *Historical Register and Dictionary of the United States Army, From Its Organization, September 29, 1789, to March 2, 1903*. 2 vols. Washington, D.C.: U.S. Government Printing Office, 1903.

History of Tennessee with an Historical and Biographical Sketch of Maury, Williamson, Rutherford, Wilson, Bedford, and Marshall Counties. Nashville: Goodspeed Publishing Co., 1887.

Hoole, William Stanley, ed. *Alabama Tories: The First Alabama Cavalry, U.S.A., 1862-1865*. Tuscaloosa, Ala.: Confederate Publishing Co., 1960.

Hopkins, Donald A. *Horsemen of the Jeff Davis Legion: The Expanded Roster of Men and Officers of the Jeff Davis Legion, Cavalry*. Shippensburg, Pa.: White Mane, 1999.

——. *The Little Jeff: The Jeff Davis Legion, Cavalry, Army of Northern Virginia*. Shippensburg, Pa.: White Mane, 1999.

Horwitz, Lester V. *The Longest Raid of the Civil War*. Cincinnati: Farmcourt Publishing, 1999.

Hughes, Nathaniel Chears. *Bentonville: The Final Battle of Sherman and Johnston*. Chapel Hill: University of North Carolina Press, 1996.

——. *General William Hardee: Old Reliable*. Wilmington, N.C.: Broadfoot Publishing, 1987.

Hunt, Roger D. and Jack R. Brown. *Brevet Brigadier Generals in Blue*. Gaithersburg, Md.: Olde Soldier Books, 1989.

Jeffries, C. C. *Terry's Texas Rangers*. New York: Vantage Press, n.d.

Jones, Virgil Carrington. *Eight Hours Before Richmond*. New York: Holt, 1957.

Kayne, Sharyn and Richard Keeton. *Fiery Dawn: The Civil War Battle at Monroe's Crossroads, North Carolina*. Fort Bragg, N.C.: U.S. Army, 1999.

Keenan, Jerry. *Wilson's Cavalry Corps: Union Campaigns in the Western Theatre, October 1864 Through Spring 1865*. Jefferson, N.C.: McFarland & Co., 1998.

Kinney, Anders M. *Joseph Wheeler: Uniting the Blue and the Gray*. Lincoln, Neb.: Writers Club Press, 2002.

Klotter, James C. *The Breckinridges of Kentucky, 1760-1981*. Lexington: University of Kentucky Press, 1986.

Krick, Robert E. L. *Staff Officers in Gray: A Biogaphical Register of the Staff Officers in the Army of Northern Virginia*. Chapel Hill: University of North Carolina Press, 2003.

Krick, Robert K. *Lee's Colonels: A Biographical Register of the Field Officers of the Army of Northern Virginia*. Dayton, Ohio: Morningside, 1992.

Lloyd, Lewis. *Sherman, Fighting Prophet*. New York: Harcourt, Brace and Company, 1932.

Longacre, Edward G. *Gentleman and Soldier: A Biography of Wade Hampton III*. Nashville, Tenn.: Rutledge Hill, 2003.

——. *The Cavalry at Appomattox: A Tactical Study of Mounted Operations during the Civil War's Climactic Campaign, March 27-April 9, 1865*. Mechanicsburg, Pa.: Stackpole Books, 2003.

Lowry, Thomas P. *The Story the Soldiers Wouldn't Tell: Sex in the Civil War*. Mechanicsburg, Pa.: Stackpole, 1994.

Lucas, Marion Brunson. *Sherman and the Burning of Columbia*. College Station, Texas: Texas A&M University Press, 1976.

Marshall, Vera Lee Kearl. *Proud to Remember; Genealogy and History on Four Ancestral Lines of Lula Barzilla Humphrey Kearl*. Provo, Utah: Brigham Young University Press, 1964.

Martin, Samuel J. *Kill-Cavalry: Sherman's Merchant of Terror—The Life of Union General Hugh Judson Kilpatrick*. Madison, N.J.: Fairleigh-Dickinson University Press, 1996.

——. *Southern Hero: Matthew Calbraith Butler—Confederate General, Hampton Red Shirt, and U.S. Senator*. Mechanicsburg, Pa.: Stackpole, 2001.

Matthews, Byron H., Jr. *The McCook-Stoneman Raid*. Philadelphia: Dorrance & Co., 1976.

McMurry, Richard M. *Virginia Military Institute Alumni in the Civil War: In Bello Praesidium*. Lynchburg, Va.: H. E. Howard Co., 1999.

Miller, R. *Wheeler's Favorites: 51st Alabama Cavalry*. DePew, N.Y.: Patrex Press, 1991.

Moore, Mark A. *Moore's Historical Guide to the Battle of Bentonville*. Mason City, Iowa: Savas Publishing Co., 1997.

——. *Moore's Historical Guide to the Wilmington Campaign and the Battles for Fort Fisher*. Mason City, Iowa: Savas Publishing Co., 1999.

Morrill, Dan. *The Civil War in the Carolinas*. Charleston, S.C.: The Nautical and Aviation Publishing Co. of America, 2002.

Murrah, Jeffrey D. *None but Texians: A History of Terry's Texas Rangers*. Burnet, Texas: Eakin Publications, 2002.

Nevin, David and the Editors of Time-Life Books. *Sherman's March: Atlanta to the Sea*. Alexandria, Va.: Time-Life Books, 1986.

The New Handbook of Texas. 6 vols. Austin: The Texas State Historical Assoc., 1996.

Northern, William J. *Men of Mark in Georgia*. 6 vols. Atlanta: A. B. Caldwell, 1907-1912.

Oates, John A. *The Story of Fayetteville and the Upper Cape Fear*. Charlotte, N.C.: The Dowd Press, 1950.

Poole, John Randolph. *Cracker Cavaliers: The 2nd Georgia Cavalry Under Wheeler and Forrest*. Macon, Ga.: Mercer University Press, 2000.

Reid, Whitelaw. *Ohio in the War; Her Statement, Generals and Soldiers*. Columbus, Ohio: Eclectic Publishing Co., 1893.

Robertson, Emma G. B. and Thomas C. Robertson. *History of Aberdeen*. Aberdeen, N.C.: Malcolm Blue Historical Society, 1976.

Robertson, John, comp. *Michigan in the War*. Lansing: W. S. George & Co., 1882.

Rosen, Robert N. *The Jewish Confederates*. Columbia: University of South Carolina Press, 2000.

Rowell, John W. *Yankee Cavalrymen: Through the Civil War With the Ninth Pennsylvania Cavalry*. Knoxville: University of Tennessee Press, 1971.

Scott, Douglas D. and William J. Hunt, Jr. *The Civil War Battle of Monroe's Crossroads: A Historical Archaeological Perspective*. Fort Bragg, N.C.: U.S. Army, 1998.

Spencer, Cornelia Phillips. *The Last Ninety Days of the War in North Carolina*. New York: Watchman Publishing Co., 1866.

Starnes, H. Gerald. *Forrest's Forgotten Horse Brigadier*. Bowie, Md.: Heritage Books, 1995.

Starr, Stephen Z. *The Union Cavalry in the Civil War: The War in the West 1861-1865*. Baton Rouge: Louisiana State University Press, 1985.

Symonds, Craig L. *Joseph E. Johnston: A Civil War Biography*. New York: Norton, 1992.

Todd, Glenda M. *First Alabama Cavalry, U.S.A.: Homage to Patriotism*. Laurel, Md.: Heritage Books, 1999.

Union Forces in Anson County Under the Command of General William Sherman: March, 1865. Wadesboro, N.C.: Anson County Historical Society, 1990.

Vetter, Charles Edmund. *Sherman: Merchant of Terror, Advocate of Peace*. Gretna, La.: Pelican Publishing Co., 1992.

Warner, Ezra J. *Generals in Blue: The Lives of the Union Commanders*. Baton Rouge: Louisiana State University Press, 1964.

———. *Generals in Gray: The Lives of the Confederate Commanders*. Baton Rouge: Louisiana State University Press, 1959.

Weatherbee, F. W., Jr. *The 5th (1st Middle) Tennessee Cavalry Regiment, U.S.A.* Carrollton, Miss.: Pioneer Pub. Co., 1992.

Wellman, Manly Wade. *Giant in Gray: A Biography of Wade Hampton of South Carolina.* New York: Charles Scribner's Sons, 1949.

——. *The Story of Moore County: Two Centuries of a North Carolina Region.* Southern Pines, N.C.: Moore County Historical Assoc., 1974.

Wilson, Harold S. *Confederate Industry: Manufacturers and Quartermasters in the Civil War.* Jackson: University Press of Mississippi, 2002.

Wittenberg, Eric J. *Gettysburg's Forgotten Cavalry Actions.* Gettysburg, Pa.: Thomas Publications, 1998.

——. *Glory Enough for All: Sheridan's Second Raid and the Battle of Trevilian Station.* Dulles, Va.: Brassey's, 2001.

——. *Little Phil: A Critical Assessment of the Civil War Generalship of Philip H. Sheridan.* Dulles, Va.: Brassey's, 2002.

——. *Protecting the Flank: The Battles for Brinkerhoff's Ridge and East Cavalry Field, July 2-3, 1863.* Celina, Ohio: Ironclad Publishing, 2002.

——. *The Union Cavalry Comes of Age: Hartwood Church to Brandy Station, 1863.* Dulles, Va.: Brassey's, 2003.

Young, Bennett. *Confederate Wizards of the Saddle.* Boston: Chapple Publishing Co., 1914.

INDEX

Abbott, Pvt. David D., 239

Abingdon, VA, 42

Acker, Col. George S., 76, 233

Adams, Capt. Charles F., 7

Adams, Pvt. James M., 239

Adams, Pvt. Mat, 251

Ahrens, Capt. John, 282

Aiken, SC, engagement at, 9,
12-13, 216

Alabama military units: 1st Cavalry
(Confederate), 46-47, 234, 236; 1st
Cavalry (Union), 19-, 20, 82, 113, 122,
139, 152-153, 163, 168-169, 175, 221,
234, 238; 3rd Cavalry, 47, 135, 143, 170,
236, 248; 4th Infantry, 55; 9th Cavalry,
47, 236; 12th Cavalry, 47, 236; 19th
Infantry, 27; 51st Partisan Rangers, 47,
127, 135, 143, 163, 236; 53rd Partisan
Rangers, 47, 236, 248; Montgomery
Mounted Rifles, 46

Albany, GA, 56

Albertson, Pvt. John M., 239

Aldie, VA, battle of, 21

Alger, Russell A., 228, 298

"Alice," Kilpatrick's girlfriend, 9, 141-142,
149-150, 179, 199, 215-216, 252-253,
262, 288

Allen, Gen. William W., 46-47, 137, 143,
159, 170, 235, **photo,** 45

Allen, W. G., 120, 122

Allen's Division, 46, 126-127, 132, 137,
141, 163, 223, 235

Allison, Col. Robert D., 235

Allison's Squadron, 235

Alvis, Pvt. William, 241

Anderson, Lt. L. C., 234

Anderson, Lt. Col. Paul, 247

Anderson, Gen. Robert H., 48, 137, 236,
photo, 48

Anderson's Brigade, 48, 58, 84, 117, 126, 135,
137, 164, 236, 248

Andersonville Prison, 1, 193

Antioch Church, 93

Appel, Maj. Charles A., 150, 234, 246

Appomattox Court House, VA, xiii, 209,
220, 257

Arkansas, 3rd Cavalry, 44, 235

Arlington National Cemetery, 231

Armies: Georgia, 62, 198; Kentucky, 18;
Northern Virginia, xiii, xvi, xxii, 10, 31-32,
34-35, 42, 54-56, 209, 219, 267, 296;
Tennessee, xxi, 25, 43, 45, 207, 234;
Cumberland, 18, 27; the Potomac, 1, 4, 7,
216, 219; the South, 207; the Tennessee, 62;
the West, 43; Virginia, 4, 21

Ashby, Col. Henry M., 44-46, 170, 235, 281;
photo, 44

Ashby's brigade, 125-126, 168, 235

Atkins, Gen. Smith D., 18-19, 71, 111, 130,
164, 205, 233, 280; **photo,** 18

Atkin's Brigade, 96, 104-105, 110, 117,
128-129, 177-178, 180, 201, 233

Atkinson, Thomas, 78

Atlanta Campaign, 6, 18-20, 23, 29, 43, 46, 48,
52, 60

Atlantic & North Carolina Railroad, 61

Atlee's Station, VA, battle of, xv, 5, 216

Augusta, GA, 11, 25, 27, 30, 32

Averasboro, NC, battle of, xxii,
201, 203, 205-207, 215, 217-218, 295

Avery, Col. Issac, 236

Bailey, S. W., 166-167

Baker, Cornelius, 66, 70, 208

Ball, Pvt. O. P., 141, 244

Ballard, Pvt. Calvin W., 245

Bartley, Pvt. Wilson H., 241

Bartram, Pvt. Edwin, 246

Baseter, Pvt. William R., 239

Batey, Pvt. William T., 239
Baxter, Pvt. William R., 239
Beauregard, Gen. P. G. T., xxi, 11, 32, 80, 257
Beebe, Capt. Yates V., 23, 234
Bell, Pvt. Daniel, 245
Belle Isle Prison, 5
Bellinger, W. H., 191, 290
Bennett Place, xiii, 78, 185, 201, 210, 232
Bentonville, NC, battle of, xxii, 207-208, 215, 217-219, 226, 295
Bethel Church, NC, 72, 76, 79, 92
Bethesda Church, 111, 130
Bethuen, Lt. S. D., 143
Bice, Cpl. Nathaniel, 239
Big Bethel, VA, battle of, 2
Bird, Col. Edward, 236
Black River, 201
Blackwell, Sgt. John G., 239
Blackwell, Maj. William H., 235
Blair, Gen. Frank, 20
Blakey, Col. David T., 236
Bland, Rev. S. C., 78
Blanford, Lt. Charles, 72
Blevins, Pvt. John, 239
Blue, Belle, 109
Blue, Malcolm, 109-110, 117, 278
Blue, Neill, 174, 180
Boling, Sgt. William C., 238
Bolton, Lt. Hugh L., 239
Bondure, Pvt. William H., 245
Booker, Pvt. Jesse, 242
Boozer, Marie, 252-254, 262, 299
Bostick, Capt. Samuel D., 120, 132, 142, 217
Bowen, Pvt. Archie, 238
Boyd, Pvt. Tilmon S., 239
Bradshaw, Pvt. James, 239
Bragg, Gen. Braxton, 11, 27,-28, 46, 51, 55, 93, 207
Brandy Station, VA, battle of, 4, 54, 146
Brannam, Cpl. Milton, 241
Breckinridge, Gen. John C., 50, 59, 185
Breckinridge, Joseph C., 51
Breckinridge, Rev. Robert J., 50-51
Breckinridge, Col. William C. P., 50-52, 171, 235; **photo,** 50
Broadwater, Pvt. Abe, 147
Bromley, Capt. W. L., 235

Brooks, Ulysses R., xvii, 91, 145-146, 155, 282, 284, 292
Brown, Pvt. William, 246
Bryant, Cpl. James E., 241
Bryant, Pvt. Jesse S., 242
Bryant, Pvt. John, 241
Buchan, Archibald, 110
Buckland Mills, VA, battle of, 5
Bullock, Silas, 150-151
Burgess's Mill, VA, engagement at, 36
Bushong, Pvt. Henry C., 242
Butler, Capt. James, 146, 249
Butler, Gen. Matthew C., xvi, 37, 42, 65, 116-118, 126, 131, 142, 145, 147, 149, 173, 177, 183, 222, 236, 270, 285; Hampton's protégé, xxii; captures "bummers", 40; biography, 54-55; wounded at Brandy Station, 54; Sherman's destination, 80; plans for a dawn assault, 118-120; wanted to capture Kilpatrick, 123; getting men into position, 128; Monroe's Crossroads, 132, 158, 165, 167-168, 170, 176, 221; attacked by Union soldier, 146; men plunder's enemy camp, 154; grows frustrated, 155; needs Wheeler's support, 155; John P. DeVeaux, 161; almost captured by Duncan, 198; great plan to defeat Kilpatrick, 222; assessment of Monroe's Crossroads, 224-225; postwar, 228; Spanish American War, 228; death, 229; **photo,** 53
Butler's Brigade, 236, 250
Butler's Division, xvi, xxii, 58, 63-64, 66, 80, 82, 91-92, 95, 101, 105, 107, 115, 134, 140- 141, 146, 150, 152-154, 158, 177, 188, 223, 236, 249
Butler, Capt. Nathaniel, 146-147, 249, 284

Caldwell, Pvt. Lafayette, 141, 244
Calhoun, Charles M., 31, 120, 153, 165, 224
Callicotte, Pvt. Wade, 242
Cape Fear River, xviii, 61-62, 79-80, 82, 92-93, 187-188, 190-192, 196, 200-201, 203, 206, 215
Cape, Pvt. John, 242
Carleton Medical College, 48
Carolinas Campaign, 9, 11, 19-20, 45-46, 61, 126, 208, 217, 221, 225, 231, 298

Caruthers, W. G., 143
Casteel, Cpl. James H., 239
Catawba River, 62
Cato, Pvt. Joe, 248
Caughman, Capt. A. H., 250
Cedar Creek, VA, battle of, 263
Centre College, 51
Chambersburg, PA, 51
Champion, NY, 19
Chancellorsville, VA, battle of, 104
Chapin, Adjutant, 130
Charleston Mercury, 29,
Charleston, SC, 11, 63, 65, 205, 257
Charlotte, NC, 14, 59, 62-63, 66, 68, 82, 87
Chase, Salmon P., 230
Chastain, Pvt. David D., 239
Chattanooga, TN, siege of, 52
Cheek, Maj. Christopher T., 140, 150, 160, 177, 234
Cheraw, SC, 65-66, 80
Cheshire, CT, 27
Chesnut, Mary, 38, 252
Chester, SC, 39
Chesterfield, SC, 65-66
Chickamauga, GA, battle of, 17-18, 28, 45, 52, 56, 264
Chicken Road, 104, 111, 177-178, 181
The Citadel, military college, 115, 161
Clay, Henry, 51
Cleveland, Pvt. Jackson, 246
Cobb's Legion Cavalry, 56-57, 120, 132, 134, 165-167, 237, 249
Coffee, Pvt. Quintis, 242
Cogburn, Pvt. Fayette, 251
Columbia, SC, 11-12, 14, 16, 30, 37-38, 40, 54, 56, 62-63, 165, 209, 228, 252-253, 254, 262
Columbus, GA, 220
Committee on Expenditures, 229
Compton, Scout Lou, 123
Confederate military units: *Charleston Light Dragoons*, 191, 253, 256, 294; *3rd Cavalry*, 236; *5th Cavalry*, 137; *7th Cavalry*, 211; *8th Cavalry*, 48, 236, 248; *10th Cavalry*, 48, 236, 249
Cook, Pvt. Robert, 242
Cooke, Col. Gustave, 235, 247
Corinth, Mississippi, 19
Corps, Army; 14th, 62, 65, 79, 92, 163, 171, 181, 196, 207, 287; 15th, 62, 181; 17th, 20, 62, 193; 20th, 62, 65, 207, 216; 23rd, 93
Cothern, Pvt. George W., 239
Cothran, Sgt. Sam, 251
Cottington, Pvt. Samuel B., 239
Cox, Gen. Jacob D., 93, 216
Cramer, Maj. Francis L., 152, 234, 239; **photo,** 153
Crews, Col. Charles, 48-49, 236; **photo,** 48
Crews's Brigade, 49, 236
Crow, Pvt. George W., 242
Cumberland River, 28
Curtin, Andrew G., 17
Custer, Gen. George A., 232
Cuthbert, GA, 48

Dahlgren, Col. Ulric, 5
Dalton, GA, 50
Dalzell, Capt. John, 233
Dana, Charles A., 293
Danville, VA, 63, 219, 296
Darlington, SC, 55
Dauphin County, PA, 16
Davidson, Tug, 198
Davis, Col. Zimmerman, 144, 236
Davis, Flynn, 144-145
Davis, Glenn E., 138, 161
Davis, Pvt. James K., 244
Davis, President Jefferson, 5, 30, 36-37, 59, 210-212, 257-258
Davis, Gen. Jefferson C., 171, 181
Davis, W. H., 135
Davitte, Col. Samuel W., 236
Day, David F., 193-194, 290, 292
Dayton, Col. L. M., 291
Decatur, AL, 229-230
Deckertown, NJ, 2
Deep Creek, 96
DeLoach, Z. T., 105, 164
Departments: North Carolina, 54; South Carolina, Georgia, and Florida, 59-60, 234; Tennessee and Georgia, 59
DeVeaux, Lt. John P., 161, 250
Devil's Gut, 96, 111
Dibrell, Gen. George G., 50, 117, 127, 155, 164, 173, 235, 299; **photo,** 49
Dibrell's Brigade, 53, 235
Dibrell's Division, 49, 132, 155, 171, 173, 176, 224, 235

Dickinson College, 16
Dickson, Capt. M. C., 250
Dillahay, Pvt. Haywood, 242
Dixon, Capt. M. C., 165
Dobbs, Capt. S. P., 236
Dockery, Alfred, 86, 89, 274
Dodge, Gen. Grenville M., 19
Dowling, Richard, 203
Downing, Capt. C. T., 235
Doxon, Pvt. William, 239
Drowning Creek, 95, 99
Dukes, Sgt. J. H., 250
Duncan, Capt. William H., 188, 190,
    192-194, 198, 205, 291-292
Durham Station, NC, xiii, 7, 54

Earle, Capt. William E., 237
Eison, Pvt. D. C., 250
Eller, Pvt. Jacob F., 242
Elliott, Pvt. Francis M., 242
Ellis, Pvt. Francis M., 242
Ellis, Cpl. Jeremiah S., 241, 243
Emberton, Cpl. John I., 241
Emerick, Lt. George W., 239
Emerson, Pvt. John, 239
Ernest, Pvt. William C., 239
Essex, NJ, 21
Estes, Maj. Llewellyn G., xiv, 7, 122, 177
Evins, Pvt. William C., 239

Falling Waters, VA, battle of, 17
Fallis Creek, 174
Farish, Maj. John D., 135, 170, 236, 248
Farnsworth, Gen. Elon J., 4
Farrell, Pvt. Thomas, 245
Fayetteville, NC, xv, xvi, xviii, 14, 16, 60-
    61, 63, 65, 76, 80, 82, 84, 92-93, 95, 101,
    104, 107, 130, 180, 183, 185, 187, 190-
    191, 194, 196, 198, 200-201, 203, 205,
    213, 215, 217, 271, 278-279, 281, 292
Feaster, Amelia, 252-253
Ferguson, Maj. Thomas, 165
Fishburne, William H., 191, 290
Florence, SC, 92
Forrest, Gen. Nathan B., 6, 28, 49-50,
    52-53, 256, 268
Fort Delaware Prison, 212, 229
Fort Fisher, NC, 96
Fort Sumter, SC, 17

Francis, Pvt. Walter S., 245
Franklin, TN, 52
Froelich, Pvt. Gustave, 244

Galey, Dandridge T., 229
Gallagher, Pvt. Thomas, 243
Gannon, Andrew J., 242
Gardner, J. H., 163
Garfield, James, 231
Garrett, Pvt. William, 242
Gatch, Capt. Asbury P., 218
Geague, Lt. Louis, 157
Gentry, Pvt. John T., 242
Georgia military units: *1st Cavalry*, 49, 236;
    2nd Cavalry, 48-49, 143, 236; *3rd
    Cavalry*, 48; *4th Cavalry*, 36, 49; *5th
    Cavalry*, 48, 105, 137, 164, 208, 236; *6th
    Cavalry*, 48, 117, 140, 236; *12th Cavalry*,
    49, 236; *20th Cavalry Battalion*, 57
Gettysburg, PA, battle of, 4, 34, 56
Glore, Capt. John A. P., 169
Goldsboro, NC, 11, 14, 60-62, 91, 93, 187,
    198, 200, 206-209, 219
Gordon, Gen. John B., 256
Gore, Col. Mounce L., 235
Graber, H. W., 88
Graham's Bridge, 82
Graniteville Manufacturing Company, 30
Grant, Gen. Ulysses S., 10-11, 13-14, 63,
    200, 210, 218-220, 227, 231, 263, 293,
    296
Grassy Island Ford, 92
Graydon, Nell S., 253
Great Pee Dee River, 65-66, 79, 82, 84, 86,
    89, 92-93
Green Springs, 110
Greensboro, NC, 63, 211-212, 220, 260
Greenup, Pvt. James, 242
Greenville, SC, 54
Griffin, Lt. Amos M., 76, 78, 144
Grove, Pvt. George, 246
Groves, Sgt. Patterson, 239
Guild, Pvt. George B., 135, 170, 195, 224
Guin, Sgt. Jason, 239
Guthry, Pvt. Jacob J., 240
Guyse, Cpl. Enoch M., 238

Hagan, Col. James, 46-47, 170, 236, 248,
    269; **photo,** 47

Hagan's Brigade, 46, 126-127, 135, 143, 170, 224, 236, 248

Hagerty, Scout John, 123

Haldesman, Lt. Lee, 243

Hall, Pvt. Richard W., 240

Hamilton, Posey, 127, 135, 138, 152, 159, 176

Hamilton, Col. William D., 79-80, 129, 177, 233

Hampton, Lt. Col. Frank, 34

Hampton, Gen. Wade, xiv, xxi, 30, 38, 57, 63, 65, 70, 79, 91, 93, 105, 115, 118, 129, 139, 144, 149, 174, 210, 222, 236, 280, 290-291, 294; Judson Kilpatrick, meeting with, xiv, xv, vi; Kilpatrick's shoddy dispositions, xvii; one of war's most fascinating figure, xvii; strike prolongs war, xviii; requests transfer to South Carolina, xxii, 36-37; defeats Kilpatrick at Atlee's Station, 5; arrives in South Carolina, 13, 37; Sherman blames for Columbia fire, 14; marauding cavalrymen, 16; cavalry a powerful force, 25; biography, 32-37; requested by Beauregard, 32; wounded at First Manassas, 33; Gettysburg, 34; wounded at Gettysburg, 34; wounded at Seven Pines, 34; James Longstreet, 35; thrashed Sheridan at Trevilian Station, 35, 54; "Beef Steak Raid", 36; commands ANV Cavalry Corps, 36; promoted to Lt. General, 37; refuses to serve under Wheeler, 37; looking forward to working with Johnston, 38; denies burning Columbia, 39; home destroyed by Sherman, 39; vendetta with Sherman, 40; letter to Sherman, 41-42; cavalry, Johnston's most effective arm, 42; Matthew C. Butler, 54; Gilbert J. Wright, 56; Johnston relies on, 61; plans to join Wheeler, 65; Wheeler to operate on Sherman's flank, 65; orders for Wheeler, 68; sees advantage, 68; Wheeler requests reinforcements, 72; has a larger force than Kilpatrick, 74; remains active, 79; must delay Sherman's army, 92; Kilpatrick's troops trapped between Hampton and Hardee, 95; searching for way to attack

Kilpatrick, 101; Kilpatrick wants to intercept, 104; troops make good time, 105; worried about Kilpatrick's disposition, 105; looking for Kilpatrick, 107; Wheeler did not know plans, 117; plans for a dawn assault, 118-120, 123; has isolated Kilpatrick, 130; Monroe's Crossroads, battle of, 131-132, 166, 168, 170-171, 178, 221; first to enter Kilpatrick's camp, 132; meets "Alice", 149; men capture artillery, 149; Law's brigade in reserve, 154; orders withdrawal, 173; rallies his men, 173; withdrawal from battlefield, 174-175; losses, 177, 183; Fayetteville, 183-184, 190-194; Kilpatrick vows revenge, 183; writes account of battle, 185; achieved strategic goal, 187; in Fayetteville, 188; shoots two enemy troopers, 191; opportunity to rest, 198; post-battle, 199; Averasboro, 201; returns Kilpatrick's horse, 201; Bentonville, 207-208; attacks Paine's Division, 209; blames Sherman for Columbia fire, 209; ordered to contact Sherman, 209; argument with Kilpatrick, 210, 260; vows to fight on, 210-211; paroled, 211-212; assessment of Monroe's Crossroads, 213-215, 217, 224-225; lost battle of Monroe's Crossroads, 213; claim's victory at Monroe's Crossroads, 217; enemy camp in chaos, 218; great plan to defeat Kilpatrick, 222; postwar, 227, 232; death, 228; outranked Wheeler, 255-258; surrender, 260; grudge against Lee, 267; plundering of Kilpatrick's camp, 285; intended to hang Day, 292; **photo,** 33

Hampton Jr., Lt. Wade, xiv, 36

Hampton, Lt. William P., 36

Hampton's Cavalry Corps, 42, 96, 141, 234

Hampton's Legion, 33-34, 54

Hannon, Col. Moses W., 236, 248

Hanshew, Sgt. George J., 239

Hardee, Pvt. William, 295

Hardee, Gen. William J., 63, 66, 68, 82, 84, 86, 91, 93, 104, 128-130, 183, 187-188, 199, 213- 214, 281, 295; clears Rockingham, 80; wins race to Cape Fear River, 93; Kilpatrick's troops trapped between Hampton and Hardee, 95; searching for way to attack Kilpatrick, 101; Cavalry Corps, 184; troops cross Cape Fear River, 187;

Fayetteville, 192; opportunity to rest, 198; crosses Cape Fear River, 200; Averasboro, 201, 205-206; Bentonville, 207; able to join with Johnston, 215; assessment of Monroe's Crossroads, 217; **photo,** 64

Hardee's Corps, 65, 80

Hardie, A. F., 124

Harmon, Pvt. D. P., 250

Harper, Pvt. Fleming M., 242

Harper, Pvt. John, 243

Harrell, Pvt. Martin D., 243

Harrisburg, Pennsylvania, 17

Harrison, Pvt. B. Porter, 248

Harrison, Gen. Thomas, 43-44, 170, 234, 247; **photo,** 44

Harrison's Brigade, 43, 88, 125-126, 132, 152, 168, 170, 234, 247, 268

Hart, Col. John R., 236

Hayes, Cpl. M., 169

Hayes, Rutherford B., 227

Helm, Dr. Clinton, 123, 148

Hendricks, Pvt. Moses J., 239

Hill, Pvt. D. C., 250

Hill, Gen. Daniel H., 30

Hinchey, Capt. John J., 71-72

Hinchey, Pvt. Patrick, 243

Hinds, Capt. Jerome J., 152, 169

Hodges, Sgt. Gabriel M., 138

Hogin, Lt. James E., 249

Hoke, Gen. Robert, 207

Holman, Natt, 125

Homan, Pvt. Andrew J., 240

Homan, Pvt. William D., 240

Honneck, Pvt. John, 243

Hood, Gen. John B., 56, 87

Hood, Sgt. Nathaniel A., 135, 143, 163

Hornbeck, Lt. Joseph H., 239

Hornsboro, SC, 66, 68

Horseheads, NY, 18

Howard, Gen. Oliver O., 7, 11, 16, 190, 192, 196, 254, 262

Howard, Lt. Wiley C., 167

Hoy, Pvt. John, 243

Hoyt, Pvt. Clark, 246

Hulse, Pvt. John, 243

Humes, Gen. William Y. C., 38, 126, 139, 170, 221, 234, 247, 268; biography, 42-43; serves under Longstreet, 43; **photo,** 125

Humes's Division, 38, 42-43, 45, 125-126, 132, 141, 152-153, 234

Humphreys, Pvt. John L., 240

Humphreys, Capt. Moses B., 115-118, 138, 161; **photo,** 116

Hurlbut, Gen. Stephen A., 18

Illinois military units: *10th Cavalry*, 190; *11th Cavalry*, 18; *92nd Mounted Infantry*, 12-13, 18-19, 74, 129, 175, 198, 233, 287

Indiana military units: *3rd Cavalry*, 17, 99, 233; *8th Cavalry*, 17, 71-72, 74, 89, 96, 111, 130, 183, 206, 233, 245

Island No. 10, TN, 42

Jack, Pvt. Jim, 250

Jackson Jr., Pvt. George W., 242

Jackson, Pvt. John, 242

Jackson, Gen. Thomas H., 21

Jaggers, Sgt. James W., 240

Jarmon, Scout R. A., 123

Jeff Davis Legion Cavalry, 57, 80, 96, 134, 196, 237, 249

Jenkins, Lt. George C., 168, 221, 239

John, Enoch, 88

Johnson, Gen. Bradley T., 257

Johnson, Pvt. Pascal J., 243

Johnson's Island Prison, 42

Johnson's Mountain, 101

Johnston, Gen. Joseph E., xiii, 29, 38, 42, 50, 54, 56, 63, 68, 84, 91, 93, 105, 187, 200, 209, 212, 217, 219-221, 234, 256-258; Virginia, 17; cavalry a powerful force, 25; assumes command in North Carolina, 59-60; Longstreet's appraisal, 59; several oppose his appointment, 59; daunting task, 60; no illusions about command, 60; relied on Hampton, 61; size of his army, 61; not easily fooled by Sherman, 63; Hardee's instructions, 82; orders Hampton to delay Sherman's army, 92; begins to concentrate forces, 93; desperate plight in North Carolina, 199; Averasboro, 206; Bentonville, 207-208; nearly defeats Sherman at

Bentonville, 207; has Hampton contact Sherman, 209; meets with Sherman, 210; surrenders to Sherman, 210, 260; able to join with Hardee, 215; Wade Hampton, xiv; Bennett Place, xvi; replaces Beauregard, xxi; **photo,** 38

Jones, Col. Fielder A., 233

Jones, Pvt. John W., 240, 244

Jones, Pvt. Joseph A., 126, 246

Jones, Pvt. Martin, 242

Jones, Pvt. Schontz, 245

Jones, Thomas H., 229

Jordan, Col. Thomas J., 72, 74, 91, 97, 99, 128, 130, 201, 206, 221, 233; biography, 16-17; First Brigade commander, 16-17; prisoner of war, 17; tried to warn Kilpatrick, 130; **photo,** 16

Jordan's brigade, 70-71, 99, 103-105, 111, 130, 178, 180, 206, 233

Judd, Cpl. Nathaniel J., 241-242

Kautz, Gen. August V., 35

Keim, Gen. William H., 17

Keith, Pvt. M., 240

Kemmerly, Sgt. John, 245

Kennedy, Edward, 137

Kentucky military units: Confederate: *1st Cavalry,* 52, 235; *2nd Cavalry,* 52, 235; *4th Cavalry,* 52; *9th Cavalry,* 51-52, 235; *5th Mounted Infantry,* 52, *9th Mounted Infantry,* 52; Union: *2nd Cavalry,* 17, 233, 246; *3rd Cavalry,* 17, 97, 233, 245, 246; *5th Cavalry,* 20, 76, 111, 118, 140, 150, 153, 160, 169, 177, 234, 241

Kilpatrick, Gen. Judson, xvi, 6, 22-23, 25, 36, 39, 62, 70-71, 74, 78, 84, 86, 91, 95, 99, 101, 111, 117, 141-142, 176, 181, 185, 193, 199, 216, 233, 280; Johnston's surrender, xiv; Wade Hampton, meeting with, xiv-xvi; "Shirt-Tail Skedaddle," xvi, xviii, 181, 198, 232; notable personality, xvii; shoddy dispositions at Monroe's Crossroads, xvii-xviii, 74; joins Sherman, 1; relieved of command in the Army of the Potomac, 1; 2nd New York Cavalry, 2; 5th New York Infantry, 2; Peninsula Campaign, 2; serves with McClellan, 2; West Point, 2; youth, 2; charged with conduct unbecoming an officer, 4; commands 3d Cavalry Division, Army of the Potomac, 4; commands a brigade, 4; Elon J. Farnsworth, 4; Gettysburg, 4; jailed, 4, 21; New York draft riots, 4; Stoneman Raid, 4; Atlee's Station, 5; "Buckland Races", 5; "Kill-Cavalry", xxii, 5; plan to liberate prisoners from Libby Prison, 5; removed from command of Third Cavalry Division, 5; wounded at Resaca, 6; eye for women, 7; fiery temper, 7; girlfriend "Charlie", 7-8; girlfriend "Frank", 7; notorious profanity, 7; girlfriend "Alice", 8-9, 99, 101, 105, 122, 130, 141-142, 149-150, 179, 199, 215-216, 252-254, 288; girlfriend "Molly", 8; Aiken, SC, 12-13; Sherman has little faith in, 13, 16, 23; four competent brigade commanders, 16; Thomas J. Jordan, 16-17; Smith D. Atkins, 18-19; George E. Spencer, 19-20; troops lack of discipline, 20; "bummers", 39-40; men captured and killed by Wheeler's men, 39; retaliates for killing of his men, 39-40; orders from Sherman, 65, 91-92; didn't realize danger, 66, 68, 70; claims he was attacked on March 3, 70; Bethel Church, 76, 79; waits to cross Great Pee Dee, 79; reward for Shannon's capture, 89; Shannon's Scouts, 89; arrives in Rockingham, 92; troops trapped between Hampton and Hardee, 95; division struggles to keep up, 96; kind to the McLeod family, 97; riding in a wagon with Alice, 99; troops strung out across the countryside, 101; arrives at Monroe's Crossroads, 104, 122; no General Lee, 104; wants to intercept the enemy, 104; nervous about another meeting with Hampton, 105; looking for Hampton, 107; briefs Col. Way, 109; men foraging, 110; has Confederate troops sandwiched, 111; lack of diligence, 111; camp virtually unguarded, 118-120, 122-126; headquarters in Monroe house, 124; camp sound asleep, 127; plan to capture him, 127; Atkins and Jordan try to warn, 130; Confederates attack camp, 132; Hampton's wishes to capture, 132; Monroe's Crossroads, 132, 163, 167, 178, 223; escapes capture, 135, 138, 140, 143, 145, 148, 157; surprised, 142; camp was chaos, 145, 147-148, 152, 178, 183;

enemy plunders his camp, 154; regains advantage, 155; rallies his men, 157-159, 167-168, 170-171, 173; impressed by 1st Alabama Cavalry, 168; does not pursue, 173-174; improper disposition, 176; losses, 176, 214; requests help from infantry, 179; post-battle, 180, 187-188; vows revenge on Hampton, 183; fails Sherman again, 196, 198; claim's victory at Monroe's Crossroads, 199, 217-218; requests Hampton return prize horse, 201; swallows pride, 201; catches rear of Hardee's column, 203; Averasboro, 205-206, 218; poor relationship with Sherman, 206; presses Hardee, 207; not at Bentonville, 208, 219; livid about Monroe's Crossroads, 209; argument with Hampton, 210; displeasure about Monroe's Crossroads, 210; message from Joe Johnston, 210; assessment of Monroe's Crossroads, 213, 216, 225; won a tactical victory, 214; had good fortune, 215; paradox, 215; shoddy dispositions, 216, 220-222; Bentonville, 218; postwar, 231-232; death, 232; conversation with Hampton, 260; excuse for being asleep, 282; **photo,** 3

Kilpatrick's Division, 66, 72, 78-79, 103, 107, 115
Kilpatrick, Col. Milton L., 236
Kimmel, Lt. Col. David H., 70, 233
Kindrick, Pvt. William A., 240
King, Lt. Col. Barrington S., 165-167, 237, 249, **photo,** 166
King, Capt. John L., 190-192
King, Lt. Col. Robert H., 97, 233
Kinston, NC, 93
Kirk, Capt. M. J., 237
Kittering, Pvt. Lewis, 243
Knapp, Pvt. James W., 245
Knight, Ed, 127, 159
Kuhn, Lt. Col. John H., 235
Kyle, Mrs. James, 184

Lagash, Pvt. Marquis, 243
Lake, Pvt. Elisha, 240
Lambrecht, Sim, 143
Landis, Lt. Isaac D., 70
Lathrop, Dr. C. C., 150

Lathrop, Pvt. Carnet C., 246
Latta, Capt. John, 139, 239
Law, Gen. Evander M., 55-56, 223, 236, **photo,** 55
Lawrenceville, GA, 56
Law's Brigade, 58, 115, 120, 131-132, 145, 148, 154
Lebanon, TN, 52
Lee, Gen. Fitzhugh, 35, 298
Lee, Gen. Robert E., xiii, xxi, 10, 30, 32, 35-37, 59, 63, 104, 185, 199-200, 209-210, 219-221, 267, 296, 298
Leman, W., 30
Lentz, Sgt. Abraham J., 239
Leonard, Pvt. John, 244
Leonard, Sgt. W. C., 175
Lewis, Maj. Ivey F., 249
Lewis, Lt. Col. James H., 235
Libby Prison, 5, 17, 22
Lighting Brigade, 18, 264
Lincoln, President Abraham, 17, 68, 70, 212, 219-220
Livingston, Pvt. Aaron, 240
Long, Pvt. James, 245
Longstreet Church, 101, 208
Longstreet, Gen. James, 35, 43, 59
Longstreet, NC, 184
Looney, Capt. George C., 236
Loring, Gen. William W., 230
Louis, Pvt. Lavin, 242
Lovejoy Station, GA, battle of, 23
Lowndes, Capt. Rawlins, 209-210
Lowry, Sgt. William, 240
Lucas, Pvt. James W., 246
Luckin, Pvt. George B., 243
Lupo, Pvt. D., 250
Lumber River, 93, 99
Lumley, Pvt. William, 244
Lutarall, John A., 241
Lyman, Col. Theodore, 7
Lynch River, 91
Lynch, Scout Emmitt, 123
Lynchburg, VA, 14
Lynch's Creek, SC, xv, 40

MacArthur, Gen. Arthur, 230
Macon, GA, 1
Mahan, Dennis Hart, 113, 115
Mallory, Stephen R., 59

March to the Sea, 6, 10, 17, 19-20, 23, 43, 46, 48, 52, 60
Marion, Gen. Francis, 99
Market House, Fayetteville, NC, 194-196
Martin, Cpl. Bill, 138
Massachusetts military units: *1st Cavalry*, 7
Massengale, Lt. Joe, 247
Mateen, Pvt. John, 245
McArthur, Aleck, 143
McBride, Francis, 243
McBride, Maj. James G., 70-71, 74, 76
McCain, Warren, 99
McCarty, Pvt. Henry, 245
McClellan, Gen. George B., 2
McClellan, Maj. Henry B., 117, 260
McClusky, Pvt. Aaron, 241
McDaniel, Pvt. R. P., 251
McElroy, Pvt. Andrew J., 240
McKenzie, Col. George W., 120, 122, 235
McKnabb, Pvt. John, 240
McKnight, Edward H., 86
McLaws, Gen. Lafayette, 183, 194, 281, 291
McLemore, Col. William S., xix, 52-53, 163, 171, 173, 235, **photo,** 52
McLemore's Brigade, xix, 70, 173, 249, 268
McLeod, Evander, 96-97
McMurtry, Pvt. Richard M., 242
McNamee, Pvt. Thomas, 245
Meade, Gen. George G., 219
Medal of Honor, 193-194, 286, 292
Medlin, Sgt. James P., 240
Meek, Pvt. Hosea H., 245
Melton, Pvt. James L., 241
Mestney, Pvt. Frederick, 244
Metzel, Pvt. Jacob, 246
Mexican War, 43, 46
Meyer, Henry C., 7
Michaels, Pvt. Henry, 241
Michigan military units: *1st Cavalry*, 20-21; *5th Cavalry*, 228; *9th Cavalry*, 12, 19-21, 60, 66, 70-71, 74, 150, 200, 203, 216, 221, 233, 245-246; *1st Engineers*, 200;
Miley, Pvt. Benjamin F., 245
Military Division of the Mississippi, 233
Military Division of the West, 31-32
Miller, Capt. James H., 8
Miller, Capt. Robert, 169, 288, 298

Miller, Lt. Col. Lovick P., 237
Miller, Pvt. Amos, 246
Miller, Pvt. William, 245
Mims, Capt. Wilbur F., 135
Minot, Nelson, 203
Mississippi Military Units: *Jeff Davis Legion Cavalry*, xiv
Mitchell, Gen. John, 171, 174, 178-179
Mitchell, Lt. William, 241
Mize, Pvt. James R., 238
Mobile, AL, 27, 43, 46
Monroe, Charles, 101, 103-104, 110-111, 113, 119, 122-123, 139
Monroe house, 135, 137, 141, 143-144, 146, 148, 151-153, 159-160, 179-181, 185, 208, 212, 223, 225, 253, 277
Monroe, Neill, 103, 139
Monroe's Bridge, 82
Monroe's Crossroads, NC, battle of, 101, 103, 111, 120, 127, 129-130, 151, 154, 173, 176, 178, 183, 187, 199, 208, 210-226 233, 252-254, 256, 275, 278, 286, 289, 293, 297
Montgomery, AL, 46, 220
Moody, Cpl. Charles W., 242
Moore, Pvt. John G., 240
Morgan, Gen. James D., 171, 207
Morgan, Gen. John H., 20-21, 28, 51, 264
Morgan, Pvt. John J., 241-242
Morganton Road, 101, 103-104, 110-111, 115, 117-120, 122, 124, 128, 130-132, 143, 277
Morven's Post Office, 79, 82
Mosby, Col. John S., 88
Moses, Pvt. Isaac H., 138
Moutau, Francis, 246
Mt. Morris, Illinois, 18
Mullen, Pvt. Thomas, 244
Mullins, Pvt. Granville, 242
Mullins, Cpl. Henry, 242
Munford, Col. Thomas T., 35
Murphy, Pvt. James D., 240
Murry, Pvt. John A., 242
Myers, Pvt. Henry K., 246
Myers, Pvt. Howell, 240

Nance, James B., 86
National Tribune, 163
Neuse River, 198
New Bern, NC, 14, 61-62, 200
New Gilead, NC, 65, 82

New Orleans, Louisiana, 46, 229
New York military units: *2nd Cavalry*, 2, 4, 7, 21, 264; *5th Infantry*, 2; *77th Infantry*, 196
New York draft riots, 4
Newsom, Reubin D., 248
Nichols, George W., 141
Nicholson Creek, 103, 119, 125-126, 132, 158, 169, 223
Niernsee, Frank, 144
Niernsee, Reuben, 144
Norman, Roland T., 243
North Carolina Standard, 60
Northrop, Capt. Theodore F., xix, 76, 78, 103, 141, 158-159, 203, 205, 233, 264, 284, 286; scout detachment commander, 21-22; wounded, 21; biography, 22-23; captured, 22; Southern residents hate, 23; **photo,** 22

Ohio military units: *4th Cavalry*, 190; *5th Cavalry*, 8-9, 20, 113, 134, 139, 150, 169, 234, 243, 298; *9th Cavalry*, 12, 19, 79, 129, 151, 157, 175, 177, 218, 233, 245; *10th Cavalry*, 19, 96, 105, 128-129, 178, 196, 233, 245-246; *38th Infantry*, 151; *52nd Infantry,* 92; *57th Infantry*, 193; *94th Infantry*, 196; *98th Infantry*, 179; *121st Infantry*, 171, 179; *McLaughlin's Squadron,* 19, 66, 233
Old Capitol Prison, 4
Onlicker, Pvt. John, 246
Otto, Pvt. William, 243
Overland Campaign, xxi, 56
Overturf, Capt. Joseph E., 169
Owens, Pvt. George T., 240

Page, Pvt. John W., 242
Page, Pvt. Samuel H., 242
Paine, Gen. Charles J., 209
Park, Cpl. James M. B., 242
Parker, Lt. William, 249
Patterson, Pvt. James L., 245
Patton, Capt. Charles U., 233
Peak, Pvt. James, 240
Pearson, Sgt. John, 240
Peebles, Scout B., 123-124
Pelote, Pvt. —, 12, 164, 173
Peninsula Campaign, VA, 2

Pennsylvania Military Units: *9th Cavalry*, 17, 66, 70, 89, 91, 141, 150, 203, 206, 208, 214, 233, 244-246, 260
Pensacola, Florida, 27, 46, 55
Perry, Commodore Oliver H., 54
Perryville, KY, battle of, 27, 46
Peter, Pvt. Wilbur, 241
Peters, Pvt. Harry, 245
Peters, Lt. Martin, 243
Petersburg, VA, 219-221, 263, 296
Philadelphia Public Ledger, 217
Philippine Insurrection, 230
Phillips Legion Cavalry, 57, 237
Phillips's Cross Roads, 70
Pickens, Francis W., 54
Picker, Pvt. Henry, 242
Pierce, Sgt. Isaac W., 246
Pitts, William, 203
Plank Road, 171, 178
Pleasonton, Gen. Alfred, 4-5
Pointer, Lt. Col. Marcellus, 236
Pontiac, Michigan, 20
Poole, Pvt. Joel J., 240
Pope, Gen. John, 4, 21
Porter, Adm. David D., 219
Powell, Cpl. Oliver, 245
Prather, Lt. Col. John S., 137, 236
Preston, William C., 51
Price, Gen. Sterling, 43
Princeton University, 46
Pritchard, W. W., 198

Quarterman, Pvt. Samuel, 250
Quinn, Pvt. Charles, 245

Rader, Maj. George H., 113, 139, 153, 169, 234
Radical Republican Reconstruction, 227
Raleigh, NC, 11, 60-61, 187, 199-201, 206-207, 220-221
Ramey, Pvt. William P., 239
Rannells, David, 243
Ray, John M., 110
Reams Station, VA, battle of, 35
Reconstruction, 227
Redderick, Pvt. W. S., 143
Reese, Pvt. Samuel F., 241
Resaca, GA, battle of, 6
Reynolds, Lt. Henry C., 8, 99, 101, 117,

148, 165, 170

Rhett, Col. Alfred, 203, 205, 264

Rice, Capt. Howard M., 71

Rich, Pvt. Benjamin F., 241

Richardson, Pvt. John W., 240

Riddle, Pvt. Joseph F., 241

Riggs, Capt. John B., 234

Right, Lt. John, 241

Robins, Capt. Joseph, 248

Robinson, Maj. Aaron B., 171, 179

Rock River Seminary, 18

Rockfish Church, 111

Rockingham, NC, 80, 82, 89, 91-93

Rogers, Scout Joe, 123-124

Roland, Pvt. Arch, 247

Roman, Col. Alfred, 31-32, 50, 57-58, 256-257, 270

Rome, GA, 19

Roosevelt, Col. Theodore, 230

Rosecrans, Gen. William S., 27-28

Rosin Road, 120, 122, 150, 158, 279

Ross, Mathew S., 89

Roswell, GA, 165

Rowell, Pvt. William J., 240

Rudicil, Pvt. Michael, 244

Rutledge, Col. B. Huger, 236

Salisbury, NC, 220

Salley, Joel T., 138

Sanderson, Col. Thomas W., 233

Sandy Grove Church, 178

Santee River, 61

Savannah Campaign, GA, 11

Savannah River, 11-12, 36

Savannah, GA, xxi, 10, 48

Sayers, Capt. Billy, 247

Schaffner, Pvt. John, 244

Schaum, William, 272

Schneider, Pvt. Martin, 245

Schofield, Gen. John M., 62-63, 107, 200, 207, 218

Scott, Capt. Hugh H., 115, 119, 132, 188, 190-191, 194, 278, 290

Scott, Gen. Winfield, 17

Searlet, Pvt. Robert, 245

Seddon, James A., 29

Sego, Pvt. Tom, 251

Selma, AL, 220

Selma, AL, battle of, 6

Seven Pines, VA, battle of, 38

Seward, William H., 231

Sewell, William F., 208

Shadburne, George, 209

Shailer, Alice, 2, 7

Shannon, Capt. Alexander M., xix, 78-79, 87-89, 115, 118-119, 123-124, 236, 274-275, **photo,** 87

Shannon's Scouts, 88-89, 99, 101, 117, 137, 144, 148, 236, 284

Shaw, Lt. E. H., 243

Shaw, William, 183

Sheal, Pvt. William, 250

Shelly, Pvt. Henry, 239, 245

Sheridan, Gen. Philip H., 14, 35, 218-221, 263, 296

Sherman, Gen. William T., 11, 36, 40, 65, 80, 101, 141, 187, 205, 209, 215, 233, 293; Johnston surrenders, xiii, xvi, 210; Carolinas Campaign, xxi, 11, 61; new cavalry commanders, 1; picks Kilpatrick to command cavalry, 5-6; March to the Sea, 10, 60; Savannah, 10; orders Kilpatrick to Aiken, 12; lack of faith in Kilpatrick, 13, 16, 23, 199, 215, 218, 222; blames Hampton for Columbia fire, 14, 39, 209; had to rely on Kilpatrick, 14; occupies Columbia, 14; army is unstoppable, 36; Columbia, SC, 38, 40; burns Hampton's homes, 39; vendetta with Hampton, 40; letter to Hampton, 41; Atlanta Campaign, 60; size of his army, 61; Army of Georgia, 62; Army of the Tennessee, 62; advancing into North Carolina, 65, 93; hears from Kilpatrick, 91; orders Kilpatrick to pursue Hardee, 91-92; Fayetteville is destination, 107; orders capture of Cape Fear bridge, 188; Kilpatrick fails again, 196, 198; awaiting supplies, 200; merges army with Schofield, 200; respects property rights in North Carolina, 201; Averasboro, 206; relationship with Kilpatrick, 206; Bentonville, 207-208; contacted by Johnston, 209; plan to capture, 209; meets with Johnston, 210, 260; message from Joe Johnston, 210; never again trusted Kilpatrick with important assignment, 218; informs Sheridan of plans, 219; Sheridan resists joining, 219-221; Marie Boozer,

252-254; burns part of Fayetteville, 278; **photo,** 10

Shiloh, TN, battle of, 44, 46, 47

Short, Pvt. John, 242

Shuman, George, 147

Sibley, Gen. Henry H, 87

Sims, Pvt. John M., 242

Sisters Ferry, GA, 12, 36

Slocum, Gen. Henry W., 11, 16, 91, 196, 198, 218, **photo,** 12

Smith, Col. Baxter, 235

Smith, Lt. James A., 234

Smith, Capt. John D., 241

Smithfield, NC, 206-207

Sneedsboro, NC, 82

Snyder, Pvt. George, 245

Solemn Grove, NC, 65, 103, 109, 111

Solomon's Grove, see Solemn Grove, 103

South Carolina military units: *1st Cavalry*, 56, 236; *2nd Cavalry,* 34, 54; *4th Cavalry*, 56, 118, 120, 131, 134, 142, 165, 171, 191, 236, 250, 285; *5th Cavalry*, xvii, 56, 144, 146, 236, 250; *6th Cavalry*, 31, 56, 80, 91, 95, 115, 120, 138; *6th Cavalry*, 147, 153, 161, 165, 176, 224, 237, 251; *11th Infantry*, 282; *19th Cavalry Battalion,* 56, 237; *Charleston Light Dragoons*, 191, 211, 253, 256, 294; *Earle's Battery,* 237; *Furman Light Artillery*, 237

South Carolina College, 33, 54

South Carolina General Assembly, 228

South Side Railroad, 219

Sowers, Pvt. Albert, 246

Spanish American War, 228-230, 298

Sparta, TN, 49

Spear, Pvt. Downan, 242

Spencer repeating carbine, 13, 18, 23, 163, 167, 201, 203, 205, 222, 268

Spencer, Col. George E., 19, 66, 82, 95, 103-104, 110-111, 113, 122-123, 128, 140, 148-150, 160, 175-177, 181, 215, 221, 234, 279-280; biography, 19-20; Third Brigade, 20; Morganton Road unguarded, 115; unit's dispositions, 115; escape from Monroe house, 174; postwar, 230; death, 231; **photo,** 19

Spencer's Brigade, 66, 68, 95, 96, 103, 105,

109-110, 113, 128, 139-140, 153, 159, 180, 206, 214, 234, 238

Springfield rifled muskets, 23, 57, 163

St. Clair, Pvt. John, 244

Stahel, Gen. Julius, 4

Stallings, Pvt. Micajah, 240

Stallings, Pvt. William J., 240

Stancill, Pvt. Francis M., 212, 240

Stanton, Edwin M., 200, 212

Stanton, Pvt. John G., 242

Star, Maj. Owen, 233

Starnes, Col. J. W., 53

Stener, Pvt. J. T., 250

Stephens, Alexander, 30

Stetson, Lt. Ebenezer, 66, 113, 159-161, 163, 165-166, 175, 177, 223-224, 278-279, 286

Stettler, Cpl. Christian, 245

Stevens, Pvt. Joshua B., 242

Stewart, Pvt. Jonathan M., 239

Stewart, Pvt. Lemuel L., 240

Stewart, Lt. Tom, 127, 135, 138

Stone, Pvt. John, 240

Stoneman Raid, 4

Stoneman, Gen. George, 1, 5-6, 218

Stones River, TN, battle of, 27, 44-46

Stough, Lt. Col. William, 151-153, 157, 163-165, 171, 175, 221, 234, 287, **photo,** 151

Stout, Pvt. John J., 245

Streight, Col. Abel D., 53

Strzingfellow, Pvt. William, 240

Strong, Col. William E., 196

Stuart, Gen. James E. B., xxi, 5, 27, 34-35, 267

Summer, Gen. Samuel S., 230

Sun Tzu, 113, 118

Suveal, Pvt. Christopher, 240

Swaaving, Dr. John G. C., 240

Swartz, Sgt. John W., 160, 183, 246, 286

Sweat, Pvt. Christopher, 240

Sweat, Pvt. James, 240

Sylvan Grove, GA, engagement at, 216

Taliaferro, Gen. William, 203

Taliaferro's Division, 203, 205

Tarbet, Pvt. John M., 245

Tayloe, Lt. E. Thornton, 198

Taylor, Pvt. Henry, 244

Taylor, Pvt. John J., 240

Tennessee military units: *1st/6th Consoli-dated Cavalry*, 46, 235; *2nd Cavalry*, 45-46, 235, 281; *3rd Cavalry Battalion*, 45; *4th Cavalry*, xix, 52-54, 86, 163, 249, 268; *4th/8th Consolidated Cavalry*, 44, 170, 195, 224, 235, 247; *5th Cavalry*, 46, 93, 120, 143, 235; *8th Cavalry*, 49, 268; *9th Cavalry Battalion*, 235; *13th Cavalry*, 54, 235; *Allison's Squadron*, 54; *Hamilton's Battalion*, 54; *Shaw's Battalion*, 54

Teppe Jr., Pvt. William, 250,

Terry, Gen. Alfred, 209

Texas military units: *8th Cavalry*, 36, 44, 86, 88, 125, 235, 247, 268, 295; *11th Cavalry*, 44, 235; *Terry's Texas Rangers*, 44, 87, 125-126, 235

Thomas, Gen. George H., 17

Thomas, Pvt. J. J., 240

Thomas, Maj. W. W., 237

Thomasson, Pvt. J. M, 211

Thompson, Pvt. James S., 96

Thompson, Col. Robert, 236

Thompson's Station, TN, battle of, 269

Thrasher, Pvt. William D., 240

Toombs, Robert, 30

Tramel, Maj. Sanford, 82, 152

Trans-Mississippi Department, 210, 212

Transylvania University, 52

Trevilian Station, VA, battle of, 35, 54, 138, 161

Troue, Pvt. George, 243

Tullahoma Campaign, TN, 17, 53

Tuskegee, AL, 55

Union Pacific Railroad, 231

United States Military Academy, 2, 25, 27, 48, 113, 117, 216, 232

United States Troops, military units: *1st Mounted Rifles*, 27

van Buskirk, Lt. Col. Matthew, 233

Van Dorn, Gen. Earl, 28

Vanderbilt, George, 231

Vanhoose, Sgt. Robert F., 238

Vason, Col. William J., 236

Vaughn, Gen. Alfred J., 268

Vaughn, Sgt. Carey A., 246

Vines, Pvt. John J., 238

Virginia Central Railroad, 219

Virginia Military Institute, 42

Vonders, Pvt. Peter, 246

Wadesboro, SC, 66, 68, 70-71, 74, 76, 78-79, 144

Wakefield, Pvt. Booker, 242

Walker, Pvt. John F., 240

Walker, Pvt. Jonathan, 240

Walker, Lt. Col. William A., 236

Walker, Gen. W. H. T., 48

Wall's Ferry, 92

Walls, Sgt. David H., 243

Walsh, Pvt. Jesse, 239

Walsh, Pvt. John, 244

Ward, Williamson D., 89, 111

Waring, Col. J. Fred, xiv, 80, 134, 175, 196, 237, **photo,** 134

Warren, Gouverneur K., 2

Watkins, E. W., 140, 154

Way, Lt. Col. William B., 20-21, 68, 72, 74, 99, 103, 105, 109, 113, 123, 148-151, 170, 174-176, 234, 279, **photo,** 21

Way's brigade, 78, 113, 175, 180, 214, 221, 234, 244, 285

Waynesboro, SC, 13

Webster, Pvt. Charles E., 246

Welch, Pvt. Robert A., 242

Weldon, NC, 11

Wells, Edward L., 120, 131, 142, 165, 171, 191, 196, 211-212, 253-254, 256, 285, 290, 292

West, Cpl. William H., 244

West, Pvt. Moses, 240

Western Democrat, 87

Westmoreland, Pvt. White W., 242

Wharton, Gen. John, 28

Wheeler, Gen. Joseph, xvi, 8, 17, 19, 25, 42, 45, 47-50, 52, 57-58, 65, 68, 84, 86, 89, 91, 115, 117-118, 123-124, 143-144, 149, 195, 203, 205, 222, 297; harries Kilpatrick's advance, 9; vs. Kilpatrick at Aiken, SC, 12-13; marauding cavalrymen, 16; biography, 25, 27-30, 32; Bragg's "pet", 28; captures gunboat and transports, 28; Chickamauga Campaign, 28; demeanor, 28; experienced cavalry commander, 28; Forrest refuses to serve with, 28; has the respect of his men, 28; other generals refuse to work with, 28; Atlanta Campaign, 29; men's poor reputation, 29-32; men precipitate a riot, 30; poorly organized units, 31; public opinion, 31; Beauregard requests his relief, 32; outranked by Hampton, 37; outranked Hampton, 37; troops protest Hampton, 38; troops capture and kill Kilpatrick's men, 39-40; William Y. C. Humes, 43; Thomas Harrison, 44; James Hagan, 47; ordered to operate on Sherman's flank, 65; attacks Jordan's camp, 71; Bethel Church, 72, 74, 79; requests reinforcements, 72; surrounds most of Kilpatrick's division, 72; pursuit impresses civilians, 87; must delay Sherman's army, 92; Cape Fear River crossings, 95; Kilpatrick's troops trapped between Hampton and Hardee, 95; searching for way to attack Kilpatrick, 101; did not know Hampton's plans, 117; plans for a dawn assault, 118-120; wanted to capture Kilpatrick, 123; orders to Harrison, 125; plan for attacking Kilpatrick's camp, 125-126; getting men into position, 128; Monroe's Crossroads, 131-134, 151, 158, 163-165, 168-170, 223; pitched into fight, 148; men plunder's enemy camp, 154; needed to support Butler, 155; rallies his men, 170; orders withdrawal, 173; blamed for Confederate loss, 176; losses, 177; Fayetteville, 191, 194, 196; refused to surrender, 212; surrenders, 212; assessment of Monroe's Crossroads, 215, 224-225; Kilpatrick's shoddy dispositions, 216; great plan to defeat Kilpatrick, 222; postwar, 229-230, 274; Spanish American War, 229-230, 298; death, 230; what was his rank?, xviii, 255-258, 265; Shannon's scouts, 284; **photo,** 26

Wheeler's Cavalry Corps, xvi-xxii, 50, 52, 80 92, 95, 101, 115, 117, 154, 188, 211, 214, 234

Whisler, Pvt. Daniel, 245

White, Pvt. J., 240

Whitehouse, Pvt. Jesse, 241

Wilder, Col. John T., 18

Wilkeson, Pvt. Nathan H., 241

William, Pvt. Thomas, 243

Williams, Pvt. Dan L., 246

Williams, Col. Edward C., 17

Williams, Gen. John S., 52

Williams, Pvt. Thomas A., 242

Williams's brigade, 235

Wilmington & Weldon Railroad, 61

Wilmington, NC, 14, 61-62, 65, 93, 198, 207, 271

Wilson, Gen. James H., 5-6, 18, 35

Wilson, Pvt. John W., 244

Wilson, Sgt. Josiah D., 175

Winchester, VA, 14

Wisconsin military units: *10th Artillery*, 23, 113, 177, 234, 246

Woldridge, Pvt. Alexander, 242

Woldridge, Sgt. John F., 241

Woodall, Pvt. William, 246

Wool, Gen. John E., 4

Worth, Josephine B., 184, 194

Wright, Col. Gilbert J., xv, 56-57, 120, 145, 167, 211, 224, 237, **photo,** 57

Wright's Brigade, 58, 91, 96, 132, 134, 165, 249

Wyse's Fork, NC, battle of, 93

Yadkin Road, 103-105, 117

Yellow Tavern, VA, battle of, 35

Yorkville, SC, 212

Young, Gen. Pierce M. B., 56-57

Young's brigade, 237

Youngs, Pvt. Amaziah D., 245

Zerphy, PVt. Henry, 245

Zilfa, Belle, 230